EXPLAINING
UNIFICATION
THOUGHT

UNIFICATION THOUGHT INSTITUTE
NEW YORK

ISBN 0-9606480-0-3

Library of Congress Catalog Card Number: 80-54858

Unification Thought Institute
481 8th Avenue,
New York, N.Y. 10001
©1981 by Unification Thought Institute. All rights reserved.

Scriptural quotations are from the Revised Standard
Version of the Bible, copyrighted 1946, 1952, ©1971, 1973
and used by permission of the Division of Education and
Ministry of the National Council of the Churches of Christ.

Printed in the United States of America.

EXPLAINING UNIFICATION THOUGHT

SHORT CONTENTS

PREFACE	xvii
INTRODUCTION	xxi
1 THEORY OF THE ORIGINAL IMAGE	3
2 ONTOLOGY	45
3 THEORY OF ORIGINAL HUMAN NATURE	97
4 EPISTEMOLOGY	133
5 LOGIC	171
6 AXIOLOGY	199
7 THEORY OF EDUCATION	215
8 ETHICS	231
9 THEORY OF ART	245
10 THEORY OF HISTORY	279
11 METHODOLOGY	327

CONTENTS

xv   ILLUSTRATIONS
xvii   PREFACE
xxi   INTRODUCTION

1 THEORY OF THE ORIGINAL IMAGE

3   I. THE CAUSE OF THE UNIVERSE – VARIOUS VIEWPOINTS
6   II. THE CONTENTS (ATTRIBUTES) OF THE ORIGINAL IMAGE
6   A. DIVINE IMAGE
6   1. *SUNG SANG* AND *HYUNG SANG*
6   (A) *SUNG SANG*
10   (B) *HYUNG SANG*
13   (C) DIFFERENCE
16   (D) REMARKS
17   2. POSITIVITY AND NEGATIVITY
           (*YANG* AND *EUM*)
18   3. INDIVIDUAL IMAGES
21   B. DIVINE CHARACTER
21   1. HEART
23   2. LOGOS
26   3. CREATIVITY
28   SUMMARY OF THE CONTENTS (ATTRIBUTES) OF THE ORIGINAL IMAGE
28   III. STRUCTURE OF THE ORIGINAL IMAGE
28   A. QUADRUPLE BASE
28   1. QUADRUPLE BASE
31   2. IDENTITY MAINTAINING AND DEVELOPING
34   3. INNER STRUCTURE OF THE LOGOS
37   4. QUADRUPLE BASE AND REAL PROBLEMS
38   B. *CHUNG-BOON-HAP* ACTION
39   C. STRUCTURAL UNITY OF THE ORIGINAL IMAGE
41   IV. CRITIQUE OF TRADITIONAL PHILOSOPHIES
41   A. MARXIST PHILOSOPHY
43   B. THE PHILOSOPHIES OF LIFE

2 ONTOLOGY

45   I. INDIVIDUAL TRUTH BODY
45   A. UNIVERSAL IMAGE
45   1. *SUNG SANG* AND *HYUNG SANG*
51   2. POSITIVITY AND NEGATIVITY
54   3. LOGOS AND POSITIVITY AND NEGATIVITY
57   4. SUBJECT AND OBJECT

58	5. DIFFERENCE BETWEEN UNIFICATION THOUGHT AND TRADITIONAL PHILOSOPHY REGARDING THE CONCEPT OF 'SUBJECT AND OBJECT'
58	(A) TRADITIONAL PHILOSOPHY
60	(B) UNIFICATION THOUGHT
	(C) TYPES OF 'SUBJECT AND OBJECT' IN UNIFICATION THOUGHT
61	6. PAIRED ELEMENTS AND OPPOSING ELEMENTS
68	B. INDIVIDUAL IMAGE
68	1. LOCATION AND MONOSTRATIC NATURE
72	2. INDIVIDUALIZATION OF THE UNIVERSAL IMAGE
72	3. THE INDIVIDUALIZATION OF *CHUNG-BOON-HAP* ACTION
73	4. INDIVIDUAL IMAGE, IDEA AND CONCEPT
74	5. UNIVERSAL IMAGE AND THE INDIVIDUAL
75	6. INDIVIDUAL IMAGE AND THE ENVIRONMENT
76	II. CONNECTED BODY
76	A. CONNECTED BODY AND DUAL PURPOSES
79	B. CONNECTED BODY AND THE ORIGINAL IMAGE
80	III. EXISTING MODE AND EXISTING POSITION
80	A. EXISTING MODE
83	B. EXISTING POSITION
84	C. VARIOUS TYPES OF CIRCULAR AND DEVELOPING MOTION
84	1. CIRCULAR MOTION
85	2. DEVELOPMENT AND SPIRAL MOTION
87	3. DIRECTION OF DEVELOPMENTAL MOTION
89	4. PURPOSE AND DIRECTION
91	IV. COSMIC LAW AND A NEW VIEW OF VALUE
91	A. SEVEN NATURES OF COSMIC LAW
91	1. CORRELATIVE ELEMENTS
91	2. PURPOSE AND CENTRALITY
91	3. ORDER AND LOCALITY
91	4. HARMONY
92	5. INDIVIDUALITY AND RELATIONSHIP
92	6. IDENTITY-MAINTENANCE AND DEVELOPMENT
93	7. CIRCULAR MOTION
93	B. ESTABLISHMENT OF A NEW VIEW OF VALUE BASED ON COSMIC LAW

③ THEORY OF ORIGINAL HUMAN NATURE

97	I. TASK OF THE THEORY
99	II. ORIGINAL HUMAN NATURE
99	A. A BEING WITH DIVINE IMAGE
99	1. UNITED BODY OF *SUNG SANG* AND *HYUNG SANG*

101	2. HARMONIOUS BODY OF POSITIVITY AND NEGATIVITY
103	3. A BEING WITH INDIVIDUALITY
104	B. A BEING WITH DIVINE CHARACTER
105	1. HEART
106	2. LOGOS
107	3. CREATIVITY
108	C. A BEING WITH POSITION
108	1. OBJECT-POSITION
109	2. SUBJECT-POSITION
112	3. POSITION OF MEDIATOR
113	D. CONCLUSION
114	III. CRITIQUE OF EXISTENTIALIST VIEWS OF MAN
114	A. SÖREN KIERKEGAARD
114	1. VIEW OF MAN
117	2. CRITIQUE
119	B. FRIEDRICH NIETZSCHE
119	1. VIEW OF MAN
121	2. CRITIQUE
123	C. KARL JASPERS
123	1. VIEW OF MAN
124	2. CRITIQUE
126	D. MARTIN HEIDEGGER
126	1. VIEW OF MAN
127	2. CRITIQUE
129	E. JEAN-PAUL SARTRE
129	1. VIEW OF MAN
130	2. CRITIQUE
131	F. UNIFICATION THOUGHT AND EXISTENTIALIST PHILOSOPHY

4. EPISTEMOLOGY

133	I. TRADITIONAL EPISTEMOLOGIES
133	A. SOURCE OF COGNITION
134	1. EMPIRICISM
135	2. RATIONALISM
136	B. ESSENCE OF THE OBJECT OF COGNITION
136	1. REALISM
136	2. SUBJECTIVE IDEALISM
138	C. METHOD OF COGNITION
138	1. KANT'S TRANSCENDENTAL METHOD
142	2. DIALECTICAL METHOD OF MARXISM
143	II. UNIFICATION EPISTEMOLOGY
143	A. SOURCE OF COGNITION
144	B. ESSENCE OF THE OBJECT OF COGNITION

145	C. NECESSARY CONDITIONS FOR COGNITION
145	1. CONTENT AND FORM
146	2. AUTONOMY OF THE PRINCIPLE AND PROTOCONSCIOUSNESS
148	3. FORM AND CATEGORY
152	D. METHOD OF COGNITION
152	1. GIVE-AND-TAKE BETWEEN SUBJECT AND OBJECT
154	2. ACTIVENESS OF SUBJECT
156	3. PRIORITY AND DEVELOPMENT OF PROTOTYPES
157	III. COGNITION AND PHYSIOLOGY IN UNIFICATION EPISTEMOLOGY
158	A. MIND AND BRAIN
161	B. INNER WORLD AND CYBERNETICS
167	C. TRANSMISSION OF INFORMATION
168	D. SPIRITUAL COGNITION
168	IV. CRITIQUE OF EPISTEMOLOGIES
168	A. KANT
169	B. MARX

5 LOGIC

171	I. TRADITIONAL LOGIC
171	A. FORMAL LOGIC
171	1. BASIC PRINCIPLES OF THINKING
172	2. CONCEPT
173	3. JUDGEMENT
173	4. INFERENCE
174	B. DIALECTICAL LOGIC
174	1. HEGEL
177	2. MARX
178	C. SYMBOLIC LOGIC
178	D. TRANSCENDENTAL LOGIC
179	II. UNIFICATION LOGIC
179	A. BASIC STANDPOINT
179	1. STARTING POINT AND DIRECTION OF THOUGHT
179	2. STANDARD OF THINKING
180	3. INTERRELATED FIELDS
180	B. LOGICAL STRUCTURE OF ORIGINAL IMAGE
182	C. TWO STAGES IN THINKING AND THE FORMATION OF QUADRUPLE BASES
185	D. BASIC FORMS OF THINKING
187	E. BASIC LAW OF THINKING
190	III. CRITIQUE OF TRADITIONAL LOGIC
190	A. FORMAL LOGIC
190	B. SYMBOLIC LOGIC
192	C. HEGEL'S LOGIC
194	D. MATERIALISTIC DIALECTIC

6 AXIOLOGY

199	I.	NECESSITY OF AXIOLOGY
199		A. TO PREPARE FOR FUTURE SOCIETY
200		B. TO SAVE WORLD FROM CONFUSION
200		C. TO UNIFY ALL TRADITIONAL CULTURES
200	II.	AXIOLOGY AND THE MEANING OF VALUE
201	III.	THEORETICAL FOUNDATION OF AXIOLOGY
203	IV.	TYPES OF VALUE
203		A. TRUENESS, GOODNESS, AND BEAUTY
204		B. LOVE
205		C. HOLINESS
205	V.	ESSENCE OF VALUE
205		A. PURPOSE OF CREATION
206		B. GIVE-AND-TAKE HARMONY BETWEEN CORRELATIVE ELEMENTS
206	VI.	DETERMINING ACTUAL VALUE AND THE STANDARD OF VALUE
206		A. ACTUAL VALUE
208		B. STANDARD OF VALUE
210	VII.	VALUES IN TODAY'S WORLD
211		A. WEAKNESS IN TRADITIONAL VIEWS
212		B. ESTABLISHMENT OF A NEW VIEW

7 THEORY OF EDUCATION

215	I.	FUNDAMENTALS OF EDUCATION
221	II.	METHOD OF EDUCATION
221		A. EDUCATION OF HEART
225		B. EDUCATION OF NORM
226		C. EDUCATION OF DOMINION
227		D. IDEAL IMAGE OF MAN
229		E. GOAL OF EDUCATION
229		F. UNITY AND INDIVIDUALITY

8 ETHICS

231	I.	UNIFICATION ETHICS
231		A. FOUNDATION OF UNIFICATION ETHICS
232		B. ETHICS AND MORALITY
233		C. QUADRUPLE BASE AND ETHICS
236		D. ETHICS, ORDER, AND THE HEAVENLY WAY
236		1. ETHICS AND ORDER
237		2. ETHICS AND THE HEAVENLY WAY

238	E. ORDER AND EQUALITY
241	II. CRITIQUE OF TRADITIONAL VIEWS OF GOODNESS
241	A. BENTHAM'S VIEW
242	B. KANT'S VIEW

9 THEORY OF ART

246	I. WHAT IS ART?
247	II. JOY AND RESEMBLANCE
248	A. RESEMBLANCE AND PROTOTYPE
249	B. *SUNG SANG* RESEMBLANCE
250	C. *HYUNG SANG* RESEMBLANCE TO THE *SUNG SANG* OF A WORK OF ART.
251	III. WHAT IS BEAUTY?
251	A. DEFINITION OF BEAUTY
252	B. DETERMINATION OF BEAUTY
255	C. CAUSE OF THE FEELING OF BEAUTY – HARMONY
256	D. RELATIONSHIP BETWEEN BEAUTY AND GENERAL VALUES
257	IV. TYPES OF BEAUTY
258	A. KANT'S CLASSIFICATION
258	B. UNIFICATION THOUGHT VIEW
261	V. DUAL ASPECTS OF ARTISTIC ACTIVITY AND OF PURPOSE AND DESIRE
263	VI. REQUISITES FOR CREATIVE ACTIVITY
263	A. SUBJECT REQUISITES (ARTIST)
263	1. ESTABLISHMENT OF MOTIVE, THEME, AND PLAN
264	2. ATTITUDE OF THE ARTIST
265	3. INDIVIDUALITY
266	B. OBJECT REQUISITES (WORK OF ART)
266	C. TECHNIQUE AND METHOD OF CREATION
266	1. TECHNIQUE
267	2. FORMATION OF OUTER QUADRUPLE BASE
269	3. METHOD
270	VII. REQUISITES FOR APPRECIATION
272	VIII. UNITY IN ART
274	IX. ART AND ETHICS
275	X. CRITIQUE OF SOCIALIST REALISM

10 THEORY OF HISTORY

279	INTRODUCTION
282	I. TRADITIONAL VIEWS
282	A. CYCLIC VIEW
282	B. PROVIDENTIAL VIEW
283	C. PROGRESSIVE VIEW

284		D. REVOLUTIONARY VIEW
286		E. PHILOSOPHY-OF-LIFE VIEW
286		F. CULTURAL VIEW
290		G. PROVIDENTIAL VIEW AND REVOLUTIONARY VIEW
291		1. BEGINNING OF HISTORY
291		2. MOTIVE POWER OF DEVELOPMENT
291		3. OPPONENTS AND STRUGGLE
292		4. EVENTS AT THE END OF HISTORY
292		5. ENDING OF HISTORY
292		6. NEW WORLD AFTER THE END OF HISTORY
293	II.	UNIFICATION VIEW OF HISTORY
293		A. FUNDAMENTAL POINTS
294		B. ORIGIN, DIRECTION, AND GOAL
296		C. LAWS
296		1. LAWS OF CREATION
297		(A) CORRELATIVITY
298		(B) GIVE-AND-TAKE ACTION
299		(C) DOMINION OF THE CENTER
302		(D) COMPLETION THROUGH THREE STAGES
303		(E) PERIOD OF THE NUMBER SIX
306		(F) RESPONSIBILITY
307		2. LAWS OF RESTORATION
307		(A) INDEMNITY
307		(B) SEPARATION
309		(C) RESTORATION OF THE NUMBER FOUR
310		(D) CONDITIONED PROVIDENCE
312		(E) FALSE PRECEDING THE TRUE
313		(F) HORIZONTAL REAPPEARANCE OF THE VERTICAL
314		(G) SYNCHRONOUS PERIODS
315		D. BASIC LAWS OF HISTORICAL CHANGE
315		1. DEVELOPMENT AND GIVE-AND-TAKE; TURNING *AND REPULSION*
320		2. WILLED ACTION
321		E. CULTURAL HISTORY

11 METHODOLOGY

327	I.	HISTORICAL APPROACHES
327		A. HERACLITUS (DYNAMIC)
328		B. ZENO OF ELEA (STATIC)
329		C. SOCRATES (DIALOGIC)
330		D. PLATO (CLASSIFICATION OF IDEA)
330		E. ARISTOTLE (DEDUCTIVE)
331		F. BACON (INDUCTIVE)
332		G. DESCARTES (METHODICAL DOUBT)
332		H. HUME (IDEALISTIC EMPIRICISM)

333	I. KANT (TRANSCENDENTAL)
334	J. HEGEL (IDEALISTIC DIALECTIC)
335	K. MARXISM (MATERIALISTIC DIALECTIC)
336	L. HUSSERL (PHENOMENOLOGICAL)
337	M. ANALYTIC
338	II. UNIFICATION METHODOLOGY — GIVE-AND-TAKE LAW
338	A. KINDS OF GIVE-AND-TAKE ACTION
339	1. IDENTITY-MAINTAINING AND DEVELOPING
341	2. INNER AND OUTER
343	B. SPHERE OF GIVE-AND-TAKE ACTION
345	C. TYPES OF GIVE-AND-TAKE ACTION
345	1. BILATERAL AUTONOMIC
345	2. UNILATERAL AUTONOMIC
345	3. UNCONSCIOUS
346	4. HETERONOMOUS
346	5. CONTRAST (COLLATION)
347	D. CHARACTERISTICS OF GIVE-AND-TAKE ACTION
347	III. CRITIQUE OF TRADITIONAL METHODOLOGIES
347	A. HERACLITUS
347	B. ZENO
347	C. SOCRATES
348	D. PLATO
348	E. ARISTOTLE
348	F. BACON
349	G. DESCARTES
349	H. HUME
349	I. KANT
350	J. HEGEL
351	K. MARXISM
352	L. HUSSERL
353	M. ANALYTIC METHOD
354	A CONCLUDING REMARK
357	APPENDIX: VARIOUS TYPES OF CATEGORY

ILLUSTRATIONS

12	1.	THE UNIVERSAL PRIME FORCE ACTING BETWEEN SUBJECT AND OBJECT
15	2.	THE ABSOLUTE GOD AND THE APPEARANCE OF HIS DUAL CHARACTERISTICS IN THE PHENOMENAL WORLD
18	3.	*SUNG SANG–HYUNG SANG* AND POSITIVITY–NEGATIVITY RELATIONSHIPS
30	4.	INNER QUADRUPLE BASE AND OUTER QUADRUPLE BASE
32	5.	IDENTITY-MAINTAINING QUADRUPLE BASE AND DEVELOPING QUADRUPLE BASE
36	6.	THE TWO-STATE STRUCTURE OF CREATION
47	7.	STEPPED STRUCTURE OF *SUNG SANG* AND *HYUNG SANG* IN EXISTING BEINGS
52	8.	POSITIVITY AND NEGATIVITY AS THE ATTRIBUTES OF *SUNG SANG* (MIND) AND *HYUNG SANG* (PHYSICAL BODY) OF MAN
59	9.	SUBJECT AND OBJECT ELEMENTS IN ALL LEVELS OF INDIVIDUAL TRUTH BODIES
65	10.	PAIRED ELEMENTS AND OPPOSITES
70	11.	STEP BY STEP CREATION FROM PROTOZOA TO MANKIND
78	12.	CONNECTED BODY AND DUAL PURPOSES
94	13.	VERTICAL AND HORIZONTAL ORDERS IN THE COSMOS
95	14.	VERTICAL AND HORIZONTAL ORDERS IN HUMAN SOCIETY
148	15.	A MODEL OF THE ORIGIN OF PROTOCONSCIOUSNESS
153	16.	GIVE-AND-TAKE ACTION BETWEEN SUBJECT AND OBJECT IN COGNITION
154	17.	COGNITION THROUGH THE FORMATION OF A QUADRUPLE BASE
159	18.	DIVISION OF WORK IN MAN'S CEREBRAL CORTEX (LEFT CEREBRAL HEMISPHERE)
163	19.	THE NEOCORTICAL SYSTEM, LIMBIC SYSTEM, BRAIN STEM, AND SPINAL CORD SYSTEM
164	20.	PATHWAY FOR STIMULI AND RESPONSES OF THE UPPER AND LOWER NERVE CENTERS
181	21.	THE INNER DEVELOPING QUADRUPLE BASE
183	22.	THE OUTER DEVELOPING QUADRUPLE BASE

185	23. SPIRAL DEVELOPMENT IN RATIONAL-STAGE THINKING
189	24. COLLATION-TYPE GIVE-AND-TAKE ACTION BETWEEN TWO PROPOSITIONS
191	25. LOGICAL, COGNITIVE, DOMINATING, AND EXISTING STRUCTURES
197	26. A COMPARATIVE VIEW OF UNIFICATION LOGIC, FORMAL LOGIC, MATERIALISTIC DIALECTICAL LOGIC, AND TRANSCENDENTAL LOGIC
208	27. DETERMINING ACTUAL VALUE
249	28. APPRECIATION AND COGNITION THROUGH GIVE-AND-TAKE ACTION BETWEEN SUBJECT AND OBJECT
250	29. *SUNG SANG* RESEMBLANCE AND *HYUNG SANG* RESEMBLANCE TO *SUNG SANG*
258	30. VARIETIES OF BEAUTY
268	31. THE TWO-STAGE STRUCTURE IN THE CREATION OF A WORK OF ART
320	32. HISTORY AND THE STRUGGLE BETWEEN GOOD AND EVIL
325	33. THE STREAMS OF HEBRAISM AND HELLENISM
339	34. THE QUADRUPLE BASE AND *CHUNG-BOON-HAP* ACTION
342	35. THE INNER QUADRUPLE BASE AND THE OUTER QUADRUPLE BASE OF A FAMILY
342	36. EXAMPLES OF INNER QUADRUPLE BASES AND OUTER QUADRUPLE BASES
344	37. THE GIVE-AND-TAKE ACTION BETWEEN MAN AND THE CREATION, AND BETWEEN MEN
344	38. THE GIVE-AND-TAKE ACTION IN MAN'S MIND
348	39. GIVE-AND-TAKE ACTION THROUGH DIALOGUE
351	40. KANT'S TRANSCENDENTAL METHOD (IN UNIFICATION NOTATION)
351	41. THE DIALECTIC OF THESIS-ANTITHESIS-SYNTHESIS
353	42. HUSSERL'S PHENOMENOLOGICAL METHOD AND ITS CORRESPONDENCE IN UNIFICATION THOUGHT

PREFACE

The primary object of *Explaining Unification Thought* is to set forth a philosophic application of the teachings of the Reverend Sun Myung Moon. It is intended as a presentation of Unification Principle as a philosophical system, comparing it with traditional thought systems. The material is presented in the form of a lecture series; I hope to be able to publish a more academic edition in the near future.

Dogmatic certainties have no place in philosophical discussions; yet this book will show, I am sure, that the teachings of the Reverend Sun Myung Moon do bring new and fresh insights into old philosophical questions. I have decided to publish it for three major reasons: first, to prepare Unification Thought to become—as I hope it will—a guiding light for every philosophical field, and thus for all mankind; furthermore, to provide an effective way to overcome communist ideology, which has eroded every philosophical field; finally, to manifest the comprehensive nature of Reverend Sun Myung Moon's thought, as well as its applicability to all philosophical areas.

Today we are fighting an ideological war. With so many different kinds of philosophical outlooks on life calling us from all directions, we must be well-equipped with clear ideas in order to maintain a course of righteousness. My aim has been to satisfy the needs of persons that are sincerely looking for truth, in order to prepare them for the task they are called upon to fulfill today: to help build a world of true peace, harmony, and happiness for all mankind.

Part of the material presented here grew out of several seminars for Unification Church staff members, conducted in Tokyo, Japan, and in Seoul, Korea, as well as out of my own personal reflections in the course of several years. A seminar for Japanese staff members was held in Tokyo in April 1974; again for Japanese staff members, in Seoul, in June 1977; for Korean staff members, in Seoul, in May 1979; for Japanese staff members, in Tokyo, in September 1979; finally, for Western staff members, in July and August 1980.

I treated part of the material contained here at the various seminars, but part of it developed in the process of preparing this edition. This is hardly surprising. Since the Unification Principle has such a broad applicability, continuous development is to be expected. My chief concern in this text has been to preserve the integrity of the core of the Unification Principle, while seeking for wider and wider application of it to philosophical areas. While substantially identical with my other book, *Unification Thought* (New York: Unification Thought Institute, 1973), the present book differs in scope, including new chapters, new concepts, and new expressions of old concepts. Four new chapters have been added: "Logic," "Theory of Education," "Theory of Art," and a newly constructed "Methodology." Furthermore, "Theory of the Original Image," previously dealt with as a section of "Ontology," has now become a chapter by itself. Thus, the book has now eleven chapters, covering almost all fields of traditional philosophy.

The ideas set forth here represent an effort to compress twenty-four years of study and reflection I have had the opportunity to do after becoming a follower of the Reverend Sun Myung Moon. There has been a growing interest in Unification Thought in Korea, Japan, the United States, and other countries. I have, therefore, continued to deepen and strengthen the content of this thought. Reverend Sun Myung Moon's guidance has been invaluable at every step of the way. He has often instructed me, providing clear answers to questions about the Unification Principle and other matters. He showed me such amazing instances of give-and-take action, that again and again I was surprised at his superior, high-level thought.

A large part of the material of the present book was translated from the Japanese edition of *Explaining Unification Thought*. The contents, however, have been expanded with material given in seminars after the Japanese book was published; moreover, the literary expression has been greatly improved upon, through several consecutive revisions.

I am deeply grateful to the Reverend Sun Myung Moon, the originator of the Unification Principle and Unification Thought, without whose support, guidance, and loving encouragement this work could never have been completed.

Until a more academic edition is published, I trust that this book will be of help to readers in their effort to understand Unification Thought.

I pray for your happiness and health.

SANG HUN LEE
President, U.T.I.

INTRODUCTION

I. UNIFICATION THOUGHT AND THE UNIFICATION OF THOUGHTS

What is Unification Thought? Some say that it is the unification of traditional thoughts; others, that it is a system of ideas based on the Unification Principle.* Since the purpose of the Unification Principle is to unify religions and thoughts, both opinions are acceptable. Unification Thought, then, which is based on the Unification Principle, also addresses itself to the unification of thoughts. It is not formed, however, from the synthesis of traditional thoughts; it is a new-dimensional, revealed thought, which encompasses traditional thoughts.

Since man is fallen, or separated from God, his thought has become profanized, or separated from "heavenly" thought. Many thinkers have formed their philosophies according to the needs of their age and environment. Their thoughts can be viewed as making a kind of lineal movement, although they themselves were not aware of it. This movement, ascending with each new age, has formed a kind of ladder, or a set of stairs, which extends from earth to heaven. Each thought—be it Plato's, Kant's, or Hegel's—forms a rung of the ladder, or a step of the stairs. Thinkers throughout history have searched for the truth, the heavenly thought, ascending these stairs step by step.

The unification of thoughts is the ordering of thoughts, or the

---

*In *Explaining Unification Thought* I would like to use the term "Unification Principle," instead of "Divine Principle." The expression "Divine Principle" does not convey the exact meaning of the Korean expression *Tong-Il Wol-Ni*, where *Tong-Il* means "Unification" and *Wol-Ni* means "Principle." Thus, "Unification Principle" is a more correct translation.

forming of "stairs of thought." The purpose of Unification Thought is to complete this process, and to answer the fundamental questions that traditional thoughts have left unanswered.

Traditional thoughts, of course—those of Plato, Aristotle, and others—have not disappeared, but are still alive today. All the past thoughts, which have appeared vertically in the time axis, can be arranged horizontally, constituting a portion of the new thought.

Plato's theory of *Idea* corresponds to the Inner *Hyung Sang* of God in Unification Thought; Aristotle's form *(eidos)* and matter *(hylé)* correspond—not exactly, but approximately—to the *Sung Sang* and *Hyung Sang** in Unification Thought; Thomas Aquinas's concept of God can be traced back to the Logos of the Greek philosophers, especially Aristotle. With regard to the concept of God as Logos, we must say, from the viewpoint of Unification Thought, that Aquinas considered only the *Sung Sang* aspect of God, neglecting His *Hyung Sang* aspect.

Hegel's absolute spirit *(Absoluter Geist)* also corresponds to the *Sung Sang*. Descartes, who said, "I think, therefore I am" *(Cogito, ergo sum)*, doubted the existence of all things; for him, only thinking remained as proof of one's existence. Thinking itself belongs to the Inner *Sung Sang* of God, in Unification Thought.

Locke's empiricism, dealing with experiences and sensations, corresponds to the part of Unification Epistemology dealing with the *Hyung Sang* aspect of all things. Marx said that the origin of the universe is matter, which corresponds to the *Hyung Sang* of God in Unification Thought.

Li (理), in the Oriental *Li-ch'i* theory (理気説), corresponds to reason in the *Sung Sang;* and *Ch'i* (気) corresponds to the *Hyung Sang* in the Original Image.

Unification Thought, then, contains the essence of past thoughts —it does not nullify them. It is not, however, the result of their synthesis. The essence of it has been presented by the Reverend Sun Myung Moon, as he received it through revelation.

---

*Sung Sang and *Hyung Sang*, used throughout this book, are Korean terms and can be roughly translated as "internal character" and "external form." They will be explained in detail in ch. 1, sec. 2, (1) d.

II. SOLVING MAN'S PROBLEMS

Another important point we must consider is the purpose for which the various thoughts have appeared. In every age, both in the Occident and in the Orient, people have searched for a thought to solve their problems—political, economic, educational, familial, and so on. Quite obviously, however, these problems have not been solved at the roots, although valiant stop-gap efforts have been made. New problems have appeared one by one, becoming progressively more complicated than the old ones.

Nevertheless, we cannot give up with a shrug of resignation. Man will always seek a solution to his problems, in order to realize peace, happiness, and well-being.

It is important, though, to analyze the problems themselves—not just their manifestations. In Unification Thought, the first problem is that of "existence," and the second concerns how all existing beings interrelate, i.e., the problem of "relationships."

Using politics as an example, the first problem is what the policies of a nation should be; the second concerns how the relationships between the different parties, the different politicians, and between the government and the people should be. In the field of economics, what should the economies of, for example, Korea, Japan, the USA, and even the whole world be like? Then, what should the relationship between various types of enterprises, between manufacturer and consumer, between economy and science, between economy and politics, and so on, be like? Similarly in education, what should the education of Korea, Japan, the USA be like? What should the relationships between teacher and student, between teacher and teacher, between teacher and parents—what should all these relationships be like? Furthermore, what should the relationship between education and other fields be like? In society, consider how the society should be, and what the relationships between societies and between members of the society should be like. Consider what a family should be, and what the relationships between members of a family—parents and children, husband and wife, child and child—should be like. What should an individual be like? What should his relationships with others be like? As we can see, every problem can be classified either under "existence" or under "relationship." The fact that no thought has ever actually solved mankind's problems indicates to us that these two problems have not yet been solved.

It is the position of Unification Thought that national and societal problems have been caused by "non-principled" man, or fallen man, for societies and nations are formed of such people. Natural phenomena, operating in accordance with cosmic principles, do not reflect those problems. Clearly, man has become a non-principled being. If it is certain that today's problems have been caused by non-principled men, the solution to the problems, then, is to change non-principled man into principled man.

What do we mean by principled man? The Unification Principle, quoting the Bible, says that man is created in the image of God. We must, therefore, understand the Original Image, in order to understand correctly what the principled existence and relationships of man should be, even in the levels of family, society, nation, and world.

We come to the conclusion that we must understand God, in order to solve today's increasingly complicated problems at their roots. A great number of theologians have written about God, not for the purpose of solving real problems, but just to present the results of their research. The explanation of God in Unification Thought is presented for the purpose of solving real problems, and not as a mere religious doctrine.

People often try to solve today's problems through science, or common sense, without making any reference to God, assuming that the theory of God has nothing to do with reality. We will not, however, be able to find a basic solution to our problems, unless we deal with God correctly. Kant, Hegel, and others dealt with God, but were not able to find complete answers. In contrast, Unification Thought presents the Theory of the Original Image, in order to do just that.

Neither school teachers nor university professors can give adequate guidance to today's youth—who have fallen into a crisis of values—since they themselves do not know what a principled man or a principled society is. We can repair a broken watch if we understand how it is supposed to function; a doctor can cure his patients because he knows what a healthy man is like. Similarly, we can guide an immoral man into a life of righteousness only if we know what man's original or principled state is supposed to be. Going one step further, we can build the original ideal world only if we know the original ideal for the family, society, nation, and world.

EXPLAINING UNIFICATION THOUGHT

1 THEORY OF THE ORIGINAL IMAGE

True knowledge, directly or indirectly, results in action; it is not an end in itself. Unification Thought is written, not to satisfy man's appetite for knowledge, but to reform our lives, society, and the world, in accordance with the Providence of God. Intellectuals today tend to think phenomenally and to care only about results. This way of thinking never gets to the roots of man's problems. Let us, then, consider such problems in the light of our new theology, the Unification Principle. According to this view, society resembles man; in order to solve social problems, we need to understand the ideal for society—i.e., the original man. The Unification Principle states also that everything in the created world was made in the image of man. So, in order to understand creation, we need to understand the ideal for creation—i.e., the original man. Finally, man was created in the image of God; in order to understand man, we need to understand the ideal for man—i.e., God Himself.

Unification Ontology comprises the theory of God and the theory of existing (created) beings. I will deal with them separately, calling the former the "Theory of the Original Image," and the latter, simply "Ontology." I would like to stress the importance of the former.

I. THE CAUSE OF THE UNIVERSE—VARIOUS VIEWPOINTS

One's viewpoint concerning the cause of the universe profoundly influences the way one solves actual problems. The fact that the problems of the universe and human life have not been solved, indicates, we believe, that the cause of the universe has never been correctly understood.

If, for example, one considers force to be the cause of the universe, one is led to think that power is supreme in the actual world. One's political and economic theories will insist that all the problems of the world can be solved by power.

Those who regard life or will as the cause of the universe—such as Schopenhauer, Nietzsche, Dilthey, and Bergson—are the "philosophers of life." Schopenhauer said that the cause of the universe is a blind will to live *(blinder Wille zum Leben)*. All things are expressions of the will; the eye is an expression of the will to see; the mouth, an expression of the will to eat. Moreover, goodness and happiness are accidental, not essential; they are like the pleasant feeling one gets when watching a movie, and which fades when the movie is over. What we experience is pain, pain that is caused by the blind cosmic will, which has no purpose. With such a philosophy, men of power are justified in doing anything they please. Followers of Schopenhauer's philosophy, however, usually have a pessimistic outlook on life.

Nietzsche considered the will to power *(Wille zur Macht)* to be the cause of the universe. Contrary to Schopenhauer's pessimistic blind will, Nietzsche's is an active will, or the will to grow. The ideal expression of this will is called the superman *(Übermensch)*. Christian morality is slave morality, he maintains. God is dead. Man should continuously strive at becoming a superman. This is Nietzsche's view of life, derived from his view of the cause of the universe. This theory can be used by dictators to justify their use of power; Adolf Hitler, for instance, made use of it to maintain his dictatorship.

For Hegel, the cause of the universe is reason. He developed quite a few theories relating to actual problems and expected the appearance of a rational nation, which would be realized by the self-development of the absolute spirit *(Absoluter Geist)*, or reason. According to his prediction, Prussia was to be reformed by the absolute spirit, but his expectation was never realized. Consequently, anti-Hegelian thinkers, such as Marx, soon appeared. Without presenting here a detailed analysis of this view, let us just say that those who regard reason as the cause of the universe are liable to think that reason is almighty. It is very difficult to find concepts such as "heart" and "love" in Hegel's writings; for him, the ideal man is like a puppet being manipulated by the absolute spirit. Obviously, he valued reason too highly.

The *Li-ch'i* theory of China originated from the monistic theory of *ch'i*. First, then, I shall briefly discuss the *ch'i* theory. Proponents of this philosophy are Chou Lien-ch'i (周濂溪), Chang Hêng Ch'ü (張橫渠), and Ch'êng Ming-tao (程明道), among others. For Chou Lien-ch'i, the cause of the universe is *T'ai chi* (太極 —the Absolute Origin); for Chang Hêng Ch'ü, it is *Taihshyuer* (太虛 —the Great Void); for Ch'êng Ming-tao, it is *Chiarnyuarn* (乾元 —Heaven). In reality, *T'ai chi, Taihshyuer,* and *Chiarnyuarn* are *ch'i*, which is the union of *Yin* and *Yang* (陰陽 —negativity and positivity). These theories are close to materialism, since *ch'i* means matter.

The *Li-ch'i* theory, formulated by Ch'eng I-ch'uan, says that the universe consists of *Li* (理) and *ch'i* (気). *Li* corresponds to natural laws, and is more essential than *ch'i*. This view was completed by the philosopher Chu-tzu (朱子), who developed the dualism of *Li-ch'i* into his *Shihnglii hsüeh* (性理学). Chu-tzu considered *Li* to be ethical laws in addition to natural laws, inserting a spiritual dimension into the otherwise "physical" *Li-ch'i* theory. His theory corresponds in part to Aristotle's theory of *eidos* and *hylē*.

What kind of way of life has originated from Oriental ontology? Orientals tend to be onlookers in their relationship to historical development (with a few exceptions, of course), and to nature; for man must not interfere with the laws of the universe. Westerners, on the other hand, influenced by Western and Christian thought, have been urged to take positive action in relationship to nature, for Christianity has within itself the spirit of dominion over all things. This is the philosophical reason for science having developed more in the West than it did in the East.

Thus, the way one views the nature of society, politics, and economics—as well as their mutual relationships—derives from one's view of the cause of the universe. Only a correct understanding of the cause of the universe can lead to real and fundamental solutions to actual problems.

Finally, I would like to discuss a few basic points of Unification Ontology. God, man, and the whole of creation are beings; their positions, however, differ from one another. First, God differs from man and the creation because He is the Creator, while the others are created beings. Second, man also differs from the rest of creation, because he is in the position of dominating creation. Thus, God is called Original Being, since He is the original and causal existence;

man and the rest of creation are called existing beings.

What kind of existence is God? Some will say, "God is love"; others, "God is omniscient and omnipotent"; and also, "God is the Creator of the universe," and so forth. These are a few of God's attributes, which form a vast field of study. Unification Thought attempts to arrange the attributes of God in an understandable way, in what we call the "Theory of Original Image."

True understanding of God leads to a true understanding of original man, and that leads us to a true understanding of society and history. (Since man is fallen, however, it is often easier for him to gain some understanding of God through nature.) In this sense, understanding God is not an end in itself, but is related directly to solving practical problems. We should, therefore, take the theory of God very seriously.

Next, I would like to discuss the nature of God, starting with the "contents" (attributes), followed by the "structure" of God.

II. THE CONTENTS (ATTRIBUTES) OF THE ORIGINAL IMAGE

A. DIVINE IMAGE

1. Sung Sang and Hyung Sang*

Unification Thought says that the Original Image is the united body (Neutral, or Harmonious Body) of *Sung Sang* and *Hyung Sang*. Simple though this explanation may seem, it does give us an accurate picture of God. Philosophers, thus far, have explained the cause of the universe as either spirit (*Sung Sang*), or matter (*Hyung Sang*), but never as the united body (Harmonized Body). In the following section I will explain the importance of this concept.

(a) **Sung Sang**

First, let us remember that in discussing ontology we do not, and cannot, deal with God Himself, but only with the attributes of God. Consequently, our ontology is called "Theory of the Original Image," and not "Theory of the Original Being." The *Sung Sang* of God (Original *Sung Sang*) is the mind of God, or the attribute of

---

Sung Sang and *Hyung Sang*, which are Korean terms, cannot be accurately translated into English, and will, therefore, be used in their Korean form throughout this book, as explained in item A (1) d) of this section.

God that constitutes the fundamental cause of the invisible, functional aspects of all existing beings (i.e., their mind, instinct, life, etc.). The *Sung Sang* of God consists of Inner *Sung Sang* and Inner *Hyung Sang*. The Inner *Sung Sang* is the functional part of the mind (*Sung Sang*), and has the three functions of intellect, emotion, and will. Here, intellect refers to the function of cognition; emotion, to the function of feeling; and will, to the function of decision.

There are three stages of cognition in the intellect: sensibility, understanding, and reason. In saying that God has sensibility, we do not mean that God recognizes material objects by looking at them with His eyes, or by hearing them with His ears; for God has neither eyes nor ears. Rather, we mean that the intellectual function in the *Sung Sang* of God is manifested through the sensibility, understanding, and reason of the mind of created man.

To illustrate this point, let us take the example of a seed. Though there are no stems, branches, leaves, flowers, or fruits in the seed itself, yet they are there as latent potentialities. When the seed is sown and begins to grow, those potentialities become actualized in a stem, branches, and so forth. This example may help to clarify our understanding of God. Although God is the transcendent dimension of cause, and the creation does not actually germinate from God, we can think that the sensibility, understanding, and reason of man are the actualization of latent potentialities within the Inner *Sung Sang* of God.

The Inner *Hyung Sang* is the objective part of the mind (*Sung Sang*); it refers to ideas*, concepts, original law, and mathematical principles. In the Unification Principle, *Hyung Sang* is called the Second *Sung Sang*. Why? The answer is that in the *Sung Sang* of God there is already an element of *Hyung Sang*—i.e., the Inner *Hyung Sang*. The Inner *Hyung Sang* is projected into the *Hyung Sang*, and causes the *Hyung Sang* to resemble it. This is in accordance with the Unification Principle, which states that "though the internal character [*Sung Sang*] cannot be seen, it assumes a certain form [Inner *Hyung Sang*], so that the external form [*Hyung Sang*] resembles the internal character as its visible form."† Consequently, the *Hyung*

---

*'Idea' in Unification Thought is regarded as almost identical with 'Idea' in Plato's philosophy.

†*Divine Principle*, 2nd ed. (New York: The Holy Spirit Association for the Unification of World Christianity, 1973), p. 22.

Sang (i.e., the second *Sung Sang*) exists only because there is an Inner *Hyung Sang*.

When we look at a flower, a bird, or a mountain, we retain images of these things in our mind, even though our eyes may be closed. These images form our ideas and concepts, as do the memories of events we have experienced. Consequently, the ideas and concepts in our mind are formed from real experiences. In God, however, ideas, concepts, laws, and mathematical principles existed prior to the beginning of creation. In the creation narrative in the Bible, God said "Let there be light," and there was light; He called for the appearance of dry land, and it appeared. We see, then, that everything was created according to ideas in God's mind. So, both from the Bible and from the Unification Principle, we conclude that first God had the idea for each thing—then He created it.

The *Sung Sang* of God, though absolute, is manifested to varying degrees in the *Sung Sangs* of all the different entities that make up the creation. Minerals, molecules, and atoms, though obviously serving a vital purpose, might seem to lack any manifestation of the Original *Sung Sang* (God's mind); yet, in an atom, that which directs the force causing the electrons to orbit the nucleus is the *Sung Sang* of the atom, manifesting some part of the Original *Sung Sang*. In plants, life and growth are an additional manifestation of *Sung Sang*. In animals, instinct is a higher manifestation of *Sung Sang*. Finally, in the mind of man—speaking specifically of a person who has accomplished the purpose of creation—almost all the Original *Sung Sang* functions of God are manifested.

Knowing that the *Sung Sang* of God, though absolute, manifests itself in the *Sung Sang* of created beings, let me mention that the absolute God can also manifest Himself as the relative God. Rev. Sun Myung Moon once said that God felt sorry—or felt a sense of personal responsibility—when Abraham failed to make his offering correctly. The God who felt such a sense of responsibility was the relative God (from the standpoint of the absolute God).

In Aristotle's dualism of *eidos* and *hylē* (form and matter), *eidos*—that which makes a thing be what it is—corresponds, to some extent, to *Sung Sang* in Unification Thought. The *eidos* of *eidos (prote eidos)* then, would correspond to the *Sung Sang* of the *Sung Sang*—i.e., the Original *Sung Sang* lying behind all things. Aristotle said that the *eidos* of *eidos* is God. Accordingly, prime matter *(materia prima, prote hylē)* has nothing to do with God, and

Aristotle was never able to give a reasonable explanation of the origin of matter.

Thomas Aquinas, who applied Aristotle's philosophy to Christian theology, regarded the *eidos* of *eidos* as the only cause of the universe—God. This means that he elevated the position of *Sung Sang*, compared to that of *Hyung Sang*. The Gospel of John says, "In the beginning was the Word, and the Word was with God, and the Word was God," (John 1:1) The phrase "The Word was with God" does not mean "God = Word"; it means that the Word came from God. The phrase, "the Word was God," however, does mean "God = Word." Aquinas emphasized the latter, and concluded that "God = Logos" (Word, spirit), thereby excluding the material factor from the cause of the universe. When asked, "Where does matter come from?" he answered that God created matter from nothing, since God is omniscient and omnipotent. This is known as *creatio ex nihilo* (creation from nothing), a term first used by Augustine. In his monism, Aquinas could not but exclude matter from the causal world, thereby precluding any causal explanation of its existence.

Hegel, on the other hand, regarded God as the absolute spirit. How did God think before the creation? God thought in a three-stage process: affirmation—negation—negation of the negation, or thesis—antithesis—synthesis. The starting point is reason, or Logos, where "God = Logos" (Word). Consequently, his logic developed in the wrong direction. Unification Thought says that Logos is the multiplied body formed in the *Sung Sang* of God. "The Word was with God." We do not, however, say that the Word was with God from the beginning, since that would create a God-Word dualism. We maintain that the Word was born, or derived, from God. It is not wrong to say "the Word was God," since the Word is an essential attribute of God; we should, however, give "the Word was with God" priority over "The Word was God." Hegel is considered to have started with "God = Logos," thus going in the wrong direction. It is clear, then, that the way we understand the *Sung Sang* of God may influence the direction of our whole system of thought.

Descartes, with his *Cogito, ergo sum* ("I think, therefore I am"), denied the existence of that which we can see with our eyes and hear with our ears. Having negated the universe, he was left only with thinking, which can be regarded as the Inner *Sung Sang* before creation, in Unification Thought. Nevertheless, to think is a transitive verb, and as such it needs an object. This implies that *Sung Sang* consists of an Inner *Sung Sang* (function of thinking) and an Inner *Hyung Sang* (thought). Even within the system of *methodical doubt* proposed by Descartes, it is possible to verify this.

The phenomenologist Husserl discussed the structure of pure consciousness—or non-experience-born consciousness—by excluding memories and ideas formed in our mind as the result of experience. He said that there is both a functional part and an objective part (a thinking part and a thought part) in consciousness. The former he called *noesis,* and the latter, *noema.* This also refers to the Inner *Sung Sang* and Inner *Hyung Sang* in Unification Thought. Husserl discussed man's consciousness taken all by itself, without in any way relating it to God. Unification Thought, however, maintains that the structure of man's mind originates from the structure in the *Sung Sang* of God, since man is created in the image of God. Correct understanding of man's mind, therefore, cannot be achieved without reference to God.

(b) Hyung Sang

The *Hyung Sang* of God (Original *Hyung Sang*) is the attribute of God that constitutes the fundamental cause of the material aspect of all existing beings (i.e., their mass, shape, structure, and so on). The essence of the *Hyung Sang* of God may be considered a kind of energy latent in God. This latent energy is considered as manifested in the matter of the created world and in its physical force. This energy, however, is not the actual physical energy that we observe in the created world, but the "prior-stage energy" that will eventually appear in the created world. Accordingly, this energy can be called *pre-energy.*

What is the essence of the matter of the universe? The *archē*, or ultimate cause of the universe was considered to be different things by different ancient Greek philosophers. It was considered to be water by Thales; fire by Heraclitus; air by Anaximenes; *apeiron* (boundless or infinite) by Anaximander; *eînai* (being) by Parmenides; the four elements of earth, air, fire, and water by Empedokles; *spermata* (seeds of existence) by Anaxagoras; and the atom by Democritus. Democritus conceived of a fundamental, irreducible particle, which he called atom.

I think we should entrust the study of the essence of matter to scientists, since they study the material aspect of the universe. Modern physics has clarified that atoms are formed from elementary particles, and elementary particles from energy. After this point, it seems nothing is clear. For the present, the essence of matter is said to be energy, which has the nature both of waves and of particles.

When pre-energy (Original *Hyung Sang*) is engaged in give-and-take action with the emotional impulse (Original *Sung Sang*) centered on Purpose, an energy is generated as a multiplied body. Here there are two purposes: one is the purpose to generate the energy to form all things, and the other is the purpose to generate the energy to make all things interact with one another. The energy generated according to the former purpose can be called *forming energy*, and the energy generated according to the latter purpose, *acting energy*. The existence of forming energy can be confirmed by Einstein's equation $E = mc^2$ (E = energy, m = mass, c = speed of light), which expresses the convertibility of energy E into mass m. Accordingly, the Original *Hyung Sang*, or pre-energy, can be said to be *pre-matter*, when seen from its potential to manifest itself as mass.

The acting energy is nothing but the *Prime Force*, which will give rise to the *Universal Prime Force*.* The Universal Prime Force is the force that acts among correlative elements (subject and object) in the created world; it is also the force that is generated by the give-and-take action between them. We can understand, therefore, that God's love is working behind all natural phenomena—even if scientists cannot recognize it—since Prime Force consists of the emotional element and the energetic element.

The Universal Prime Force acts between subject and object, and vice versa. This results in a subject-object union. This union, which is an individual entity in itself, further relates to other individual entities in a subject-object relation. Then, again, the universal prime force acts between the new individual entity and is

---

*In *Explaining Unification Principle*, which was published in the early times of the Unification Church, it is written that the universal prime force is generated when subject and object become engaged in give-and-take action (in other words, it belongs to the created world), and that love, which originates from the give-and-take action among persons, is also a universal prime force. On the other hand, in *Divine Principle*, which was published later, it is written that the universal prime force seems to be a kind of physical force that belongs to God. These explanations seem to be in disagreement. What we have here, though, is simply that *Divine Principle* expresses only the causal aspect of the process of operation of the acting energy (Prime Force), whereas *Explaining Unification Principle* expresses only its resultant aspect. The unitive view cannot but be the Unification Thought view as explained above.

related to other individual entities. The Universal Prime Force is called *the force of give-and-take action* when it is considered as a result of the give-and-take action between the subject and object. (Fig. 1).

Fig. 1   The Universal Prime Force Acting between Subject and Object

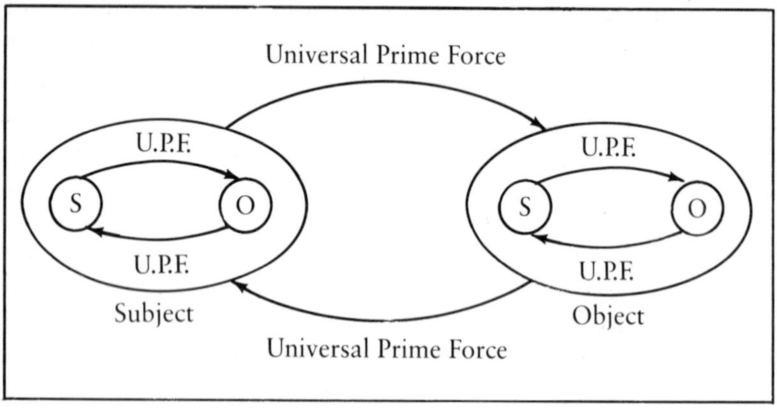

```
                    Universal Prime Force
        ┌─────────────────┐      ┌─────────────────┐
        │      U.P.F.     │      │      U.P.F.     │
        │   S ────→ O     │      │   S ────→ O     │
        │      U.P.F.     │      │      U.P.F.     │
        └─────────────────┘      └─────────────────┘
              Subject                    Object
                    Universal Prime Force
```

The Universal Prime Force acting *between* the subject and object is caused directly by the Universal Prime Force acting *within* the subject and object. If we pursue the cause of the Universal Prime Forces in nature, we will come to the atomic level. The Universal Prime Forces acting between the atoms are caused by the Universal Prime Forces acting within each atom, i.e., the Universal Prime Force acting between elementary particles. The cause of the Universal Prime Forces acting between elementary particles is the Prime Force, or the Force in God. There is a series of causes and effects in the forces of the created world. The forces acting between elementary particles are resultant forces, when we consider the Prime Force, but are causal forces, when we consider the forces acting between atoms. A force, when considered as a cause, is called a universal prime force, and when considered as a result, is called a *force of give-and-take action*.

Hyung Sang, which is a Korean word, contains the concept of form, whereas pre-energy, or pre-matter, has no form. Why, then, is *Hyung Sang* said to be the same as pre-energy, or pre-matter? Let us make an analogy with water. Water takes the form of a wave when the wind blows over it. Why does it do this, even though the wind is blowing in a straight line? Because it has the potential of taking a wave form. Moreover, water can take any form, according to the vessel in which it is put.

Likewise, *Hyung Sang*, which has both wave and particle properties, has the potential of manifesting itself in any form, according to the working of the Logos upon it. This does not mean the *Hyung Sang* is actually waves or particles; it means, however, that it does have the potential of taking these forms. Poetically stated, the *Hyung Sang* will manifest itself in various forms when the wind of Logos blows over it. It should be made clear, however, that the concepts of *Sung Sang* and *Hyung Sang* are not the results of my own analytical thinking and systematization: they were originally revealed by Rev. Sun Myung Moon.

Regarding the essence of the material world, traditional philosophers have dealt with matter as an entity completely separate from form. Aristotle, for example, discusses form *(eidos)* separately from matter, or pure material *(hylē)*. In the Unification Thought view, God's *Hyung Sang*, or pre-energy or pre-matter, cannot be completely separated from God's *Sung Sang*, as explained above.

(c) Difference Between Sung Sang and Hyung Sang

Sung Sang and *Hyung Sang* must share something in common in order to perform give-and-take action between themselves.* If they were fundamentally and essentially different, no relationship would be possible between them, and we would have a case of dualism.

Malebranche and Geulincx, followers of Descartes's dualism, doubted that two essentially different elements could assume a mutual interaction. They questioned how spirit—which is essentially different from matter—can recognize material beings, and even control a physical body. In their theory of *occasionalism*, they had no choice but to introduce God as the medium for the interaction between spirit and matter.

Descartes's dualism considered spirit (thinking) and matter (extension) to be completely heterogeneous, united with a higher being—God. In contrast, Unification Thought does not treat the origins of spirit and matter as ultimate realities in the causal world.

---

*Give-and-take action refers to the giving and receiving between subject and object when they are in a reciprocal relationship. There are five kinds of give-and-take actions in the created world, which originate from the give-and-take action between *Sung Sang* and *Hyung Sang* in the Original Image. They will be explained in Ch. 11, Methodology.

Though spirit and matter may seem quite different in the phenomenal world, they originate as relative attributes of One God.

A Korean professor of theology once criticized the Unification Principle as being a dualism of *Sung Sang* and *Hyung Sang*. The recognition, however, that give-and-take action between the *Sung Sang* and *Hyung Sang* is possible refutes such a criticism. They must have something in common, for them to relate at all. A husband and a wife must have something in common in order to relate meaningfully. The fact that *Sung Sang* and *Hyung Sang* have something in common indicates that *Sung Sang* has in itself a *Hyung Sang* element. This is not in the sense that *Sung Sang* has an Inner *Hyung Sang*, but in the sense that it has a material element—pre-energy. Likewise, the *Hyung Sang* has *Sung Sang* elements, such as reason.

Energy has no mass and no form, and in this respect pre-energy is the same as spirit. Yet energy is neither ambiguous nor accidental. It forms definite particles—such as electrons, protons, and neutrons—which have definite charges and masses. When we describe energy in terms of electromagnetic waves, we say that each kind of energy has a characteristic wavelength. Pre-energy, then, must have a kind of direction or purpose, a *Sung Sang* element, to cause energy to form sometimes particles, and other times, waves.

Conversely, *Sung Sang* has an energetic or *Hyung Sang* element in itself. Some psychologists and medical scientists refer to it as the "dynamic effect of the spirit." When a child is not loved or is ill-treated by his parents, his dissatisfaction accumulates. This accumulated dissatisfaction has a dynamic effect, which can be expressed either physically—causing the child to be openly defiant—or mentally, in the form of neurosis or mental illnesses. Also, through hypnotism we can make a person sleep, move his hands and legs, etc., just as we wish. Furthermore, we can move our own hands and legs by the decision of our mind. These facts demonstrate that our mind, which is insubstantial, has an energetic element.

We can definitely say, then, that there is a *Hyung Sang* element in the *Sung Sang*, and a *Sung Sang* element in the *Hyung Sang*. Put in another way, *Sung Sang* and *Hyung Sang* have something in common and are not essentially different elements in the world of the ultimate cause. Thus, the Unification Principle says that God is the united body (Harmonious Body) of the dual characteristics of *Sung Sang* and *Hyung Sang*, which means, first, that they are essentially of the same nature, and second, that they are united in God.

Actually, God is absolute, and thus cannot be separated into elements. He is not a composite being as finite beings are. The theory of dual characteristics objectifies God into the world of time and space, for the purpose of obtaining a convenient and correct understanding of God. Figuratively speaking, the attributes of the absolute God can be likened to a point: from a point, two rays can be drawn; likewise, from the absolute God, two directions can be objectified—*Sung Sang* and *Hyung Sang*. (Fig. 2)

Fig. 2 The Absolute God and the Appearance of His Dual Characteristics in the Phenomenal World

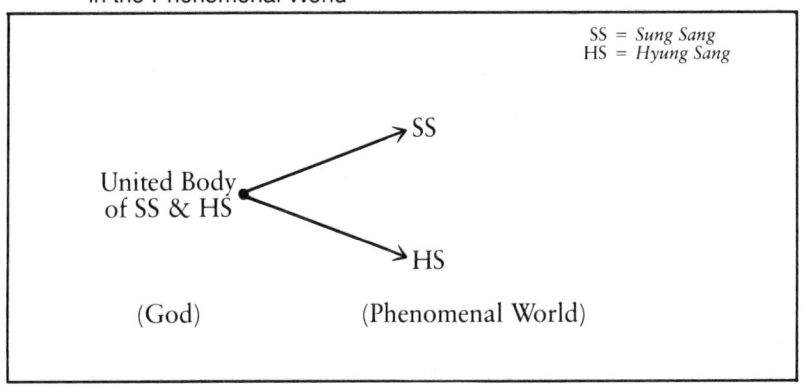

```
                                          SS = Sung Sang
                                          HS = Hyung Sang

                              ↗ SS
         United Body
         of SS & HS ●
                              ↘ HS

         (God)              (Phenomenal World)
```

Coming from one point, *Sung Sang* and *Hyung Sang* are essentially of the same quality, with only a relative, not an absolute, difference. Their relationship is that of subject and object—i.e., dominating and dominated—with one taking the controlling and active role, and the other, the obeying and passive role. Unification Thought is neither dualism, nor spiritualism, nor materialism: it is Unitism* (in Korean, *Yu-il Ron* "Theory of Oneness"), or Unificationism.

When we look at an object, light comes into our eyes and stimulates the optic nerves. The stimulation is then transmitted to the brain, where the physical process becomes a mental process. The process reverses itself when, with our minds, we move our physical body into action. Until we understand that the origin of mind and matter are essentially of the same quality in the ultimate cause, we cannot understand these phenomena.

---

*More precisely, Unitism is called "give-and-take Unitism," since it is based on the give-and-take action of *Sung Sang* and *Hyung Sang*.

(d) Remarks Concerning the Terms 'Sung Sang' And 'Hyung Sang'

In the Unification Principle, the terms *Sung Sang* and *Hyung Sang* are translated as "character" and "form" ("internal character" and "external form", to be exact). In the Unification Thought translation, however, these terms have been kept in their Korean form, since the English translation does not accurately represent their meaning.

Sung Sang means "mind", which, as explained before, has a subjective, functional part consisting of intellect, emotion, and will (Inner *Sung Sang*); as well as an objective part consisting of ideas, concepts, original laws, and mathematical principles (Inner *Hyung Sang*). Sung (性) expresses the functional part of the mind, and Sang (相), which means image, or figure, expresses the objective part of the mind. The Korean expression, therefore, is full of contents. Its English translation, "character," is inadequate, first, because it does not mean "mind"; also, because it does not contain the idea of forms.

Moreover, the relationship between *Sung Sang* and *Hyung Sang* cannot be adequately expressed by the relationship between character and form. As explained in the Unification Principle, the relationship between *Sung Sang* and *Hyung Sang* is as that between internal and external, invisible and visible, cause and effect, subject and object, vertical and horizontal. With regard to their relationship to God, we say that *Sung Sang* is closer to God than *Hyung Sang*. The reason is that the core of God is Heart, and Heart lies in the very depth of *Sung Sang*. Based on this relationship, the Unification Principle considers *Sung Sang* to be "Abel-like" and *Hyung Sang* to be "Cain-like." In the Unification Thought chapter on the "Theory of History," Hebraism is said to be a *"Sung Sang* culture," and Hellenism, a *"Hyung Sang* culture."

It is evident, therefore, that character and form could never portray such a variety of contents. (One could not, for example, say that Hebraism is a "character culture," and Hellenism is a "form culture.") Consequently, in the present book we have decided to keep these terms in their Korean form.

2. Positivity and Negativity (Yang and Eum*)

In addition to *Sung Sang* and *Hyung Sang*, the Unification Principle ascribes another set of dual characteristics to God, namely positivity and negativity. These dual characteristics relate between themselves as subject and object. Before describing them, does this mean that God has four-fold characteristics? Actually, it does not. Positivity and negativity are not direct attributes of God, but attributes of God's *Sung Sang* and *Hyung Sang*. We may describe them as attributes of attributes. Both *Sung Sang* and *Hyung Sang* contain positive and negative attributes.

The positive aspects of man's *Sung Sang* (mind) include perspicacity, good memory, cheerfulness, activeness, and so on. The negative aspects include obtuseness, poor memory, melancholy, passiveness, and so on. With regard to man's *Hyung Sang* (physical body), the positive aspects include jutting and protruding features, convex parts, and the front side. The negative aspects include sunken, hollow, and concave parts, as well as the back side.

Although both *Sung Sang* and *Hyung Sang* are attributes of God, they seem to exist as two distinct entities in the phenomenal world. Positivity and negativity, however, do not appear as entities in the phenomenal world, for they are attributes of *Sung Sang* and *Hyung Sang*. Rather than saying that man is a positive being and woman is a negative being, we should say that man is the united being of *Sung Sang* and *Hyung Sang* characteristically positive (masculine), whereas woman is a united being of *Sung Sang* and *Hyung Sang* characteristically negative (feminine). (For further details, see ch. 2, A, 2.) (Fig. 3)

The Oriental philosophy of Yin and Yang (negativity and positivity) deals with yin and yang as entities, rather than as attributes. Man is a positive being; woman is a negative being. The sodium ion would be a positive being; the chloride ion, a negative being. Unification Thought says that the sodium ion is a union of *Sung Sang* and *Hyung Sang*, having more positive characteristics. The *Sung Sang* (cause of the structure) of the sodium atom has more positive characteristics, and so does the *Hyung Sang* (the structure itself). Positivity and negativity act as modifiers of *Sung Sang* and *Hyung Sang*, and not as independent entities—this is the difference

---

*Yang and *Eum* are Korean terms and correspond to the Chinese terms Yang and Yin.

between the concept of positivity and negativity in Unification Thought and that in Oriental philosophy.

Unification Ontology seems to be the union of Occidental ontology (*eidos* and *hylē*, or spirit and matter) and Oriental ontology (Yin and Yang, or negativity and positivity). The culture that will be developed based on Unification Thought will be the union of Occidental and Oriental cultures—a unified culture. We should, however, keep in mind what was mentioned previously—i.e., that Unification Thought was not created by a deliberate, skillful, well planned welding of those two concepts.

Fig. 3 *Sung Sang – Hyung Sang* and Positivity – Negativity Relationships.

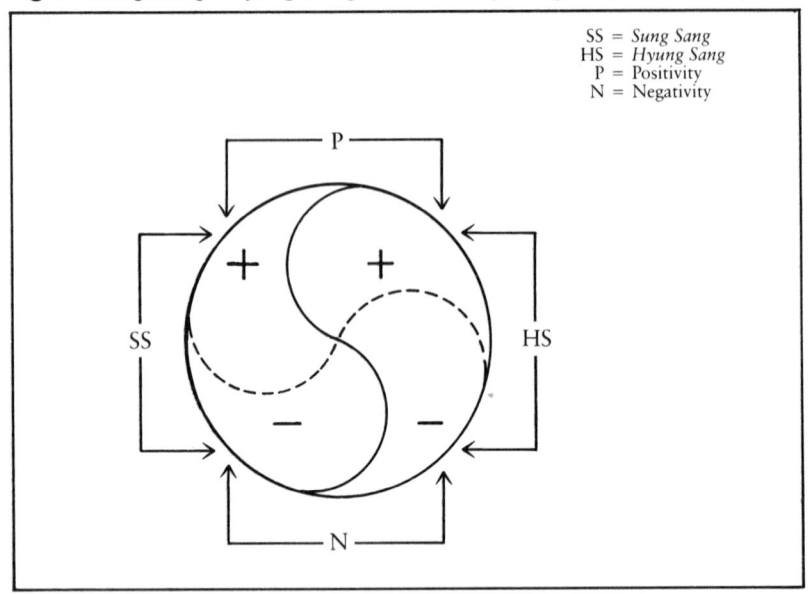

SS = *Sung Sang*
HS = *Hyung Sang*
P = Positivity
N = Negativity

The dual characteristics of *Sung Sang* and *Hyung Sang*, positivity and negativity are called *Universal Image*, since they are images of God that appear universally in every created being. In God, however, we also find Individual Images, which are explained in the next point.

3. Individual Images

As indicated above, every existing being contains the universal image of *Sung Sang* and *Hyung Sang,* positivity and negativity. Besides, every existing being has some individuality, or individual image, which comes from the Individual Image in God. From the countless Individual Images in God comes the individuality of each person and each being in creation.

Why did God give each being individuality? As it will be explained later, God's most essential character is Heart, or the emotional impulse to seek joy through loving an object. Thus, He created man and all things as His objects. How monotonous it would have been, however, if all individuals were exactly the same! One person or a million—joy would not have been any greater. Consequently, God's infinite "appetite" for joy necessitated His giving man and all things individuality.

Here is an anecdote concerning individuality, the story of Chung Suk Wong, an old Korean woman and a member of the Unification Church in Korea. Every time she saw her face in the mirror, she would feel really bad, because she thought her face looked so ugly. She would feel sorry even for sitting in the presence of Rev. Sun Myung Moon. One day, Rev. Moon said, looking around at all the faces of the church members, "God has created every person for His joy." Chung Suk Wong wondered if God really felt joy in her case, because she felt so ugly. Worrying about this, she went back to her room and prayed: "Why, Heavenly Father, have you made my face so ugly? Couldn't you have made it better?" Then the voice of Heaven came to her: "It is my face, good or bad." Her face is one of the individual images of God. She told her story to Rev. Moon, who said, with a smile, "It is true." Ever since that time she has never suffered because of her face again.

One day I visited the Ueno Park Zoo in Japan. There were many kinds of animals there, and some of them seemed very ugly. I wondered if God felt joy in seeing them and decided that He must, since He created them according to the Purpose of Creation.

Man has been given remarkable individuality. Created as the highest being, he can give the greatest joy to God. Can we also find individuality in a bacterium? Some biologists say that even a bacterium seems to have a male or a female individuality, although we would expect its individuality to be much more obscure, since it is one of the lowest forms of life we know. Birds of a certain species seem almost identical to us, yet it is said that even in a large flock a bird can recognize its mate.

That man has remarkable individuality means that his individuality should be highly valued, as well as the fact that he is the supreme being to give the greatest joy to God. Man's individuality is not acquired a posteriori, but is part of the original nature bestowed by God; if God means anything to us, then we certainly must treasure man's individuality.

Communism criticizes the democratic way of thinking, saying it has no basis for asserting the importance of individuality as it does. Man is nothing but a higher animal, evolved from other animals. Individuality may be respected for the sake of convenience in social life, but should never be regarded as absolute. Those who oppose the revolution may be disposed of with no qualms of conscience. The result of such a way of thinking, however, has been mass slaughter, which can easily be born from an ideology that makes light of man's individuality.

The way we understand the cause of the universe influences the way we understand the phenomenal world and the way we act in society. In denying the existence of God—the source of individuality—communists can easily find justification for killing those who oppose the revolution, whom they call reactionary elements. Their view that the universe, including man, originated from matter and consists only of matter further supports this justification.

According to Lenin, for example, an artist that disobeys party policy in his artistic activity must be punished. We maintain, however, that true art must not be subservient to the dictates of party policy; rather, it should display the artist's individuality, in order to be truly appreciable. We should use our God-bestowed creativity to the full, creating pictures, sculpture, music, etc., thus imitating God, who created everything as His work of art. As God has thrown Himself into creating each being, we should, likewise, throw ourselves into creating each work of art. All fine art, then, bears the stamp of individuality. This explains why most works of art are accompanied by the name of the artist, such as *The Unfinished Symphony*, by Schubert; *Missa Solemnis*, by Beethoven; or *The Angelus*, by Millet. Our original mind has subconciously known the need to respect individuality; now we are aware of the philosophical foundation for this need.

Where in God are the Individual Images located? They belong to the *Sung Sang*; more precisely, the Inner *Hyung Sang*. As already mentioned, the only direct attributes of God are *Sung Sang* and *Hyung Sang*. Positivity and negativity are attributes of the *Sung Sang* and *Hyung Sang* (attributes of attributes). These (the Universal Image), together with the Individual Images, we call the *Divine Image*.

B. DIVINE CHARACTER (DIVINITY)

Divine Character means the character of God. Heart, Logos, and creativity are three representative aspects of God's character, although there are others, such as omniscience, omnipotence, judgeship, paternity, truth, and goodness. Let us look at Heart, Logos, and Creativity in detail.

1. Heart

That which lies deeper than intellect, emotion, and will is Heart, which in Unification Thought, means the emotional impulse to seek joy through love. This impulse wells up from the bottom of the mind; it is irrepressible, even for God Himself. In order to obtain joy, there must be an object of love, related to the subject. God, therefore, having Heart, seeks objects, in order to fulfill His impulse for joy. This explains why God created man and all other creatures.

Since man is created in the image of God, he, too, has heart, or the emotional impulse to seek joy through love. Accordingly, like God he seeks objects to love. Even an infant, although contented at first simply with suckling, will gradually begin to look for objects, such as toys. If the parents deny expression to the impulses of the child's heart, the child's mind may become distorted.

By the way, what is love? It is an emotional force that the subject gives to the object and which makes the object rejoice. Accordingly, heart is "the emotional impulse to seek joy through being loved" on the part of the object, while it is "the emotional impulse to seek joy through loving" on the part of the subject.

Then, doesn't the object love his subjects? Yes, he does. For instance, a child loves his parents. In this case, the subject regards the object's love as beauty and becomes joyful by receiving it. So, both the subject and the object experience joy through loving and through being loved.

It must be noted here that the love I mean, is not mundane love (self-centered love), but true love, which is centered on God. The kind of joy that is obtained through mundane love is relative and temporary, while the kind of joy that is obtained through God-centered love is absolute and eternal.

One studies; another runs a business; others do something else —but everyone acts in order to seek joy. Fallen man, however, is not aware that true joy can be obtained through love, or he has an illusion that it can be obtained through material things, power, knowledge, and so on.

Heart, the emotional impulse to seek joy, is causal, and emotions are resultant. Everyone acts, deep in his mind, according to the impulse of heart. One feels joyful or pleasant when his impulse of heart is fulfilled, and one feels sad or angry when it is not.

At this point, I would like to discuss the relationship between Heart and love. Though both are of an emotional nature, Heart is the inner emotional impulse to obtain joy, while love is the outer emotional force that brings about a union between the subject and the object. Heart, seeking an object, or seeking a subject, is the "starting point of love," or the "source of love."

The closer the relationship between subject and object, the more the subject loves the object and the greater joy the subject can obtain. God, therefore, created man and all things in His image. Although all of creation resembles God's nature to some degree, God can obtain the greatest joy from man, who resembles Him directly and fully.

If God did not have Heart, He might have never created the universe. No religion has managed to explain why God created the universe. They normally take creation as an accomplished fact and limit their discussions to the process of creation. The explanation presented in Oriental Philosophy, also, assumes an already-accomplished creation. In the beginning was *Tai ch'i* (太極 -The Absolute Origin), from which appeared *yin-yang* (negativity and positivity). *Ssu Hsiang* (四象 —four emblematic symbols) appeared from *yin-yang*; *Baguah* (八卦 —eight trigrams of divination) from *Ssu Hsiang*; and finally all things appeared from *Baguah*. Nevertheless, the questions, "Why does *Tai ch'i* bring forth *Yin-yang?*" and "Why doesn't *Tai ch'i* remain as it is forever?" remain unanswered. Though they explained the cause of the universe, nevertheless Oriental philosophers were unable to explain the reason for its creation, for they did not know that God has Heart, neither did they understand what Heart is.*

---

*The word "Heart" can be used in both a general and in a special meaning. In its general meaning, Heart corresponds to "feeling," "emotion," "affection," "or deep (sincere) mind"; this is also referred to as the mundane meaning of Heart. In its special meaning (unique to the Unification Principle and Unification Thought), Heart is the "emotional impulse to seek joy through love." The latter meaning is causal; the former, resultant. The Unification Principle and Unification Thought make use of the word Heart in both of its meanings. Above, Heart is taken in its special meaning; but in the "Theory of Education," I will use this term also in its mundane meaning, when, for instance, I refer to "God's Heart at the Fall of Man," or "God's Heart during Restoration History."

This explanation may seem unsophisticated; its merit becomes evident, however, when we see it along side other thoughts. For instance, if we do not consider the Heart of God, it will be difficult for us to go beyond communist thought.

According to Feuerbach—whose ideas have been used by communist theorists—God is said to have such qualities as goodness, love, truth, dignity, perfection, and righteousness, because man has such qualities, though perhaps undeveloped. Everyone wants to do good, to love others, to become perfect, to live according to the truth, and so on. Such ideals can be traced back to our human essence, or generic essence. People objectify their human essence—the source of their ideals—and call this objectified human essence God, just as the painter objectifies his image as a picture on canvas. Man made God and worships Him. Feuerbach, consequently, tried to solve social problems with human love—without God. When the reason for Creation is not clarified, this approach can be convincing. We may well think "God exists for convenience' sake only," or "God may or may not exist—it does not really matter." What an unreliable God!

We said before that God could not but create objects resembling Him, in order to obtain joy. Man, created as the supreme object of God, has been given almost all the attributes of God, including Heart. For this reason, we have an irrepressible impulse to seek joy through love, regardless of time and place. Communism says that the so-called "original nature" of man is no more than the nature that is formed in bourgeois society. This original nature, however, is God-given: the more it is suppressed, the more it will resist suppression.

Many thinkers have tried to solve the problems of the world, nation, society, family, and individual—but their efforts have been in vain. If the Purpose of Creation is clarified, the purpose of human life, family, society, etc., will be clarified. This will enable us to find out how we should lead our lives, and how families, societies, etc., should be. Consequently, we lack true standards and true direction because no one has ever known the reason for the creation of the universe.

2. Logos

The Gospel according to John says, "In the beginning was the Word, and the Word was with God, and the Word was God. He was in the beginning with God. All things were made through him, and without him was not anything made that was made." (John 1:1-3).

Here 'Word' means 'Logos.' Many philosophers have tended to move away from 'the Word was with God' towards 'the Word was God'. Hegel, for example, developed his theory assuming God to be Logos. Unification Thought, however, says that Logos is created by God, as a Multiplied Body (New Body). It is the Word uttered by God. The Unification Principle says that Logos is an object of God, containing dual characteristics.

Logos is the Multiplied Body formed by give-and-take action between Inner *Sung Sang* and Inner *Hyung Sang*, centering on purpose. Inner *Hyung Sang* refers to idea, concept, original law, and mathematical principle; Inner *Sung Sang*, on the other hand, refers to intellect (sensibility, understanding, and reason), emotion, and will. Reason, in the Inner *Sung Sang*, and law, in the Inner *Hyung Sang*, play the most important role in the formation of the Logos. Accordingly, we call Logos 'reason-law' (理法 *Ih-Bup*).

Reason is the faculty that enables thinking and practice. We make a plan to do something, then we put our plan into practice. Reason operates in freedom. The nature of law, however, is necessity and inevitability; there is no freedom in law. Freedom and necessity are united in reason-law, Logos. In the natural world, the evidence of law is more pronounced than that of reason, whereas the reverse applies to man. Traditionally, Logos has been called *Law* or *natural law* or the *rule of Heaven* when referring to the natural world, but we cannot ignore the workings of reason.

Scientists say the universe has been developing for billions of years. We recognize that this development has been directional— i.e., the earth was formed, plants appeared, animals came to exist, and finally man was created. The question arising here is whether the development of the universe has been accidental or not. The earth started as swirling gas, gradually cooled, liquified, and finally solidified. Is this development accidental? Is it similar to the changes occurring, say, in water? Upon heating, water vaporizes; upon cooling, it turns into ice. If vapor is cooled, it becomes water again; ice, when heated, also becomes water. This process is repeatable. Does the development of the universe occur in similar patterns of predictable repetitions?

There are various views concerning this question. Accidentalism, for instance, stresses contingency, or the idea that the universe will eventually go in one of many possible directions. In contrast, a second view maintains that the universe could only have developed in a single direction, according to natural law. This view is characterized by inevitability. A third view proposes the theory of the autonomous development of the universe in one direction, excluding other *possible* directions. This view is characterized by the unity of freedom and necessity.

Needless to say, materialism and communism base their theories on the second view. They maintain that we can thoroughly explain the direction of the development of the universe, as long as we understand the exact laws at work in that development—which is similar to applying mathematical formulae to mathematical problems.

Unification Thought takes the third view. It explains the development of the universe from the standpoint of creation by Logos (reason-law). Reason in Logos works freely; it influences the direction of the development of the universe, while preserving the efficacy of laws.

The development of a tree can illustrate the point of reason in Logos. First, there is a seed, which grows into a stem; then, it develops branches, leaves, flowers; finally, fruits appear. The plant possesses a kind of "mind"—or latent consciousness—which makes it grow in a definite direction, displaying the "intellectual" functions of selectivity and adaptability to the environment.

By extension, we can say that the universe itself has a kind of latent consciousness, or life, which can be called *cosmic life* or *cosmic consciousness*. This seems to be a more scientific and reasonable explanation than saying that the universe has developed solely according to the necessity of law. When Logos is considered merely as natural law, freedom (or selectivity) is excluded. When it is considered as the union of Inner *Sung Sang* (reason) and Inner *Hyung Sang* (law), both freedom (or selectivity) and natural law are included. Unfortunately, however, a great number of scientists today only pursue laws, neglecting the contribution of reason.

As mentioned before, the work of law (necessity) is very obvious in the natural world, whereas that of reason is more apparent in man. Although man is endowed with great reason, and thus with freedom, he should still obey laws. In the various meetings of the International Conference on the Unity of the Sciences, Rev. Sun Myung Moon has been stressing the importance of values. As I see it, values in science are related to reason working in nature. As stated above, reason influences the development of the natural world; similarly, we can control or change the direction of the development of the sciences by using our reason and wisdom. This is the purpose behind the International Conference on the Unity of the Sciences, which seeks to formulate a values-oriented viewpoint that can guide the direction of the development of the sciences.

3. Creativity

Everyone has an innate tendency and desire to invent new things, develop new ideas, and live a creative life. This is a reflection of God's own character and ability to create new things, which is called Creativity. It was this character of God that enabled Him to create human beings and all things.

According to the Unification Principle, God has given us His creativity. We say, then, that our desire and tendency to create have come from God. In order to understand the purpose and nature of our creativity, we need to understand God's own Creativity.

The first expression of God's Creativity is His ability to form the Inner Quadruple Base, or Logos, which takes place through the give-and-take action between God's Inner *Sung Sang* and Inner *Hyung Sang*, centering on purpose. Next, God's Creativity is manifested in the formation of the Outer Quadruple Base,* which takes place when the Logos, formed in the *Sung Sang* of God, enters into give-and-take action with the *Hyung Sang*, in order to form a new body (multiplied body). God's Creativity, then, is described as the ability to form those two quadruple bases.

With regard to the creative act, one might think that it is a kind of energy. Creativity, however, has two aspects: one is the energetic aspect; the other, the aspect of will, which is a spiritual aspect and is more significant than the first. Thus, creativity in God takes place primarily due to the action of the will within the Inner *Sung Sang*.

Quadruple bases are formed centering on purpose. At this point I would like to discuss purpose, which is the center of the Quadruple Base. What is the origin of purpose? Purpose is grounded in, and established by, Heart. Heart is described as the emotional impulse to seek joy through loving an object. Heart is the very reason for the establishment of the Purpose of Creation; without

---

*The Quadruple Base, which includes both the Inner Quadruple Base and Outer Quadruple Base, is explained in the next section of this chapter.

Heart, there can be no Purpose of Creation. When we say that God created the universe according to the Purpose of Creation, we should acknowledge the underlying role of Heart. We must conclude, then, that Creativity itself is also motivated by, or is grounded in, Heart.

According to the Unification Principle, God's ultimate purpose in bestowing His Creativity on man was to set him up as the dominator over all things (See *Divine Principle*, Part I, ch. 2, Section VI, 3.) Man, however, was to receive God's Creativity only after passing through the three stages of growth (Formation, Growth, and Completion Stages). It is important to note here that God intends to endow man with His own Creativity, not just with creativity in general. When I queried the Reverend Sun Myung Moon about this, he answered that there is no true creativity apart from God's Creativity. The fundamental characteristic of God's Creativity is that it is based on Heart (love). This, of course, raises the question about fallen man's creativity. Fallen man does exhibit a sort of creativity; since, however, it is not based on Heart (love), his creativity is quite different from that of God.

As stated above, the purpose of man's creativity is to enable him to dominate all things. 'Dominion' has various shades of meaning. It may imply 'ruling', 'controlling', 'dealing with', or 'protecting'. Consequently, various human activities fall under the category of dominion. For instance, industrial production, commercial enterprises, farming, scientific research, artistic creativity—all these can be considered under the concept of 'dominion'.

We should be reminded, however, that dominion of all things with love can only be accomplished through the Creativity given by God. After the fall, man lost the original Creativity given by God. He now expresses creativity without Heart, which is only the *Hyung Sang* aspect of God's Creativity. Scientific research, commercial enterprises, and so on, are undertaken without any love for the creation or for mankind. They are undertaken for individual purposes, or, at best, for the nation; hence, we have been plagued by the evils of war, pollution, etc.

This is in sharp contrast to God's Creativity. When God created man and all things, He took exceedingly good care not to harm them, for His creativity is based on love. This, again, brings up the point of the International Conference on the Unity of the Sciences. The purpose of the Conference is to give scientists an opportunity to discuss the relationship between science and values, as an attempt to reconnect scientific research with true Creativity (God's Creativity). It is hoped that scientists will finally realize that they must conduct their research on the basis of love for mankind and for all things.

Summary of the Contents (Attributes) of the Original Image

Sung Sang and *Hyung Sang*, positivity and negativity, and Individual Images are called *Divine Image*. Heart, Logos, and Creativity are called *Divine Character*. The Divine Image and the Divine Character constitute the ORIGINAL IMAGE.

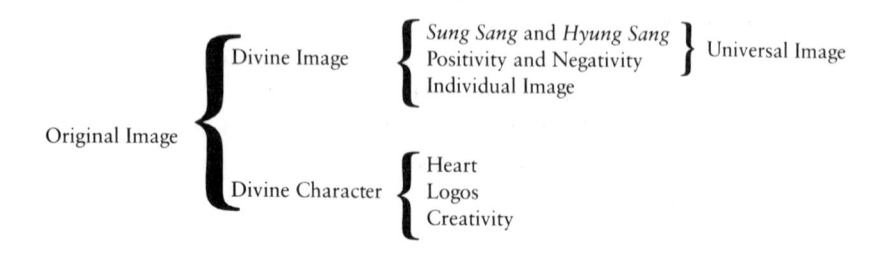

Original Image
- Divine Image
  - *Sung Sang* and *Hyung Sang*
  - Positivity and Negativity
  - Individual Image
  } Universal Image
- Divine Character
  - Heart
  - Logos
  - Creativity

III. STRUCTURE OF THE ORIGINAL IMAGE

The structure of the Original Image refers to the relationships between the various attributes of God. A watch is composed of many parts, and each has its fixed position and maintains a specific relationship with other parts. Similarly, each attribute of God has its position and maintains a specific relationship with other attributes. Of course, it is not really appropriate to discuss the transcendent God by using such temporal terms as 'structure' and 'position', and we must bear in mind that if God were a composite being of *Sung Sang* and *Hyung Sang*, or Positivity and Negativity, He would no longer be God. Nevertheless, with the limitations of our words, which have been developed in space and time, we cannot but explain the absolute God, for the benefit of our own understanding, as if He were an objectified being.

A. QUADRUPLE BASE

1. Quadruple Base (Four Position Foundation)

In the Original Image, *Sung Sang* and *Hyung Sang* form a

United Body, or Harmonious Body, through give-and-take action centered on Heart. The structure of the Original Image is the Quadruple Base (Four-Position Foundation), which is made up of four components: Heart, *Sung Sang*, *Hyung Sang*, and United Body (Harmonious Body). Heart, actually, lies deep within the *Sung Sang*, but we put it in the central position, since it is the motive, or starting point, for the give-and-take action between *Sung Sang* and *Hyung Sang*. Centering on Heart, *Sung Sang* is in the subject position, while *Hyung Sang* is in the object position. The relationship between subject and object is as that between active and passive, controlling and obeying, central and dependent, creating and conserving, initiating and responding, dynamic and static. In the Original Image, *Sung Sang*, which is subject, actively controls and works on *Hyung Sang*, which takes an objective, passive position.

Let us discuss the center of the Quadruple Base. I explained in the "Introduction" that many of today's social problems arise from unclarity as to (a) how something should be, and (b) how its relationships should be. There is no relationship without a center, for the center is the standard or motive for establishing the relationship. *Sung Sang* and *Hyung Sang* relate with each other centering on Heart. In the same way, members of a family must relate with one another centering on the Purpose of Creation, or centering on the parental will, if their relationship is to be harmonious and meaningful.

Give-and-take action between *Sung Sang* and *Hyung Sang* originally should be harmonious and smooth, without the slightest strain or angularity. For this reason we refer to the United Body resulting from the give-and-take action between *Sung Sang* and *Hyung Sang* as a 'Harmonious Body' or 'Neutral Body'.

According to Unification Principle the give-and-take action between a subject and an object is initiated through the agency of the universal prime force. This might give the impression that there is something like a physical force at the center of the Quadruple Base in God; that is not the case, however. To be sure, a force is present in the initiation of give-and-take action between a subject and an object in the physical world. This is the universal prime force, which may be likened to the Newtonian universal force of gravitation. The origin of the universal prime force lies in God; this origin is called *Prime Force*, in Unification Thought.

The Unification Principle says that the universal prime force is the center of the Quadruple Base and the initiating factor of the give-and-take action between subject and object. This, however, is liable to be misunderstood, if we happen to consider the universal prime force as nothing but a physical force. In this case, we would be led to the inevitable conclusion that force is the most essential element in the universe, including social life. We would have to say that give-and-take action occurs centering on power, and would have to agree with the proposition, "Might makes right." In doing this, we would lose the philosophical basis for valuing love and goodness and would find ourselves—like the communists—justifying dictatorial power. The most essential and central attribute of God is Heart. God created all things motivated by Heart. Heart is the center of the Quadruple Base in the Original Image. By showing that Heart and love have the highest value, we can protect people from false philosophies.

Finally, let me explain the Quadruple Base in the *Sung Sang*. *Sung Sang* consists of Inner *Sung Sang* (subject) and Inner *Hyung Sang* (object). The Quadruple Base that is formed by the give-and-take action between Inner *Sung Sang* and Inner *Hyung Sang* is called the *Inner Quadruple Base*. Needless to say, the center of the Inner Quadruple Base is Heart, and the United Body is nothing other than *Sung Sang* itself. The Quadruple Base that is formed by the give-and-take action between this *Sung Sang* and the *Hyung Sang* is called the *Outer Quadruple Base,* to distinguish it from the Inner Quadruple Base. (Fig. 4)

Fig. 4 Inner Quadruple Base and Outer Quadruple Base

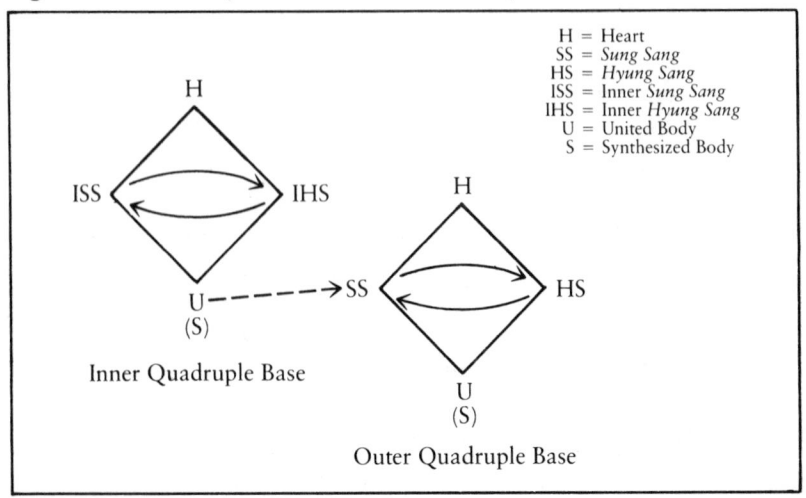

H = Heart
SS = *Sung Sang*
HS = *Hyung Sang*
ISS = Inner *Sung Sang*
IHS = Inner *Hyung Sang*
U = United Body
S = Synthesized Body

Inner Quadruple Base

Outer Quadruple Base

Structure of the Original Image

In the Original Image, *Sung Sang* and *Hyung Sang* are engaged in harmonious give-and-take action centering on Heart to form the United Body or Synthesized Body. This aspect of the Original Image is eternal and unchanging, and the Quadruple Base thus formed is called the *Identity-Maintaining Quadruple Base* or *Static Quadruple Base*.

In the creation of the universe, however, the Purpose based on God's Heart becomes significant. Heart is the emotional impulse to seek joy, and in this process the *Sung Sang* and *Hyung Sang* enter into give-and-take action centering on the Purpose based on Heart—the Purpose of Creation.

2. The Identity-Maintaining Quadruple Base and the Developing Quadruple Base

The aspects of *Sung Sang* and *Hyung Sang* that are engaged in give-and-take action centering on Purpose are different from those engaged in maintaining the identity of God. Intellect, emotion, and will in the *Sung Sang* are mobilized to realize the Purpose in the process of Creation; in maintaining identity, however, they are silent. When God decided to create something—a bird, for instance—He thought of a concrete image, including such things as the type of feathers, the location of the beak, and the shape and location of the eyes. This means that the contents of *Sung Sang* (Inner *Sung Sang* and Inner *Hyung Sang*) are changing. The form, or image, of the bird is "stamped" onto the *Hyung Sang*, so that it, too, is changing. Change in the Original Image means development, for the New Body or Multiplied Body is formed as the result of this change. Through give-and-take action, God's *Sung Sang* and *Hyung Sang* are multiplied, so that the New Body results. The Quadruple Base, consisting of Purpose, *Sung Sang*, *Hyung Sang* and Multiplied Body (New Body), is called *Developing Quadruple Base* or *Dynamic Quadruple Base*. (Fig. 5)

The fact that both the Developing and the Identity-Maintaining Quadruple Bases appear in the Original Image indicates that God created the universe while maintaining His immutability. Changeability and unchangeability are united in God. Man and all of creation, being created after the Original Image, necessarily and simultaneously have both identity-maintaining and developing quadruple bases.

For example, man, on one hand, grows and changes both

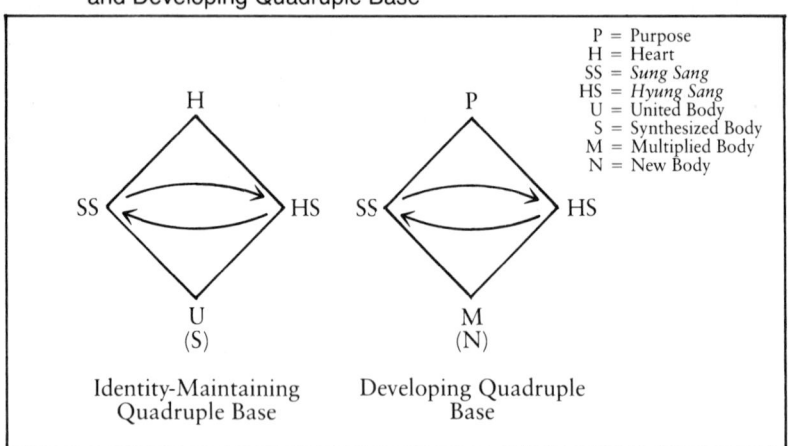

Fig. 5 Identity-Maintaining Quadruple Base and Developing Quadruple Base

```
         H                    P              P  = Purpose
                                             H  = Heart
                                             SS = Sung Sang
                                             HS = Hyung Sang
 SS <======> HS     SS <======> HS           U  = United Body
                                             S  = Synthesized Body
                                             M  = Multiplied Body
                                             N  = New Body
         U                    M
        (S)                  (N)

  Identity-Maintaining    Developing Quadruple
    Quadruple Base              Base
```

mentally and physically; on the other hand, he maintains his character and identity: he cannot change into another man, no matter how long he lives. A cherry tree grows branches, produces flowers, and bears fruit; yet it maintains its identity as a cherry tree: it can never change into a pear tree or an apricot tree. A tree grows from being a seed into a sprout through the give-and-take action between the embryo and albumen; its growth continues to fructification. This is the developing aspect of the tree. Throughout its growth, however, it remains the same tree. This is the identity-maintaining aspect of the tree.

In the Original Image, the Identity-Maintaining Quadruple Base is centered on Heart; the Developing Quadruple Base, involved in the Creation process, is centered on Purpose. This Purpose, however, is the Purpose of Heart, and the two are not essentially different. When we say 'Purpose', we are referring to 'Heart with Purpose'; when we say 'Heart', we are considering 'Heart' minus the 'Purpose' factor.

In the created world, however, both the identity-maintaining and the developing quadruple bases are centered on Purpose. In a timepiece, for instance, it is obvious that there is purpose in its maintaining its identity, since it was made by man for the purpose of telling time. Likewise, there is purpose in every existing being's maintaining its identity. Animals, plants, and even inorganic matter have purpose—the Purpose of Creation. Man was created with a purpose; in a family, the husband and wife love each other, forming an eternal unity centering on the Purpose of Creation. Not knowing one's purpose can be the source of great anxiety. In fact, numerous problems in life are due to people's ignorance of the purpose of life.

The developing quadruple base in created beings is also centered on purpose. A growing seed, for instance, has the purpose of becoming a new plant and bearing fruit; an incubated egg develops to realize the purpose of becoming a chicken; husband and wife bear children centered on the Purpose of Creation—the realization of God's love through the family (developing quadruple base of the family).

Philosophical trends of the past have tended to emphasize either the identity-maintaining or the developing aspect of the quadruple base. In either case, the resulting world view becomes distorted. The materialism of the 17th and 18th centuries, for instance, called *mechanical materialism,* only dealt with the identity-maintaining aspect of repetitive motion in every being. Communists criticized this philosophical trend, saying that it did not recognize development in the universe, even though it recognized motion. In fact, communists consider mechanical materialism to be a prop for maintaining the capitalist system. In the communist philosophy itself, on the other hand, dialectical materialism emphasizes development, with the specific purpose of justifying the changing of capitalist society into a communist one. When such a high priority is given to the developing aspect of the universe, the political undercurrents become very strong.

Communists also criticize traditional metaphysics, which deals with unchanging essences. According to this type of metaphysics, a bud, for instance—which seems to be constantly changing through the stages of becoming a flower, then withering and dying—has an unchanging essence, for the same flower will bloom again in the following year. Stalin challenged this idea, saying, "Contrary to metaphysics, dialectics holds that nature is not a state of rest and immobility, stagnation and immutability, but a state of continuous movement and change, of continuous renewal and development, where something is always arising and developing, and something always disintegrating and dying away."*

---

*J. Stalin, *Dialectical and Historical Materialism* (New York: International Publishers, 1975), p. 7.

To be sure, motion and change are, in fact, real aspects of the universe. Nevertheless, dialectical thought, also, is one-sided. In Unification Thought, everything has both changing and unchanging aspects, since there are both Identity-Maintaining and Developing Quadruple Bases in the Original Image.

3. The Inner Structure of the Logos

The Inner *Sung Sang* and the Inner *Hyung Sang*, centering on Heart, make up the *Sung Sang*. When Purpose appears in the Heart, both the Inner *Sung Sang* and the Inner *Hyung Sang* move toward its accomplishment. Hence the Identity-Maintaining Quadruple Base in the *Sung Sang** becomes the Developing Quadruple Base.

The Inner *Sung Sang* consists of intellect, emotion, and will. I will now explain these terms in greater detail.

First, 'intellect' refers to the function of recognition, which includes sensibility, understanding, and reason. When Isaac Newton, for example, saw an apple fall to the ground, he recognized that it had fallen. This is cognition based on sensibility, or perceptual cognition. Then he wondered, "Why do apples fall?" He tried to acquire a deeper cognition, through understanding. Next, he began to think beyond the mere incident of the apple: "Why does anything fall to the ground?" "How can this be understood?" He looked for a universally applicable truth, and finally discovered the law of universal gravitation. He had applied 'reason' to the problem. Sensibility corresponds to formation-stage intellect; understanding, to growth-stage intellect; and reason, to completion-stage intellect. The origin, or prototype, of the three-stage intellectual faculty of man is the intellect of God.

Second, 'emotion' refers to the function of feeling—feeling joy, sadness, etc. It is different from Heart, for Heart lies deeper than emotion, intellect, and will. Heart is the cause; emotion, the effect. God feels joy when His Heart is satisfied, and sadness when it is not. Joy and sadness are not emotion itself, but emotional states; emotion refers to the function of feeling them.

Third, 'will' refers to the function of intent, or the decision to

---

*The Identity-Maintaining Quadruple Base in the *Sung Sang* is called the Inner Identity-Maintaining Quadruple Base, and the Identity-Maintaining Quadruple Base formed between the *Sung Sang* and the *Hyung Sang* is called the Outer Identity-Maintaining Quadruple Base. The establishment of these Quadruple Bases enables God to exist eternally.

do something. The will of man originates from the will of God, which is expressed as the decision to realize the Purpose of Heart.

Once the Purpose for creating something—such as a bird—is formed by Heart, the Inner *Sung Sang* (intellect, emotion, and will) interacts with the idea or image in the Inner *Hyung Sang*. God thinks with His intellect (especially with reason), "How can I realize the idea of a bird? What color should it be? What should the shape and structure of the feathers be like? How should the bones and muscles be constructed?" Next, He makes a specific plan for creating the bird. Seeing the plan, He feels with His emotion, "It is not good," or "It is fine." If the plan is unsatisfactory, He corrects it. Then He decides, with His will, to realize the plan. In forming and carrying out the plan, intellect, emotion, and will are all mobilized; of these three, however, intellect plays the most important part in forming the plan.

Besides the idea, the other aspects of the Inner *Hyung Sang*, —i.e., original law and mathematical principle—are also mobilized. Law plays the most important part in this process. It may be said, in fact, that the plan of anything is formed through the give-and-take action between reason and law. (There are, of course, other factors, too.) The concrete plan of the bird, for instance, is its logos. Logos is the unity of the dual characteristics of Inner *Sung Sang* (reason) and Inner *Hyung Sang* (law).

As explained before, the quadruple base formed by the give-and-take action between Inner *Sung Sang* and Inner *Hyung Sang* is called Inner Quadruple Base. We also said that the Quadruple Base centering on Purpose is called Developing Quadruple Base. So, the quadruple base that forms Logos by the give-and-take action between Inner *Sung Sang* and Inner *Hyung Sang*, centering on the Purpose of Creation, is called Inner Developing quadruple Base. Logos, therefore, is the New Body formed by this Quadruple Base. This is the inner structure of Logos. Logos is the very *Sung Sang* of God in Creation. Human creativity follows a similar pattern. When we want to make something, first we form a plan in our mind—the blueprint. Besides the blueprint, we need materials to realize the plan. The same can be said with regard to God. In order to realize the Logos of a bird, for instance, God needs matter to make bones, muscles, feathers, and so on. The actual bird is the result of the give-and-take action between Logos and *Hyung Sang* (pre-matter). Logos is in the subject position; pre-matter, in the object position.

Thus, the purpose arising from Heart can finally be accomplished.

In sum, God created the universe through give-and-take action of two successive quadruple bases: first, the Inner Quadruple Base; second, the Outer Quadruple Base. Both are centered on Purpose and are called Developing Quadruple Bases. The structure involving these two Quadruple Bases formed during the Creation process is called the *two-stage structure of Creation.* * (Fig. 6)

Fig. 6 The Two-Stage Structure of Creation

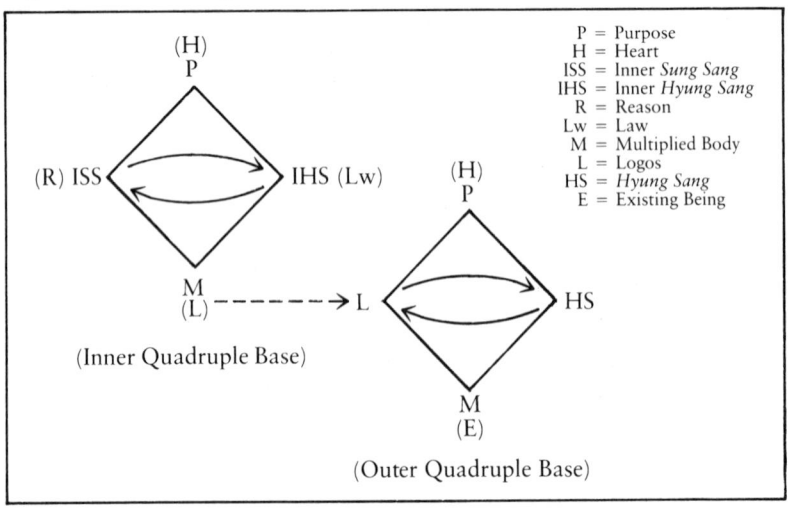

```
P   = Purpose
H   = Heart
ISS = Inner Sung Sang
IHS = Inner Hyung Sang
R   = Reason
Lw  = Law
M   = Multiplied Body
L   = Logos
HS  = Hyung Sang
E   = Existing Being
```

(Inner Quadruple Base)

(Outer Quadruple Base)

Following the pattern of God, man, also, has a two-stage structure both in his creative process and in his existence. Specifically with regard to his creative process, first he thinks and makes a plan for what he wants to make; then he makes it, through using all the necessary materials.

Here I would like to reemphasize the proper position of reason in the Quadruple Base of God. Heart, or Purpose, occupies the central or highest position; *Sung Sang,* which contains reason, is in the second position; *Hyung Sang* (pre-matter) is in the third position; and the United Body, or the Multiplied Body, is in the fourth position. Reason, to say nothing of matter, is not the motive, but the

---

*In a similar manner, the process of forming the Inner and Outer Identity-Maintaining Quadruple Bases for the eternal self-existence of God can be called the *two-stage structure of existence.*

means, to accomplish the Purpose of Creation. Even the attributes of omniscience and omnipotence are related to Heart, for God is said to be omniscient and omnipotent because He can always accomplish the purpose of Heart. In all respects, therefore, Heart is the most essential attribute of God.

4. The Quadruple Base and Real Problems

The Inner Quadruple Base has two forms: the Inner Identity-Maintaining (Static) Quadruple Base, and the Inner Developing (Dynamic) Quadruple Base. Moreover, there is the Outer Quadruple Base, which also has two forms: the Outer Identity-Maintaining Quadruple Base and the Outer Developing Quadruple Base. In all, then, there are four kinds of Quadruple Bases.

Understanding these Quadruple Bases is very important for solving real problems. The inner quadruple base of man is formed by the give-and-take action between his spirit-mind and his physical mind. This give-and-take action will be harmonious only when the spirit-mind is in the subject position and the physical mind is in the object position. The function of the spirit-mind is to seek the values of love, trueness, goodness, and beauty; it also directs man to live according to the Purpose of Creation. The function of the physical mind is to seek the basic physical necessities of life, such as food, clothing, shelter, and reproduction. One should seek a life of spiritual values first, and physical necessities second.

While forming a correct Inner Quadruple Base (proper way of life within oneself), one should also make Outer Quadruple Bases through establishing give-and-take action with others (such as family members and co-workers). Harmonious relationships with parents, spouse, children, superiors, inferiors, and so on—through the establishment of relationships of subject and object—will bring unity and prosperity to one's family, business enterprise, organization, etc. This is related to 'how each being should be' and 'how relationships should be'—questions which I raised in the Introduction. There is no harmonious give-and-take action if the participants do not occupy their correct positions—if, for example, students in a school oppose their teachers and go on strike; or the teachers do not care about the well-being of their students. Harmonious give-and-take action is based on love and on the observance of position. Teachers should teach their students with love; students should study seriously and show respect for their teachers.

We can see, therefore, that both the theory of dual characteristics and the theory of Quadruple Bases in the Original Image have been proposed, not for the sake of theorizing, but in order to be practiced in daily life.

Finally, I would like to give an additional explanation about the Identity-Maintaining and Developing Quadruple Bases. The Identity-Maintaining Quadruple Base is characterized by unchangeability, whereas the Developing Quadruple Base is characterized by changeability. These two Quadruple Bases are not separate from each other, but represent dual features of the one Quadruple Base. Every existing being simultaneously has both identity-maintaining and developing aspects in its quadruple base. In our specific case, for example, some aspects of our character and appearance remain the same throughout our whole life; on the other hand, we are constantly growing and changing from birth. Indeed, the unity of changeability and unchangeability constitutes an important aspect of existence.

B. THE *CHUNG-BOON-HAP* ACTION*

The structure of the Original Image is the Quadruple Base, which has four components and is centered on Heart. Let us consider the process of forming the Quadruple Base in the Original Image. First, God is the Absolute, or the Oneness. Furthermore, He has the correlative aspects of *Sung Sang* and *Hyung Sang*. Finally, these correlative aspects enter into give-and-take action to form the United Body or Multiplied Body. This means that there are three stages in the formative process of the structure of the Original Image—i.e., the Absolute, the Correlative, and the United. The Absolute is represented by Heart (or Purpose), since Heart is the essence of God. This formative process of the structure of the Original Image, which goes through these three stages, is called *Chung-Boon-Hap* action (Origin-Separation-Union action), abbreviated as C-B-H action (O-S-U action). Both the Quadruple Base and the *Chung-Boon-Hap* action are relative views of the structure of the Original Image: the former is a spatial approach; the latter, a temporal approach.

**Chung-Boon-Hap is a Korean expression that may be translated as "Origin-Separation-Union."

Structure of the Original Image

Since God transcends time and space, He actually has neither a forming process nor a spatial structure. He is the oneness, or the "point," from which time and space have developed. Such a view of God, however, will help us to understand the forming processes in the world of space and time.

There are Inner and Outer Quadruple Bases, as well as Identity-Maintaining and Developing Quadruple Bases in the Original Image. Similarly, there are Inner and Outer C-B-H actions, as well as Identity-Maintaining and Developing C-B-H actions. *Chung* (Origin) in the Identity-Maintaining C-B-H action is Heart, whereas *Chung* (Origin) in the Developing C-B-H action is Purpose. In the created world, however, Purpose constitutes *Chung* for both the identity-maintaining and the developing C-B-H actions, just as Purpose is the center for both the identity-maintaining and the developing quadruple bases in the created world. Purpose, or motive, is the prerequisite for give-and-take action between a subject and an object. The result is a United Body, or Multiplied Body. When seen from the time perspective, then, give-and-take action is none other than C-B-H action. The earth, for example, orbits the sun based on the Purpose of Creation, and together with the other planets, forms the solar system. The center of the give-and-take action between the planets and the sun is the Purpose of Creation; the result, the solar system. This process is the identity-maintaining C-B-H action. In the family, a husband and wife who love each other form an eternal unity, centering on the Purpose of Creation. This is the identity-maintaining C-B-H action. The bearing of children, however, is a developing C-B-H action.

C. THE STRUCTURAL UNITY OF THE ORIGINAL IMAGE

We have discussed the attributes and structure of the Original Image from the viewpoint of time and space. As we noted, however, there is neither time nor space in God. Thus, our explanations about attributes and structure in God are figurative and metaphorical. God's attributes and structure are actually unified in one point. In God, there is no difference between front and back, right and left, above and below, here and there, inside and outside. God exists in one locus, yet simultaneously, in an infinite number of loci. He exists simultaneously in the present and in the future. The world of the Original Image, therefore, is the infinite "here" and the eternal "now."

The four positions in the Quadruple Base are actually one position; the three stages of C-B-H action are actually one stage. *Sung Sang* and *Hyung Sang,* Inner Quadruple Base and Outer Quadruple Base, Identity-Maintaining Quadruple Base and Developing Quadruple Base—all these are totally united and harmonious in God.

Without describing the Original Image as we have, however, our understanding would not develop. We can better understand the structural unity of the Original Image by thinking of a roll of movie film. When we watch a movie, the part of the film that has already been projected on the screen belongs to the past; the part that we watch now belongs to the present; and the part that remains to be seen belongs to the future. There is a past, a present, and a future as we watch the movie; yet all are united in the one roll of film. People, animals, trees, and so on, have positions on the screen and are separated from one another, but come from the same roll of film.

In a similar—though essentially different—manner, everything that exists in the universe, from the greatest heavenly bodies to the minutest particles, originates from one point—God. (God's attributes themselves are united in God.) Every existing being in the universe has its own position. But there is one (united) position within God; hence, the whole universe forms a united, organic body.

Consequently, all the existing beings in the universe are related. The solar system, for example, would become disordered if just one planet, such as the earth, were taken away. With regard to physical health, a man with a stomach ailment, for example, will find his whole well-being affected. In the physical body, the cells and the organs are related to one another, since the body is the result of successive cell divisions from the original fertilized egg-cell. Furthermore, all the bodies of the universe are related to one another, for all of them have been projected from the one origin—God.

Engels said that metaphysicians cannot see the forest for the trees. They do not realize the universal relatedness of all things. His description of mutual relationships is only natural from the Unification Thought viewpoint. Unification Thought, however, goes on to clarify why all things cannot but be mutually related; Engels offered no such clarification.

I have pulled God down to the temporal world, by describing Him in temporal language. Still our concept of structure is effective, since the relationships among God's attributes do in fact exist, even though God is beyond time and space. The structural unity of the Original Image is a critical and essential concept for a correct understanding of the absoluteness and oneness of God.

IV. CRITIQUE OF TRADITIONAL PHILOSOPHIES
A. CRITIQUE OF MARXIST PHILOSOPHY

Marxism has held sway over the philosophical world for almost a century. I would like to point out the shortcomings of this philosophy—dialectical materialism—and its harmful influence on man and the world.

The Marxist dialectic maintains that development is realized by "the unity and struggle of opposites." This, actually, differs from Hegel's original thought. In his writings, contradiction—the extreme condition of opposites—is the motive of development; there is no mention of the concept of struggle, except in an explanatory note.* In Marx, Engels, and Lenin, however, the concept of struggle became an essential factor of development. In Lenin's words, "The unity (coincidence, identity, equal action) of opposites is conditional, temporary, transitory, relative. The struggle of mutually exclusive opposites is absolute, just as development and motion are absolute."† Accordingly, in the communist dialectic the unity of opposites has become no more than an ornament; the struggle of opposites has become the essence of the dialectic.

In contrast, Unification Thought says that development is realized through the harmonious give-and-take action between subject and object. Subject and object have a common purpose; give-and-take action is centered on that purpose. Engels said that he verified the dialectic through his study of the natural world, but that is not exactly true. All he did was to observe the existence of two elements in every natural phenomenon; his conclusion that they are opposites was hasty, unfounded, and illogical. Since the two elements share a common purpose, they do not exist in a state of

---

*Hegel, *Hegel's Science of Logic*, trans. by A.V. Miller, (London: George Allen & Unwin Ltd., 1969), p. 435-438.
† V.I. Lenin, *Collected Works*, Vol. 38: *Philosophical Notebooks*, (Moscow: Foreign Languages Publishing House, 1961), p. 360.

opposition, contradiction, or struggle. On the contrary, they exist in the correlative relationship of subject and object, centering on their common purpose.

Yet it is difficult for man to form and keep meaningful relationships with his fellow man, for the common purpose—the Purpose of Creation—has been lost because of his Fall, and many struggles and wars have occurred in human history. Struggles, however, have never brought about development, but only stagnation and the decline of culture and economy. In the fallen world itself, development has been realized by the give-and-take action between subject and object, even when they were centered on a "non-principled" purpose.

The origin of the subject and object in every existing being is the Subject and Object (*Sung Sang* and *Hyung Sang*) in the Original Image, for every existing being is created taking after the Original Image. But fallen man is separated from God; the relationship between subject and object in human society has become disordered, from within the individual level to the level of family, society, nation, and world. (No such disorder is found in the natural world.) So, the relationships between government and people, teachers and students, parents and children, and so on, must be corrected, if we are to bring about the world of harmony, centered on the Purpose of Creation.

In sum, in order to bring about an ideal individual, family, society, nation, and world, as well as an ideal school and an ideal education system, it is imperative to establish proper relationships between subject and object and to maintain harmonious give-and-take action between them. This gives us the basis for solving the problems raised in the Introduction. Furthermore, it should help us to realize that Unification Thought is not just a matter of semantics and high-flown ideas: it is immediate and practical.

By saying that struggle in nature and in human history is absolute, the communist dialectic can easily justify class struggle as something inevitable. It scatters the seeds of unbelief and hatred into families, societies, nations, and the world, striving at establishing a communist dictatorship on earth. Peace and happiness, however, can never be realized by such philosophical principles. (More on the communist dialectic in ch. 2, Sec 1, 1, [5])

These views, however, can be overcome by the theory of *Sung Sang* and *Hyung Sang*. The shortcomings of materialism, as well as the excelling qualities of the Unification Thought view, will be discussed in ch. 2, "Ontology," and in ch. 4, "Epistemology." At this point, I will limit my comments to the image of man based on materialism. Communist materialism considers economy as the basis for society, or the *infrastructure* of society, classifying it in the category of matter. On the other hand, politics, religion, art, philosophy, and so on, are placed under the category of ideology, which, in their view, constitutes the *superstructure* of society. Naturally, then, economic activity is regarded as the most central aspect of human concerns. In other words, labor is the essence of man. Engels, in fact, says this about labor: "It is the prime basic condition for all human existence, and this to such an extent, in a sense, that we have to say that labour created man himself."*

Based on their view of man, communists have attacked intellectuals, managers, artists, religious persons, and others in non-communist societies, saying that they are not laboring, but exploiting laborers, especially manual laborers. Is this view of man correct and satisfactory?

In Unification Thought, labor is viewed as a creative activity. True creativity originates from God's Creativity, which is based on heart and love. Labor, therefore, should be based on heart and love, should be pursued for the realization of love—the Purpose of Creation. Unfortunately, heart and love are left out of the communist idea of labor. Their concept of labor is different from our view of labor as a creative activity. Hence, their attack on intellectuals, managers, and so on, in non-communist societies. From the Unification Thought point of view, however, not only manual laborers, but also other members of society such as managers, scientists, and artists should express their creativity for the realization of the purpose of creation, the Kingdom of Heaven on earth.

B. CRITIQUE OF THE PHILOSOPHIES OF LIFE

At this point I would like to criticize the philosophical trends that designate 'life' as the ultimate cause of the universe. Schopenhauer, Nietzsche, Bergson, Simmel, and others, can generally be classified under this category, if we account for specific variations in their views. In Unification Thought, life-force corresponds to the creative force (will), or simply to energy. As such, it cannot be the ultimate

---

*F. Engels, *Dialectics of Nature* (Moscow: Progress Publishers, 1976), p. 170.

cause of the universe, because Heart lies even deeper than will and energy. In fact, subject and object cannot achieve a harmonious give-and-take action centering on force alone. History shows that those who have based their philosophies on force have failed to solve real human problems.

Hitler and Mussolini reportedly used Nietzsche's philosophy of force in order to strengthen their dictatorships. General Kanji Ishihara, seeking to justify the Japanese occupation of Manchuria, said, "All living things struggle for existence. It is natural for the strong to prey upon the weak. A strong nation, therefore, is justified in occupying a weak nation in order to protect her, for the weak nation might be destroyed, if left alone."

Despotic rulers can easily make use of philosophies that justify hegemony; those trends that designate life, force, or will as the cause of the universe are especially suitable for their purposes.

Life alone could never be the basis for an ideal world, for life without heart and love can easily take a destructive direction. Animals, for example, without man's dominion of love, may kill one another recklessly. It must have been so before the appearance of man on earth. (Since, however, that was the process of creation, it could not be helped.) Struggles among the animals continue until today, but they are due to the human fall. If man had not fallen, but instead had realized the Purpose of Creation, he would have dominated all things with love, preventing needless struggles among animals. The fact of struggle, however, illustrates the point that life (force, will) that is not based on heart and love inevitably leads to conflict and strife. We maintain, therefore, that the philosophies of life, force, and will should be connected with, and supplemented by, the philosophy of heart and love.

The French theologian Teilhard de Chardin, while admitting that God has various attributes, said that the motivating essence behind the creation is force. Polish communists have made use of this statement to substantiate their view that Marxism and Christianity are in effect the same, for both designate force as the cause of the universe. They criticize Teilhard de Chardin, however, for failing to recognize the character of struggle within force. Clearly, philosophies of force, or theologies of force, can invite utilization by those who would propagate the "revolution of the proletariat."

2 ONTOLOGY

Traditionally understood, ontology is the study of all beings—i.e., God, man, and creation (all things). In Unification Thought, however, God is dealt with in "Theory of the Original Image"; man, in "Theory of Original Human Nature"; and creation, in "Ontology."

The Unification Principle says that all things were created in God's image, according to the Law of Resemblance. But man was also created in God's image; consequently, nature must resemble man, though symbolically. Through studying the principles that rule nature, we can perceive some aspects of man's original nature, which but for the human fall he would have fully developed. This gives us a basis for understanding ourselves as well as our society, in its aspects of politics, economics, and so on.

As stated in ch. 1, God's Original Image contains the aspects of Universal Image and Individual Image. Existing beings, also, must exhibit a resemblance to these characteristics. When a being does contain the aspects of universal image and individual image, we call it an Individual Truth Body, as explained below.

I. THE INDIVIDUAL TRUTH BODY
A. UNIVERSAL IMAGE
1. Sung Sang and Hyung Sang

Every existing being has both the invisible aspects of function and character, and the visible aspects of matter, structure, and shape. (The latter are visible at least through scientific registration.) The invisible aspects are called *Sung Sang,* and the visible aspects, *Hyung Sang.* The *Sung Sang* and *Hyung Sang* of existing beings are derived from the *Sung Sang* and *Hyung Sang* of the Original Image.

In minerals, the physicochemical character of the constituent matter is the *Sung Sang,* while the atomic and molecular structure of the constituent matter corresponds to the *Hyung Sang.*

Plants contain minerals; thus, they have both a physicochemical character and a molecular or atomic structure. Plants, however, have additional *Sung Sang* and *Hyung Sang* characteristics. The additional *Sung Sang* elements are function and life, and the additional *Hyung Sang* elements are cell structure and tissue structure, which include the cortex, xylem, phloem, pith, and shape.

Animals, also, contain minerals, so they have physicochemical character and molecular or atomic structure. In addition, they contain all the *Sung Sang* and *Hyung Sang* characteristics of plants, namely, function, life, cell and tissue structure, and shape. In addition, animals have *Sung Sang* and *Hyung Sang* characteristics of a higher dimension: sense and instinct in its *Sung Sang,* and sense organs and nerves in its *Hyung Sang.*

Man contains minerals in his physical body, so he has characteristics corresponding to the *Sung Sang* and *Hyung Sang* of minerals. (It is said that we must ingest about forty different kinds of minerals to be well nourished.) Man also contains the *Sung Sang* and *Hyung Sang* aspects of plants. So, he has life, cells, tissue structure, and shape. Since man also contains the *Sung Sang* and *Hyung Sang* aspects of animals, he has sense and instinct (functions of the physical mind) as well as organs and nerves. Furthermore, man has *Sung Sang* and *Hyung Sang* characteristics of yet a higher dimension— i.e., a spirit-mind *(Sung Sang)* and a spirit-body *(Hyung Sang).*

As we can see, then, the *Sung Sang* and *Hyung Sang* characteristics of existing beings form a kind of staircase, which is called the *Stepped Structure of Sung Sang and Hyung Sang in Existing Beings.* What is the significance of this? It is related to the Unification Principle teaching that man is the integration of the universe (microcosm). Here we can see that man has all the elements of the universe—i.e., the *Sung Sang* and *Hyung Sang* of minerals, plants, and animals; but he also has higher characteristics, a spirit-mind and a spirit-body. The stepped structure view of the *Sung Sangs* and *Hyung Sangs* of existing beings can help us to understand man as the integration of the universe, or man as the microcosm. (Fig. 7) Stepped structure of *Sung Sang* and *Hyung Sang* in Existing Beings

Fig. 7 Stepped Structure of *Sung Sang* and *Hyung Sang* in Existing Beings

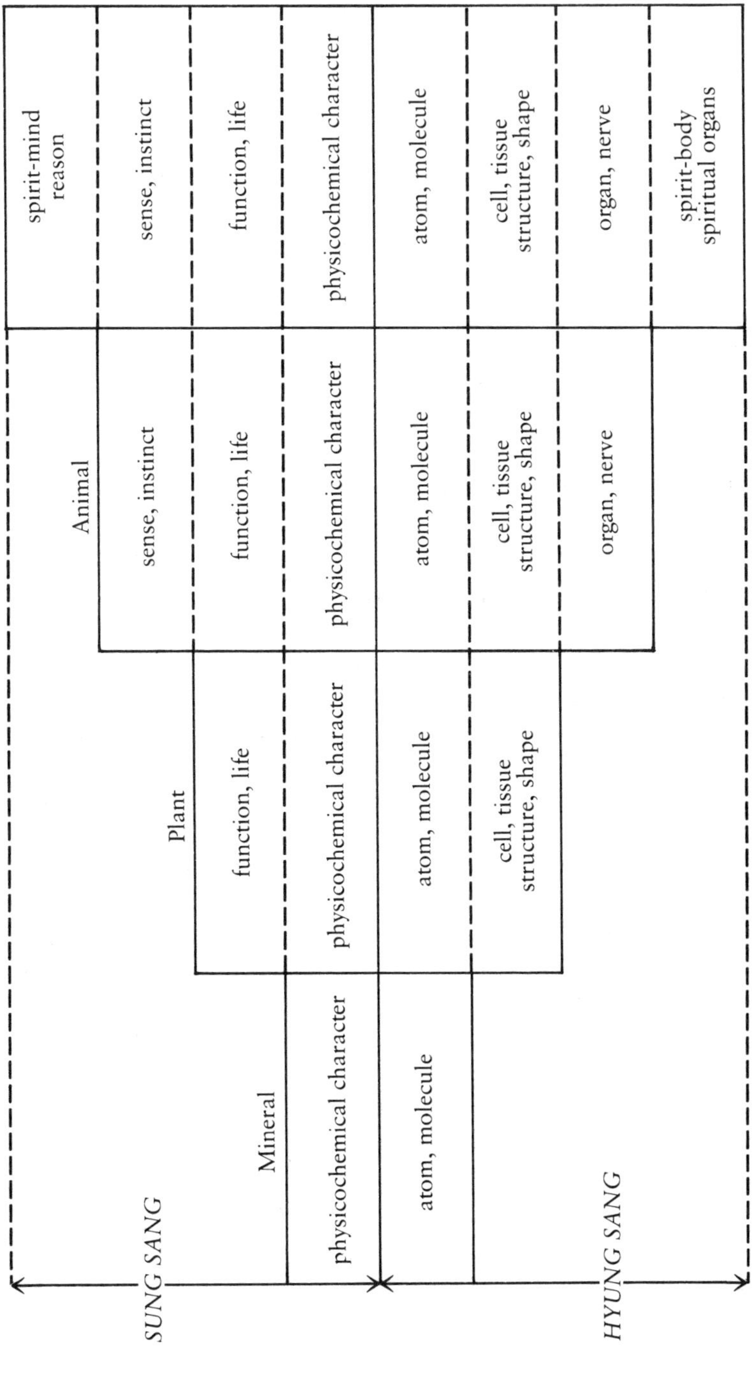

Today, studies about life are flourishing; there is a good deal of controversy about life's origin and the existence of God. Several decades ago, religious persons had an advantage over materialists in explaining the mysteries of life, in that scientists, in spite of great scientific progress, had not been able to create life. For those who defend the spiritual side of reality, life can only be created by God. For them, as well as for theologians, this creation theory was the last fortress against the assault of materialism and atheism. It seems, however, that modern science is on the verge of synthesizing life. If such be the case, it would appear that we cannot but accept the materialistic theory of evolution. Proponents of this view say that in the early stages after the formation of the earth, several elements gathered accidentally to form organic substances, including amino acids. (Amino acids have actually been synthesized from inorganic gases in recent experiments.) Proteins were then synthesized from amino acids, with the help of nucleic acids (which also appeared by chance), over the period of hundreds of millions of years. Since proteins are the essential substance of life, it is claimed we do not need God to explain the appearance of living creatures.

Unification Thought rejects such a conclusion and presents a different philosophical interpretation of scientific data, based primarily on a clear understanding of the Stepped Structure of the *Sung Sang* and *Hyung Sang* of existing beings. Next, I shall present such data, with a concomitant interpretation.

Many scientists regard the catalytic action of enzymes, which are proteins, to be life itself. This is not correct, from the Unification Thought viewpoint. The catalytic action of enzymes takes place in every part and function of the body—such as in food digestion, in the absorption of nutritious substances into the blood—and even in the thinking process of the brain. Without enzymes we would die immediately.

Proteins, which include enzymes and many of the important structural components of the cell, are created by the work of genes, or DNA (deoxyribonucleic acid). The DNA is formed of four chemical bases, aligned in pairs: adenine and thymine, guanine and cytosine. It is the arrangement and sequence of these bases that will instruct the cell to manufacture proteins. This arrangement is the genetic code, stored in the DNA, which will determine the specific characteristics of every living being. This code is transferred from parent to offspring. The arrangement of the four bases—Science tells us—can be altered, thereby changing the genetic code and the whole functioning of the cell.

Scientists can also explain how the information is transferred from the DNA to the specific area of the cell where proteins are produced, through the work of molecules of ribonucleic acid (RNA). Based on such a thorough understanding of the work of the DNA, materialists conclude that life can be totally explained by physico-chemical processes alone. Moreover, it has been reported that scientists are now able to synthesize simple DNA, or part of DNA. Consequently, materialists conclude that we no longer need God to explain life.

There seems, however, to be a jump of logic here. It is up to scientists to say, "The results of the scientific experiment are such and such," and it is up to philosophers, upon this basis, to say, "So, God exists" or "God does not exist." If Science concludes that God does not exist, without any proof, it will cease to be Science. As yet, Science has been unable to verify the existence of God; nevertheless, we cannot deny the possibility of such verification in the future. Materialists deny the existence of God—whereas we affirm it—on the basis of identical scientific explanations.

With regard to reports that scientists can synthesize simple DNA, what do they actually mean? From the Unification Thought point of view, that which scientists can synthesize—the DNA molecule—is only the *Hyung Sang* part of DNA. There must also be a *Sung Sang* aspect, because all existing beings, including DNA, have the dual characteristics of *Sung Sang* and *Hyung Sang*. Accordingly, no one can say that life itself has been synthesized. For the DNA molecule is not life itself, but only the base for life, or that which carries life.

We can liken DNA to a radio: a radio is merely a device to intercept electromagnetic waves, and to transform them into sound waves. The origin of the sound waves is not the radio itself, but the radio station. In a similar way, DNA has the ability to intercept, not electromagnetic waves, but life. From among the immense variety of electromagnetic waves, the radio picks up only those that are suitable; similarly, DNA picks up a suitable life form from a *life field*. The whole universe is diffused with life, which comes from the *Sung Sang* of God. We can say that God created DNA molecules, which pick up life, just as engineers make radio sets, which pick up electromagnetic waves. The DNA molecule is the *Hyung Sang* part, which "captures" the *Sung Sang* part—life.

If the behavior of DNA were regulated merely by physicochemical laws, it would be entirely mechanical. DNA, however, manifests selectivity and purpose. Enzymes themselves manifest selectivity and purpose. This indicates that behind the DNA molecule there is reason and will. According to Unification Thought, life is reason and will latent in the physical body. We conclude, then, that there is life behind the DNA molecule, and life gives it selectivity and purpose. Actually, a considerable number of scientists are now ready to include the life-factor in their theories connected with DNA behavior.

Can life, then, be synthesized under laboratory conditions? As we know, every created being has *Sung Sang* and *Hyung Sang* aspects, whose origin lies in God's united *Sung Sang* and *Hyung Sang*. From recent discoveries in the field of Biology, it has become clear that now scientists can manipulate the DNA molecule to a degree never thought possible before. Besides, these discoveries are very recent, and future possibilities are wide-open. Any such manipulations, however, are only dealing with the *Hyung Sang* aspect of DNA. So, scientists cannot synthesize life, even if they can synthesize a DNA molecule. As explained above, the structure of the DNA molecule is nothing but a "receiver" of life. The Genesis account of the creation of man may help us to understand this point. It says: "...then the Lord God formed man of the dust from the ground, and breathed into his nostrils the breath of life; and man became a living being." (Gen 2:7) We can think of life entering the DNA molecule in a similar way: the molecular structure, once prepared, can receive life, which comes from God.

Life, however, does not enter all molecules indiscriminately. It is captured only by a suitable molecule, DNA, as electromagnetic waves are captured only by a suitable apparatus, the radio set. The more developed the molecule, the higher the form of life it can accommodate. This can be seen through the Stepped Structure of *Sung Sang* and *Hyung Sang* of existing beings, as discussed above. Life exists abundantly in the whole universe, but can only be captured by a suitable structure. The more complex the structure, the higher the form of life it will be able to receive. Here we can see that man has the highest form of life, because he has the most complex structure. (See Fig. 7—Stepped Structure of *Sung Sang* and *Hyung Sang* in Existing Beings.) For this reason, man is called the integration of the universe (integrated being), having within himself the *Sung Sangs* and *Hyung Sangs* of all existing beings.

There is yet another way of looking at the *Sung Sang* and *Hyung Sang* of created beings, different from the Stepped Structure thus far discussed. We can regard man simply as having mind and body (dual being); animals as having instinct and body; plants as having life and body; and minerals as having physicochemical character and atomic or molecular constituents. Existing beings, then, have a single layer of *Sung Sang* and a single layer of *Hyung Sang*, when observed from this perspective. Here, the various *Sung Sangs* and *Hyung Sangs* form a double column or row, as opposed to the ladder-like formation of the Stepped Structure. We call this the *Monostratic Structure*, or *Horizontal Structure*, of the *Sung Sang* and *Hyung Sang* of existing beings.

The above two approaches relate man's *Sung Sang* and *Hyung Sang* to those of all existing beings. There are two other ways of looking at man's *Sung Sang* and *Hyung Sang:* as the united body of spirit-man and physical man (dual man), and as the possessor of spirit-mind and physical mind (dual mind). In the former, the spirit-man is *Sung Sang* and the physical man is *Hyung Sang*. In the latter, the spirit-mind is *Sung Sang* and the physical mind is *Hyung Sang*. From the aspects of *Sung Sang* and *Hyung Sang*, then, Unification Thought has four conceptions of man: the integrated man, the dual being, the dual man, and the possessor of dual mind.

Let it be noticed in passing that, when living in the spirit-world, the spirit-man is an individual truth body in his own right. The spirit-mind is *Sung Sang*, and the spirit-body is *Hyung Sang*.

2. Positivity and Negativity (*Yang* and *Eum*)

As previously mentioned, positivity and negativity are attributes of *Sung Sang* and *Hyung Sang*. Here, I will briefly sketch the positivity and negativity of *Sung Sang*, or mind (intellect, emotion, and will), and the positivity and negativity of *Hyung Sang*, or body.

Positive aspects of the intellect are perspicacity, keen perceptiveness, imaginativeness, good memory, and so on; negative aspects are obtuseness, dullness, unimaginativeness, poor memory, and so on. Positive aspects of emotion are pleasantness, cheerfulness, brightness, and so on; negative aspects are unpleasantness, melancholy, gloominess, and so on. Positive aspects of the will are activeness, decisiveness, creativeness, and so on; negative aspects are passiveness, indecisiveness, conservativeness, and so on. Similarly, we also find positive and negative aspects in the *Hyung Sang*. Jutting, protruding, and convex parts, as well as front side, and so on, are positive aspects; sunken, hollow, and concave parts, as well as back side, and so on, are negative aspects. (Fig. 8)

Fig. 8 Positivity and Negativity as the Attributes of *Sung Sang* (Mind) and *Hyung Sang* (Physical Body) of Man

		POSITIVITY	NEGATIVITY
Sung Sang (mind)	intellect	perspicacity keen perceptiveness imaginativeness good memory	obtuseness dullness unimaginativeness poor memory
	emotion	pleasantness cheerfulness brightness	unpleasantness melancholy gloominess
	will	activeness decisiveness creativeness	passiveness indecisiveness conservativeness
Hyung Sang (physical body)		jutting part protruding part convex part front side	sunken part hollow part concave part back side

These characteristics of positivity and negativity can be found in a man and in a woman. Now, let me explain the difference of positivity and negativity of man and of woman. This difference brings about the relationship of man and woman as the relationship of positivity and negativity. Both man and woman have positivity and negativity in their *Sung Sang*s and *Hyung Sang*s, but they are not the same. The positivity and negativity of man's *Hyung Sang* and those of woman's *Hyung Sang* are different quantitatively: man has more positive characteristics than woman, and woman has more negative characteristics than man. The positivity and negativity of man's *Sung Sang* and those of woman's *Sung Sang* are different qualitatively. For instance, the brightness of man's mind is different qualitatively from the brightness of woman's mind.

The positivity of man's *Sung Sang* can be called masculine positivity; the positivity of woman's *Sung Sang*, feminine positivity.

The Individual Truth Body

The negativity of man's *Sung Sang* can be called masculine negativity; the negativity of woman's *Sung Sang*, feminine negativity. For the sake of a better understanding of this, we can compare masculine positivity and feminine positivity to tenor and soprano; likewise, we can compare masculine negativity and feminine negativity to bass and alto, in vocal music.

Another important point must be mentioned here. The relationship between positivity and negativity is originally that between subject and object. In the case of man and woman, however, the relationship of subject and object applies basically to the husband-and-wife relationship. When their relationship is not of husband and wife, woman can at times have the subject position, and man, the object position. For example: the relationships between mother and son, elder sister and younger brother, female senior officer and male junior officer, and female teacher and male student.

Next I shall discuss the relevance of positivity and negativity with regard to the identity-maintaining and developing quadruple bases of the *Sung Sang* and *Hyung Sang*.

The identity-maintaining quadruple base enables man to have a congenitally fixed status, both in his *Sung Sang* and in his *Hyung Sang*. This explains man's unique character *(Sung Sang)* and unique appearance and constitution *(Hyung Sang)*. These unique features, however, can only be expressed through the attributes of positivity and negativity. One person may be sociable, active, and cordial, while another is aloof, quiet, and reserved. Likewise, each person's *Hyung Sang*, or appearance and constitution, will display positive and negative characteristics; these are a reflection of the positive and negative characteristics of the *Sung Sang*, or mind. It is possible, therefore, to know a great deal about a person's internal character simply by looking at his external appearance. Hence, only through positivity and negativity can the *Sung Sang* and *Hyung Sang* characteristics be expressed in the identity-maintaining quadruple base. Since the *Sung Sang* and *Hyung Sang* have unchanging aspects, the attributes of positivity and negativity, also, have unchanging aspects.

The give-and-take action between *Sung Sang* and *Hyung Sang* in the developing quadruple base produces a changing aspect that is both expressed through, and affected by, positivity and negativity. For example, man's mind, which is expressed through the attributes of positivity and negativity, changes when he acquires new knowledge. There are both positive kinds of knowledge and negative kinds of knowledge. A positive or negative emotional environment, also, has a marked effect on man's mind. Likewise, man's body is also affected by the physical environment. Some types of physical environment are positive, such as the seaside or a tropical country; others are negative, such as shady valleys deep in the mountains or a cold country. Positive and negative kinds of food, also, affect man's body. In conclusion, we can see that the changing aspect of the developing quadruple base, which is expressed through positivity and negativity, is also affected by the positivity and negativity of the environment.

Positivity and negativity can be seen in all beings, not only in man. A plant grows in the spring and is dormant in the winter. This is positivity and negativity in the life of a plant. A leaf has both convexity and concavity, an upper surface, which faces the sun, and an underside, which is away from the sun. Animals are active and restless sometimes, but docile and languid at others. Needless to say, their bodies, also, have positive and negative parts. Minerals have positivity and negativity both in their *Sung Sang* and in their *Hyung Sang*. Sodium chloride (NaCl), for example, consists of sodium ions (Na+) and chloride ions (Cl-), which are the positive and negative aspects of the *Hyung Sang* of sodium chloride. The *Sung Sang* part of sodium chloride, also, has both positive and negative aspects in its physical and chemical behavior.

3. Logos and the Harmony Between Positivity and Negativity

Logos is formed through the give-and-take action between Inner *Sung Sang* and Inner *Hyung Sang*, centering on purpose. In the formation of Logos, both the Inner *Sung Sang* and the Inner *Hyung Sang* are expressed through the attributes of positivity and negativity. The positivity and negativity of the Inner *Sung Sang* comprise the positive and negative aspects of the emotion, intellect, and will, as explained previously. The positivity and negativity of the Inner *Hyung Sang* can be described, figuratively, as the Inner *Hyung Sang's* convexity and concavity. More precisely, the Inner *Hyung Sang* has the potentiality of assuming positive and negative features.

In the Outer Quadruple Base that is formed by the give-and-take action between Logos and *Hyung Sang*, the effect of Logos over *Hyung Sang* is manifested through positive and negative aspects. As we know, *Hyung Sang*, which is pre-energy (or pre-matter), has no convexity or concavity in itself. Why, then, is it said to have positivity and negativity? Because *Hyung Sang* has the potentiality of expressing positivity and negativity. We can compare the *Hyung Sang* of God with water. Water has no definite form in itself, but it assumes a square form when it is put in a square vessel, or a spherical form when put in a spherical vessel, or even the form of a wave, when the wind blows over its surface. Even if the wind blows uniformly, water takes the form of a wave, with crests and troughs. This means that water has the latent possibility of expressing positivity (crests) and negativity (troughs). This parallel may help us to understand the meaning of the positivity and negativity in the *Hyung Sang*.

Thus, the principle of positivity and negativity has been operational in the process of Creation, both in the first stage—the creation of the Logos—and in the second stage—the creation of existing beings.

Not only in the creation of the universe has Logos been operational, but also in its development. In the development of the universe from a gaseous state to a solid state; in the growth of all living things, such as the growth of a plant from a seed to a fruit-bearing tree; everywhere Logos has been working through the principle of positivity and negativity. Thus, *Sung Sang* and *Hyung Sang* can neither exist, nor enter into give-and-take action, without the attributes of positivity and negativity.

Furthermore, there is yet another reason why positivity and negativity are at work in the creation process and in the development of the universe. That is to realize the unity and harmony of the universe. The Unification Principle says that all things were created as objects of beauty for man. But beauty can only be realized by harmony, such as the harmony of colors, shapes, and sounds. Harmony here can be defined as a pleasing combination of positivity and negativity. For example, flowers of many colors are usually more beautiful than flowers of a single color. Beauty, therefore, can be found where there is *harmony in variation* or *unity in variety*. Harmony in variation comes from the give-and-take action between positivity and negativity, such as positive and negative colors in the above example.*

Flowers of many colors in a flower-bed are an example of the harmony of positivity and negativity in *space*. Likewise, the harmony of successive high and low notes, of long and short notes, and of strong and weak notes in music, represent harmony of positivity and negativity in *time*. The development of the universe, therefore, has not been monotonous, but harmonious and full of variety, largely because of the principle of positivity and negativity. All the indescribable beauty of creation exists for the joy of man, and God enjoys man's being joyful.

I would like to give an additional explanation about the harmony of positivity and negativity in the created world. When a husband and wife relate between themselves through give-and-take action centering on the Purpose of Creation, the husband is said to be a "positive substantial body," who has a relatively positive *Sung Sang* and a relatively positive *Hyung Sang;* the wife, on the other hand, is said to be a "negative substantial body," who has a relatively negative *Sung Sang* and a relatively negative *Hyung Sang*. The give-and-take action between husband and wife forms a family quadruple base. Here we have an identity-maintaining quadruple base (the eternal unity of the loving husband and wife) and a developing quadruple base (the birth of children—i.e., multiplied bodies).

In the animal kingdom, there are identity-maintaining and developing aspects in the give-and-take action between male and female; in the plant kingdom, the same is true with regard to the give-and-take action between stamen and pistil. These give-and-take actions are expressions of the harmony and unity between positivity and negativity, or, more precisely, between "positive substantial bodies" and "negative substantial bodies."

In nature, we can see the harmony between mountains and plains, land and lakes, white cloud and blue sky, flying birds and a tranquil sea, and so forth. A picture contains harmonious elements, such as colors, positions, and shapes. When harmony is achieved, the picture can be called good. In dancing, there is harmony among the various kinds of costumes, among the various types of movements (such as moving to and fro, twirling around, and moving in a

---

*The statement, "harmony in variation comes from the give-and-take action between positivity and negativity," means that man, the appreciator, feels harmony when he contrasts or collates positivity and negativity. This is called "contrast-type give-and-take action," to be further explained in "Methodology."

straight line), and between dance and costumes. In literature, there are ups and downs, climactic situations and ordinary events.

Thus, the principle of positivity and negativity works universally, whether it be in nature, in the creative arts, or anywhere else. Once we understand this principle, our appreciation of creation and of the arts begins to blossom.

4. Subject and Object

Every individual truth body contains the correlative aspects of *Sung Sang* and *Hyung Sang*, positivity and negativity, principal individual and subordinate individual (or principal element and subordinate element), etc. The Unification Principle says that the elements of each of these correlative aspects relate between themselves as subject and object.

In a nutshell, the relationship between subject and object is as that between dominating and dominated. In other words, it is as the relationship between active and passive, central and dependent, creating and conservative, initiating and responding, controlling and obeying, dynamic and static, extrovert and introvert, etc. This means that the relationship between *Sung Sang* and *Hyung Sang* in the Original Image is as that between dominating and dominated. We can say, therefore, that God created all things through the dominion of *Sung Sang* over *Hyung Sang*.

Accordingly, every individual truth body has subject and object elements within itself, and is, at the same time, connected with other individual truth bodies in subject-object relationships.

The "great macrocosm,"* which is also an individual truth body, comprises the spirit-world (subject) and the physical world, or universe (object). In the universe—astronomers tell us—galaxies (object) revolve around the center of the universe (subject), which has not yet been defined or clarified. In a galaxy, solar systems (object) revolve around a core system of fixed stars (subject). In a solar system, planets (object) revolve around the sun (subject). The earth, which is a planet, has a crust (object) and a core (subject), and rotates on its axis, which goes through the core.

Moreover, on earth there are nations—a kind of individual

---

*The Unification Principle says that God created a dual world, the spiritual world (invisible) and the physical world (visible), just as He created a dual man, the spirit-man and the physical man. The two worlds are integrated in a single concept, and together are called the "great macrocosm."

truth body—consisting of government (subject) and people (object). Governments consist of a head of state (subject) and ministers (object). Within the nation, families consist of a husband (subject) and a wife (object), or parents (subject) and children (object). An individual member of the family consists of spirit-man (subject) and physical man (object). The physical man consists of a brain (subject) and organs and limbs (object). Each cell has a nucleus (subject) and cytoplasm (object). In the nucleus, chromosomes (subject) are suspended in the karyoplasm (object). In a chromosome, there is DNA (subject) and a chromosomal base (object). DNA consists of the four bases (subject) and sugar and phosphate groups (object). These molecules are composed of atoms, which have a positive nature (subject) or a negative nature (object). Atoms consist of the nucleus containing protons (subject) and electrons (object).

As we can see, from elementary particles to the great macrocosm, there are numerous levels of individual truth bodies, each one consisting of subject and object parts. The individual truth body of one level constitutes only a part of an individual truth body of the next level, while containing the individual truth bodies of the levels below it. For example, the solar system, which is a constituent of the galaxy, contains lower level individual truth bodies, such as Mercury, Venus, and Earth. "Individual truth body," therefore, is a relative concept: it is a constituent, when seen from a higher level, and a synthesized being, when seen from a lower level. (Fig. 9)

5. The Difference Between Unification Thought and Traditional Philosophy Regarding the Concept of 'Subject and Object'

The concept of 'subject and object' is important in Unification Thought and differs in meaning from 'subject and object' in traditional philosophy. It is necessary, therefore, to clarify the difference.

(a) 'Subject and Object' in Traditional Philosophy

Epistemologically, in the philosophy after Kant, 'subject' refers to man's consciousness, or the self, which perceives things; 'object' refers to the thing that is perceived by the 'subject'.

Ontologically, in the controversy between materialism and idealism, the concept of 'subject and object' is used for describing the reality of mental and material entities. A mental entity (consciousness) is called subject; a material entity (material thing), object.

The Individual Truth Body

Fig. 9
Subject and Object Elements in
All Levels of Individual Truth Bodies

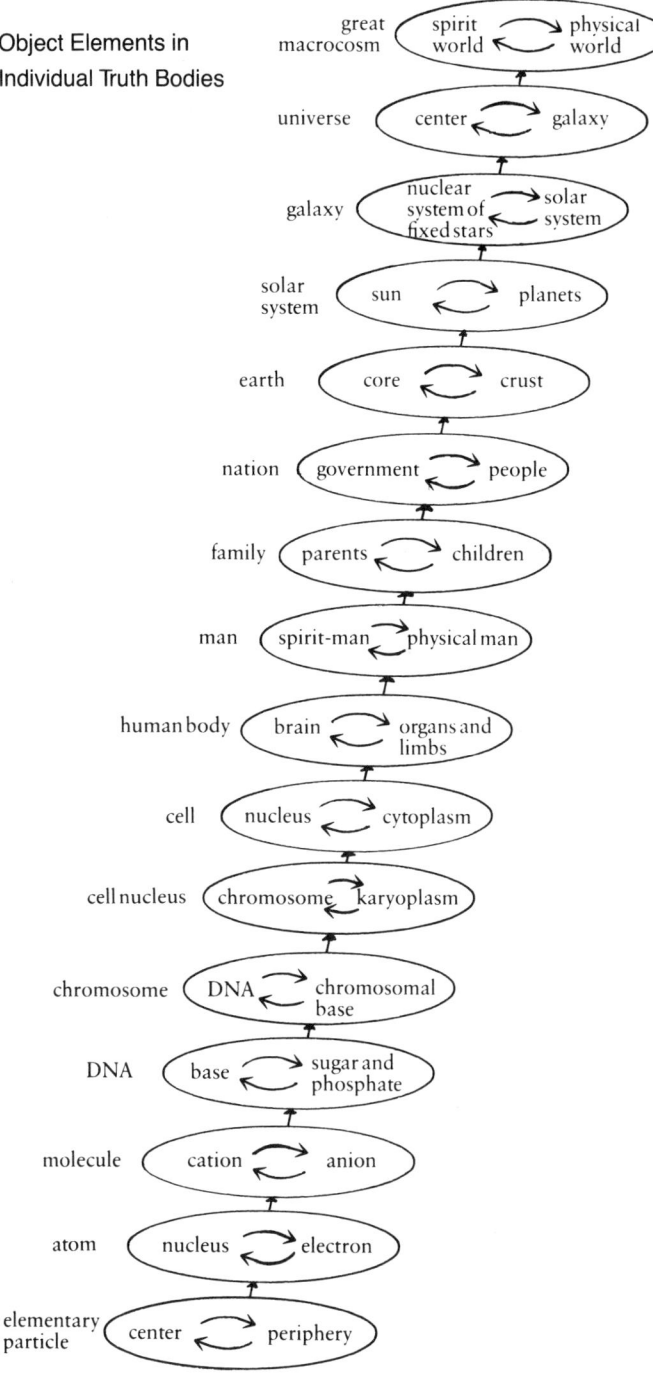

- great macrocosm: spirit world ⇄ physical world
- universe: center ⇄ galaxy
- galaxy: nuclear system of fixed stars ⇄ solar system
- solar system: sun ⇄ planets
- earth: core ⇄ crust
- nation: government ⇄ people
- family: parents ⇄ children
- man: spirit-man ⇄ physical man
- human body: brain ⇄ organs and limbs
- cell: nucleus ⇄ cytoplasm
- cell nucleus: chromosome ⇄ karyoplasm
- chromosome: DNA ⇄ chromosomal base
- DNA: base ⇄ sugar and phosphate
- molecule: cation ⇄ anion
- atom: nucleus ⇄ electron
- elementary particle: center ⇄ periphery

Concerning man's practice in the various fields, man is regarded as subject, while the things that are dealt with by man are regarded as object.

In sum, the concept of 'subject and object' in traditional philosophy is used primarily to explain the relationship between man and things.

(b) 'Subject and Object' in Unification Thought

According to the Unification Principle, 'subject and object' can be defined as follows: "when the dual beings, or dual elements, give and take something to each other, forming a reciprocal relationship, the being (or element) that is chiefly dominating, active, or central is called subject; and the being (or element) that is chiefly dominated, passive, or dependent is called object." In any reciprocal relationship, one of these dual beings (or elements) will necessarily take the subject's position; the other necessarily takes the object's position, except in the phenomenon of repulsion.

Different from traditional philosophy, the concept of 'subject and object' in Unification Thought applies to relationships not only between a person and a thing (being), but also between person and person, thing and thing (or being and being), element and element, and so on. In addition, it also applies to the relationship between the functional part of the mind *(Inner Sung Sang)* and the non-functional part of the mind *(Inner Hyung Sang)*.

(c) Types of 'Subject and Object' in Unification Thought

The types of 'subject and object' that can be derived from the Unification Principle are as follows.

(1) Original Type

The original type is the eternal and universal relationship of 'subject and object' seen from the viewpoint of God's creation. For instance, the relationships between husband and wife, parents and children, teacher and students, star and its planets, nucleus and cytoplasm (in a cell), nucleus and electron (in an atom) belong to this type. When the reciprocal relationship of 'subject and object' is viewed from this point of view, the subject bears the purpose and the direction of an action within that relationship.

(2) Temporary Type

The temporary type refers to relationships of 'subject and object' that are effective only temporarily; such relationships occur frequently in our daily lives. For instance, the relationship between lecturer and listener belongs to this type, since it is effective only while the lecture is going on.

Note that the positions of subject and object in an original-type relationship may be reversed in some cases, as for example, in a family where the wife is responsible for the family (instead of the husband) or a son or daughter makes a living (instead of the parents). Such relationships can also be regarded as being of a temporary type, but they are not effective apart from their original type. In order to be effective, these relationships must be based on the original type.

(3) Alternate Type

In the cases where the positions of subject and object alternate between themselves, the relationship is called alternate-type 'subject and object'.

A dialogue is an example of this type of relationship. The speaker is in the subject position; the listener, in the object position. As the positions of speaker and listener alternate, so do the positions of subject and object.

(4) Undetermined Type

The undetermined type refers to a relationship of 'subject and object' in which a human being may freely decide what has the position of subject and what the position of object. In a relationship between an animal and a plant, for instance, the animal gives carbon dioxide to the plant and receives oxygen from it. If someone sees this relationship from the viewpoint of the flow of oxygen, the plant can be considered the subject; if he sees it from the viewpoint of the flow of carbon dioxide, the animal can be considered the subject. Thus, in this type of relationship, the position of subject and object are determined by man.

6. Paired Elements and Opposing Elements

The subject and object elements in an individual truth body perform give-and-take action between themselves, and are called *Paired Elements*, or *Correlative Elements*, in Unification Thought.

The Unification Principle, however, says that in order for a subject and an object to perform give-and-take action, they must first establish a reciprocal relationship. When this relationship is established, give-and-take action can occur; the subject and the object form a reciprocal base, constituting an individual truth body. A reciprocal base can only be established when there is a common factor at the center, a common purpose, motive, or cause. Without a common factor, no reciprocal relationship is formed, and no give-and-take action can take place. Paired elements, or correlative elements, then, refer to a subject and object that do have a common factor.

The concept of paired elements is a contrast to the notion of *opposites* in Marxian philosophy. Unification thought and Marxian philosophy are in agreement as far as recognizing that everything has two elements. Unification Thought, however, says that they are correlative and cooperative, whereas communist philosophy says that they oppose each other. Communist philosophy claims also that development is brought about by the struggle between the opposing elements, and this principle is called the *dialectic*. Unification Thought says that development is the result of harmonious give-and-take action between subject and object, and this principle is called the *law of give-and-take action*, or briefly, the *give-and-take law*. Which concept is more reasonable: opposites or paired elements?

Marx, who first expounded dialectical materialism,* did not base his theory on the natural sciences. He supported his theory by citing the history of class struggles, especially the struggles between the productive forces and the relations of production in Europe. True philosophy, when dealing interrelatedly with the causes of natural and socio-historical development, should explain natural phenomena first, and socio-historical phenomena next. Marx, however, without any prior clarification of the causes of development in nature, insisted that socio-historical development, accompanied by class struggle, has followed the law of natural development. This is a weak point in his philosophy.

It was Engels who approached dialectical materialism through the natural sciences. After prolonged studies in physics, chemistry, mathematics, astronomy, and so on, he observed that there are two

---

*Dialectical materialism is, of course, the world view of Marxism, but Marx himself never used the term. It is said that the term was first used by G.V. Plekhanov, who was the first Russian communist, preceding Lenin.

elements in every natural phenomenon and being. Then, he hastily concluded that these elements are opposites, or contradictions. That was a jump of logic.

In order to determine whether two elements are in contradiction or in harmony we need to find out whether or not there is a common factor or common purpose between them. If no common factor or purpose is found—and instead there are contradictory factors or purposes—we can say that the two elements are in contradiction. If, however, a common factor or purpose does exist, then the two elements are in harmony and can be called paired elements.

In order to substantiate his theory of opposites, Engels gives the following description of polarity in nature:

> A magnet, on being cut through, polarises the neutral middle portion, but in such a way that the old poles remain. On the other hand, a worm, on being cut into two, retains the receptive mouth at the positive pole and forms a new negative pole at the other end with excretory anus; but the old negative pole (the anus) now becomes positive, becoming a mouth, and a new anus or negative pole is formed at the cut end.*

The north and south poles of a magnet, as well as the mouth and anus of a worm, cannot exist independently of each other, but always exist in pairs. Engels concluded from this that they are in opposition, without any further explanation. This is the jump of logic we referred to before. We should examine whether or not a common factor or purpose exists between the two elements—N-pole and S-pole, mouth and anus—before drawing any conclusions.

If you spread iron filings around a magnet, they will form curved lines from the N-pole to the S-pole. This is the magnetic field, which the two poles form around themselves, showing that they are mutually attractive and complementary. The N-pole needs the S-pole for a partner, for it cannot make a magnetic field by itself. The same is true for the S-pole. Making a magnetic field, then, is a common factor, or purpose, between them, and we conclude that they are paired elements. If the two poles opposed each other, the iron filings would not make a line from one to the other, but would scatter in repulsion.

As for the mouth and anus of a worm, we can recognize their

---

*F. Engels, *Dialectics of Nature* (Moscow: Progress Publishers, 1976), p. 217.

common purpose also. Although the ingestive function of the mouth and excretory function of the anus are different, they serve a common purpose: to support the life of the worm. So, it is not correct to say that they have an antagonistic relationship, but we should say, instead, that they are paired elements.

Engels cites many other examples of opposition, such as positive and negative electricity in physics; addition and subtraction, multiplication and division, roots and powers in mathematics; life and death in biology. A careful examination of these opposites, however, reveals that every pair has a common purpose—the common purpose of making an electric field, of making mathematical calculations, and so on. Accordingly, these, also, are paired elements.

The chicken egg is another frequently presented example of opposites.* The egg, containing embryo, yolk, white, and shell, brings forth a chicken, supposedly through a struggle among the elements. Are these, however, real opposites? Is there not any common purpose among them?

The function of the embryo is to grow into a chicken. The yolk and the white serve as nourishment for its growth, while the shell protects it, until it is ready to emerge as a brand-new chicken. Accordingly, the various elements have a common purpose—making a chicken in the egg—and there is no clash of interests among them. Struggle will only occur if there is a clash of interests—if one element profits at another's expense—but no such clash can be seen here.

We can further explain this point by discussing the breaking of the shell at hatching. When the embryo has grown into a chicken, after the period of twenty-one days, the protective role of the shell comes to an end. At this point, the shell must be broken, in order to allow the chicken to come out; it becomes very thin and easy to break. The embryo does not grow into a chicken by struggling with the shell, for it is already a chicken before it starts pecking at it from the inside. The breaking of the shell, therefore, is not a sign of struggle, but a sign that the chicken is fully developed, and is ready to come out, through the cooperative phenomenon of hatching.

Through the Unification Thought view, we can recognize the

---

*I first disputed this example with a Marxist theoretician, when I visited him while detained in prison in Taejon, Korea. Since then, I have made frequent use of this example in my discussions.

flaws in the concept of opposites. The two elements have a common purpose, the purpose for the whole. Accordingly, they are not opposites, but are paired elements of subject and object. There is no struggle between subject and object. If we find struggle, it will be only between subject and subject, as explained below. (Fig. 10)

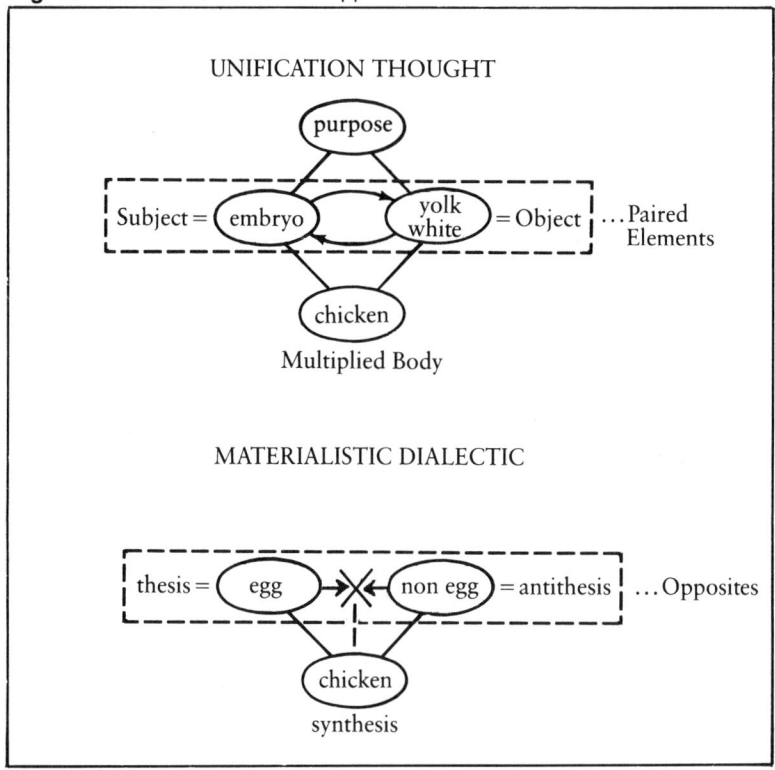

Fig. 10 Paired Elements and Opposites

UNIFICATION THOUGHT

Subject = embryo ⇄ yolk/white = Object ... Paired Elements

purpose

chicken

Multiplied Body

MATERIALISTIC DIALECTIC

thesis = egg →✗← non egg = antithesis ... Opposites

chicken

synthesis

It is not a mere conjecture to say that communists are involved in all major wars today, since the communist philosophy is one of struggle. Where there is communist philosophy, there we shall find struggle—among families, social groups, and nations. Before we can even hope to end struggles, we must eradicate the ground of dialectical materialism, which is the very basis of the communist philosophy. Unification Thought, with its concept of paired elements and law of give-and-take action, is an adequate counterproposal to it.

Undeniably, there have been numerous struggles in the course of human history, but they owe their existence to man's Fall—that is, man's deviation from principles. If man had not fallen, history would not have been marred by struggle. In the Unification Thought view, the struggles in human history took place for the purpose of restoring the sovereignty of goodness. The history of mankind should, therefore, be understood as the history of struggle between good and evil.

We have been deluded into believing that struggles occur between the ruling class and the ruled class, since we have heard it from the communists so many times. This is nothing but fiction. They depict the ruling class as being evil and exploitive and as giving the ruled, exploited class a miserable life. In the Unification Thought view, however, the relationship between ruling and ruled is not inherently evil; originally, this relationship should be as that of subject and object. The important question here is whether or not the ruling class is governing in a principled way.

Here I will present a brief sketch of the Unification Thought view of the history of struggle; this view will be dealt with in greater detail in the chapter on Theory of History. When society is in a state of disorder, and people no longer believe in the government, a new leader appears from among the people. When he makes himself known to the people, some will decide to follow him, while others will remain with the old leader. We have here, then, two leaders, in the position of subjects, and two groups of people, in the position of objects. The new leader, leading the new group, will then struggle with the old leader, leading the old group. The struggle is not between subject and object, since the object follows the subject. The struggle here, as in every case, takes place between two subjects. (We should note that in the natural world only the laws of Creation continue to apply; the situation there is different from that in human society, because there was no fall in the natural world.)

Someone might point out that there are numerous instances of struggle in the animal kingdom, where the strong prey upon the weak. But the struggles in the animal kingdom and those in human society are essentially different, since those among the animals are struggles between different families, whereas those in human society are struggles within the same family—the family of man. A cat, for instance, eats a rat; a snake eats a frog; a crab eats a shrimp, and so forth. Cats and rats belong to the class of mammals, but are of different order and family. Snakes and frogs are vertebrates, and thus belong to the same phylum, but are of different class, order, and family, Crabs and shrimps belong to the animal kingdom, but are of different phylum, class, order, and family. Under normal circumstances, a cat does not kill another cat; a rat does not eat another rat. In human society, however, it is not unusual for people to fight or kill one another.

Occasionally we can see struggles within the same family of animals. When a new lion comes into a group of lions, for example, there may be an actual struggle between the newcomer and the head of the group. Still, this kind of struggle is no more than a process for deciding which lion should be the head. When the decision is made, peace is restored. Such struggles, therefore, are only temporary.

Even the instances of violence now perceived among families of animals can be removed, if man—who was supposed to dominate creation with love, but failed to assume his proper position because of the Fall—finally perfects himself and dominates them well. Thus, man's restoration will affect even nature itself. (Isaiah 65:25)

From among the major Marxist theoreticians—such as Marx himself, as well as Engels, Lenin, Stalin, and Mao Tse-tung—no one ever said that the two opposing elements are subject and object. Maurice Cornforth, an English communist, wrote in his *Dialectical Materialism* that the relationship between two opposing elements is that of ruling and ruled. 'Ruling' and 'ruled', however, are not to be taken as 'subject' and 'object', since no struggle can take place between two beings that are in the position of subject and object. Cornforth's explanation of social change is based on the Law of the Transformation of Quantitative into Qualitative Changes in the dialectic. According to this law, a sudden qualitative change occurs when quantitative change reaches a certain point. Cornforth said that although the relationship of ruling and ruled is invariable during the process of quantitative change, the relationship is reversed upon the attainment of qualitative change. Since a struggle does take place, however, we can say that the relationship of ruling and ruled is, in fact, of subject and subject. As a matter of fact, Marx, Engels, and Lenin considered the two opposing elements to be equal in position, and not to have the relationship of ruling and ruled. Accordingly, we can say that in their view the opposing elements are in the relationship of subject and subject. This further substantiates the Unification Thought view of socio-historical struggle, as explained above.

B. INDIVIDUAL IMAGE

1. The Location and the Monostratic Nature of the Individual Image

The Bible describes the creation of man and the universe in the following words:

> And God said, "Let there be light," and there was light... And there was evening and there was morning, one day... And God made the firmament and separated the waters which were under the firmament from waters which were above the firmament. And it was so... a second day... and God said, "Let the earth put forth vegetation, plants yielding seed, and fruit trees bearing fruit..." And it was so... a third day. And God said, "Let there be lights in the firmament of the heavens..." And it was so... a fourth day. And God said, "Let the waters bring forth swarms of living creatures, and let the birds fly above the earth across the firmament of the heavens." ... a fifth day. And God said, "Let the earth bring forth living creatures according to their kinds; cattle and creeping things and beasts of the earth according to their kinds." And it was so... God created man in his own image, in the image of God he created them; male and female he created them... And it was so... a sixth day. (Genesis 1:3-31)

The words, "it was so," mean that all things were created according to the images in God's mind. These mental images can be called ideas. Since every created being has its own specific characteristics, we can infer that the mental images in God's mind, also, have specific characteristics and are the model for each being. These are the Individual Images of God. The location of the Individual Images, or mental images, of God is in the object-part of God's mind, that is, in the Inner *Hyung Sang*—as explained in "Theory of the Original Image."

What are the specific contents of the individual image of a man? Let us take a Korean as an example. First of all, this man is a living being. He is also an animal and a vertebrate. He belongs to the mammalian group of vertebrates. Of the mammalian groups, he is a primate. Among the primates, he belongs to the anthropoid apes. Among the anthropoid apes, he is a human being. Ethnically, he is oriental, and more specifically, a Korean. Thus, he has the general characteristics of living beings, animals, vertebrates, etc.

You might think, then, that the Individual Image of man consists of many levels of characteristics, or that it is *polystratic*. (Polystratic image implies that the various characteristics were

The Individual Truth Body

added one by one, beginning with the most generic ones, down to the most specific.) Unification Thought, however, does not share such a view, for it would lead us to the Theory of Evolution. Instead, Unification Thought maintains that the Individual Image is *monostratic*—i.e., of a single layer.

In order to understand this concept, let us refer again to the process of Creation. According to the Bible, God created man on the last day of Creation. It is the Unification Thought point of view, however, that in His mind, God conceived the image of man first. Then He conceived the images of animals, plants, and finally minerals—taking the image of man as the standard. This is the *downward* process of creation of images (Logos) in the mind of God. It explains why man is the integration of all things. In the phenomenal world, however, God created everything starting from the minerals, then plants, animals, and finally man. This is the *upward* process of creation of substantial beings.

The image of man, therefore, was the first to be created in the mind of God and was the standard for all other images. The original Individual Image of man in the Inner *Hyung Sang* of God (before the creation of the universe) was none other than the image of Adam himself. It was neither vague nor abstract, but specific and concrete. Adam's image had both a spiritual aspect (spirit-mind and spirit-body) and a physical aspect (instinct, sense, organs, nerves, tissues, cells, molecules, and atoms). Of course, Adam's individual character and appearance, also, were included in the original Individual Image. God then thought of another human, Eve, the helper for Adam, based on the image of Adam. The image of Eve was conceived so as to enable her to be a wife to Adam. Their relationship was to be as that of positivity and negativity. The new image had additional aspects of new individual character, leaving out Adam's individuality. In other respects, the images were quite the same.

Then God conceived the images of animals, leaving out the spiritual aspects of the image of man. Next He conceived the images of plants, leaving out the instinct and nervous system of the animals. Finally, He conceived the images of minerals, leaving out the life, tissues, and cells of the images of the plants.

We can see, then, that the individual image of man was originally conceived by God before the images of animals, plants, and minerals. The individual image of man, therefore, which includes heart, reason, instinct, organs, cells, atoms, etc., was not formed by a process of piling up successive layers of other images; it is monostratic. God conceived all the elements of man simultaneously. The images of animals and plants, conceived through a gradual elimination of certain aspects of the image of man, are also monostratic. (Fig. 11)

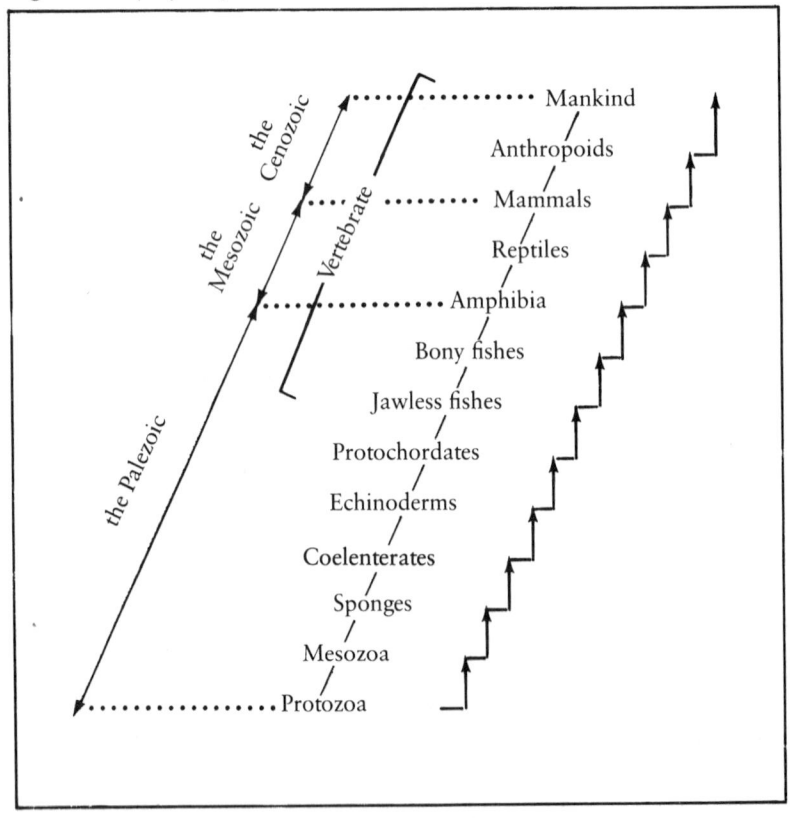

Fig. 11 Step by Step Creation from Protozoa to Mankind

The theory of continuous evolution says that protozoa evolved into mesozoa, sponges, coelenterates, echinoderms, protochordates, and cyclostomes (jawless fish). These evolved into bony fish, which evolved into amphibia, reptiles, mammals, anthropoids, and finally into mankind. There are many problems with this theory. One is that there should be no protozoa now, if they had evolved, according to the "survival of the fittest," into mesozoa, sponges, etc. This is not the case: there are still protozoa on earth today. Another problem is that there should be intermediate beings, showing slight and gradual

The Individual Truth Body

changes, if evolution is to be a continuous process. If there had been intermediate beings, they would have been fitter to survive than those that had existed before them, for they would have been the very ones that had survived by natural selection. Actually, we cannot find such creatures, even amongst the fossils. If the "survival of the fittest" were true, the fossils of such intermediate beings would be easily found, since the fossils of even more primitive beings have already been found. Evolutionists may point to the archaeopteryx as being an intermediate between reptiles and birds. This is the only example they can cite, and even then it is extremely difficult to establish that it actually is an intermediate. Because of these two incongruities, we must seriously question the theory of continuous evolution.

What about the theory of mutation, as presented by Hugo de Vries? This theory says that higher beings have evolved from lower beings by successive random mutations. Mutation is understood to be caused by changes in the gene structure of the cell. Genes can be affected by heat, radioactive rays, chemical agents, etc. Mutation evolutionists conclude that animals and plants have evolved as the result of countless genetic mutations over a period of millions of years, brought about through irradiation by cosmic rays or by other means, such as crossing over during cell replication.

This explanation, also, poses some difficulties, the most important of which is that there is no definite direction in the change of the genetic structure, with such accidental causes. In other words, the direction of change will be completely at random. We know that random mutations can cause changes within a species or lead to degradation; but can they bring forth higher beings, even if repeated an infinite number of times? Some people may bring up the *principle of natural selection* and claim that meaningful changes—that is, those with a better chance to survive—have been selected. But even in evolution by mutations, a change cannot be so drastic as to bring forth a new and higher species instantly, but it should be a slight and gradual change, since mutations are completely at random. Accordingly, there should have been intermediate beings showing the footprints of evolution. Such beings, however, were apparently unfit to survive, as shown by the absence of their fossils. Clearly, there is a contradiction here; this claim cannot be considered as valid.

According to the Unification Thought view, plants and animals have not evolved by chance and accident, although a superficial observation of the phenomenal world might suggest that opinion. Every existing being was created by God, following His plan. Unification Thought accepts genetic mutations as a possible factor in the appearance of new species. Such mutations, however, were caused, not by chance and accident, but by the work of God.

2. The Individualization of the Universal Image

The individual image in all beings is not, and cannot, be separated from the universal image of *Sung Sang* and *Hyung Sang*, positivity and negativity. The individual image is in actual fact the individualization of the universal image.

In the case of human beings, for example, one person may express his joyfulness by laughing, another by joking. This is an example of the individual image in the positivity of the mind *(Sung Sang)*. As for the positivity of the body *(Hyung Sang)*, one person may have a large nose and long fingers, while another has a snub nose and short fingers. Negativity of the mind and of the body are similarly individualized. The individual image, therefore, is the individualized *Sung Sang* and *Hyung Sang*, or individualized positivity and negativity.

3. The Individualization of *Chung-Boon-Hap* Action

What is the relationship between the individual image and C-B-H action? To state the conclusion first, the individual image is the individualization of C-B-H action.

As previously mentioned, C-B-H action in the Original Image is the structure of God's attributes when seen from the perspective of time. Similarly, in the created world, subject and object conduct give-and-take action centering on purpose, bringing about either a united body or a multiplied body. The time process of this give-and-take action constitutes the C-B-H action of all things.

Since each created body is individualized, or has an individual image, the C-B-H action is also individualized. Let us take man's digestive process as an example. The digestive process is not an isolated action, but is the cooperative give-and-take action of the heart, brain, liver, pancreas, etc. The heart sends blood to the digestive areas; the liver and the pancreas secrete digestive enzymes; the brain controls the process. This process of C-B-H action is slightly different from person to person, because it is individualized. One person can easily eat eggs; another develops an allergy eating them.

As another example, let us use the give-and-take action between the spirit-mind and the physical mind (C-B-H action in the *Sung Sang)*. The spirit-mind seeks the values of trueness, goodness, beauty, and love, while the physical mind seeks food, clothing, and shelter, following instinctive desires. The spirit-mind should be the subject, and the physical mind, object. Original man pursues a life of spiritual values first, considering food, clothing, shelter, etc., as means for attaining those values. He eats and lives in order to love other persons, his nation, and all mankind.

In fallen man, however, the relationship between the spirit-mind and the physical mind has been reversed. He seeks to gratify the desires of his physical mind more so than to attain a life of spiritual values. Furthermore, the give-and-take action between spirit-mind and physical mind is different from individual to individual, showing unique characteristics. Thus, the C-B-H action in the mind *(Sung Sang)* is also individualized.

Another level of give-and-take action is that between the mind and the brain. According to the Unification Principle, the human mind is the united body of the give-and-take action between spirit-mind and physical mind. The mind then enters into give-and-take action with the brain in order to cause mental activity. This is clearly different from the materialistic view, which says that the mind (spirit) is a product of the brain (matter). (Our critique of this materialistic view is explained in detail in ch. 4, Sec. IV, B.) As stated above, the give-and-take action, or C-B-H action, in the mind is individualized. Then, the individualized mind enters into give-and-take action with the brain, which is also individualized in shape, structure, function, and so on. Consequently, the give-and-take action between mind and brain, also, is individualized. Mental activity, therefore, is different from person to person; in other words, the C-B-H action of the mental process is individualized.

4. Individual Image, Idea, and Concept

'Individual Image' is an expression peculiar to Unification Thought. 'Idea' and 'concept', on the other hand, are terms from traditional philosophy, where idea is considered to be individual, and concept, universal. 'Idea and concept', 'individual and universal', would seem to correspond to 'Individual Image and Universal Image' in Unification Thought, but this is not the case. In God, the

Individual Image does in fact correspond to idea—i.e., the mental image of each thing to be created. Universal Image, however, is quite different from concept.

Concept can be defined as the mental image of—or a name given to—the common properties abstracted from a group of individuals. The common properties are called intension (connotation), whereas the things that belong to the same concept are called extension (denotation). In the concept of 'animal', for example, intension includes sense organs, nerves, mobility, etc.; extension includes dogs, chickens, fish, birds, and so on. Extension indicates the range of the concept. The extension of 'animal' is greater than that of 'bird', and the extension of 'living being' is greater than that of 'animal'.

The word 'universal' is often used in the same way as 'concept'. 'Universal image', however, is different from 'concept', since it is not derived from abstracting the commonness of a certain group of individuals. Universal Image refers to the common attributes *(Sung Sang* and *Hyung Sang,* positivity and negativity) that every being necessarily possesses.

5. The Universal and the Individual

An important philosophical argument took place in the Middle Ages as to which is first, or more essential, idea or concept, i.e., individual or universal. The argument is known as the *Universalienstreit* (dispute about universals). This is the same as asking which is first in the *Sung Sang* of God, the Individual Image (idea), or the concept. Did God think of a universal man first, or did He think of an individual (Adam) first?

Realism supports the priority of the universal, and *nominalism* supports the priority of the individual. Nominalists say that a concept is a man-made label given to classify the commonness he finds in certain individuals, and there is nothing like a concept in the ultimate existence.

According to Unification Thought, God originally conceived a concrete image, or idea, of Adam, in His Inner *Hyung Sang*. From the image of Adam, God derived the concept of man, animal, plant, and mineral. In this sense, the idea of Adam is called the *original idea,* or the *standard idea.*

The concept of man was derived from the idea of Adam, through eliminating Adam's individual characteristics. The ideas of

Eve, Cain, and Abel were formed by adding appropriate individual characteristics to the concept of man. The concept of animal, on the other hand, was derived from the concept of man, through leaving out the spirit-man, thereby eliminating spiritual characteristics, such as heart and reason. From the concept of animal, ideas of specific kinds of animals were derived, such as cow, horse, dog, hen, elephant, anchovy. These ideas came about by the process of imitating and transforming the concept of animal, which was set up as a standard. The various ideas are called *ideas of similarity*, and the concept of animal is called the *standard concept*.

Likewise, the concept of plant was derived from the concept of man, through eliminating specific characteristics pertaining to man and to animals. The idea of each kind of plant was formed by setting the concept of plant as the standard. The formation of the concept of minerals—and the ideas of the various kinds of minerals—follows a similar pattern.

In conclusion, there was an idea as the standard in the beginning. Concepts were derived from it, and finally the ideas for all created beings were formed, all within the *Sung Sang* of God.

6. The Individual Image and the Environment

The individual image of every existing being, which, to a large extent, is determined a priori, can change to a certain degree through give-and-take action with the environment. Accordingly, everything has a priori, determined features, as well as a posteriori, changing features. The determined features are essential and basic, since they originate from the Individual Image in God.

Our environment comprises both natural and social beings. Under natural beings we have animals, plants, minerals, mountains, the sea, etc.; under social beings we have family members, neighbors, groups, institutes, political parties, and so on. Throughout our whole lives, we are constantly engaged in give-and-take action with the environment, whereby we both influence, and are influenced by, persons and things we come in contact with. The effect of the give-and-take action between one constituent of the environment and another is called *individual effect*. Owing to the countless individual effects, our individual images are continuously changing, although our basic and essential features remain unchanging.

II. THE CONNECTED BODY

As already mentioned, there are content and structure in the Original Image. Content refers to each Divine Image (*Sung Sang* and *Hyung Sang,* Positivity and Negativity, and Individual Image) and to Divine Character (Heart, Logos, and Creativity); structure, on the other hand, refers to Quadruple Base and C-B-H action. Every existing being is created in the direct or indirect image of God, so it resembles God both in content and structure.

Let us consider the resemblance in content. In Unification Thought, man is the direct image of God's Divine Image and Divine Character, but the rest of creation is the indirect image of God, reflecting only His Divine Image. Accordingly, this view may be called *Pan-Divine-Image Theory.* It must not be misapprehended as Pantheism, which says, in effect, that all things are the direct expression of God. In Unfication Thought, creation is not God Himself. God is the subject, and all created beings are His substantial objects.

Next, let us consider the resemblance in structure, that is, the quadruple base. Man has an inner quadruple base, formed within him by the give-and-take action of spirit-mind and physical mind (together making the original mind). All other created beings, also, have an inner quadruple base, since they, too, have correlative elements within themselves. Any being that has an inner quadruple base is called an *individual truth body.* When we say that a being resembles God, we mean that it is an individual truth body.

In addition, beings conduct give-and-take action with other beings also. A man, for example, has give-and-take action with his wife, thereby establishing an outer quadruple base—a family centering on the Purpose of Creation. In this case, he is called a connected body, as he has both inner and outer quadruple bases. He is called an individual truth body when we consider only his inner quadruple base, independent of other individuals. A connected body is an individual who has established both the inner and the outer quadruple base. The term does not mean two connected individuals.

A. CONNECTED BODY AND DUAL PURPOSES

The connected body is called a *being with dual purposes,* when seen in the light of purpose. It simultaneously has a purpose for the individual and a purpose for the whole. The purpose for the individual seeks self-preservation and self-development; the purpose for the whole seeks to contribute toward the preservation and development of the whole.

In concrete terms, an atom, for example, exists for the purpose of making a molecule, by forming an outer quadruple base through give-and-take action with other atoms. It exists for itself also, by forming an inner quadruple base through give-and-take action between its nucleus and electrons. Similarly, molecules exist for the purpose of making a cell, as well as for their own purpose. Cells exist for the purpose of making the tissues and organs of a plant or an animal, as well as for themselves. Other molecules exist for making minerals, which form the earth; the earth exists for forming the solar system; the solar system, for forming the galaxy; the galaxy, for forming the universe. And all of these exist for themselves as well.

For what purpose, then, do plants, animals, and the universe exist? They exist for man. What about man? For what purpose does he exist? He exists for God. Thus, every existing being has both a purpose for the whole and a purpose for the individual. Each being is a whole, when seen from below; it is a component, when seen from above.

Incidentally, within the purpose for the whole, there is both *"Sung Sang* purpose" and *"Hyung Sang* purpose." The purpose for the whole of the earth, for example, is to orbit the sun in order to form the solar system: this is *Hyung Sang* purpose. It is also the earth's purpose to provide a suitable dwelling place for man: this is *Sung Sang* purpose. An electron orbits the nucleus, in order to form an atom: *Hyung Sang* purpose. On the other hand, an electron helps to make the physical body of man and the environment for man, the earth: *Sung Sang* purpose. In other words, through the *Hyung Sang* purpose, an existing being contributes to the individual being of the next higher stage; through the *Sung Sang* purpose, it contributes to the existence of man. (Fig. 12)

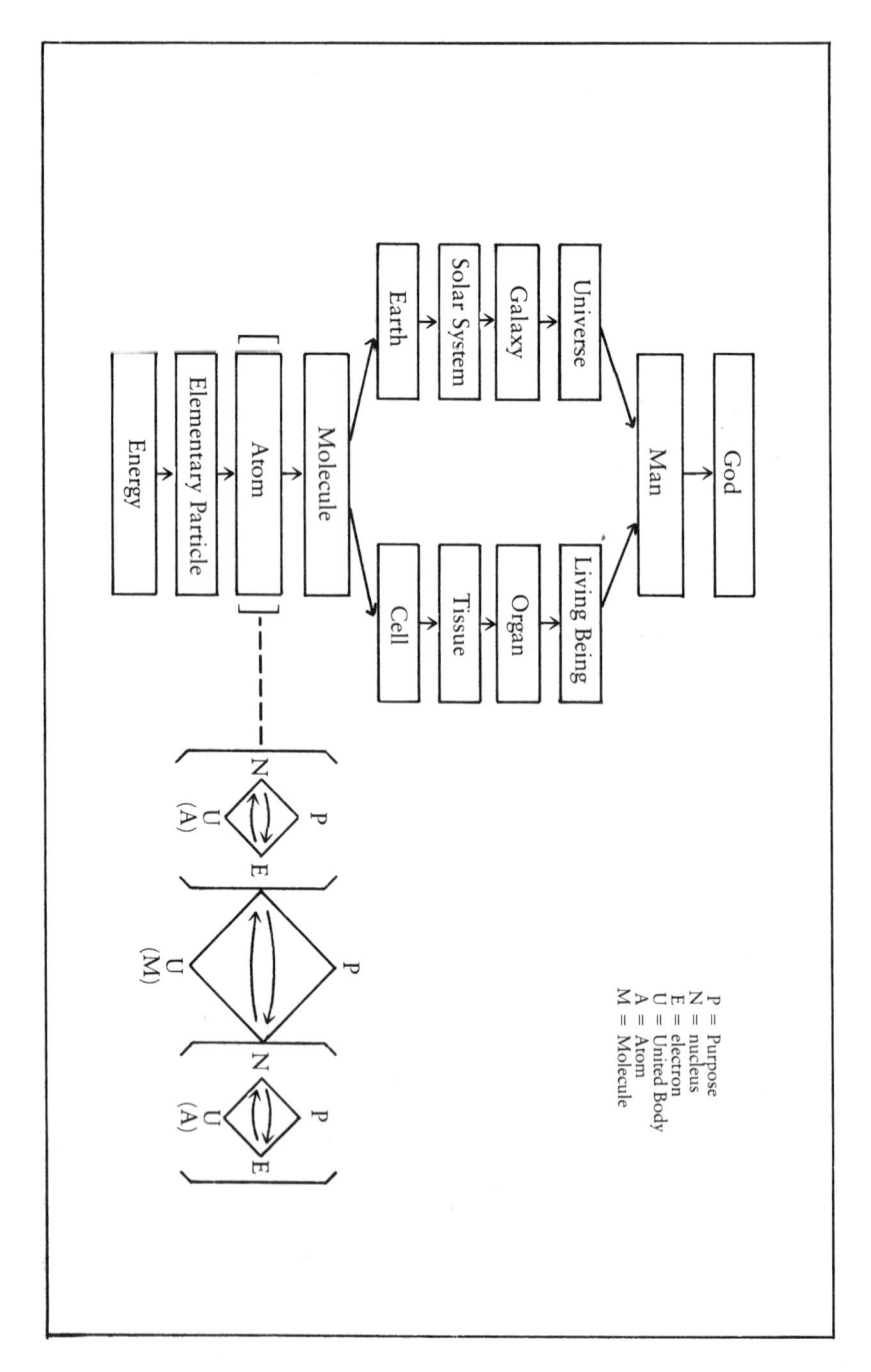

Fig. 12 Connected Body and Dual Purposes

B. THE CONNECTED BODY AND THE ORIGINAL IMAGE

Every existing being forms both inner and outer quadruple bases, just as both Inner and Outer Quadruple Bases are formed in the Original Image. Man's inner quadruple base is established by the give-and-take action between his spirit-man and his physical man (essentially, spirit-mind and physical mind); his outer quadruple bases are established by give-and-take actions with other persons, such as spouse, children, friends, and fellow citizens. These relationships should be characterized by harmony. A value-centered life will bring harmony to the inner quadruple base, whereas an atmosphere of love will bring harmony to the outer quadruple base.

Though the Quadruple Bases in the Original Image are non-dimensional (in other words, they are of the absolute dimension), man, who lives in the world of three dimensions, forms quadruple bases in six directions: front and back, right and left, above and below. In front, he has teachers, leaders, and seniors; behind, pupils, followers, and juniors. His brothers and sisters and friends will be to his right, whereas his competitors and those whom he finds it difficult to get along with, to his left. Above him he will find his parents, superiors, and the head of his nation (king or president); below, he will find children and subordinates. During one's lifetime, one should develop harmonious give-and-take action in all the six directions. The six directions, plus the spot in the center where the individual is located, make the number seven, which symbolizes man's forming relationships in three dimensions. (In the Unification Principle, the number seven also symbolizes perfection.) These are the relationships necessary for man to enter into family and social life. This is the *Sung Sang* aspect of original man's relationships as a connected body.

Moreover, man has relationships with his natural surroundings. Even distant stars influence us; scientists tell us that cosmic rays penetrating the earth's atmosphere influence the physiological processes of living beings. We gain much from nature and influence it as well. We are, therefore, connected with nature, and even with the whole universe, directly or indirectly. This is the *Hyung Sang* aspect of original man's relationships as a connected body. As we can see from the above, the concept of 'connected body' is indeed very significant.

III. THE EXISTING MODE* *(YANG SANG)* AND THE EXISTING POSITION
A. THE EXISTING MODE

In Sections I and II, I expounded the Unification Thought view on the content and structure of existing beings. In this section, I would like to discuss motion in existing beings. How do existing beings move? The answer to this question lies in the explanation of the "existing mode" of existing beings. To say the conclusion, existing mode is defined as the *circular motion* that results from the give-and-take action between subject and object.

As there is no effect without a cause, we would expect to find a causal motion in the Original Image corresponding to the motion of every existing being. Of course, motion can only take place in the world of time and space, so there can be no actual motion in the transcendent God; nevertheless, there is some essentiality, or cause, in God that corresponds to circular motion in the phenomenal world. This essentiality, or cause, is the harmonious give-and-take action between *Sung Sang* and *Hyung Sang* (subject and object), centering on Heart. The harmony or smoothness of this give-and-take action in the Original Image is reflected in circular motion in the phenomenal world.

According to the Unification Principle, man was created as God's substantial direct image, while the rest of creation was created as God's substantial indirect image. Thus, man is referred to as "figural individual truth body," whereas creation is referred to as "symbolic individual truth body." A brief explanation of the terms 'truth', 'figural', and 'symbolic' may be useful at this point.

'Truth' means true character, or true attributes—that is, the attributes of God. Accordingly, an 'individual truth body' is an individual body with God's attributes. 'Figural' indicates that man is the figure, or the image, of God. In other words, man expresses, directly, the attributes of God—that is, Divine Image *(Sung Sang* and *Hyung Sang,* Positivity and Negativity, and Individual Image) and Divine Character (Heart, Logos, and Creativity). 'Figural', therefore, means "of direct likeness or similarity."

With respect to creation, it is said to be the symbol of God,

---

*The term "mode" is a translation of the Korean term *Yang Sang,* which is also a special expression in the Unification Principle (like *Sung Sang* and *Hyung Sang*). Here, the English term is used, since "mode" seems correctly to convey the meaning of *Yang Sang.*

since it represents God only indirectly. In a certain sense, every existing being is the image of God. Creation, however, is the indirect image—more precisely referred to as the symbol—of God, whereas man is the direct image of God.

The terms 'symbol' and 'figure' can have a wide variety of application. The Korean flag, for example, is the symbol of Korea; the Korean map, on the other hand, can be considered a figure of Korea, as it resembles the shape and proportions of Korea. In the Unification Principle we can find other examples: in its second flight, the dove set free by Noah after the flood was a symbol of Jesus. By contrast, the Temple of Jerusalem (or even the Tabernacle, which was a pre-stage of the Temple), was a figure of Jesus, since it expressed the structure and function of original man.

Likewise, iron can be a symbol of the hardness of the Original Image; water, of its softness. The sea is symbolic of its breadth; sunlight is symbolic of its brightness; heat is symbolic of its warmth; and green or blue colors are symbolic of its youth. Circular motion is the symbol of the harmony and smoothness of give-and-take action in God. Moreover, love, the most essential attribute of God, is symbolized by harmonious roundness with no angularity. In fact, if we were to draw a representation of the Original Image, it would have to be a circle.

Although God has no definite form, He has the original form, which is expressed in an infinite variety of ways in the creation. God has infinite forms, united into one form; He has an unlimited form. The example of water may be helpful again. Water has no form, but can assume the form of a cube, of a sphere, or of any other container. In a similar manner, God, who has no form, can manifest Himself in the created world in any kind of form.

Although God's manifestations in the created world can take any kind of form—such as a tree, a flower, or a bird—the most representative form is the sphere, just as the spherical drop of water is the most representative form of water. Every existing being makes circular motion, taking after the Original Image.

There are additional reasons for the necessity of circular motion in all things. Everything exists by forming quadruple bases through the give-and-take action between subject and object. Of the four elements in the quadruple base—purpose, subject, object, and united body (or multiplied body)—purpose itself does not engage in give-and-take action directly, because it is not a substantial being;

neither does the united body (or multiplied body), because it is a resultant being, derived from the very give-and-take action. Consequently, only the subject and the object participate directly in the circular motion caused by give-and-take action. The center of the circular motion lies in the subject, and the object revolves around the subject. If the motion were linear, instead of circular, it would eventually come to an end; the object would be either separated from the subject, or absorbed by it. Give-and-take action would be impossible. Without give-and-take action, however, nothing can exist, since existence, multiplication, and the force of action can only be realized through give-and-take action—as explained in the Unification Principle (Principle of Creation). The object must not be separated from the subject; it must maintain a fixed distance from, and revolve around the subject.

The necessity of circular motion can also be grasped from the perspective of dual purposes. From our explanation of Connected Body and Dual Purposes, we can conclude that there is a graded series of centers, or subjects, in the created world. The subject on one level relates to the subject of the next higher level as its object. The new subject, in turn, relates to the subject of a still higher level as its object—and so forth. This graded series of centers, of subjects, is only possible because of the circular motion of the object around the subject on each level.

The moon revolves around the earth as its object; the earth revolves around the sun, as the sun's object; the sun, along with other stellar groups, revolves around a nuclear system of fixed stars, as their object—taking two hundred and fifty million years for one revolution. The galaxy, in turn, revolves around the center of the universe (macrocosm), as the object of this macrocosmic center. At the other end of the spectrum, we have the electron revolving around the nucleus, as its object. We can see, then, that this pattern is identical at every level of the phenomenal world.

The supreme center of the created world is man. Although man is less than microscopic, when compared with the heavenly bodies, his value is greater than the whole universe. Hence, the universe revolves around man, the highest center in the series of circular movements. Of course, this revolution is not physical, but is referred to as *Sung Sang* motion (purposeful motion). There is harmonious give-and-take action in all creation. If man had not fallen, he, too, would be enjoying circular motion now—i.e., a harmonious life through complete give-and-take action centering on the Purpose of Creation.

What is the purpose of give-and-take action? What is the purpose of circular motion? The purpose of these things is none other than the realization of the Kingdom of Heaven on earth—the fulfillment of the Purpose of Creation.

Although the rest of creation performs give-and-take action solely according to the autonomy of the Principle, man's harmonious give-and-take action requires his own creative effort and responsibility. Human history has developed through circular motion (harmonious give-and-take action between subject and object), even in the fallen world of wars and struggles. How much more would it have developed in the original world, with circular motion based on the Purpose of Creation!

B. THE EXISTING POSITION

All beings in the natural world are individual truth bodies. The numerous complex phenomena in the natural world are caused by the countless interactions between these individual truth bodies. No matter how complex, there is order in all these interactions. All parts of an organism are related to one another in a certain order. 'Order' means a hierarchy of positions: it is realized when things are positioned or ranked. For example, in man's physical body, the cells, tissues, and organs make a hierarchy of positions, with the brain in the highest position.

Since society is to be formed after the model of man, it must have order as well. The same applies to the universe, also made after the model of man. Accordingly, there is order in the solar system, in the galaxy, and in the universe—no matter how large these things may be.

Order within the created world is a reflection of the order within the Original Image. In the Quadruple Base, Heart is in the first position; *Sung Sang*, in the second; *Hyung Sang*, in the third; and the United Body (or Multiplied Body), in the fourth. Man takes after the orderly structure of the Original Image; creation—i.e., the universe and human society—takes after the orderly structure of man.

Each cell in man's body lives for the whole (the tissue or the organ) as well as for itself. The same applies to each tissue or organ. Cells, tissues, and organs are linked to one another through harmonious give-and-take relationships of subject and object. Warm blood runs through every part of the body without discrimination.

Similarly, in society, every man should live for the whole (his family, his nation, and the world), as well as for himself. Men should relate to one another through orderly and harmonious give-and-take relationships of subject and object. Love should be communicated from person to person without any discrimination, just as warm blood runs through every part of the body. (Blood can thus be considered a symbol of love.) With the correct understanding of original man—or by setting original man as the standard—we can rescue society from its present confusion.

Man has always underestimated his own value, considering it only a little greater than that of the animals. Consequently, we have been unable to realize that circular motion—resulting from harmonious give-and-take relationships at all levels of creation—is for the sake of man himself. Electrons revolve around the nucleus for man, as does the earth around the sun, and so forth. For what purpose, then, does man himself exist? Man exists for God.

Note that by 'man' I do not mean an individual person: I mean 'husband and wife', for without realizing the unity of husband and wife through marriage man cannot be the center of the universe.

C. THE VARIOUS TYPES OF CIRCULAR MOTION AND DEVELOPING MOTION
1. Types of Circular Motion

As I have explained, circular motion is the existing mode of existing beings. There are numerous kinds of motion, however, that are not literally circular. In the atom, for example, the electrons revolve around the nucleus, performing a spherical movement; yet atoms and molecules in minerals and living things do not move circularly, for they establish relatively fixed structures.

The atoms and molecules that constitute the earth's crust, mantle, and core are strongly bound to one another, in order to solidify the earth—our dwelling place. If they moved circularly, the earth would be gaseous, and thus unfit to be man's dwelling place. Water, on the other hand, needs to have a liquid form, with loose bonding, in order to fulfill its numerous functions; by being liquid, it can form part of the blood, which flows through all the parts of the body. In contrast, a house fulfills its purpose by being stationary.

In living things, neither cells, nor tissues, nor organs make circular movements. (Body fluids, however, such as blood and lymph, move circularly.) The cells that form the walls of the heart must be tightly bound together; they need to facilitate muscle contraction, which pushes blood out of the heart and around the body. Without this, we would be unable to live. Furthermore, people do not move around in circles: they walk on their legs and move their arms freely. If we were to move circularly, we would become extremely dizzy, to say the least, and would be quite unable to dominate the creation.

Since all things in creation act in order to accomplish the Purpose of Creation, they have various kinds of shape and perform various kinds of motion suitable to their specific purposes. When a created being cannot fulfill its Purpose of Creation through actual circular motion or with an actual spherical shape, its movement and shape will be modified as needed, becoming non-circular and non-spherical. We should, however, regard such non-circular motion and non-spherical shape as modified circular motion and modified spherical shape. Actual circular motion can be seen most clearly on the microcosmic (atomic) and macrocosmic levels, while the majority of intermediate forms of motion are modified, in order to accomplish the Purpose of Creation. Thus, there are two kinds of circular motion in the universe: actual circular motion and modified circular motion.

2. Development and Spiral Motion

The concept of development involves a changing process with a definite forward direction. A seed grows a sprout, then a stem, branches, leaves, flowers and fruits, which yield a lot more seeds than existed before. During this process, we see a change from simple to complex, from low to high and from old to new: this is development.

In the change from simple, low, and old, to complex, high, and new, we can see direction. The direction of development is determined by a purpose, or a goal. There is also a time period needed for growing and for realizing the purpose. There are three stages in the development (growth) process. In the plant, for example, there are the stages of sprouting, leafing, and flowering (including fruitage), which is the goal of the plant. Besides intragenerational development, there is also intergenerational development, which is especially significant in the case of man. Thus, there are three necessary elements in developmental motion: purpose, time, and stages.

A seed grows into a fruit-bearing tree, manifesting several stages, as mentioned above. Its new fruit falls to the ground, and seeds are dispersed again. The new seeds grow; the process repeats itself. Likewise, a young chick hatches from an egg, grows into an adult bird, and lays eggs, which hatch; the process repeats itself. Developmental motion, therefore, progresses toward a purpose (becoming a fruit-bearing tree or an egg-laying hen) and at the same time revolves, with each circle being represented by one generation. We can figuratively express this motion, which is characteristic of all living beings, with a spiral; thus, we call it "spiral motion" or "circular motion in time." Without exception, then, spiral motion contains purpose, time, and stages.

On the other hand, the revolution of the moon around the earth, for instance, or of the earth around the sun, is "circular motion in space." The movements of molecules, cells, tissues, and organs, which have been modified by the Purpose of Creation, are also types of circular motion in space.

Why is circular motion in time characteristic only of living beings? All created, non-living beings (such as the moon and the earth) perform circular motion in space in order to maintain their eternity. Living beings, however, do not live eternally through the circular motion in the space of (the components of) their physical bodies. They maintain their eternity through succeeding generations by spiral motion—circular motion in time.

Why should it be so? An explanation of the process of Creation may be appropriate here. Although inorganic beings were created almost infinite in number, living beings were created from a single source—just as mankind came from Adam and Eve—and they multiplied all over the earth, as the Bible says: "And God blessed them, saying, 'Be fruitful and multiply and fill the waters in the seas, and let the birds multiply on the earth.' " (Genesis 1:22) This means that the multiplication of living beings is performed according to the plan and order of God.

Since all things were created as the object of man—as the Unification Principle tells us—their numbers should increase proportionally to those of man, in order for man to live with them and have dominion over them. (This is related to the problem of natural resources.) Thus, living beings should multiply, as well as maintain their eternity, which they can do intergenerationally—i.e., by circular motion in time.

The multiplication of living things has two characteristics: *diversification of features* and *numerical increase.* All beings in creation are objects of beauty, as well as of dominion, for man. As explained before, beauty is realized by harmony in variation. Consequently, the diversification of features is necessary for creating beauty in nature. (When we look at puppies in a litter, for example, the variety of markings, hair color, and individual features is very beautiful.) Finally, with regard to numerical increase, I have already discussed what it means.

By the way, why do plants and animals not live forever? It is because they are the objects of man's dominion, and they need not live eternally, even if man does live eternally in the spirit-world. The purpose of maintaining their eternity and multiplication can be carried out intergenerationally. It is doubtful that a dog would become more beautiful simply by living a long time—say, a hundred years or more—growing bigger and bigger and outliving its master. It would become ugly and repulsive. By contrast, how lovely a litter of puppies is!

3. The Direction of Developmental Motion

The Unification Principle says all living things grow according to the autonomy and dominion of the Principle. Growth here actually means development. All living things produce offspring when they become mature. Multiplication is development, as well. In living beings, development is irreversible; in contrast, change in inorganic things is reversible. Water, for instance, changes into vapor or ice, and back into water again. But this cannot be called development; change in inorganic things is not developmental motion.

Here I would like to discuss the concepts of autonomy and dominion of the Principle. These are essential characteristics of life. What is life, then? Life is consciousness, will, or reason latent (hidden) in the body of a living being.

Autonomy, the opposite of heteronomy, means doing something of one's own will. The earth, for instance, does not move around the sun according to its own will, but according to mechanical laws. Living things, however, clearly have their own will and purpose, and do not merely follow mechanical laws. Even a plant has its own latent will: when physical objects impede its growth, the plant will grow around them.

Dominion means the governing or influencing action of a subject over objects. If a seed is sown in good soil, it will grow shoots and leaves, according to its autonomy. At the same time, it influences its surroundings. It takes in water, carbon dioxide, and nutrients, and releases oxygen, thereby influencing its environment. This is dominion. Thus, life is autonomous when seen from the perspective of growth, and has dominion when seen from the perspective of influencing objects.

As a seed grows and bears fruit, its developmental movement has a definite direction and purpose. There must be a force behind growth in order for the purpose to be realized. This force is "life." The direction and purpose of develoment is determined by life at the starting point of growth, for life is the will latent in material—in the above instance, in the seed.

Let us consider the development of the universe. We are told that there was a big bang in the beginning, about 15 billion years ago. A gaseous whirlpool appeared, and then emerged various bodies, such as the stars and the earth. Plants, animals, and finally man appeared on earth. This process has taken fifteen billion years and has been guided through the workings of physicochemical laws. Of course, when we look at each individual stage, or when we observe only short periods of time, we can see only the workings of physico-chemical laws; yet if we look at the development of the universe as a whole (through fifteen billion years), we will recognize direction and purpose (the purpose of forming the earth). The direction of the development of the universe has been determined by a certain will or reason latent behind it, which may be called *cosmic will,* or *cosmic life*.

The universe has developed in a fixed direction. Plants, animals, and man have appeared along this line of direction. There are atheists who say that this development has been purely accidental, but this is unreasonable, for in spite of an infinite number of possibilities, the universe has not only developed, but has developed in a fixed direction. In the Unification Thought view, this development has been determined by cosmic life. Cosmic life is none other than reason (or consciousness). On the other hand, it is also obvious that laws are at work in the universe. We can, therefore, conclude that Logos (reason-law) has controlled the development of the universe.

Thus, it may be said that the universe has grown according to the life latent within it, just as a seed grows according to the life within. The earth, where man, the dominator of the universe, lives, may be likened to the fruit of a seed: it is the final goal in the development of the universe, just as the fruit is the final goal in the growth of the seed.

I said before that developmental motion is limited to living beings; now I have just explained that the inorganic universe has also developed over the course of billions of years. In the light of the ideas explained here, I would like to amplify what I said before and state that all things develop according to the autonomy and dominion of the Principle (Principle of Creation).

4. Purpose and Direction

There is purpose in every development. Communists, however, will not recognize purpose. They say that there is only law, necessity, and direction in development. Why are they so adamant in their denial of purpose in development? When one recognizes purpose, the next obvious question is, "Who has established this purpose?" —for only will or reason is able to do that. The development of the universe, then, would strongly suggest the existence of God, which is anathema to the communists. So, they cannot but deny purpose.

Unification Thought recognizes direction, necessity, and law in development. We emphasize, however, the existence of purpose. Direction, necessity, and law cannot be separated from purpose. Direction should be toward purpose, and there is no direction without purpose. The necessity of phenomena (i.e., the working of physical laws) is also related to purpose. For example, the necessity of the sprouting of a seed is identical to the necessity of the attainment of its goal (purpose): to develop to the fruit-bearing stage. The physical laws at work within it are for the realization of its purpose. Laws have been prepared beforehand by God for realizing the Purpose of Creation.

There are numerous physicochemical activities in our body. If we examine our blood with scientific instruments, we will be able to see these physicochemical activities, but never life itself. The direction of these physicochemical activities is controlled by life. All laws directing these physicochemical activities, therefore, are for the realization of the purpose of the body. Should we disregard the purpose, the laws would become meaningless.

Materialists generally deny any purpose in the development of the universe. The heavenly bodies and the earth are supposedly formed by chance; plants, animals, and man appeared accidentally. These processes, they insist, are merely the results of physicochemical actions and have not been controlled by reason or will.

What is the significance of this "accidental" man? What basis is there for morals, values, and ethics in an "accidental" human society? Such would be a world of survival of the fittest, where the strong and powerful prey upon the weak. There would be no eternal peace on earth. Actually, the dignity of man's life has no meaning until we accept that man and all things have purpose.

Let me refer again to the example of the chicken and the egg. The embryo of the egg grows into a chicken. Materialists may say that this happens purely through the necessity of physicochemical laws. When I discussed "subject and object," however, I mentioned that all elements of the egg have a common purpose. The shell is created to protect the contents. The yolk and the white are created as nourishment for the growing embryo. The embryo, which contains life, grows into a chicken. All cooperate for the common purpose of bringing a new chicken into life. If these elements existed accidentally, there would be no necessity of having a yolk and a white in the egg. There could just as easily be stones or sand in it. I am sure none of you have ever seen an egg with stones and sand instead of yolk and white. We should recognize the purpose of the egg. Direction, necessity, and law in the growth of an embryo cannot be reasonably explained until we do.

In the "Theory of the Original Image," the first step of Creation is the formation of the Logos (Inner Developing Quadruple Base) by the give-and-take action between the Inner *Sung Sang* (reason) and Inner *Hyung Sang* (law), centering on Purpose. In this Quadruple Base, the center (Purpose) is first established by Heart. Next, reason and laws come to be engaged in the give-and-take action, as subject and object, in order to form Logos, centering on this Purpose. Laws are located in the Inner *Hyung Sang* in order to realize the Purpose of Creation. Accordingly, it is the Unification Thought view that laws are prepared beforehand, in expectation of the realization of the Purpose of Creation.

IV. COSMIC LAW (HEAVENLY WAY, *CHEON-DO* 天道) AND A NEW VIEW OF VALUE
A. THE SEVEN NATURES OF COSMIC LAW

The cosmos is vast and boundless, containing innumerable heavenly bodies. This vast and boundless cosmos, nevertheless, is controlled by one single law, namely, the Give-and-Take Law. This law is characterized by seven natures, which I would like to discuss next.

1. Correlative Elements (Paired Elements)

In order for give-and-take action to be established, there must be correlative elements of subject and object. This is a prerequisite for the cosmic law, because when there is only a single element, no give-and-take action can take place.

2. Purpose and Centrality

In order for give-and-take action between subject and object to occur, there must be a common purpose and a center between them. Since purpose and center are located in the subject, give-and-take action is performed centering on the subject.

3. Order and Locality

Since the subject's position differs from that of the object, another prerequisite of the cosmic law is the establishment of order and locality. Every being has a specific position from which to engage in give-and-take action, and cannot perform principled give-and-take action apart from its position. If a teacher in a school, for example, leaves his position, he is no longer a teacher. The establishment of position is a necessary condition for give-and-take action. In making quadruple bases, purpose (Heart), which is the center of the subject and of the object, obviously occupies the first position; subject and object are in the second and third positions; and the united body (or multiplied body), which will be established after the give-and-take action takes place, will be in the fourth position.

4. Harmony

When the above three requirements are met, harmonious give-and-take action can be carried out; harmony, therefore, is the fourth nature of cosmic law. The materialistic dialectic attempts to explain relationships in terms of opposites, or of struggle, but this can never be the essence of give-and-take law. From celestial bodies in the cosmos all the way down to particles in an atom, all actions we see are harmonious give-and-take actions.

5. Individuality and Relationship

No being can exist or develop (change) without being engaged in give-and-take action internally and externally. Though every being relates with other beings and with the environment—and thus can be said to have relationships—each being, nevertheless, has its own individuality. For example, in the cosmos there are countless stars and planets, which are related to one another, but each one is different from the other. Likewise, in human society people are related to one another, yet every person is different from the others, both in mind and in physical constitution, and shows remarkable individuality.

6. Identity-Maintenance and Development

As explained in the "Theory of the Original Image," there are two kinds of Quadruple Base in God. One is the Identity-maintaining Quadruple Base and the other, the Developing Quadruple Base.* Accordingly, every existing being has such quadruple bases, showing unchangeability and changeability. Traditional philosophies have generally been one-sided, stressing either the aspect of unchangeability or that of changeability. By contrast, Unification Thought considers that every existing being has both aspects in harmonious unity.

Here I would like to add an explanation about development. Unquestionably, multiplication is development, but so is withering away. It may be regarded as negative development. Once I asked Reverend Sun Myung Moon if growing old is development. He answered, "Yes, it is." Then, why? Man has a physical man and a spirit-man. Even though the physical man may be growing old and infirm, the spirit-man is still developing. Moreover, when a person is

---

*To be exact, there are four kinds of Quadruple Bases in the Original Image: Identity-maintaining, Developing, Inner, and Outer Quadruple Bases. The Identity-maintaining and the Developing Quadruple Bases are the Quadruple Bases seen from the perspective of time

maturing, his children and grandchildren are growing up. On the whole, then, aging is development.

7. Circular Motion

When the subject and object enter into give-and-take action, a circular motion is produced, whereby the object goes around the subject. Every motion in the cosmos is circular motion—either actual or modified, and either in space or in time—expressing harmony, eternity of existence, and duality of purposes. The materialistic dialectic, also, asserts that all things move, yet it has been unable to clarify either what kind of motion they have or the reason for such motion.

This concludes my explanation about the seven natures of cosmic law (give-and-take law). These seven natures rule the cosmos and can be called secondary laws of the cosmos, when we consider the give-and-take law the primary law of the cosmos.

B. THE ESTABLISHMENT OF A NEW VIEW OF VALUE BASED ON COSMIC LAW
The Vertical Order and the Horizontal Order

The characteristic of order and locality is one of the seven natures of the cosmic law. There are two kinds of order in the cosmos: vertical order and horizontal order. (Fig. 13)

The cosmos was made in the image of man; as regards the relationships among heavenly bodies, they were patterned after the image of a family. Accordingly, the order of the cosmos and the order of the family are similar, and we can derive the view of value, or the standard of conduct, of man by observing the cosmos. The law of nature—which is the law of force—and the law of the family—which is the law of love—correspond to each other. (Fig. 14)

In the cosmos there is vertical order; in the family, likewise, there is vertical order and vertical love: parental love (downward) and children's love (upward). A school, a commercial company, a social organization, and a nation are extended forms of a family in the Unification Principle view. Accordingly, they should display the same kind of order. In a school, teachers should observe the duties of teachers and should love their students (downward); students should respect and obey their teachers (upward). In a commercial company, a superior official should give directives to his subordinates with

Fig. 13 Vertical and Horizontal Orders in the Cosmos

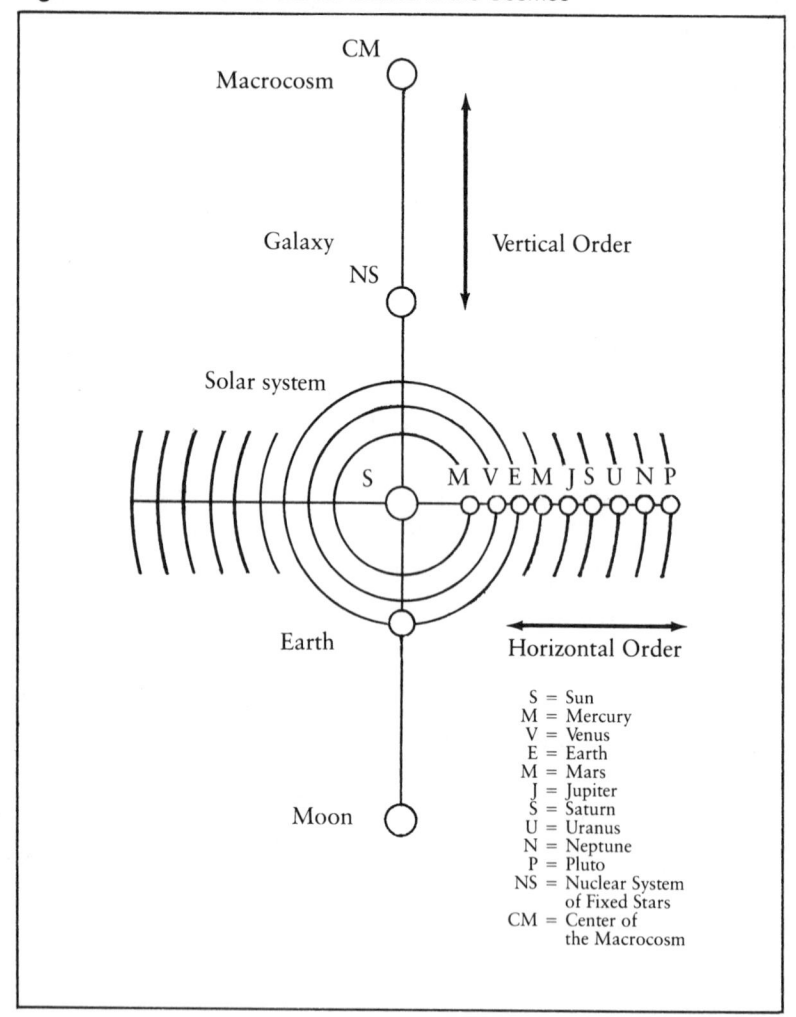

```
S  = Sun
M  = Mercury
V  = Venus
E  = Earth
M  = Mars
J  = Jupiter
S  = Saturn
U  = Uranus
N  = Neptune
P  = Pluto
NS = Nuclear System
     of Fixed Stars
CM = Center of
     the Macrocosm
```

love and dignity (downward); subordinates should obey their superiors (upward). In a social organization, seniors should take care of juniors (downward); juniors should respect their seniors (upward). In a nation, the government should have clemency toward the people (downward); the people should express loyalty to the nation (upward). These are the vertical views of value, or vertical standards of conduct in human relationships.

As there is horizontal order in the cosmos, so there are horizontal order and horizontal kinds of love in the family: conjugal love

Cosmic Law and a New View of Value

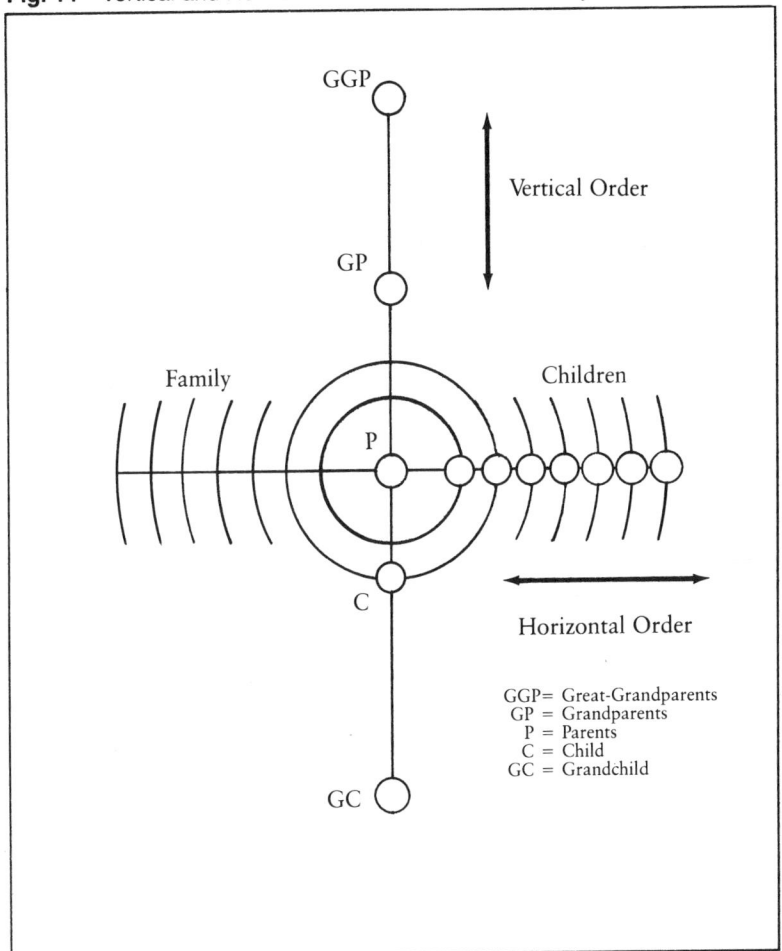

Fig. 14 Vertical and Horizontal Orders in Human Society

```
                    GGP ○
                        │
                        │        ↕ Vertical Order
                        │
                     GP ○
                        │
          Family        │         Children
        ))))))))────────○────────○○○○○○((((((
                        P
                        │
                        │         ←————→
                      C ○
                        │         Horizontal Order
                        │
                        │     GGP = Great-Grandparents
                        │     GP  = Grandparents
                        │     P   = Parents
                        │     C   = Child
                        │     GC  = Grandchild
                     GC ○
```

as well as love among siblings. Horizontal order can be perceived among neighbors, colleagues, brethren, and human beings in general. Accordingly, our lives should reflect the virtues of reconciliation, tolerance, justice, sincerity, courtesy, modesty, compassion, helpfulness, service, and understanding. These are horizontal views of value, or horizontal standards of conduct, in human relationships.

The order and the values (different kinds of love) thus established in a family become the basis of all order and values in society, nation, and world; they can be called "Basic order and values." On the other hand, the order and the values established in society, nation, and world can be called "applied order and values," or "order and values of resemblance," since society, nation, and world resemble the family.

According to individuality and relationship, which are characteristics of the cosmos, every being in the cosmos has relationships with others and, at the same time, has its own characteristics, occupies its own position, and rotates around its axis to maintain its existence. In human society we should likewise establish our individuality and perfect our personality, by realizing the values of purity, honesty, righteousness, temperance, courage, wisdom, self-control, endurance, self-reliance, self-help, independence, dignity, diligence, innocence, integrity, etc. These virtues, then, should become part of our daily lives. These are individual views of value, or individual standards of conduct, which every individual should endeavor to keep.

Thus, there are three kinds of views of value: vertical, horizontal, and individual. Oriental society has generally emphasized the vertical view of value, whereas Western society has emphasized the individual view of value. To a certain extent, however, both societies have recognized other views of value.

Today, there is a lot of confusion in the family, society, nation, world, as well as within ourselves, chiefly because the views of value taught by traditional religions have lost their persuasive power. Since the views of value of traditional religions offer no reasonable explanations for the teachings, it is increasingly difficult for them to be accepted by people today, who are inclined to think in a logical and analytical way. Unification Thought, however, can establish a solid basis for such views and can unite them into a new view of value, by offering philosophical explanations such as those presented above. Cosmic law is absolute and unchanging; if we fail to obey it, we will be harmed as a result. Likewise, if we disregard values in our lives, there will be harmful and detrimental consequences to our family, society, nation, world, and to ourselves. We should, therefore, establish order and realize values in our lives, in order to realize happiness, peace, and prosperity—the Kingdom of Heaven on earth.

3. THEORY OF ORIGINAL HUMAN NATURE

I. THE TASK OF THE THEORY OF ORIGINAL HUMAN NATURE

The Theory of Original Human Nature deals with the nature of man, disregarding the fact of the human fall. Since, however, the fall did occur, man has inherited properties that discord with his original human nature, causing him often to feel dissatisfied with life. Nevertheless, man also feels that he has something like an original self buried inside, although he may not clearly perceive what it is. Certain thinkers who pondered on these problems began a movement in the nineteenth century called existentialism, but existential philosophy has not given us an exact picture of the original man—the ideal man of creation. The "Theory of Original Human Nature" does that. This theory is unique to Unification Thought; we can look upon it as the anthropology of the Unification Principle.

As a result of the Fall, man became unable to realize not only his original nature, but also the original world (ideal world). After that, and often quite unaware of it, man has been attempting to restore his lost self and the lost world, the world never realized. He tries to improve himself and his family; he wishes to deepen his friendship with those around him, in an effort to make this a better world; yet he dies without fully actualizing his hopes. In a nutshell, this has been the story of human life.

Fish swim and eat freely, apparently quite satisfied with their life; birds fly in the sky, seemingly contented, singing and eating as they please. If these creatures, however, were taken out of their natural environment, what would happen? If a fish were taken out of the sea and thrown on the ground, it would feel extraordinary agony and would long to return to its home, the sea; it would have lost its original environment. If we were to catch a bird and put it in a cage, it would feel discontented and would long to fly freely in the sky. Similarly, man feels restless and craves to realize an ideal. This means that he has lost his ideal self and the ideal world for which he was created. The painful disappointment and despair that result from shattered hopes and unrealized ideals have often led people to resign themselves to a world and life that do not bring true satisfaction. Some, however, have not given up. These are the philosophers and religious persons. We cannot but respect those who have seriously struggled with man's problems, seeking an ideal way of life, even at the expense of their wealth and social position.

Gautama Buddha, for example, forsook his riches and worldly position in order to seek the answers to questions such as: 'What is man?' 'How should he lead his life?' 'Why is man born?' 'Why does he live and die?' Only after years of searching and meditation did he finally receive spiritual enlightenment.

So it was with Jesus. Even though when we read the Bible we are apt to think that Jesus was endowed with complete wisdom from the beginning and was just biding his time until he started his messianic mission, Jesus actually had to find answers to the same fundamental questions. On that foundation he stood as the Messiah.

Jesus was born in accordance with God's dispensation; he had, however, to accomplish his mission as a man. In order fully to discover the original or true nature of man, Jesus put himself in the same position as that of fallen man, experiencing all the sufferings that man had gone through during history. He put himself in the place of fallen man and suffered, so that others would not have to suffer as he did. By doing so, he received revelations from God and proclaimed these to mankind as God's representative.

Rev. Sun Myung Moon,* also, has suffered terribly in his search for solutions to mankind's problems. His revelations have come neither accidentally nor easily. The Unification Principle has been compiled with tears, sweat, blood, and suffering; only those

---

*This chapter contains several references to Rev. Moon and the Unification Church. Please note again that the contents of this book have been compiled from lectures on Unification Thought given to staff members of the Unification Church. Some parts, therefore, are presented in the form of guidance for the life of faith of church members; these parts are not necessarily expressed in strictly academic style.

who have searched and suffered to find the true way of life can understand its contents.

Few of us have deeply suffered over the question, 'What is life?' Few of us can really appreciate the tribulations of past sages and the foundations they have laid for us. This grieves Rev. Moon, for it means that we cannot really appreciate what he is trying to tell us. With regard to the question, 'What is man?', a warning may be appropriate: if we lack an honest and deep yearning to find the answer, we may fail to grasp its true meaning when we happen to find it.

As we have seen in "Ontology," man is a created individual truth body. Some scholars have considered man as a creature like any other—a higher animal evolved from the apes. Unification Thought, however, seeks to liberate man from being just a cog in the wheel of nature, and to restore him to the position of the person who rules creation with love and wisdom.

If man is a creature, yet stands apart from the rest of creation, then in what lies his uniqueness? The "Theory of Original Human Nature" deals primarily with this question.

II. ORIGINAL HUMAN NATURE
A. A BEING WITH DIVINE IMAGE
1. A United Body of *Sung Sang* and *Hyung Sang*

Man is a being with divine image resembling the Divine Image. The Divine Image contains the Universal Image *(Sung Sang* and *Hyung Sang,* Positivity and Negativity) and the Individual Images.

First and foremost, man is a United Body of *Sung Sang* and *Hyung Sang.* There are four ways of comprehending the *Sung Sang* and *Hyung Sang* aspects in man: (1) as the integration of all the *Sung Sangs* and *Hyung Sangs* of creation (integrated man); (2) as the union of mind and body (dual being); (3) as the union of spirit-man and physical man (dual man); and (4) as the union of spirit-mind and physical mind (dual mind).

In the original man, the spirit-mind and the physical mind participate in give-and-take action centering on Heart, forming a united body. The give-and-take action between spirit-mind and physical mind in fallen man differs from what it would have been in the original man, in two aspects: (a) it is not centered on Heart; (b) the positions of subject and object are usually reversed.

The purpose of the spirit-mind is to pursue a life of trueness, beauty, goodness, and love, in order to give joy to God. Man pleases God by being true, beautiful, and good. The basis for trueness, beauty, and goodness is love; so a life of trueness, beauty, and goodness centering on love is a life of values. A life of values is a life lived 'for' the family, 'for' the nation, and so forth—the highest 'for' being 'for God'. The physical mind, on the other hand, centers on the physical necessities of life, such as food, clothing, shelter, and sex. It pursues 'physical life.'

The 'life of values' should be subject, and the 'physical life' should be object. In other words, the life of values comes first, and the physical life, second. We must, however, keep in mind that food, clothing, and shelter are a necessary foundation for achieving and maintaining a life of values. The original man has the ability to maintain the correct relationship between his spirit-mind and his physical mind. His heart has grown to become centered upon, and united with, the fullness of the Heart of God. The give-and-take action between his *Sung Sang* and *Hyung Sang*, like the give-and-take action between God's *Sung Sang* and *Hyung Sang*, is harmonious and perfect, because it is centered upon Heart.

Because of the fall, however, man has been unable to maintain this relationship; the original positions have become reversed. Food, clothing, and shelter—and in general a life of physical pleasures—have become a primary concern for man, whereas the values of trueness, beauty, goodness, and love have become secondary. Sometimes man even tries to love his fellow man and to do good, but often only for the purpose of gaining physical pleasure, wealth, or political power.

I do not wish to imply that there are no spiritual values in this world; the point here refers to correct order. Values in this world often serve a self-centered purpose, for man's spirit-mind has become subservient to his physical mind. Furthermore, his heart—the center of the give-and-take action—is not fully developed.

Although the spirit-mind is continually trying to return to its original position, man has been unable to become what he truly wishes to be. After the fall, man has had an impulse (desire) to go back to the original self and the original position. He persists in his search for an ideal because of that very impulse. Nature itself shows a similar impulse to grow: a young sapling will often continue to grow even under most severe circumstances. This is similar to fallen man's situation. After the fall, his natural growth has become obstructed, but he never ceases to pursue his original ideal. Man's situation is more complicated, however, since he does not clearly perceive which direction his growth should take; he only feels vaguely that things are not as they should be.

We must receive the Word of God in order to change our direction and be re-created. This explains why an increasing number of persons in today's world are demanding a new understanding of values.

2. A Harmonious Body of Positivity and Negativity

In "Ontology" I said that positivity and negativity are attributes of *Sung Sang* and *Hyung Sang*. Man is a substantial being with relatively positive characteristics, and woman is a substantial being with relatively negative characteristics. The harmony between positivity and negativity in the case of mankind means the harmony between man and woman—that is, conjugal harmony.

Plants, animals, and minerals are created through the combination of positivity and negativity, but to think that this is the only reason man and woman should unite is to ascribe to them a mere biological existence. In certain advanced countries of the world today men and women begin to question whether marriage should be a lasting relationship, as soaring divorce rates indicate. People marry and soon separate, in what is often little more than a biological relationship. What should be the true relationship between husband and wife? Is the ideal of eternal marriage just a holdover from the feudal ages? Problems related to the family are very complex indeed.

Moreover, since one cannot easily find the correct answer to questions such as "What does man exist for?" or "What does woman exist for?" a great number of people choose not to marry at all, opting for a life of total dedication to God. Our answer to these problems is clear. In their relationship, the ideal husband resembles one essential aspect of God (positivity), and the ideal wife resembles another essential aspect of God (negativity). Neither is complete or fulfilled without the other. Only when united do they substantially resemble the harmonious positivity-negativity relationship in God. Positivity and negativity, as well as *Sung Sang* and *Hyung Sang*, are the attributes of dual characteristics that every existing being has. Man is born as the united being of *Sung Sang* and *Hyung Sang* characteristically positive (masculine), while woman is born as the united being of *Sung Sang* and *Hyung Sang* characteristcally negative (feminine). Only when united can they be harmonized and perfected. Man was created as the encapsulation of the universe, but he can represent only half of the universe; the same is true of woman. Consequently, only through the union of man and woman can mankind become the loving dominator of all creation.

Each individual can fully represent not only half of the universe, but also half of all mankind. The population of the world today is estimated to be about four billion, four hundred million. Since one half of these people are men and the other half women, each human being has such value as to represent two billion, two hundred million people. This means that the husband and the wife are meeting half of the universe and half of all mankind in each other. They have to see such great value in each other. I would even predict that this view of the husband-and-wife relationship will soon prevail everywhere.

The perfection of husband and wife means the perfection of Creation. Since the husband-and-wife relationship has not been perfected, however, Creation has remained unperfected. For this reason, God has been involved in re-creating the universe until today. Re-creation means to lead man again toward the completion of the Three Blessings.* Since Adam and Eve failed to perfect themselves and to be married according to the original ideal, God has been trying to raise man and woman up to perfection, enabling them to have an ideal marriage; this would bring Creation to perfection. Originally, the marriage of man and woman would have meant the completion of the creation of the universe, the unification of all mankind, and the full manifestation of God.

The main cause of social and family problems is that husbands and wives are not as they should be. Consequently, families are in a state of confusion, as are our societies, nations, and in fact, the whole world. Harmonizing the relationship between husband and wife represents harmonizing and unifying the whole world. We can say, therefore, that the key to solving world, national, social and family problems lies in solving problems between husband and wife. Such is the significance of the relationship between you and your spouse. To see this relationship as something private, only con-

---

*God's three blessings to man are 1) perfection of individuality, 2) multiplication of children or perfection of the family, and 3) dominion over the whole creation. (Gen. 1:28)

cerning one another, is not what God wants.

In order to help us to become aware of these truths, Rev. Moon takes every possible opportunity to speak about husband and wife, man and woman. Some of you may wonder why he speaks on this subject so often. This is because you have not yet grasped that this is the problem of greatest importance in the world today. First and foremost, husbands and wives must form a harmonious unity.

Of course, in trying to actualize the Principle we will encounter great difficulties, since we have to walk the course of restoration through indemnity. Nevertheless, if we clearly grasp the theory of the original standard, we will eventually be able to create an ideal family. For this reason I have emphasized these points in the "Theory of Original Human Nature."

3. A Being with Individuality

Before creating, God had in His mind an Individual Image for each being to be created. He thought of numerous Individual Images for persons, animals, and plants. In order to receive infinite joy, God creates innumerable individuals, each one resembling the specific attributes of one of His Individual Images.

The individuality, or specific attributes, of a person is quite distinguishable from that of another. In the lower scales of creation, however, the distinction among individualities becomes less and less perceptible.* This is related to the value of a specific being. The lower the value, the less perceptible the individuality will be; likewise, a being of great value will have a clearly defined individuality. Man, who has the highest value and is to give the greatest joy to God, shows unique individuality. We need to understand, therefore, that God has given us unique individuality (individual image) in order to derive unique joy from each one of us.

Because of the Fall, man's individuality has often been abused or disregarded. Throughout history, there have been dictators and powerful leaders who used their subjects only as a means to achieve their selfish ends, often driving them like animals or machines, with little thought for their personal welfare. God, however, with love, wants to obtain joy from each person. It is not His wish for us to ignore the individuality of our fellow man.

---

*Nevertheless, some distinction always remains. Even amoebas seem to differ from one another to some extent.

In today's communist societies, man's individuality is being grossly disregarded. It is true that the citizens of those countries have a certain amount of freedom and have their individuality respected to a certain extent. This, however, is not done under the inspiration of the communist (Leninist) philosophy itself. It is reluctantly granted under pressure from the internal demands of the people, and it often represents the desire of these governments to save face in their diplomatic dealings with free nations. If our free society is destroyed, communism will quickly reveal its true nature by restricting man's freedom and disregarding his individuality; powerful leaders will dominate man in any way they please.

In a work of art, we can perceive the artist's individuality. Michaelangelo's individuality is expressed in his paintings and sculpture, as are the unique character of Beethoven, Schubert, Bach, and Tchaikovsky in their musical compositions. A special beauty can be found in each one of them. In communist countries, however, even art has largely been deprived of its role of expressing the artist's character and has been used primarily as a tool for the Communist Party to further its own causes. The kind of music to be composed and the kind of painting to be created are stipulated by the Party, and the artist must comply. Under such conditions, no true art can appear. Art without full investment of individuality is not true art; it contains neither true beauty nor true joy. This explains why some artists in the Soviet Union are so involved in anti-establishment movements.

Originally, man himself is a work of art that gives God joy to behold. During his lifetime he uses his freedom to express his individuality, thereby taking part in his own creation. His undertakings help to create his personality. God Himself takes pleasure in seeing man's creative works, for they express his individuality. Thus, in every person there is God-given individuality (individual image). Since it is a gift from God, it must be respected.

B. A BEING WITH DIVINE CHARACTER

I have explained above that man is a being with Divine Image. In addition, man is originally a being with Divine Character—Heart, Logos, and Creativity. Accordingly, man is originally a *being with heart, being with logos,* and *being with creativity.*

1. A Being with Heart

Heart, the first aspect of Divine Character, is the emotional impulse to seek joy through love. Man, who is created taking after God, has such impulse, too. How can we know that? Simply by observing that every person seeks joy through love. There is no one who doesn't, neither child nor adult. Even martyrs; those who have been martyred for their faith were willing to die because they believed that their sacrifice was important to God's Providence. They believed they were loved by God. They were seeking true joy. Most people try to obtain physical joy, whereas martyrs tried to obtain spiritual joy, through serving God, even to the point of death.

The impulse to obtain joy through love—through loving or through being loved—is irrepressible. If repressed, it will find a different way to manifest itself. Children, for instance, have the impulse to be loved by their parents; if they are not, they may become nervous or even psychologically ill. They may choose to vent their frustrations on society, thus becoming delinquents. The desire for joy through love cannot remain repressed. No matter what activities man engages himself in, no matter what methods he uses, his motivation is always the same: to find joy and happiness.

Like God, man is a being with heart. Just as God could not but create man and the rest of creation in order to seek joy through loving them, man tries to find or create his objects to love; also, he tries to find his subjects whom he is loved by, in order to be joyful. Fallen man, however, does not know how to obtain true joy. He is not aware that there is true joy only in true love, and he seeks joy through wealth, power, fame, mundane love, and so on. True love is what pleases the other first before pleasing oneself, just as God intended to please man first before pleasing Himself when He created man. True love will be realized through an original family centered on God (See Chapter 8 "Ethics").

All of us are beings with heart, but our heart is not completely united with the Heart of God and cannot be fully expressed. Only after growing through the stages of formation, growth, and perfection, and after reaching the level of God's Heart, will we be able clearly to comprehend the direction of our lives. Only when our heart is perfected will the originally intended direction of give-and-take action between our spirit-mind and physical mind be perfectly stabilized.

Since man's heart is not elevated to this level, man has been unable to find the true direction of his life. In his desperate search for happiness, he has often turned to the acquisition of money and other material things, as well as to power. The result has been new problems and increased anxiety, for man cannot find happiness in a life centered around physical things alone. True joy must be based on heart, which man must find through practicing love. Heart is man's deepest part; to develop and to improve it is his supreme task.*

2. A Being with Logos

Man is a 'being with logos'. As explained in "Ontology," logos is reason-law. Man, like the rest of creation, was created through the Logos; in other words, he was created to live a life of reason-law, following laws and norms.

The idea of laws and norms may be repugnant to those who believe that man must be free from any restrictions or laws. (Young people, especially, are attracted to this way of thinking.) Such views, however, come from their ignorance of the details of Creation. True freedom is found within rules. Freedom without rules results in licentiousness and destruction. A train is free to go either fast or slow, and to run from one place to another, but it must remain on tracks, for without them it cannot run. Tracks, therefore, represent true freedom for the train. If it goes off the tracks, not only will it be destroyed and paralyzed, but may also destroy property and injure people. Similarly, we must lead our lives according to laws. We need norms, or guidelines, on how to act as a child, as a spouse, or as a parent. These norms constitute family ethics. Since we were created with logos, it is natural for us to conform to laws. The problem is whether these laws are within the Principle or not. As long as they are, we should gladly conform to them, for ethical laws are the way to actualize love.

Every person needs to receive education of logos—that is, instruction on the various norms that guide human life. (This will be dealt with in "Ethics.") If a person is thus educated from childhood, he will become the incarnation of the norm and logos. Each one of his actions will be in accordance with the norm. Confucius, for instance, said, at the age of seventy, "I never go against the law, even

---

*Since Heart is the deepest point in the spirit, to center on Heart means to give spiritual values priority, valuing physical life subordinately.

when I pursue what I want." It was not until he reached that age that his actions became consonant with the rules of Heaven; he had attained a life of logos.

If man had not fallen, but had passed through the growth period, perfecting himself, he would have become the incarnation of reason-law, the incarnation of the norm. He would have become a *being with logos*.

3. A Being with Creativity

God's Creativity, with which He made the world, was given to man as a potentiality. Even though man has fallen, he has displayed creativity throughout history, bringing about the development of science and the arts. The creativity manifested in fallen history, however, differs from that of God: God's Creativity is based on Heart, whereas fallen man's usually is not.

As it was explained in the "Theory of the Original Image," God created the universe motivated by the element of Purpose within Heart. Purpose, therefore, was established first. Then, centering on Purpose, God's Inner *Sung Sang* entered into give-and-take action with Inner *Hyung Sang* to form the Logos. This was a manifestation of God's Creativity. After that, there was give-and-take action between Logos and *Hyung Sang* in order to create substantial beings. This was also a manifestation of God's Creativity. In the Creation process, therefore, God first established Purpose based on Heart; next, He dedicated everything He had to its realization.

Similarly, when man wants to create something, he sets up his purpose, formulates a plan, and works to carry it out. But, where is heart, which is the foundation of true creativity? Instead of setting up his purpose based on heart, man usually sets it up based primarily on reason. Consequently, his creativity has given rise to numerous ill effects.

God created the universe in order to have an object to love. Man, however, usually creates for self-centered reasons. God's Creation, which is based upon Heart, shows His love for mankind and all things. In contrast, man (fallen man) creates things out of love for himself, for his own family, or at best for his own nation, disregarding other people, other nations, as well as nature. Consequently, we have such problems as pollution and the draining of natural resources. The world around us—air, land, and sea—is suffering from problems caused by man's deficiency and disregard of heart. The damage will eventually fall back on man. If we waste and misuse the world's natural resources, instead of appreciating and conserving them, they will soon be used up.

Creativity, therefore, must be guided by a true standard of values. A scientist, for instance, should be primarily a person with a standard of values (a person of character), and secondarily a person of science. In other words, ethics should be the very basis of natural science. Man's motivation to develop science must be his love for creation and for his fellow man. Scientists, however, have often refused to establish a universal standard of values, saying that science need not concern itself with anything but phenomenal events, leaving problems of value, ethics, and morality out of its domain. The miserable condition of the world around us is the result of such thinking.

Thus, original man is a being with Divine Character and Divine Image. Knowing this, we can more easily realize the preciousness of man and the importance of a proper way of life.

C. A BEING WITH POSITION
1. A Being in the Object-Position

Man was created as the substantial object of God. God desires to rejoice through loving His substantial object—man. Man, therefore, must love God and assume the object-position in relation to Him; this is the only way for God to find true joy. Thus, man can be called a being in the object-position. The object relies upon, lives for, and seeks to please the subject; man must do these things in relationship to God.

'Position' here refers to 'relative situation' in the created world and in social life. Primarily, man is in the object-position to God; secondarily, in the subject-position to the rest of creation. Accordingly, from birth man tends to take the object-position— that is to live for, and to be ruled by, a subject.

When, for example, people find someone who truly loves them and wants to help them solve their problems, they seek this person's guidance and accept him as their leader; in some cases they may be willing to follow him unconditionally, even at the cost of their lives. This they do, not out of compulsion, but out of loyalty.

Why is man willing to follow and even die for a subject? This springs from man's original tendency to be a loyal object to God, to serve Him, and to bring Him joy. Consequently, man looks for a leader who can represent God. If a leader appears to be the person for whom they have been searching, people will follow him willingly. It is not easy, however, for a man to find a true leader in the fallen world. Even if God's representative does appear, it will be extremely difficult for people to recognize him as such.

On the contrary, history shows us that numerous false leaders have appeared, who excited and mobilized large numbers of people with their words; they were later revealed as selfish dictators, who misled and abused their followers. By exploiting the object-consciousness of the people, they received their unconditional support; later, they became arrogant and deified themselves. Soon, however, they fell, for they were false subjects.

Man originally stands in the object-position not only to God, but also to a subject on earth. The object-position is necessary in order for us to establish order, morality, and norms in our society; only through respecting and following a true person in the subject-position can order and morality be established.

In the modern world, however, most people desire to have only themselves in the subject-position, as man's object-consciousness becomes increasingly hampered, bringing about a great number of conflicts. This is very sad indeed, when we consider that the hope of all mankind is peace.

2. A Being in the Subject-Position

Man is the subject and dominator of all creation. Accordingly, man simultaneously occupies the dual positions of subject and object. He is in the subject-position not only with regard to creation, but also with regard to his wife, his subordinates, his children, those younger than him, and so forth.

While in the subject-position, man must be guided by the original subject-consciousness—that is, by love. Subject-consciousness is often misconstrued as one's tendency to oppose or dominate others by putting oneself first. The true, or original subject-consciousness, however, is love; in other words, to be a subject means to love those in the object-position. God, for example, who is the subject of mankind, has an immense love for all of us, His objects.

The word 'love' often evokes the idea of warmth or tenderness. This, however, need not always be the case. A stern order may also be an expression of love. If a leader uses only sweet words in leading his subordinates, he may eventually find that he has no authority at all.

Yet authority must accompany the subject-position. The expression of subject-consciousness, therefore, will vary according to time, place, situation, and so forth, but its origin must always be love.

In the early days of the Unification Church, Rev. Sun Myung Moon often spoke with warm and gentle words, which seemed to reach out and embrace the members. Now, he sometimes speaks forcefully and issues stern orders. Those who see him for the first time may think that he is a very cold-hearted person, but this is far from the truth. As older members will testify, he is a warm and loving person.

In the Summer of 1958, as I recall, Rev. Moon instructed us to do a seven-day fast, for the first time. For a lot of members it was their first time to fast at all; for everyone, it was a formidable obligation. Nowadays new members breeze through a seven-day fast and continue activities as usual; at that time, however, we all had to remain lying down, and would only get up to walk short distances. We felt proud of ourselves and thought we were doing a phenomenal task. It is said that Rev. Moon worried very much about us, torn inside because he had to give us such an order. But it was God's order, so he made us do it, suffering along with us and consoling us with a heart of love.

Sometimes Rev. Moon would also give us very difficult missions. He would give us strict orders, such as, "Go out immediately and evangelize for forty days. Don't take anything with you. If you don't find transportation, then walk! Don't worry if you fall down on the way." We had to manage somehow, by ourselves. The Bible tells us a similar story, that of Jesus sending out his disciples in pairs, telling them not to take anything with them. I have heard that after giving that order, Rev. Moon wept in prayer. Even though it was a necessary indemnity condition, he wept because he had to give an apparently cruel order.

Following Rev. Moon's example, the leaders of the early church sent members out to work or to evangelize under very severe conditions. Seeing them faithfully obey, the leaders would pray tearfully. Though strict, those orders were based on love.

This does not mean, however, that a leader can issue any kind of order he likes. Once the subject gives a direction, he must take responsibility for the results of the efforts of those in the object-position who have tried to follow his direction. The subject must love his object and have a genuine interest in his well-being. He must not overlook anyone—no matter how many subordinates he may have—for only through showing interest does love grow.

Once in Korea a woman itinerary worker went far into the countryside in order to visit a local church. It was a very small church, far away from the central headquarters; it could have easily been neglected. When she arrived there, she spoke and prayed together with the missionary who was leading that church. The missionary was surprised and thankful that someone had taken the trouble to come such a long way just to see him. As he thanked the itinerary worker, he wept with tears of gratitude. Indeed, love begins by showing interest in someone. When the subject shows real interest in his object, love grows, and the true subject-consciousness develops.

True subject-consciousness manifests itself in other areas as well. If you are the subject, when you give a lecture or sermon, for instance, you should not feel that you are great. Instead, you should feel that you are representing the church leader or Rev. Moon or God Himself. You must think that your subject is behind you; this will help you to maintain your object-consciousness. Only then will you remain humble, thus conveying the right impression to your audience. Of course, we also ought to show dignity as a preacher or lecturer. Our attitude must combine both the subject- and the object-consciousness.

In today's democratic societies, the subject-consciousness has been over-emphasized, and the object-consciousness largely neglected. People want to control others, while they themselves are reluctant to submit to authority. They criticize the government, disregard authority, and oppose their subjects—all because of a misunderstanding of the idea of equality. This shows that the object-consciousness has been stifled. Nevertheless, not only the objects are at fault; subjects are also to be blamed, for they have lost the consciousness of ruling with love. Their concern for the object is usually one-sided and based on selfish motives. Thus, democracies are falling into confusion; to an increasing degree, they are ignoring or becoming indifferent to man's position.

On the other hand, what should be the attitude of an object with regard to his subject? As mentioned before, the object should obey and respect the subject. This, however, does not mean that he must be servile or sycophantic. In fact, he ought to present his own ideas and opinions—with a humble attitude—whenever necessary. He should become an object with independent consciousness, for man is both an object as well as a subject. He should be a good subject to his subordinates and, at the same time, a good object to his superiors.

3. A Being with the Position of Mediator

If man had not fallen, he would have become a perfect mediator, harmonizing the physical and the spiritual worlds. Because of the Fall, however, he has been unable to attain that position. The spirit-man and the physical man have been rendered unable to harmonize; in other words, they have lost their mutual resonance.

Originally, man's spiritual senses should resonate harmoniously with his physical senses, and vice-versa. Even fallen man, if sufficiently mature spiritually, can feel the presence of the spirit-world to some degree. In fact, the spirit world is always willing to respond to, and to cooperate with, those who earnestly seek its help. This is called *Hwa-Dong* (Harmony).*

Suppose that we are listening to a fine musical concert. As we enjoy the concert we can also mediate between the physical and the spirit-world, allowing spirit-men around us to hear the music through having give-and-take action with us; thus, they will enjoy the concert as well. Here, the physical and spiritual worlds are harmonized through the concert. This is *Hwa-Dong*.

Hence, man is the mediator—the center of harmony—between the two worlds. If you give a Unification Principle lecture and really express your heart through it, the spirit-world will be moved and will listen to you. This is because man is able to dominate the spiritual as well as the physical world, even while still living on earth.

Since we are in the position of mediators, we must choose our words carefully; even a single wrong word can offend some spirit-man. Thus, we ought to think and act so as to please the spirit-world. If you act centering on the Word, the spirit-world will cooperate with you. Here, again, you are a mediator.

In summary, man is simultaneously a being with Divine Image, a being with Divine Character, and a being with position. Although this may sound simple, it actually answers the questions, 'What is

---

*In a certain sense "Hwa Dong" (和動) means "harmony"; a more exact translation, however, would be "delight felt among people" or "delight felt between the physical and spiritual worlds."

man?' and 'How should he be?' As we know, these are questions that have worried man for a long time.

D. CONCLUSION

Among the original human characteristics I have explained, the most essential one is 'a being with heart' or 'a being with love.' Man exists to love others—that is, to love his family, neighbors, society, nation, world, and God. Philosophers thus far have advocated various views of man, such as *homo sapiens* (intellectual man), *homo faber* (technical man), *homo religiousus* (religious man), *homo economicus* (economic man), *homo liberalis* (liberal man), social animal, and tool-making animal. Unification Thought, however, regards man as *homo amoris*, which means "man of love," or "man for loving." To be sure, Unification Thought does not disregard the other aspects of man's value, referred to above.

Since we have received such precious information about the original human nature, based on the Unification Principle, without really exerting ourselves to find it, we are apt to slight its value. We should, however, treasure the Unification Principle and treat it with respect. When we talk about the Unification Principle, we should do so seriously and with great effort, feeling in our hearts the value of these words. We ought to realize how much blood, sweat, and tears of righteous persons are behind them. If we speak with such an attitude, our listeners, as well as the spirit-world, will be deeply moved. Rev. Sun Myung Moon shed countless tears before making public the message of the Unification Principle. He says that we ourselves should naturally feel like crying when we understand that message deeply.

Besides the power to make an emotional impact, the Unification Principle contains also academic and rational aspects. Some members, therefore, attempt to convey it only through the use of logic; this is not what Rev. Moon wants. He has told me that unless our intellectual aspects are accompanied by the aspects of faith and heart, people will not be moved. Even if we are speaking to academic professors or students, we must speak earnestly and honestly, with heart.

As I mentioned in "Ontology," God, during the Creation, caused *Sung Sang* and *Hyung Sang* to enter into give-and-take action centering on Heart. Prior to that, the Inner *Sung Sang* and Inner *Hyung Sang* of the *Sung Sang* had formed the Logos. Within the Inner *Sung Sang* there is reason, which operates centering on Heart. Heart never arises from attitudes such as thinking that it is enough just to convey a given amount of content for a certain period of time. Heart seeks to love people, to save them from their miseries, to guide them toward knowing and carrying out God's will. Become earnest! When you speak, forget everything else and devote your whole heart and soul to your audience. This is the kind of attitude Heaven wants to see.

Heaven does not want to see you, or any teacher, selling knowledge as an "education merchant." Teachers must teach their students with their whole heart and soul, praying that through their teaching the students will grow up to become loving family members, useful constituents of society, a backbone for the nation, and good servants of mankind.

III. A CRITIQUE OF EXISTENTIALIST VIEWS OF MAN

A considerable number of philosophers have attempted to provide solutions to problems concerning the original nature of man. The group of existentialists is among them. Here I will criticize the ideas of five existentialists, whose ideas still influence people's thinking today. Understanding their theories, I think, will help you to understand the theory of the original human nature.

Existentialists are basically concerned with such problems as how man should live and what the real man is like. To most of these philosophers, man is caught up in anxiety and despair, even though some people seem not to suffer. These philosophers observed also that there are people who sincerely try to live in a true way, and yet cannot avoid suffering. Thus existentialist philosophers, like many religious persons, tried to identify the origin of human suffering, drawing their own conclusions about the meaning of life.

A. SÖREN KIERKEGARRD (1813-1855)
1. Kierkegaard's View of Man

With regard to what man is, Kierkegaard says, "Man is spirit. But what is spirit? Spirit is the self. But what is the self? The self is a relation which relates itself to its own self...."* Who enables man to

---

*S. Kierkegaard, *The Sickness unto Death*, trans. by Walter Lowrie (Princeton: Princeton University Press, 1974), p. 46.

have this relation with his own self? It must be someone other than the self. This is none other than God. Man's self, therefore, always makes man face God.

But man, who is originally related to God, has been separated from Him. How did that happen? Kierkegaard discussed the state of Adam's innocence and explained that the dread in Adam's innocence was the cause of original sin.

> In this state there is peace and repose; but at the same time there is something different, which is not dissension and strife, for there is nothing to strive with. What is it then? Nothing. But what effect does nothing produce? It begets dread. This is the profound secret of innocence, that at the same time it is dread.*

Man has tried to free himself from his dread as if it were something hanging around his neck, but he has been unable to do so. He cannot overcome despair until he becomes related to God, and until he relates himself to his own self. Belonging to the public is not true existence. Such life is limited to loving pleasures of the physical world—the world of no value. Kierkegaard, therefore, maintains that man should escape from such a world in order to become his original self—an individual that has recovered his relationship to God. Everyone should stand before God alone, as an individual.

He classified the process of the return to the original self into three stages: the aesthetic, the ethical, and the religious stages.

(a) *The Aesthetic Stage*—This stage is formed by the aesthetic attitude—i.e., the attitude of seeking after pleasures. Man in this stage lives by wit *(mit Geist)* and according to sensuous desires. The satisfaction of one desire, however, only brings about dissatisfaction soon afterwards, and a person wanders around, looking for his next satisfaction. In this stage, therefore, there is a constant alternating between satisfaction and dissatisfaction. Some pleasures are noble and others vulgar, but they all have in common their lack of seriousness toward life. However attractive, a life of seeking after pleasures is a life of despair, for it brings about the vicious circle of satisfaction and dissatisfaction.

(b) *The Ethical State*—A man enjoying the aesthetic stage will finally fall into deep melancholy. In order to escape from its vicious

---

*S. Kierkegaard, *The Concept of Dread*, trans. by Walter Lowrie (Princeton: Princeton University Press, 1973), p. 38.

circle, he must regain seriousness toward life and leap to the ethical stage. Here he takes into consideration the standpoint of other people, as well as his own. In this stage he lives by conscience, trying to be a good citizen. He finds meaning in life through performing his duties and responsibilities. Once he occupies a responsible position in his community, for instance, he will no longer fear the monotonous repetition of daily living. While the aesthetic person lives in moments, the ethical person lives in time and in history. For the aesthetic person, pleasure and displeasure, beauty and ugliness are the standards of judgment, or the decisive factors for personal conduct; for the ethical person, however, good and evil become the standard of subjective decisions and deeds. Yet man soon realizes he cannot do good however eagerly he may try. In other words, he finds sin latent within himself and thus falls into serious ethical self-contradiction.

(c) *The Religious Stage*—When man becomes aware of his sin, he also becomes conscious of his true self as well. But only in God can man become conscious of his true self, because God is the source of man's self. So, God is the medium of man's discovery of his true self. Here man enters the religious stage, in which he lives by faith and becomes a true existence facing God. As we said before, the aesthetic person lives in moments; the ethical person lives in time; the religious person, however, lives in the expectation of eternity. The religious person is not satisfied with human sincerity alone; his goal is much higher, as he seeks after internal seriousness.

According to Kierkegaard, these three stages of existence develop neither naturally nor necessarily. They can be reached only through a personal decision and a leap of faith. At the point of the leap of faith that carries man from the ethical to the religious stage, paradoxical faith emerges—i.e., a kind of faith through which man believes that which he cannot understand with reason.

For instance, in discussing the faith of Abraham, who was ordered by God to offer his only son Isaac, Kierkegaard concludes that "... Abraham was greater than all, great by reason of his power, whose strength is impotence, great by reason of his wisdom, whose secret is foolishness, great by reason of his hope, whose form is madness, great by reason of the love which is hatred of oneself."[*]

As Kierkegaard understood it, faith includes strife such as this.

---

[*]S. Kierkegaard, *Fear and Trembling*, trans. by Walter Lowrie (Princeton: Princeton University Press, 1974), p. 31.

This strife, however, is the very process of overcoming sin. He calls this process 'paradoxical dialectic'. Even beyond faith, love should guide people's lives. He said that those who have become true existences should love one another through the agency of God's love, according to Jesus' teachings, "Thou shalt love thy neighbour as thyself." (Matthew 23:39) True society can be realized by such works of love.

2. Critique of Kierkegaard

According to Kierkegaard, man has fallen into anxiety and despair because of his separation from God and the subsequent disintegration of the relation that 'relates itself to its own self'. This relation is, in the Unification Thought view, the relation between mind and body, or between spirit-mind and physical mind. What Kierkegaard is saying here is that mind and body, which originally should be united harmoniously, have been disunited because of man's fall and his separation from God. Kierkegaard's view of man as the 'relation which relates itself to its own self' corresponds to the original human nature of the 'United Body of *Sung Sang* and *Hyung Sang*' in Unification Thought. But how can mind and body be united centered on God? Unification Thought would reply that spirit-mind and physical mind can be harmoniously united when they enter into the relationship of subject and object centered on God's Heart and love.

Kierkegaard said that man must stand before God alone as an individual, and that an individual must relate absolutely to God. But why is an individual absolute? He seems to offer no explanation. His concept of the individual corresponds to 'being with individuality' in Unification Thought. Unification Thought explains the absoluteness of individuality in that God is the God of Heart, and He has created every man as His object of love; from each individual God seeks to obtain a particular joy, which cannot be acquired from any other person. Thus, each individual is unique and is created taking after a particular Individual Image in God.

Kierkegaard explained the unity of mind and body as well as the individuality of the original human nature; in the Unification Thought view, however, this is only a part of the original human nature. He was unable to understand the most essential aspect: 'a being with heart.' Furthermore, he was unable to understand man as 'the harmonious body of positivity and negativity.' According to this characteristic, man is not complete as an individual, but only when united with a partner in a husband-wife relationship. He also failed to see man as a 'being with logos' and a 'being with creativity', where logos and creativity are centered on heart. Furthermore, Kierkegaard did not perceive man as a 'being with position,' or a being that has both subjectivity and objectivity. In the Unification Thought view, Kierkegaard's view of man as an individual who stands alone before God is, though sincere, lonely and solitary. The original human nature is, first of all, a heart full of joy.

Why has man been separated from God? It is impossible for man to restore his original self—the self of a man who has realized the Purpose of Creation—unless matters pertaining to the human Fall are clarified. Kierkegaard said that Adam fell because of the dread lying within his innocence. Is it really true that this dread is the cause of the Fall? Unification Principle says that insecurity and fear arose in Adam and Eve only as a result of their separation from their original position—accordingly, from God's love. In other words, dread appeared as the result of going off the track of the Principle; dread itself cannot be the cause of the Fall.

According to Unification Principle, the cause of the Fall is the power of non-principled love, which was generated when Eve responded to the temptation of the archangel. After falling, Eve seduced Adam, hoping to rid herself of the fear derived from the Fall; they made a premature conjugal relationship centered on non-principled love, which multiplied mankind in sin. Adam and Eve should have become husband and wife, eternally centered on God, after their perfection. Through their Fall, all mankind has been separated from God; anxiety and despair have been generated as a result. Man cannot overcome his anxiety and despair unless the problem of the Fall is solved.

Kierkegaard said that man has to meet God as an individual. The question here is whether or not the God met in this way is the true God. Can man meet the true God by going against what is "reasonable," and believing in a paradoxical dialectic? Not necessarily.

In Kierkegaard's day, the clergy was very corrupt. He felt that he had a mission to awaken Christianity, so he spoke about true faith and the true path for Christians. He was not aware, however, of what we now understand about God's Heart and the Purpose of Creation. He had only a veiled understanding of God, even though his faith was pure, and his desire to discover God was sincere.

A Critique of Existentialist Views of Man

Furthermore, his concept of love was vague. Purpose and direction are a part of the nature of love, as we know from the Principle of Creation. When God's love is expressed on earth, it takes different forms (just as white light can be broken up into different colors, when projected through a prism); this can be called *divisional love*. There is parental love, conjugal love, and children's love. These basic types of love can be developed, when applied to different situations, thus becoming love for mankind, love for one's country, love for animals, love for nature, and so on. First, however, we must have a concrete understanding of love, and a concrete experience of God's love; otherwise, problems will arise in each one of our relationships.

B. FRIEDRICH NIETZSCHE (1844-1900)
1. Nietzsche's View of Man

Nietzsche said that man suffers because of his belief in God, a view quite different from Kierkegaard's affirmation that man suffers because of his separation from God. Perhaps he had good reasons for saying that. Preachers and theologians of his day taught that man must do good and endure pain on earth in order to go to heaven after death, and that life on earth is only a preparatory period before going to heaven. Thus, man must not hate others, must not steal, and must not kill. He has to attend church regularly and live according to God's words, which are conveyed by his pastor. Man must not have desires while living on earth; he should submit to his plight. Christianity in Nietzsche's time was authoritarian, stoical, and oriented toward life after death.

Nietzsche had no need for such a religion, and had a great hatred for Christianity. It seemed to him that those who went to church regularly had surrendered their own rights to the church. Man might just as well be an ox or a horse. Such miserable people cannot assert themselves or express their own hopes; all they can do is silently and obediently follow orders from God. Since he believed that man had become diminished because of his faith in God, Nietzsche felt it was up to him to free man. He believed that man had lost his true human nature, his rights, and his freedom, thus becoming a weak and cringing creature.

For these reasons, Nietzsche declared the *death of God*, and attacked Christianity. In his view, Christian morality supports weakness, opposes strength, despises the physical body and instinct, and does not accept life's realities. In other words, Christian morality is *slave morality*.

In its place he advocated a morality that followed nature—a morality of life. Scrapping all Christian ideals—such as love, service, and compassion—he proposed a life based on the instinctive desires of the human body. According to him, there is a life-force within every living being, an impulse to grow and become great. When suppressed, this force will fight against its suppressor. Man should live according to this life-force, Nietzsche asserted.

With regard to the essence of life, he wrote, "Where I found a living creature, there I found will to power; and even in the will of the servant, I found the will to be master."*

Thus, life is not merely the will to live, but the *will to power (Wille zur Macht)*. Based on the theory of 'will to power', he established the *master morality*, or hero morality, instead of the Christian slave morality. He said that even the weak have a 'will to power', but owing to their weakness, they are unable to fulfill their desire of domination. This creates in them a feeling of resentment *(Ressentiment)*, or a desire for revenge. Master morality is challenged by this deep-seated resentment on the part of the "slaves," or "herd," who are oppressed and abused. Because of their situation, they cannot have a proper outlet of action and are forced to find their compensation in an imaginary, psychological revenge. Nietzsche regarded Christianity as a seductive life, and was appalled that Europe should be subjected to the morality of a small group of slaves, such as those who gathered around Jesus. For Nietzsche, Christianity was no more than slave morality, springing from the resentment of the herd.

In his master morality, the ideal man is *Superman*, or superior man *(Übermensch)*. The Superman is the goal of history, the meaning of the earth, the highest rung in the ladder of evolution. A few superior individuals are destined to reach the level of Superman, not by the blind force of evolution, but by a conscious effort to break away from the shackles of traditional values and then respond in freedom to the 'will to power' within. In Superman, passion reaches its highest expression, but it is carefully controlled by intellect. Only through enduring and accepting the pain of life can man reach such

---

*F. Nietzsche, *Thus Spake Zarathustra*, trans. by R.J. Hollingdale (New York: Penguin Books, 1961), p. 137.

a level. To affirm life means to accept the idea of *eternal recurrence (ewige Wiederkunft):* "Everything goes, everything returns; the wheel of existence rolls forever."* To accept the eternal recurrence means to endure fate; this is possible when we look at inevitability as beauty, and when we love fate. Thus, he advocated the *love of fate (amor fati)*. Superman is the person who always surmounts the difficulties of his actual life. This is Nietzsche's ideal image of man. He encouraged superior individuals to seek to attain the level of Superman.

2. Critique of Nietzsche

We must recognize Nietzsche's sincere efforts to rescue man, who—as he saw it—had become diminished because of an extreme Christian belief in life after death. The charges Nietzsche brought against Christianity served as a warning to the clergy that they were failing to portray the true nature of God. Nevertheless, Nietzsche has a distorted view of God, as a ruler who judges man from His throne in Heaven, rewarding the good and punishing the wicked.

His philosophy originated from this distorted view of God. The way man understands God greatly affects his philosophical thought, as well as his views on political, economic, and other social issues. For this reason have we tried clearly to state our understanding of God in the "Theory of the Original Image" of this book. We do not see God as this entity of the world after death, standing in the highest place and denying man's earthly life. God's Purpose of Creation is not to establish the Kingdom of Heaven in the world after death (the spiritual Kingdom of Heaven); rather, it is to establish the Kingdom of Heaven *on earth;* when this is done, the spiritual Kingdom of Heaven will be automatically established (by the spirit-men of those who have experienced life in the Kingdom of Heaven on earth).

We cannot deny Nietzsche's assertion that every living being has a will to power. According to the Bible, God gave man the blessing of dominion over all things (Genesis 1:28). In other words, man was given the nature of dominion and creativity. Accordingly, the desire of dominion itself is one of the characteristics of the original human nature given by God. True dominion, however,

---

*Ibid., p. 23.

means dominion by love—not by power—as already explained in 'a being in the subject-position' of this chapter. Consequently, the necessary conditions for one's dominion are the ripening of heart through the perfection of character, and the practice of the ethics of love through family life. True dominion can only be displayed on these foundations. Nietzsche, however, emphasized the will to power—the will to dominate without such foundations. This is a problem in his philosophy.

Nietzsche considered Christian morality as slave morality, or a system of thought that fundamentally opposes strength. In reality, however, Christianity does not oppose strength. Christianity has tried to teach people true love, which is the basis of dominion. In order to acquire true love, man has had to fight against an evil power, which has worked mainly through the instinctive desires of his physical body. This does not mean that the instinctive desires themselves are evil. Man's physical body should be controlled by his spirit-mind centering on heart. Fallen man, however, being controlled by this evil power, often pursues the instinctive desires of the physical body, rather than the spiritual desires of the spirit-man. The actions of the physical body are good when the spirit-man controls the physical-body. If fallen man's spirit-mind develops, this control will be easier to establish and maintain.

I must say that I feel Nietzsche's thought is quite dangerous. He nullified not only God, but also man's spiritual aspect—the spirit-man. He taught people to be concerned with the physical, rather than the spiritual; with life, rather than love; with instinct, rather than reason. Instinct acts in order to develop and preserve physical life and is an aspect of the physical man; reason and love are attributes of the spirit-man. Nietzsche's advocating the scrapping of virtually all the functions of the spirit-man amounts to killing the spirit-man altogether.

What is left after that? Nothing but the physical man. Nietzsche, therefore, has practically degraded man to the level of a mere animal. At best, he can be a powerful animal, but never a true man. Nietzsche's way of remodelling man is completely erroneous. Man is the 'united body of *Sung Sang* and *Hyung Sang*', but he emphasized only the *Hyung Sang* aspect.

Even though he was not a materialist, we can see that, in his conclusions, he tried to solve the problems of life in a materialistic way. Numerous young people today have adopted a way of thinking similar to Nietzsche's—disregarding morals and a religious view of values. They follow a very selfish way of life. As long as such a way of thinking is perpetuated, God's kingdom cannot appear.

C. KARL JASPERS (1883-1969)
1. Jasper's View of Man

For Jaspers, as for Kierkegaard, true existence is related to God, as well as to its own self. The existence that has not yet become related to God is called *possible existence (mögliche Existenz)*. Ordinarily, man is a possible existence that encounters various situations. To some of these situations he can react positively, by his own free will, but he also faces dreadful, desperate situations—the *ultimate situations (Grenzsituationen)* of death, suffering, struggle, chance, and guilt. In Jasper's own words, "I must die, I must suffer, I must struggle, I am subject to chance, I involve myself inexorably in guilt. We call these fundamental situations of our existence ultimate situations. That is to say, they are situations which we cannot evade or change."*

Death is a very serious problem for man, since he wants to live eternally, but no one can evade death. Life is a "sea of sufferings," and to live means to face these problems. Man cannot evade struggles as long as he lives and is given to the hand of chance. Man is stricken with conscience and the guilt of sin.

In an ultimate situation, man becomes anxious and falls into despair; he becomes powerless and his efforts seem meaningless, no matter how much knowledge or how many experiences he may have had. What kind of existence he will realize depends on his way of experiencing this situation. Man should not attempt to escape an ultimate situation; he must sincerely face it and endure to the end, until he has passed through it. If he does that, what seemed meaningless before becomes meaningful; it comes to life. He suddenly realizes that the *Transcendent (Transzendenz)* or the *Comprehensive (das Umgreifende)* —that is, God—is behind nature, history, philosophy, and art. Though things may once have seemed worthless to him, they now have value; through them God embraces and speaks to him.

---

*K. Jaspers, *Way to Wisdom*, trans. by R. Manheim (New Haven: Yale University Press, 1978), p. 20.

God does not speak in words that can be heard directly by the human ear, but in ciphers. Consequently, it is up to man to interpret the ciphers, or the symbols; only those who have passed through suffering and despair can do so. This is called *cipher-reading (Chiffrelesen)*. Since each person has different experiences and faces different kinds of suffering and despair, people understand the meaning of ciphers in different ways. God, therefore, uses those ciphers to communicate individually with each person. What should man do then? He should communicate harmoniously with his fellow man, and thus live his life loving others.

2. Critique of Jaspers

According to Jaspers, man is usually a possible existence—that is, someone who has not yet found the Transcendent; he can become his true self, or the existence related to the Transcendent, by passing through an ultimate situation. But why does man usually remain as a possible existence separated from the Transcendent, and why does man become related with the Transcendent when he passes through an ultimate situation? Jaspers did not say anything about this. If, however, we do not know the answers to these questions, we can understand neither what our original selves are nor how to return to our original selves.

Unification Principle says that man was created to realize the Purpose of Creation. Realizing the Purpose of Creation means completing God's three great blessings: the perfection of character, the perfection of the family, and the perfection of dominion. But, as already explained in the critique of Kierkegaard, the first human ancestors, Adam and Eve, did not believe in God's commandment and prematurely became husband and wife centered on non-principled love; they multiplied children of sin, and all mankind became separated from God.

If man had realized the Purpose of Creation, his original human nature would have been fully developed. When Jaspers asserts that true existence is related to the Transcendent as well as with his own self, he is explaining only the perfection of character from among the three blessings. (We have shown that Kierkegaard followed a similar path.) This corresponds only to the 'united body of *Sung Sang* and *Hyung Sang*' and 'being with individuality' of the original human nature in Unification Thought.

Next, why does man become related to the Transcendent when

he passes through an ultimate situation? As Jaspers points out, "In ultimate situations man either perceives nothingness or senses true being in spite of and above all ephemeral worldly existence."* From the philosophy of Jaspers, however, it is not clear why one perceives nothingness (as Nietzsche did), while someone else senses true being (as Kierkegaard did), even if both sincerely face ultimate situations.

Unification Principle offers an explanation of the difference in these results, through the Principle of Restoration through Indemnity. Because of the Fall, man was separated from God and became dominated by an evil subject—that is, Satan. It became impossible for him to go back to God unconditionally; he can do that only through a *condition of indemnity*. The Principle of Restoration Through Indemnity teaches us how to establish conditions of indemnity. (See *Divine Principle,* Part II, Introduction, I.) The pain and suffering in an ultimate situation correspond exactly to this condition of indemnity; when he endures them to the last, the condition of indemnity is completed, and he comes nearer to God. In enduring pain and suffering in an ultimate situation, however, man should have a humble objective consciousness, serving the absolute subject, just as the Bible instructs us to do: "Ask, and it shall be given you; seek, and ye shall find; knock, and it shall be opened unto you." (Matthew 7:7) As long as he continues to have a self-centered subjective consciousness, he will never meet God, even though he may pass through an ultimate situation.

Jaspers said that man meets the Transcendent through cipher-reading; the Transcendent thus met, however, is only the symbolic God. When one meets only the symbolic God, one cannot understand the Divine Character, especially Heart and love. Jaspers said that, after man becomes related with the Transcendent, he must communicate with other people by loving them. Like Kierkegaard, however, Jaspers was vague when he spoke about love. Actually, love for others can more clearly be expressed through the divisional loves; as we explained before, the divisional loves are manifested in the family. Thus, we must become aware of the specific details of the human fall; we need a clear understanding of the Purpose of Creation; and we must experience God's Heart and love, by establishing true families centered on God.

---

*Ibid., p. 23.

D. MARTIN HEIDEGGER (1889-1976)
1. Heidegger's View of Man

Heidegger called the entity of man *Dasein,* and said the essential element of *Dasein* is 'being-in-the-world' *(In-der-Welt-sein).* Man is not born on earth of his own will; he finds himself alive as though someone had thrown him into the world, so he is in a state of thrownness *(Geworfenheit).*

In everyday life, man is a trivial, unauthentic existence that may be called *they (Das Man).* When man becomes aware of the fact that he is facing *dread (Angst),* he can have the chance to overcome everyday triviality and to become a true existence. There is no particular cause for this dread; it is caused by *nothing;* dread is the dread over nothing. There is also dread over death. Should man wait for his death passively in dread? No, he shouldn't. He must project himself toward the future, that is, he must live sincerely, trying to become a true being. Even death can be a possible motive in his becoming the true existence, when he realizes that he is the *being-towards-death (Sein-zum-tode).*

Then, what is the standard by which man projects himself toward the future? It is the voice of conscience, Heidegger said. The conscience is the call of the self to itself, out of forfeiture *(Verfallen)* and to truth. For Heidegger, conscience is the standard of behavior and of value.

Heidegger explained *Dasein* from the stand-point of time, saying that the meaning of the being of *Dasein* is *temporality.* Man has three aspects: facticity, forfeiture, and existentiality. Facticity means that man is always already in the world; in other words, it means the past. Each one of us is born into a family, a society, and a nation that are the product of past events; we cannot be separated from these things. Forfeiture means that man in his everyday life is surrounded by gossipy, insincere, promiscuous people; in other words, it means the present. Being dissatisfied with the present, man tries to become a new self and to project himself toward the future. Existentiality is the anticipation of true existence and the true world; in other words, it is the future.

Heidegger said that man should not forget that he is a being-in-the-world, and that he is not here because of his choice. Man must take upon himself the burdens of the past, and escape from the forfeiture of the world around him, going on toward the possibility of the future according to the voice of the conscience.

2. Critique of Heidegger

According to Heidegger, man is a being-in-the-world who has lost his original self, and whose basic characteristic is dread. Like other existentialists, however, he did not explain exactly what he meant: why man has lost his original self, or what the original self is like. If one's understanding of man's original nature is not clear, one cannot know whether or not one is going toward true existence, even if one projects oneself toward the future. Heidegger said that the voice of conscience is calling man to become a true existence; this, however, is not a real solution. He is simply presenting a complicated expression of common knowledge. In a world where man does not recognize God, he has only two options: either to live according to his conscience (as Heidegger proposes), or according to animal-like instincts (as Nietzsche proposes).

According to the Unification Principle, man's mind has both *Sung Sang* and *Hyung Sang* aspects, where *Sung Sang* is the original mind and *Hyung Sang* is the conscience. They are similar in that they both help to direct man to lead a life of goodness, but the standard of conscience is earthly, whereas the standard of the original mind is based on God's standard. The standards of conscience will vary, depending on one's age, circumstances, religion, and so forth. The conscience of a Japanese directs him to serve the nation of Japan; that of a Korean, to serve Korea; that of a communist, to serve his Party. Heidegger tells us to live by our conscience, but this will not solve our problems. Since there are numerous kinds of standard of conscience, conflict among people is bound to happen and to continue.

What we should follow, actually, is our original mind. When people live according to their original mind, they seek to become united and to recognize God. Practically speaking, we must begin by seeking God; when we ignore God, our original mind becomes inoperative, even if we may still have it. If all men were to recognize God and to allow their original minds to work, we would have a world without conflict.

Heidegger said that man has temporality. But why does man have temporality? Why should man take upon himself the past, escape from the present, and project himself toward the future? The reason should be clarified. According to the Unification Principle, because of the Fall of Adam and Eve man has inherited "original sin"—the sin derived from the Fall of the first human ancestors;

besides, he has also inherited "hereditary sin"—the sin of ancestors transmitted to their descendants—as well as "collective sin"—the sin for which all members of a nation or a tribe are responsible. Accordingly, man has the mission of restoring his original self and the original world, which were lost because of the Fall, by freeing himself from such sins. This mission is not achieved by any one single individual; instead, it is carried out by a number of people, who hand over the baton of mission from generation to generation. This means that man should take upon himself the problems of the past (the sins of his ancestors and of his people), should liquidate them to some degree in the present, and should take responsibility for the happiness of his future descendants. This is the true meaning of man's temporality.

Heidegger said that man should not wait for the future passively, but should live for the future with a determined mind, thus freeing himself from the 'dread over nothing.' But how can man be freed from dread, if his future original self is not clarified? In the Unification Thought view, man's dread comes from his separation from God's love; he will be set free from dread and will experience peace and joy, only if he becomes 'a being with heart' *(homo amoris)*, by returning to God and by experiencing His Heart.

Furthermore, Heidegger said that man becomes free from death by realizing he is the being-toward-death; this, however, cannot be the true solution of dread over death, for the true meaning of death has not been clarified. In the Unification Thought view, man is the united body of spirit-man and physical body; the spirit-man grows on the foundation of the physical body. After man fulfills the Purpose of Creation of earth, his spirit-man becomes mature; the physical body will have fulfilled its function, and will eventually die. The spirit-man, on the other hand, will live forever in the spirit-world. Thus, man is not a being-toward-death, but a *being-toward-eternity*. After man completes his original self on earth, he is ready to start a new life in the spirit-world. The phenomenon of death, therefore, can be compared with the ecdysis of an animal. In conclusion, the dread over death originates from man's ignorance of the meaning of death, as well as from his awareness—conscious or unconscious—that he is spiritually unprepared to go to the spiritual world.

E. JEAN-PAUL SARTRE (1905-1980)
1. Sartre's View of Man

Dostoyevsky once wrote, "If God did not exist, everything would be permitted." This is the starting point of Sartre's philosophy, as he himself has said. Heidegger was indifferent to God and asserted an existentialism without Him. Sartre's existentialism is not just indifferent to God: it denies God altogether. It is atheistic existentialism.

Sartre's fundamental idea is that existence precedes essence. In his own words, "If man as the existentialist sees him is not definable, it is because to begin with he is nothing. He will not be anything until later, and then he will be what he makes of himself. Thus, there is no human nature, because there is no God to have a conception of it."*

A man-made instrument, such as a book or a paper-knife, has been made by someone who had a conception of it—including its purpose or essence—in his mind. If God exists, and if He has created man according to the conception of man in His mind, then we can say that essence precedes existence in man. But Sartre denied God, so there is no such thing as a pre-determined, essential human nature in man. Consequently, there is no original human existence in Sartre's philosophy.

Sartre said also that existence is subjectivity. Man is an accidental being who has appeared from nothing; he is not restricted by anyone and need not be ordered around by anyone. He decides by himself whether he should become a statesman, a musician, or a scientist. Subjectivity means making decisions and choices concerning one's way of life by oneself.

The essential character of existence is *anguish,* which is related to man's ability to choose for himself. When man chooses for himself, he also chooses for all men; he must make his choice with a deep sense of anguish, for he is responsible not only for himself but also for all men. Since existence precedes essence in man, he is free in his actions, but the results of his actions can be either good or bad—hence, the anguish of man. Nevertheless, he said, anguish does not prevent man's action; on the contrary, it is a condition of his action, or a part of his action. In sum, man is in anguish because

---

*Jean-Paul Sartre, *Existentialism and Humanism*, trans. by Philip Mairet (London: Eyre Methuen Ltd., 1973; reprint ed., London: Eyre Methuen Ltd., 1978), p. 28.

he is free.

Sartre said that man is subjectivity; in order to make his subjectivity operational he needs objects to dominate. If the object is a *being-in-itself (l'en-soi)*—which has no relationship with itself and all that can be said of it is that it is—there is no problem. If, however, his object is a *being-for-itself (le pour-soi)*—which is a conscious being, or a person— there will necessarily be conflicts, for the object—in this case, a person—also has his own subjectivity. For this reason, he said conflict is the original meaning of *being-for-others (être-pour-autrui)*, which is man in contact with other persons. When I stand in the presence of someone, I become a thing to be observed, an object of his looking. On the other hand, when someone stands in my presence, he becomes a thing to be observed, an object of my looking. As long as man is a being-for-itself, he is subjective to himself; when he faces others, however, he becomes a being-for-others, whose nature is conflict.

2. Critique of Sartre

According to Sartre, existence precedes essence in man; every individual chooses for himself; the concept of human nature, or essence, must be rejected. In the Unification Thought view, the original human nature does exist; we cannot, therefore, accept Sartre's idea (see section 1 of this chapter). If his idea were accepted, we would no longer have a standard of value or a judgment of good and evil. Man would be able to justify any action whatsoever, under the pretense that he made the decision responsibly and by himself.

Sartre said man is subjectivity, whereas Unification Thought asserts that man is both subjectivity and objectivity—that is, a being in the subject-position and in the object-position. Sartre considers subjectivity as the ability to choose or to decide by oneself; Unification Thought, however, views subjectivity as the ability to dominate one's objects with love. Before man can do this, he must establish his own *objectivity*, that is, his ability to experience the joy of being dominated with love by his subjects and to have the heart of thanks to his subjects. Once he has gone through this experience, he becomes able to dominate his objects with love and becomes a being in the subject-position (a being of true subjectivity). Emphasizing false subjectivity—as Sartre does—cannot save the world; in fact, it has put, and will continue to put, the world into confusion. The world of love and harmony will be realized only when man has established true subjectivity as well as true objectivity, through the harmonious give-and-take action among persons in relationships of subject and object.

These views proposed by Sartre originate from his concept of man's freedom, according to which man is essentially free, and his freedom is realized by the denial of his objects. It is similar to Thomas Hobbes's thought that the unavoidable nature of society is that of 'a war of all against all'. Unless the errors in these views are exposed and corrected, the confusion in society, especially democratic society, will not be solved.

According to the Unification Principle, freedom cannot exist apart from the Principle. In other words, keeping the Principle is a precondition for freedom. Here, Principle means the rules for the realization of true love. The Principle for the realization of true love, though a rule, does not restrain man, for the freedom that man seeks from the bottom of his heart is the freedom to realize true love. Such freedom is characterized by joy. On the contrary, Sartre's freedom is characterized by anguish, restraining man to the point of despair, instead of liberating him.

F. UNIFICATION THOUGHT AND EXISTENTIALIST PHILOSOPHY

As we have seen, the solutions that these five philosophers have reached in their attempts to escape from anxiety (dread, anguish) and from despair are either vague or incomplete or both. According to the Unification Principle, the reason for man's anxiety and despair is that he is fallen; in other words, he has lost his original position and has become unable to receive love from God and from persons around him. The fact that he has lost his original position and love explains why he is anxious.

This situation is reflected in human relationships as well. Within the family, for example, neither parents nor children are taking their proper positions. When they find their proper positions, they will find true joy and will be liberated from anxiety. In schools, teachers and students are not carrying out their proper roles. When they find their proper positions, teachers will love their students, and students will love and respect their teachers. Only when true positions are understood and kept can a true exchange of love take place; when this happens, anxiety is no more.

Hence, all men must return to their original position. This does not mean that man must go back six thousand years to the beginning of civilization; it means, rather, that man must realize he is fallen and must be re-created, thus recovering his original position in the family, which is the base of the society, nation, and world. When this is done, all problems of anxiety become solved.

As mentioned above, despair and anxiety are a result of man's having fallen and lost his original position and love. In order to recover what was lost, man must first restore his original relationship with God, especially with God's Heart. He can do this only if he finds and follows the Messiah (who perfectly embodies God's Heart as the True Parent), and forms relationships of brothers and sisters with ties of Heart. This is the way for man to restore himself and to create the world that God intended for him from the beginning.

Love is directional: the love of parents for their children is vertical (downward); the love between husband and wife is horizontal; and the love of children for their parents is vertical (upward). Unless each family member is in his or her proper position, true love cannot be realized, for the directions become confused. God's love cannot be manifested, no matter how much He longs to share His love with man.

Both Kierkegaard and Jaspers said that people ought to love one another, but their explanations about how to realize love were vague and incomplete—as I have shown in the critique of their philosophies. We need a concrete idea on how to realize true love—that is, God's love. This will be dealt with in "Ethics," where the realization of God's love through the family foundation (divisional love) will be explained in detail.

4. EPISTEMOLOGY

Many philosophers have developed epistemologies based upon their philosophical viewpoints. Although we have natural sciences for the study of the material world and the Unification Principle for the study of the philosophical world, we must, nonetheless, formulate a Unification Epistemology to clarify our standpoint on human knowledge and cognition and to point out the inadequacies of the epistemologies presented in the past.

The epistemology derived from communist philosophy is based on the *theory of reflection (teoriya otrazhenia)*, which is a philosophical means for justifying violent revolution. Besides dealing with cognition of natural phenomena, it is closely connected with practice and with politics. It deals also with non-political practices, such as scientific research and the manufacturing of goods, but these are relegated to mere expediency. The key-point in this theory is to have people clearly perceive the faults and contradictions of the capitalist system, in order to overthrow it. Unification Epistemology must point out the errors and defects of this theory. Furthermore, it must present a viable explanation that testifies to the authority of the Unification Principle, from which it is derived.

I. TRADITIONAL EPISTEMOLOGIES
A. THE SOURCE OF COGNITION

What is the source of cognition? A cognition is attained by the mutual interaction between the mind of man, which is subject, and the objective world. The objective world cannot be recognized by man's mind directly, but must first be perceived by man's senses, which relate directly to the objective world. We can say there is a flower in the objective world when we experience it with our senses. Seeing a flower means perceiving it through the sense of sight. Where exactly does the process of cognition take place? In man's sensual stage? Or does it take place in the deeper stage of understanding, or even in that of reason? Two schools of thought have contended with each other over this matter: the school of empiricism and that of rationalism.

1. Empiricism

Francis Bacon said that truth can be acquired by experiments and observations—i.e., by experiences. His successor, John Locke, established a branch of philosophy called Empiricism, which says that experiences, rather than reason, are the source of our cognitions. In his book, *An Essay Concerning Human Understanding*, Locke said that man's innate mind, or mind at birth, is like blank paper *(tabula rasa)* or like a dark room. Knowledge is the experience that is imprinted on it from the outside, just like a picture that is imprinted on white paper.

A dark room needs windows for light to enter; our mind needs windows through which knowledge can enter. There are two windows: *sensation* (physical senses) and *reflection* (internal sense). Sensation functions to form ideas from external experiences, through which we can perceive physical qualities—such as yellow, white, hot, cold, soft, hard, bitter, and sweet. Reflection functions to form ideas from internal experiences, through which we can know the operations of our mind—such as perception, thinking, doubting, believing, reasoning, knowing, and willing.

Simple ideas are formed involuntarily through sensation and reflection. In the perception of a flower, for example, each element of the sensation (color, shape, aroma, etc.) is carried to the brain, where it forms a simple idea. The sensations are fragmented, since they come via different sense organs—the eyes, the nose, the ears, etc. *Complex ideas* are formed through the activity of the mind, which combines or associates simple ideas.

There are two kinds of qualities in simple ideas: primary qualities and secondary qualities. Ideas of figure, extension, motion, solidity, number, and so on, are primary qualities; the ideas of color, sound, odor, taste, temperature, and so on, are secondary qualities. The cognition of primary qualities is objective and does not vary from person to person. The cognition of secondary qualities is subjective and varies from person to person. If two people look at the same object, both will perceive the object as having the same shape, but one may see it as a deep-colored object, while the other perceives it as a light-colored object.

Man's mind has the ability to associate simple ideas, thus forming complex ideas. The idea of 'gold', for instance, is obtained from the association of the simple ideas of color, weight, hardness, ductility, and fusibility. The idea of gold, therefore, is a complex idea. One acquires simple ideas from external experiences and obtains knowledge through associating simple ideas. This is the main point of Locke's empiricism, which influenced Berkeley and Hume.

2. Rationalism

As a method for his philosophical investigations, Descartes doubted the existence of the physical objects around him, allowing for the possibility that our senses may deceive us, or that everything we have in our minds is nothing but illusions and dreams. One thing could not be doubted: the fact that he was doubting. Hence the famous proposition, "I think, therefore I am" *(Cogito, ergo sum)* was set up. Descartes thought this proposition certain because it was 'clear and distinct'; thus, it became the first principle of his philosophy.

From this first principle he derived the general rule, "Everything that we conceive very clearly and distinctly is true." The opposite to 'clear and distinct' is 'confused and obscure'; ideas that contain something 'confused and obscure' contain falsity.

Consequently, my existence is certain. I am nothing more than a thing that thinks: I am reason. Reason is the judgment of truth. If a certain knowledge or cognition is clear and distinct in my reason, it is true. Since matter appears to be clear and distinct in my mind, its existence is certain. Here another proposition is established as certain: "Matter exists." There are two substances: the thinking substance (mind) and the extended substance (matter). According to Descartes, these two substances are entirely independent of each other. They are, however, both dependent on God—the only independent entity —and through Him they can relate to each other.

The point of Descartes's rationalism is that we have true knowledge or true cognition if reason judges it to be clear and distinct. If it is not approved by reason, it cannot be true. In this philosophy, reason is the source of cognition.

B. THE ESSENCE OF THE OBJECT OF COGNITION

Other questions to be investigated in Epistemology are: What is the essence of the object of cognition? Does the object of cognition really exist in the objective world independently of the subject, or does it merely exist in the mind of the subject (man) as an idea?

1. Realism

Realism says the object of cognition does exist in the objective world.

Naïve realism is the view that the object of cognition is the material being as we perceive it to be. A great number of people may be included in this category.

In *scientific realism,* on the other hand, scientists come to certain conclusions from experiments, but going beyond simply accepting the results of the experiments, they reflect upon them. When Isaac Newton saw an apple fall, he reflected upon it and concluded inductively that everything is subject to the force of gravitation. This type of realism is characterized by scientific reflection.

In contrast, *realistic idealism* and *objective idealism* say that it is not matter, but idea, that exists independently of the subject. Plato and Hegel are representatives of this trend. According to Plato, idea appears in the phenomenal world garbed in the robes of matter; it is the primary existence in the phenomenal world. For Hegel, the phenomenal world (nature) is the Idea *(Idee)* in the form of *otherness.* The essence of the phenomonal world is Idea, or Reason—not matter.

Communists advance the 'theory of reflection' or 'copy theory' *(teoriya otrazhenia)* to explain the process of cognition. According to this theory, objects can be reflected in man's brain, just as they are reflected in a mirror. Lenin pointed out that the process of cognizing does not end with reflections, but must continue through practice, for it is through practice that one verifies what has been reflected. This view is a kind of realism, since it emphasizes that matter exists outside the subject. Communists, however, do not usually call it realism, in order to avoid confusion with ideal realism, such as that proposed by Plato. The communist view is commonly referred to as dialectical epistemology or theory of reflection.

2. Subjective Idealism

Contrary to realism, subjective idealism says that nothing

exists outside, or independently of, the subject. Whereas Plato and Hegel recognize the existence of the idea outside man's mind, Berkeley, for instance, maintains that all things exist in the mind of man as ideas. In other words, the object of cognition is the idea within the subject. This is known as *subjective idealism,* or immaterialism. Berkeley's basic principle is "to be is to be perceived" *(esse est percipi),* implying that although things seem to exist outside the mind, they cannot actually exist except as perceived by the mind. He was suspicious of Locke's empiricism, arguing that Locke's theory would lead to skepticism. According to Locke, the primary qualities (extension, speed, solidity, etc.) are objective, whereas secondary qualities (heat, color, sound, etc.) are subjective. Berkeley said that even the primary qualities are subjective, for they are intimately connected with the secondary qualities; if the secondary qualities cannot exist without the mind, neither can the primary qualities. The image of distance, for example, which seems to be independent of the observer, is actually subjective. Suppose there is a flower in front of you. You walk towards it step by step. On your twentieth step you reach it. At that point you can recognize the original distance through the tactile sensation of walking twenty steps. Seeing the flower with your eyes, also, is a sensation. According to Berkeley, the image of distance is the synthesis of these various sensations. Distance, therefore, does not really exist in the objective world; it is only suggested by our experience.

Distance, however, does exist in the objective world, we hold. We can sense it when we observe things with both eyes (although not so well when using only one eye). When looking at an object with both of our eyes, there is an angle formed by the two lines that can be drawn between the object and each eye. This angle is wide when the object is near, and narrow when the object is far away. Through this angle our mind can judge distance, which can be said to exist objectively, since the angle itself exists objectively. This is one of the ways we can recognize distance; Berkeley, however, probably lacked this information. Thus, flaws can be pointed out in subjective idealism, even through scientific means.

Locke's empiricism became skepticism when it reached Hume through Berkeley. Hume said that every experience is subjective; the relationship of cause and effect cannot be ascertained directly from our experiences. In a thunderstorm, for instance, first we see the lightning, then we hear the thunderclap. The conclusion that the relationship between the lightning and the thunderclap is that of cause and effect is purely subjective. When we say that two phenomena are connected by the relationship of cause and effect, what we actually experience is that those phenomena are connected by the relationship of before and after. There is nothing in our experience to indicate a necessary connection.

For example, we have experienced numerous times that the sun rises soon after the cock crows. Yet people know there is no cause-and-effect relationship there. Why, then, should we ascribe a cause-and-effect relationship to lightning and thunder? Based on this analysis, Hume expressed his skepticism about the so-called law of cause and effect.

The weak point in Hume's philosophy is that he did not consider practice in his approach to cognition. According to the Unification Thought view, cognition must have give-and-take action with practice, for it is not conclusory in itself. In the example above, we can create thunder-like phenomena through an electrical discharge experiment. The relationship of cause and effect, then, is not concluded solely by cognition, but also by practice. In Unification Thought, therefore, we need not fall into skepticism.

C. THE METHOD OF COGNITION
1. Kant's Transcendental Method

Kant attempted to unify continental Rationalism and British Empiricism. He also tried to establish epistemology as a philosophical base for the natural sciences, which by that time had developed considerably.

British empiricism had fallen into skepticism, and continental rationalism had become dogmatic. In Kant's opinion, rationalism had become dogmatic because continental philosophers had established their theories without sufficient re-examination. He maintained that theories should be established by accurate and rigorous analytical (critical) methods, and not dogmatically.

Kant argues that we must examine the possibility and authenticity of man's cognition. Locke has no problems here, since he says that the cognition is, in fact, the experience. Probing even further, however, one can ask, "how is experience itself possible?" "How can ideas (such as Locke's simple and complex ideas) be formed in our mind?"

Kant's approach, called Critical Philosophy, consists of three critiques, formulated in his later years: the *Critique of Pure Reason,* the *Critique of Practical Reason,* and the *Critique of Judgment.* The Critique of Pure Reason analyzes the process of cognizing, so I will discuss it briefly.

Since cognition is nothing more than judgment, the problems of cognition are the problems of judgment. (Kant inquired about the possiblity of judgment, not the possibility of cognition.)

Judgment is a proposition; it necessarily consists of a subject and a predicate. Its form is "…is…"—such as "This flower is beautiful," where 'flower' is the subject and 'is beautiful' is the predicate. In Kant's view, judgments are either analytic or synthetic. In analytic judgment, the subject already contains the meaning of the predicate; in synthetic judgment, the subject receives new meaning from the predicate. One cannot acquire new knowledge through analytic judgments. Take, for example, Descartes's proposition, "All things have extension." ('Extension' here means size, length, thickness, etc.) The term 'all things' is the subject, while 'have extension' is the predicate. Things, however, already contain the idea of size, length, and thickness; in other words, things already contain the idea of extension. That is an analytic judgment.

On the other hand, in the proposition "This chalk is red," the subject 'chalk' does not contain the idea of 'red'. Although a chalk always contains extension, it does not contain any definite color, for it can be red, white, or some other color. Here, the subject acquires new meaning (the color red) because of the predicate. Consequently, this is a synthetic judgment, through which new knowledge is acquired.

It is through synthetic judgments that the progress of science takes place, Kant maintains. Newton, for instance, discovered that all things have gravitation. It was revolutionary new knowledge; though all things were supposed to have extension, figure, weight, and so on, gravitation was unknown then. Man's knowledge increased, and science progressed, as a result of that synthetic judgment.

In order for a synthetic judgment to be true, it must be universal—i.e., valid not just for some people, but for all people, regardless of place and age. In order to be universal, however, a judgment must be 'a priori', (prior to experience); in other words, it must be effected through the use of a priori forms of synthesis (categories).

The terms *categories (Kategorien), forms of synthesis, pure concepts of understanding (reiner Verstandesbegriff)* and *thinking forms (Denkformen)* refer to a way of thinking, a restriction of thinking, or a frame of thinking. When we see an object, we ask 'what' it is; when we see something move, we say that 'something' moves. Thus, we tend to think of an occurence in relation to the subject (substance); we tend to think that 'something' has caused the occurrence. This form is called *Substance (Substanz)*.

Another form is *Causality (Kausalität):* we tend to see successive phenomena in a cause-effect relationship. *Reality (Realität)* and *Negation (Negation)* are forms as well; we have a tendency to query whether or not something really exists, or whether something is or is not so. These are some of the a priori tendencies, or frames of thinking.

Aside from a priori forms of synthesis, there are also a priori *forms of intuition (Anschauungsform)*, or *forms of sensibility*—such as time and space. Neither time nor space exists in the objective world; what exists is our tendency (or restriction) to think of something in terms of time and space. For an a priori synthetic judgment to take place, 'forms of synthesis' must be united with 'forms of intuition'. The latter work in the stage of sensibility; the former, in the stage of understanding. There is yet a higher stage of cognition —that of reason.

The cognition of a flower, for example, comes about as follows. The flower has sensible qualities—such as color, shape, and fragrance. It also contains the 'flower-in-itself', which lies forever beyond our perception. The 'flower-in-itself', is the essence of the flower, which transmits to us its color, shape, fragrance, etc. Even though the sensible qualities of the flower are perceived by our senses, the flower-in-itself cannot be perceived. According to Kant, then, the flower sends material elements to the senses and stimulates *(affizieren)* the senses through these elements.

The elements of the flower, thus caught by the senses, are first recognized through having forms of intuition applied to them. The sense-impressions, united with forms of intuition, are then connected with the forms of synthesis; the result becomes the object of cognition.

How are the forms of intuition connected with the forms of synthesis? According to Kant, there must be a force to make this connection, which is *imagination (Einbildungskraft)*. Imagination, then, unites the two forms, thus enabling us to complete the judgment, "this is a flower."

Where does imagination come from, or what is its basis? It comes from the *transcendental unity of apperception (transzendentale Apperzeption)*, or consciousness in general *(Bewußtsein überhaupt)*, or pure self *(reines Ich)*. It is on this basis that imagination enables judgment to occur. Consciousness in general is always flowing as an undercurrent in the judgments and experiences of man. This is the main point of Kant's *Critique of Pure Reason*.

The features of Kant's epistemology can be summarized as follows: (1) Forms of intuition and forms of synthesis are applied to sense-impressions received from the thing-in-itself, in order to constitute an object of cognition. Imagination is the force that unites these two thinking forms. The object of cognition is neither subjective nor objective, for it is a synthesis of subjectivity and objectivity. (2) the *thing-in-itself (Ding an Sich)* cannot be cognized. (3) man has a priori forms before his experiences. This is a brief summary of Kant's epistemology.

Cognition, therefore, can be achieved by applying forms of intuition and forms of synthesis to sense-impressions. If any one of these elements is missing, no cognition can take place. In the case of God, for example, Kant says that we cannot determine whether or not He exists, because God cannot be an object of cognition. As there are no sensible qualities in God, He cannot be seen, heard, or tasted; our mind, therefore, cannot obtain any sense-impressions from God. Without these, no cognition can take place. Even though we may have concepts of God, we cannot have a cognition of Him or of His existence.

In spite of his exclusion of God from the world of scientific cognition—to which he clung doggedly—Kant nonetheless believed in God, and said that man postulates God's existence. How can we explain this?

The answer has to do with man's need to lead a good moral life. In order for man to live, he needs, not only cognition, but also practice. In the realm of practice, we are guided by 'practical reason', which is different from 'pure reason', or the reason needed for acquiring knowledge. Practical reason guides us in making decisions about how to live and how to behave; it presupposes man's freedom, for our decisions must be made freely. Practical reason and pure reason differ from, and do not interfere with, each other; pure reason cannot control practical reason, neither can practical reason affect pure reason.

In order to know how we should live and behave, we need the highest standard of good, which is God. Thus, we cannot but accept God as a postulate of practical reason. Practical reason directs the will, which in turn directs actions. When the will is directed by practical reason it is called 'good will'. Man's behavior should be guided by good will.

The directives of practical reason are called 'categorical imperatives', which are unconditional orders. These do not originate from some purpose—such as the purpose to make a profit or to gain popularity. They originate from practical reason and command us to do good unconditionally. Belief in God is what keeps our practical reason in the right direction; thus, God's existence must be postulated. Furthermore, we need to believe in the spirit-world, for similar reasons. Kant was well informed about the spirit-world by Emanuel Swedenborg; he believed in it at first, but denied it in the end.

2. The Dialectical Method of Marxism

Marx, Engels, and Lenin said that a cognition is the reflection of an outside object on our consciousness. In order to be complete and exact—they maintain—cognitions must be verified through practice. True cognition comes both from receiving what reflects on our consciousness from outside (natural world) and from working to practice it outside (in the natural world).

There are three stages in dialectical cognition: (1) the perceptual state of cognitions—that is, the stage of sense-perceptions and impressions; (2) the rational stage, where conception, judgment, and inference take place; (3) and the practice stage. When compared with Kant's epistemology, the second stage corresponds to the union of 'understanding cognition' and 'rational cognition'. The three stages of dialectical cognition are explained in detail in Mao Tse-tung's *On Practice*. By classifying 'practice' as the highest stage, the communist philosophy is in effect saying that the purpose of every cognition is for practice. In other words, one should study or conduct research for the sake of practice, which is understood to be the social revolution, as Mao Tse-tung spells out in *On Practice*.

Knowledge is increased and expanded through the spiral repetition of cognition, practice, recognition, repractice, and so forth. In the beginning, knowledge contains only relative truths; as the process of cognition goes on, it progresses toward absolute truth (according to Lenin).

Mao Tse-tung did not mention 'absolute truth'. He only said that knowledge increases through the spiral repetition of cognition and practice of the relative truth. Lenin, however, accepted the possibility of absolute truth, as defined by him. He did not say that knowledge is absolute (or else the progress of science would be stopped); nevertheless, he said that a system of thought can be considered "absolute truth" if it can explain things most reasonably for a given age. Absolute truth for an age, therefore, is the synthesis of the relative truths of that age. These are the main points of the dialectical theory of cognition.

II. UNIFICATION EPISTEMOLOGY
A. THE SOURCE OF COGNITION

Does cognition take place in the stage of sensation or in the stage of understanding? In other words, is the source of cognition the sensation that comes from the object, or is it the reason of the subject?

These questions are related to the controversy between empiricism and rationalism. For empiricists, cognitions originate from sensations; the role of the objects (all created beings) is stressed. For rationalists, cognitions originate from the subject's reason; the role of the subject (man) is stressed.

The Unification Thought view on the origin of cognitions is based on the Unification Principle teaching that every created being is the object of man; in other words, every created being exists for, and must be cognized by man. This implies that all things were created in the expectation of man's appearance on earth.

This view of the relationship between man and other created beings is actually unprecedented in philosophy. Kant, Hegel, and Marx, for example, took a different position, claiming that man is not the subject, but just a member of creation. They thought that all things existed by accident and for no special reason, before man's appearance; when man appeared, he utilized those things, since they happened to be available.

Schelling's *theory of identity (Identität philosophie)* says that the starting point of man and all creation is God; all beings are phenomenal forms of God. God manifests Himself, first, as nature;

next, as man. One may think that this philosophy explains the necessary relationship between man and creation, but in actuality it relegates man to the level of all creation.

In Hegel's philosophy, man and all beings are phenomenal forms of the Idea (God). Hegel's theory is, in this respect, the same as Schelling's *theory of identity*. Why does the Idea undergo self-development, giving rise to creation and to man? He explained this matter with the dialectic theory of thesis-antithesis-synthesis. In our view, however, the dialectic is not the correct explanation of the reason for the self-development of the Idea; it seems only to justify Hegel's own theory of the self-development of the Idea. Actually, neither Hegel nor Spinoza nor Schelling were able to clarify why man is necessarily distinguished from the rest of creation.

In the Unification Principle view, man cannot exist without creation, and creation is meaningless without man, since man is the subject over all created beings, which are his objects. Man is not only the subject of cognition but also the subject of dominion. The necessary relationship between subject and object was determined in God, even before man was created.

A characteristic of the subject is to have selectivity and autonomy. Man is not a passive recipient of random sensations; he selects certain elements and excludes others. Unification Epistemology maintains that man's subjectivity is involved in cognition. Of course, the sensible qualities of the object, also, are necessary for cognition to take place.

In conclusion, the impasse in the controversy between empiricism and rationalism came about because the relationship between subject and object was presumed accidental. According to Unification Thought, both reason and experience are necessary for cognition, and true cognition is based on the unity of these two. This unitive view of the source of cognition is derived from the necessary relationship between subject and object.

B. THE ESSENCE OF THE OBJECT OF COGNITION

Is either the realistic or the idealistic approach to the object of cognition correct? Here I wish to present the Unification Thought view on the essence of the object of cognition, relating it to those two traditional views.

In "Ontology" I said that man is the integration of all beings in creation, and that all these beings are made in the image of man.

There is a similarity between man and all creation. Although man (Adam) was the last to appear in the phenomenal world, he was created first in the world of idea (Logos), as the standard for all creation.

Man is the microcosm, (encapsulation, integration) of the universe. Consequently, all the elements of the universe exist in man as a "prototype," no matter how small man may be physically.

The concept of prototypes occupies a cardinal position in Unification Epistemology. I will now discuss it briefly and will present a more detailed explanation further on in this chapter. Cognition is a judgment, such as "This is ...''; a judgment can be compared with a measurement, which needs a standard. When I measure something, I must know the units of measurement in order to understand the dimensions of the thing being measured. Similarly, we need standards of judgment in cognition. Man does have such standards within himself, for he is the encapsulation of the entire creation. For example, within himself he has the standards of a flower and a tree, which correspond to a flower and a tree outside. These standards exist in man as prototypes, which correspond to the structure, elements, qualities, and so on, of all beings outside him.

Understanding that man has the whole universe (in prototype) within himself is an important key for establishing Unification Epistemology. The prototypes exist in the mind as ideas; created beings, however, exist outside. By bringing these two together, Unification Epistemology turns out to be the unity of idealism and realism.

For Berkeley, 'to be is to be perceived' *(esse est percipi)*. Thus he limited his area of concentration to ideas in the mind. The realists, on the other hand, limited their area of concentration to outside material substances. By contrast, Unification Thought says that cognition is accomplished by the union of both. This conclusion, however, has not been reached simply through putting together idealism and realism; it is a logical deduction from the Unification Principle.

C. NECESSARY CONDITIONS FOR COGNITION
1. Content and Form

Content is usually understood as those qualities in the object that can be perceived through physical senses—such as color, smell, and shape. *Form* has many interpretations, according to the various philosophers.

Kant's thinking form is transcendental—that is, existing in man's mind before his experiences. Content belongs to the object, and form belongs to the subject. In Marxism, the form in man's mind is a secondary form; it appears when an existing form in the objective world is reflected on man's brain.

In Unification Thought, the object perceived has both content and form. A flower, for instance, has content (shape, color, fragrance, etc.) and form *(Sung Sang* and *Hyung Sang,* positivity and negativity, etc.). Not only the object perceived, but also the subject (man) have both content and form. Since man has all the elements of every being within himself, he necessarily has content and form, corresponding to the content and form of all beings. Give-and-take action (collation) takes place between the content and form of the subject and the content and form of the object. The judgment that results from collation is cognition.

2. Autonomy of the Principle and Protoconsciousness

So far, we have explained that the subject has content and form, which corresponds to the content and form of the object. This does not refer only to the material aspect. For example, when we say, in seeing a flower, that the red pigment on the retina of our eyes corresponds to the red color of that flower, it does not solve all the problems of cognition, for cognition cannot be realized only through material similarity. Man's cognition is a mental judgment; thus, the mental aspect of the process of cognizing must be considered.

The material element of an object does not enter the subject (man) as it is. It stimulates the nerve, causing an impulse that forms an idea in the brain. This idea is then collated with the inner idea (prototype), in order to form a cognition.

Unification Epistemology, therefore, asserts that we are able to recognize the content and form of objects only because we already possess a corresponding content and form in our consciousness. In order to recognize a flower in the objective world, for example, we need a previous image of a flower within us. Without the content and form in our consciousness (i.e., prototype), we would be totally unable to recognize anything. Thus, we need a clear understanding of how prototypes are formed.

Plato solved this problem through the "doctrine of recollection." He said that cognition cannot be achieved by the reflection of the object on the mind of the subject. Man's soul knows everything intrinsically, since it once belonged to the world of Ideas, where it knew all Ideas; upon becoming incarnate in the body, however, the soul forgot those Ideas. When a man sees an object—a flower, for example—he remembers the Idea of a flower, which he once knew, and recognizes it as such. Thus, cognition takes place through the process of recollection.

The doctrine of recollection, however, can hardly explain how man gains new knowledge. If all we can do is to remember what we have forgotten, how can we explain the knowledge we gain through actual experiences and studies throughout our life? Unification Epistemology, on the other hand, accounts for the value of real experience.

At this point, I would like to discuss "protoconsciousness," which is the foundation for the development of prototypes. The formation of prototypes in man's consciousness is connected with the very "life" of the cells in the human body. The life of a cell, as explained in "Ontology," is the autonomy of the principle; it has perceptiveness and purpose, as well as energy. What is the origin of the life of the cell?* The life of the cell—the *Sung Sang* aspect of the cell—is the cosmic consciousness which has entered it. We can conceive of the universe as a sea (or a field) of consciousness, with cells floating in it, permeated by consciousness. When consciousness enters the cell, it conforms to its structure, in a process similar to what happens when water permeates an object: water will enter porous areas, but not dense areas, assuming a certain shape. Likewise, when consciousness enters the cell, it conforms to the shape of the structure of the cell, resulting in the particular consciousness of the cell. We call this particular consciousness "protoconsciousness," which can be defined as the autonomy of the principle (perceptiveness and purpose) received by the cell from the cosmic consciousness of the universe. (Fig. 15)

---

*This should be explained from the standpoint of the creation process, noting that the *Sung Sang* and the *Hyung Sang* aspects of the cell are formed simultaneously. Here, however, I will present only a schematic explanation—describing the *Hyung Sang* aspect of the cell as existing prior to its *Sung Sang* aspect—for a convenient understanding of prototypes.

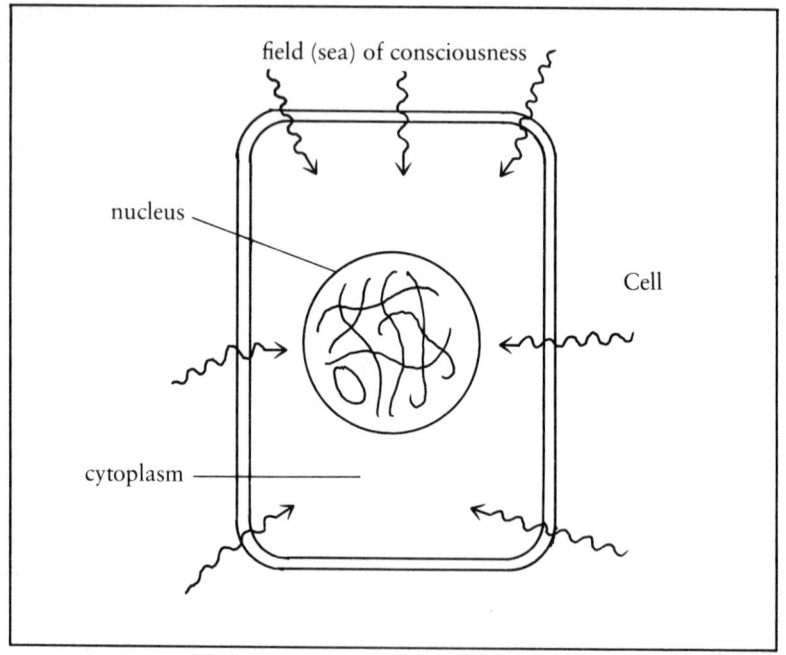

Fig. 15 A Model of the Origin of Protoconsciousness

Every cell in the body has protoconsciousness, which can be compared with the consciousness of a newborn baby just prior to any experiences with the outside world: it is intrinsic. Since it does not derive from experiences, we call it protoconsciousness, or original consciousness, or causal consciousness.

When consciousness permeates a cell, becoming its life, it also comes to know the contents and structure of that cell. Protoconsciousness has the capacity to know the structure of the cell because it has perceptiveness, just as a film has photosensitivity. This perceptiveness can be described as a transparent homogeneous screen of consciousness (or a film of consciousness), where the image of the structure of the cell is projected. Thus projected, the image of the cell is called "protoimage," which is the foundation for the development of prototypes.

3. Form and Category

In the human body, cells perform give-and-take action with neighboring cells as well as with distant cells. These mutual interactions are reflected in the film of protoconsciousness; the reflected image is called "image of form" (or image of relation).

The image of form comes from the existing form of the cell. What are the existing forms in Unification Thought? Existing forms can be understood as the conditions of existence that every created being must have as an individual truth body. From among the various existing forms, I will list the ten most fundamental ones, which are derived from the theories of give-and-take action, C-B-H action, and quadruple base, in Unification Thought.

(a) **Self-existence and Force:** Every being needs force in order to maintain its identity, or self-existence.

(b) **Sung Sang and Hyung Sang:** Every being has the dual characteristics of *Sung Sang* and *Hyung Sang*.

(c) **Positivity and Negativity:** Every being has active and passive (dynamic and static) characteristics, both within itself and in relation to other existing beings.

(d) **Subjectivity and Objectivity:** Every being exists either as a subject or as an object: nothing exists in a state of stability without taking either of these positions.

(e) **Position and Settlement:** Every being needs a certain position in order to exist, and it exists by keeping that position. For example, when a part of our body is lacerated or damaged, cells immediately multiply to fill what has been taken away, or to compensate for what has been damaged. They assume specific positions; no holes or gashes are left. Everything has the nature of settling in a definite position.

(f) **Relation and Affinity:** All beings have the potential to relate with any other being and do, in fact, relate with a few specific beings. A man, for example, has the potential to marry any woman, and vice-versa; eventually, he may marry one woman. Thus, from a wide range of possibilities, one particular relationship is developed. This relationship is called affinity.

(g) **Action and Multiplication:** Every being has the tendency to influence others as well as to change themselves and to develop.

(h) **Time and Space:** Every being exists in time and space.

(i) **Original Law and Mathematical Principle:** Every being, having been created by the Logos, has laws, which necessarily have a mathematical character.

(j) **Infinity and Finiteness:** On one hand, beings are concrete existences, and thus, finite; on the other hand, they contain a certain element of infinity. Man's mind, for instance, is connected with the infinity of God's *Sung Sang;* man's body, to the infinity of God's *Hyung Sang.* Inorganic matter performs circular motion, which is eternal; through multiplication, living beings maintain their eternity.

These are the fundamental existing forms in Unification Thought. Since our body is an existing being, it also contains these existing forms. In other words, our stomach, heart, lungs, tissues, cells, and so on, contain existing forms, because every part of the body—organs, tissues, cells, etc—is connected with every other part. The image of the existing forms in the protoconsciousness is called "image of form," as mentioned before. If man did not have images of form in the protoconsciousness of each cell of his body, he would be unable to recognize such forms in the outer world.

This explanation may seem implausible; yet modern medical science increasingly tends to accept that life (consciousness) in the body is aware of every single part and every single form of the body.

When we observe an object, the information (stimulation given to the receptor) of the content and form of that object is transmitted to the cerebral cortex, where it becomes an image. At the same time, an inner image, or prototype, corresponding to the outer image, is submitted to the consciousness, enabling the process of collation (cognition) to take place. Prototypes are submitted by the "subconscious," which can be described as a processing center for the information coming from the protoconsciousness of each cell. Subconsciousness, then, is the integration of the protoconsciousness of all cells. (The various steps in the process of cognizing will be further explained in this chapter.)

What about artificial beings, such as spaceships? How can they be cognized? Artificial beings are produced by imitating and synthesizing beings created by God. Man can produce artificial beings because of his inventiveness, which usually works through synthesizing ideas. When our senses receive some uncatalogued information, our consciousness will try to understand it through a process of synthesizing inner ideas, or prototypes, thus forming complex ideas. Brain physiology explains how the synthesis of ideas in our mind is possible: nerve fibers, which make billions of interconnections among brain cells, enable ideas to be synthesized unlimitedly.

Here I would like to present additional information about existing forms and categories. I have explained that all things (including our bodies) have existing forms, and that our protoconsciousness knows them. In their mutual relationships, cells are either controlling (dominating) or obeying (dominated); in other words, they are either subjective or objective. Consequently, the latent consciousness of the cell knows the form of Subject and Object.

Stomach functions are suppressed by the sympathetic nerves of the autonomic nervous system and stimulated by the parasympathetic nerves. Suppression is a negative action; stimulation, a positive action. Through this, the latent consciousness of the body knows the form of Positivity and Negativity.

As mentioned before, the subconsciousness is the integration of the information coming from all the cells. It can be compared with a military headquarters. The headquarters of an Army Division knows all the activities of its batallions, companies, and platoons because it receives constant information from them. Likewise, the subconscious, which receives constant information from organs, tissues, and cells, knows everything about their conditions and forms. This information is not usually sent up to the cerebrum, but is kept in the lower central nervous system. (See Section III of this chapter.) For instance, if the sympathetic nerves are acting so strongly as to impair the activities of the stomach, the autonomic center orders them to let up on their work; this shows that the autonomic nerves, which operate automatically, have a kind of latent consciousness, which knows all the existing forms and conditions of the stomach, in the above example.

The subconscious, therefore, knows the existing forms of all things. When cognition takes place, judgment is influenced by the existing forms in the subconscious, so that our thinking acquires a certain tendency, or restriction. This 'thinking tendency' in the judgment is called 'thinking form'.

When we judge something, for example, we tend to think that there must be an essence behind it. This is a thinking form. (Husserl said we grasp this essence with our intuition.) How do we acquire this tendency? Our subconscious knows the form of *Sung Sang* and *Hyung Sang,* and this affects our thinking. When we see the *Hyung Sang* aspect of a thing, we naturally look for its *Sung Sang* aspect, because we know that the two are always together. In other words, we have a thinking form of *Sung Sang* and *Hyung Sang*. For every existing form there appears a corresponding thinking form. Among the numerous thinking forms, the ten most essential ones, according to Unification Thought, are called "category." (See "Appendix" on page 357.)

D. METHOD OF COGNITION
1. Give-and-take Action between Subject and Object

Cognition operates under the law of give-and-take action. The subject (man) and the object (any being) become engaged in give-and-take action, in the process of cognizing. In order to have an actual cognition, the subject must meet these two requirements: (i) to have prototypes; (ii) to be concerned or interested. Prototypes consist of images of content and images of form within the subject. Images of content are the images of cells, tissues, and organs in the subject's body; they are formed in the subconscious of the subject through the integration of protoimages. Images of form are the reflected images of the existing forms of cells, tissues, and organs of the subject's body, in the subconscious. The images of content can be transformed or synthesized in a variety of ways in order to correspond to the content of the object. This is how the prototype of an object is established (the prototype of a flower, for example). The images of form, on the other hand, give rise to 'thinking forms', as already explained.

Besides having prototypes, the subject must also be concerned or interested, in order for cognition to take place. This matter will be further discussed in the next item.

The object must display certain characteristics in order to be cognized by the subject. The object must have content—such as shape, color, and fragrance. Furthermore, it must possess existing forms—such as *Sung Sang* and *Hyung Sang,* Positivity and Negativity, and Time and Space. When the requirements of the subject and those of the object are met, cognition can take place, through a process of matching the content and form of the subject (prototype) with the content and form of the object. (Fig. 16)

In the diagram expressed in Fig. 16, 'object' refers to the image of content (sensible qualities) and the image of form (existing form) of the object. Sensible qualities—such as shape, color, sound, and fragrance—as well as existing forms—such as *Sung Sang* and *Hyung Sang,* and Subjectivity and Objectivity—are perceived by our senses. This information is transformed into ideas (images) in the cerebral cortex. These images correspond to what philosophers have traditionally called "sense-impressions." The subject com-

Unification Epistemology

pares this image with the prototype existing in himself. This is called *collation*. When the prototype matches the image, cognition occurs.

Fig. 16 Give-and-Take Action between Subject and Object in Cognition

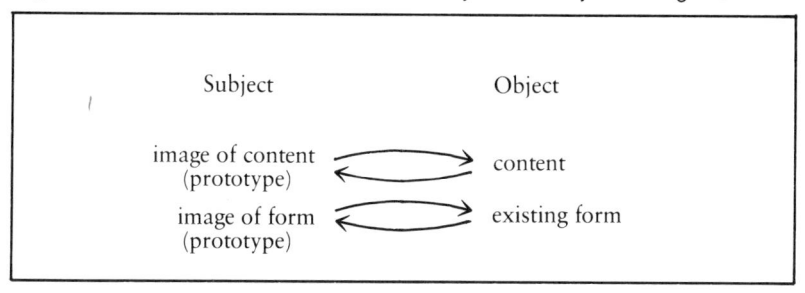

```
   Subject                          Object

   image of content  ⇌  content
   (prototype)
   image of form     ⇌  existing form
   (prototype)
```

Let us ask now how a prototype is formed in the subject. A newborn baby cannot recognize a flower clearly. The image of the flower is vague because the prototypes in his subconscious lack clarity and definition, as his nerves and brain cells have not fully developed yet. As he grows, his prototypes become clearer and more sharply defined; thus, he can recognize flowers more easily.

Nevertheless, he would still have to ask someone about aspects that he could not recognize. He would be taught that a particular flower is a rose, for example. Then the image of a rose would be inscribed in his memory. When he sees a rose again, he will recognize it at once, because the image of a rose, which has been stored in his memory, will spring to his mind immediately; by comparing the outer image with the information stored in his memory, he can recognize as a rose the flower he sees. Thus, we cannot say that prototypes exist a priori, for they are not fully established in a newborn baby; neither can we say that subconsciousness is entirely intrinsic, for it operates through nerves and cells.

When we see a flower, the prototype of a flower comes to mind immediately, but we do not necessarily know what kind of flower it is. Once the flower has been identified—as a rose, for example—its image is inscribed in our memory. This information is not conceptual, but actual; it will be stored in certain brain cells. We may forget this image after a while, but it will not disappear; the information can be retrieved whenever needed.

Since cognition in Unification Thought occurs through give-and-take action, to cognize is to form a Quadruple Base. Cognition is the result (United Body) of the give-and-take action of collating the content and form of the subject (prototype) with the content and form of the object, centering on purpose.* This is the "theory of collation," in contrast with Kant's "theory of synthesis" and with Marx's "theory of reflection." (Fig. 17)

Fig. 17 Cognition through the Formation of a Quadruple Base

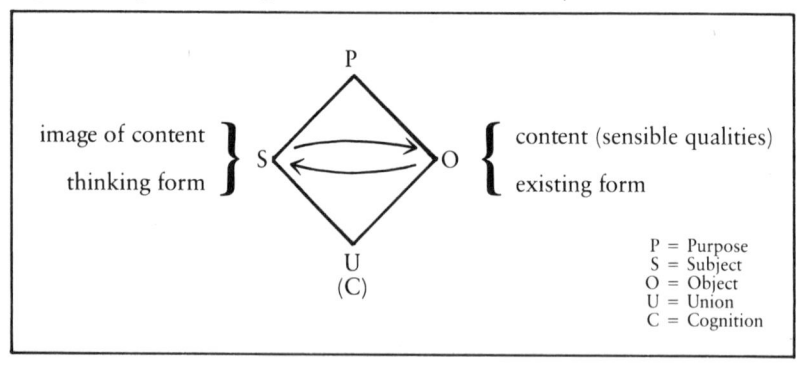

image of content
thinking form
} S

content (sensible qualities)
existing form
{

P
U
(C)

P = Purpose
S = Subject
O = Object
U = Union
C = Cognition

2. Activeness of the Subject in the Process and Development of Cognition

As the subject, man controls the process of cognition. He may simply ignore the information coming through his senses, or he may select specific kinds of information as objects of his cognition. Someone walking along a crowded street, for example, may choose to disregard sights and sounds and to concentrate on his own thoughts. One of his friends may say later, "You snob! Why didn't you answer when I said hello yesterday?" He may have seen his friend or even heard his voice, but no cognition took place because he wanted to concentrate on his thoughts.

Another example is a family working at a lighthouse. In the beginning they are disturbed by the sound of the waves and can hardly sleep at night. But after a while, they become accustomed to the noise and are no longer disturbed by it. If the baby in that family cries at night, however, the mother will wake up immediately, even though the sound level of the baby's voice is only a fraction of that of the waves. The mother is awakened, not so much by the sound itself, but by her concern for the well-being of her child.

Give-and-take action is centered on purpose; the more explicit

---

*This Quadruple Base for cognition is called "The Structure of Cognition" in Unification Thought.

our purpose, the more exact the resulting cognition. If we look at someone in order to find good points, for example, we will find them; if it is bad points that we are looking for, we will find them, too. A flower is much more beautiful if we look at it in order to see beauty. This reminds us of Jesus' saying, "Heaven is in the midst of you." Most people are not conscious of the purpose for which they are thinking, although some purpose—be it good or bad—is always there.

If someone wants to know something more thoroughly, the best way to do it is through practice. Thus, I do not disagree with the Marxist view that cognition deepens through the three stages of perception, reason, and practice, and that cognition develops in a spiral form (endless cycles). Mao Tse-tung says in *On Practice,*

> Start from perceptual knowledge and actively develop it into rational knowledge, then start from rational knowledge and actively guide revolutionary practice to change both the subjective and objective world. Practice, knowledge, again practice, and again knowledge. This form repeats itself in endless cycles, and with each cycle the content of practice and knowledge rises to a higher level.*

When the subject is concerned or interested (though unconsciously), give-and-take action leading to cognition can be initiated. The more this process of cognizing is repracticed, the more exact the resulting knowledge will be. The process of repractice develops new cognition because of the resulting association and synthesis of ideas.

In Unification Thought, also, there are three stages of cognition: the formation stage, the growth stage, and the completion stage. The *formation stage* is the perceptual stage, in which the sensible qualities of the object are received in the brain through the senses, producing an image in the mind. The mind calls up a corresponding prototype. The *growth stage* is the stage of cognition, through collation between the outer image and the prototype; through their give-and-take action, a quadruple base is formed. 'Thinking forms' are applied and the information is cognized, producing understanding. This is the stage of understanding, in which cognition is completed in one level. In the *completion stage* one thinks freely without seeing the object. In the case of a flower, for instance, one

---

*Mao Tse-tung, *On Practice* (Peking: Foreign Language Press, 1968). p. 27.

may consider when it was planted, why it was planted, and so forth.

It is said that fourteen billion brain cells are connected with one another in the brain—not in a conceptual way, but in reality—as in a network of telephone wires. Information from outside seems to come chiefly to the parieto-temporo-preoccipital association area through the various sensory areas. It may be there that the information is recognized. If it cannot be recognized, all the nerve cells in the brain seem to be ordered to send more information (prototypes) about the object. A final synthesis of information may be carried out in the frontal association area, as explained below.

3. Priority and Development of Prototypes

I would like to return to the subject of prototypes once again. When a clock was first brought to Korea in 1631, people did not know what it was. They thought it was a bell, since it rang at different times; they called it a "self-ringing bell." They had no prototype for a clock, so they applied what they had: the prototype of a bell. After much puzzling, they finally came to know that it was not a bell, but a device to tell time. Thus they acquired the prototype of a clock, and their knowledge increased. Through experiences, therefore, we gain new ideas and enrich our prototypes, mainly through the association and synthesis of old ideas.

Kant says that man has a priori forms (understanding forms); Plato maintains that man's soul knew all ideas prior to entering the human body. Unification Thought, however, says that the prototype is formed on the basis of the physical body of man. Before the ovum is fertilized by the sperm cell there are no prototypes. When a baby is born he already has prototypes, even though he has had no experiences with the outside world. He can have prototypes because he has a physical body. Subsequent experiences will add to the newborn baby's germ-like prototypes, forming a standard for later experiences.

In conclusion, prototypes comprise two types of contents: (i) "a priori ideas," or intrinsic ideas, which originate from the individual's intrinsic experience of his own physical body (cells, tissues, organs, and so forth); (ii) "pre-experienced ideas," which derive from actual experiences with the outside world through a learning process. This aspect of Unification Epistemology is referred to as "Priority of Prototypes," which contrasts sharply with Kant's "a priori forms." Man's prototypes, obscure during his childhood, develop as he grows (both in the aspect of "a priori ideas," through the growth of his nervous system and cells, and in the aspect of "pre-experienced ideas," through the expansion of his experiences) until they finally become complete.

III. COGNITION AND PHYSIOLOGY IN UNIFICATION EPISTEMOLOGY

Developing the basic framework of Unification Epistemology has been quite an adventure, so to speak. I have attempted to deduce its canons solely from the premises of the Unification Principle. At first I encountered a great deal of difficulty in organizing it, but I just had to persevere. Epistemology is so crucial to any philosophical system that without it the whole system of Unification Thought might be in jeopardy.

There were no research materials to which I could refer. No one, except Reverend Sun Myung Moon, has ever told me that a cell or an organ has life (consciousness) within it. The Unification Principle asserts that every existing being is a united body of *Sung Sang* and *Hyung Sang;* the cell and the organ are no exception. It also maintains that man's spiritual senses are matured on the basis of the physical body. I have rooted Unification Epistemology on these foundations. Moreover in the development of this theory, Rev. Moon has at times guided me even when dealing with puzzling specific issues.

My desire, of course, was to find a scientific foundation as well. It often happens that deductive explanations proposing a general truth initially lack scientific verification. In my case, also, when I assumed deductively that cells have protoconsciousness as their *Sung Sang*, I had no scientific evidence to substantiate it. On the other hand, if a theory is demonstrably logical, consistent, and free of contradictions, it can be considered true, even though it has not yet been scientifically validated. Based on the Unification Principle and on Rev. Sun Myung Moon's words, I was able to establish Unification Epistemology as a theory, under such conditions. After completing my exposition, I found that cybernetics supports our theory scientifically; I was reassured that Unification Epistemology is indeed correct.

Let us now discuss one of the vital epistemological points: the relationship between cognition and man's physiology.

A. MIND AND BRAIN

According to the Unification Principle, *Sung Sang* and *Hyung Sang* are as inseparable as two sides of a coin. The three stages of cognition— perception, understanding, and reasoning—have been explained by Kant and others as purely mental phenomena. In the Unification Thought view, however, mental processes are necessarily accompanied by physiological processes (especially cerebral processes). Accordingly, cognition is not a purely mental phenomenon, but is a complex phenomenon of both mental and material (cerebral, nervous) processes. In order to clarify the Unification Thought view, I will briefly and schematically discuss the physiological functions of the cerebral cortex, based on recent cerebral physiological discoveries.

The surface of the cerebral hemisphere is divided into four lobes: frontal, parietal, temporal, and occipital. There are many furrows on the surface of the cerebral hemisphere, and the sections separated by furrows are called gyri. The main furrows are the central fissure (fissure of Roland), which separates the frontal lobe from the parietal lobe, and the lateral fissure (fissure of Sylvius), which separates the temporal lobe from the frontal and parietal lobes.

Embryologically, the cerebral cortex consists of paleocortex, archiocortex, and neocortex. The paleocortex and the archiocortex together form the limbic cortex; the limbic cortex and the subcortical structures (including the hypothalamus) together form the limbic system, which is embryologically older than the neocortex. In the case of fish, their cerebral cortex consists primarily of paleocortex; in the case of amphibia, it consists primarily of paleocortex and archiocortex. The neocortex begins to appear in reptiles and develops most remarkably in man; it is closely related with the limbic system through the hypothalamus and mesocortex.

The neocortex of man covers almost the whole surface of the cerebral hemisphere. It comprises three parts: the motor area, the sensory areas, and association areas. The motor area, located in front of the central fissure, controls voluntary movements. The sensory areas are responsible for sensations from stimulation received through the sense organs. The sensory areas consist of the somatic sensory area, visual area, auditory area, and so on. The somatic sensory area, which lies just behind the central fissure, is responsible for the sensations of the skin. The visual area, in the occipital lobe, is responsible for the information from optic nerves; and the auditory area, in the temporal lobe, is responsible for the information from auditory nerves. Other sensory areas include the gustatory area and the olfactory area.

The remaining areas, known as association areas, are related to the higher integration faculties, such as cognition, judgment, memory, will, and integration of motions. I would like to discuss the faculties of the association areas in greater detail, since a clear understanding of them will clarify Unification Epistemology.

The association areas consist of three parts: (i) The frontal association area, which is located in the frontal lobe and is involved in the functions of reasoning, emotional control, will, creativity, and integration of movements; (ii) The anterior temporal association area, which lies in the frontal part of the temporal lobe and is responsible for memory; (iii) The parieto-temporo-preoccipital (PTP) association area, which extends from the parietal lobe to the temporal and the occipital lobes and is the locus of perception, cognition, and judgment. (Fig. 18)

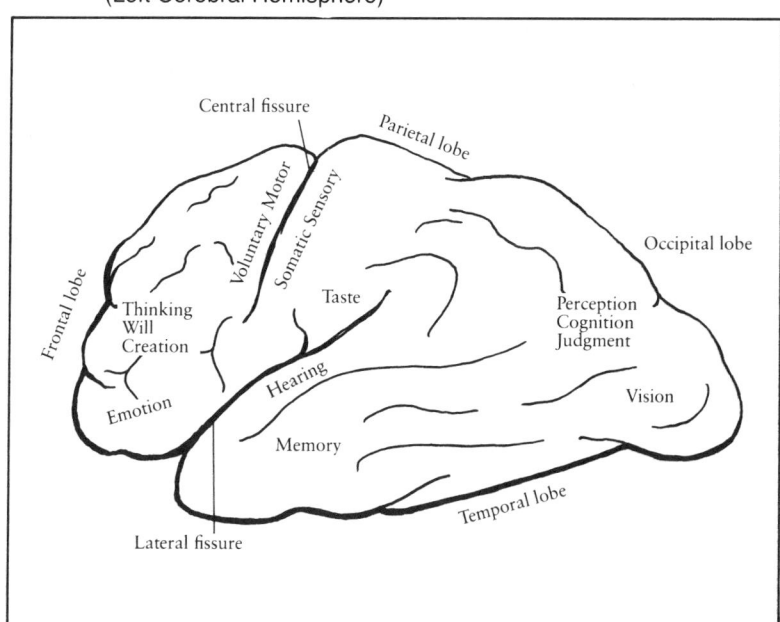

Fig. 18 Division of Work in Man's Cerebral Neocortex (Left Cerebral Hemisphere)*

---

*T. Tokizane, ed., *The Physiology of the Brain* (Tokyo: Asakura Shoten, 1966), p. 340.

Since the PTP association area is closely related to cognitive activities, damage in this area will cause failure in some aspect of the process of cognizing, even if the sensory areas themselves are working properly. If it is damaged in its parietal part, tactile agnosia may result, causing the individual to become insensitive to the things he touches, even if his skin sensation is normal. If damage occurs in its temporal part, auditory agnosia may result, causing the individual to become insensitive to sounds, even if his hearing sensation is normal. Furthermore, if the PTP association area is damaged in its occipital part, visual agnosia may result, causing the individual to become unable to distinguish things seen, even if the visual sensation is normal. In addition, since the PTP association area is also involved in the cognition of time and space, damage to the specific part where this cognition takes place may result in apraxia, making the individual unable to perform voluntary movements, even if no paralysis actually exists.

The part of the brain responsible for memory is the anterior temporal associaton area, which we may call a memory center. Memories themselves are probably not stored here but are retrieved to this area from the lower parts of the brain, especially from the hippocampal area, in the limbic system. The memory center acts as a processing center, sending information to the storage areas (subconscious) and retrieving it when necessary.

Based on the above information we can attempt a description of the pathway of the process of cognizing, which may be described in the following steps.

(i) The information from the outside world comes through the sensory organs and nerves to the various sensory areas, where it gives rise to visual images, auditory images, and so on.

(ii) Those images are transferred to the PTP association area through nerve fibers, where they are integrated and prepared for the process of collation.

(iii) Prototypes are retrieved from the memory storage areas by the memory center in the anterior temporal association area, and are sent to the PTP area for collation.

(iv) Collation takes place between the outer image and the inner image (prototype). At this point cognition occurs. After that, there are two possibilities:

(a) either the newly acquired information goes to the memory center in the anterior temporal association area and then is transferred to the subconscious in the lower parts of the brain;

(b) or the newly acquired information goes to the frontal association area in the frontal lobe, to become data for the function of reason, will, emotion, and creativity. (The information sent to the memory center can also be forwarded to the frontal association area any time it is needed.) In the frontal association area all the necessary knowledge acquired through experience can be gathered and integrated in the creation of new plans to be used in practice.

In conclusion, cerebral physiology supports the theory of three-stage cognition of perception, understanding, and reason, for it gives a clearly distinguishable physiological base for each of these theoretical stages. Furthermore, cerebral physiology also supports the theory of the unity of cognition and practice, by showing how newly acquired knowledge can be used to create new plans.

B. ELEMENTS OF THE INNER WORLD AND CYBERNETICS

Now I would like to discuss certain activities of the body, as an effort to present a scientific base for the theory of the existence of consciousness in the cell (protoconsciousness). Cybernetics is the study of the adjustments and control functions of self-regulating mechanisms. The term can be applied both to living beings and to automatic machines, as both can make appropriate responses to outside stimuli, especially through feedback. For the purpose of this discussion, feedback can be understood as the process whereby a living organism detects a stimulation and uses it to control the process producing the stimulation. (The operation of a thermostat to control room temperature can be given as an example of how feedback works.) Cybernetics can also be described as the control mechanism operating to attain and maintain homeostasis. As applied to our physical body, homeostasis refers to a tendency of organs within our body to maintain their composition and function through a coordinated response to stimuli tending to affect them. Stimuli can come from the environment (physical and social surroundings) as well as from within man himself—from organs (heart, stomach, lungs, liver, etc.), from tissues, and even from cells. Homeostasis keeps the organism stable in its relationships to the numerous stimuli from the environment and from within the body.

If the weather is hot, for example, pores at the root of the hair open, and heat is released through sweat. If it is cold, we begin to shiver in order to keep the body warm. If there is too much light, the iris contracts; if not enough light, it dilates. Pulse rate increases when a person runs and returns to normal soon after he stops running.

If someone has appendicitis, certain nerves send directives to the inflamed part to try to restore it. Soon the muscles in that area tighten in order to protect that area, which is called the MacBarne point, or the oppressive pain point. If the person is pressed in the lower right region of the abdomen, he will feel pain because of the tautness of the muscles. At the same time, white corpuscles are sent in to heal the inflammation. This again, is homeostatic, or reflex activity. Even a cell displays homeostatic functions: the nucleus responds immediately to externally caused cytoplasmic disturbances.

Homeostatic activities are controlled by the lower nerve center of the body, which is also called the reflex center. The lower nerve center (LNC) comprises the limbic system below the neocortex, the interbrain (thalamus and hypothalamus), the midbrain, the hindbrain (cerebellum, pons, medulla), and the spinal cord. The control of the dilation and contraction of the iris, for instance, takes place in the midbrain. When information cannot be handled by the midbrain, it is sent to the hypothalamus. Almost all internal information, however, is dealt with in the part of the brain below the hypothalamus. It is said that it is now certain that the hypothalamus is controlled by the limbic cortex. (Fig. 19)

This is similar to the administrative processes of a nation. In Korea, for example, information that cannot be handled by the *Myeon* (subcounty) is sent to the *Gun* (county); if it cannot be handled there, it is sent to the *Do* (province); if necessary, it can finally be sent to the central government. Almost all information, however, is dealt with below the *Do*.

The cerebral cortex is what would correspond to the central government of a nation. It is the location of the "awake" consciousness, dealing primarily with stimuli from the outer environment. When the lower nerve center (LNC) cannot deal with internal stimuli, it sends a message to the upper nerve center (UNC), metaphorically saying, "I cannot deal with this stomach ache; please do something." The UNC judges the information and may reply something like, "This needs to be treated in a hospital at once." We must recognize in this the existence of selectivity in the LNC. Selectivity implies consciousness.

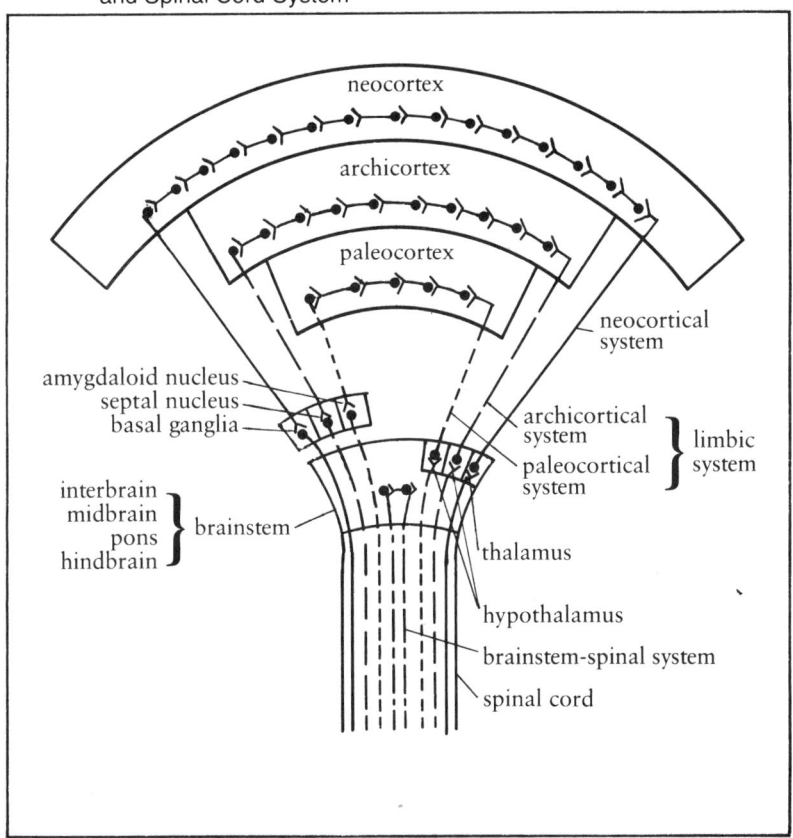

Cognition and Physiology in Unification Epistemology 163

Fig. 19 The Neocortical System, Limbic System, Brain Stem, and Spinal Cord System*

Stimuli reach the nerve centers through different nerve pathways, according to their origin and nature. Those from the outer environment go to the UNC (cortex) through the sensory nerves; a suitable response is given by the UNC through the motor nerves (moving hands, legs, or whatever). On the other hand, information from within the body reaches the LNC through the afferent autonomic nerves; the LNC, in turn, sends an appropriate response through the efferent autonomic nerves. This is the reflex pathway. Reflex actions are initiated in our subconscious mind; we are largely unaware of their operation. (Fig. 20)

---

*Ibid., p. 4

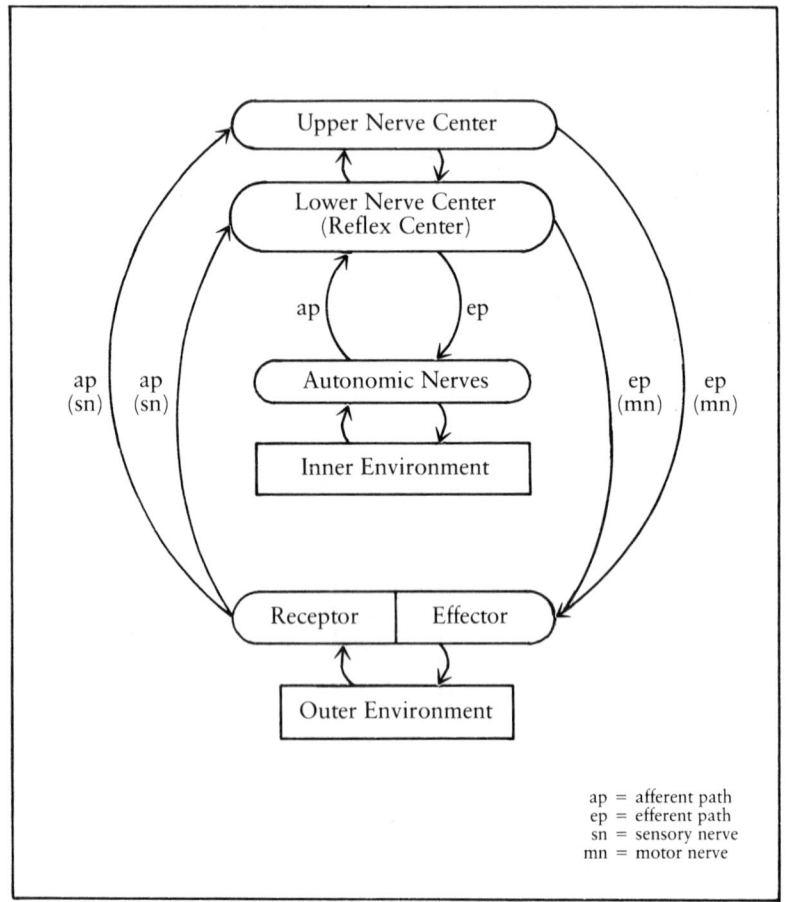

Fig. 20 Pathway for Stimuli and Responses of the Upper and Lower Nerve Centers

```
              Upper Nerve Center
                     ↕
              Lower Nerve Center
                (Reflex Center)
                   ap ↕ ep
              Autonomic Nerves
                     ↕
              Inner Environment


              Receptor    Effector
                     ↕
              Outer Environment
```

ap (sn)   ap (sn)   ep (mn)   ep (mn)

ap = afferent path
ep = efferent path
sn = sensory nerve
mn = motor nerve

As we can see, there are myriad functions happening simultaneously in order to keep our physical body balanced and well-maintained. Innumerable bits of information are received at the nerve centers, analyzed, and classified; an equally fantastic number of decisions are made, and orders are issued according to those decisions. What, then, is the subject of all these activities? What judges the information received at the nerve center and issues appropriate orders? In other words, what causes the homeostatic functions of the body to take place?

As mentioned above, the LNC usually deals with stimuli from within the body, through reflex action and control. At times, however, the LNC sends certain types of information to the UNC, to be dealt with at the cerebral cortex. This means that the LNC "knows" that there is a problem, takes action to solve the problem, and has the ability to discriminate among the various stimuli, choosing the ones to be forwarded to the UNC. The fact that the LNC can understand and analyze stimuli and can make necessary decisions—including even that of whether or not to send information to the UNC—means that it actually has consciousness. The cybernetic phenomena within a cell—that is, the cell's ability to cope with something wrong inside it or to make appropriate responses to outside stimuli—imply that even a cell has consciousness, or more precisely, protoconsciousness. This conclusion is not only derived from the Unification Principle view—which says that every existing being has both *Sung Sang* and *Hyung Sang* aspects—but is also affirmed by physiological science.

This conclusion is also supported by the fact that actions that are normally performed through the reflex control of the LNC can at times be performed through the intentional control of the UNC. Yogis, for example, who have spent a lifetime disciplining themselves, have shown that certain physiological processes can be controlled at will—such as pulse rate and the temperature of different parts of the body. In the case of the iris, it should contract when too much light is coming in and dilate when there is not enough light, as mentioned above. This is a reflex process. There are those, however, who can cause the reverse procedure through intentional control.

Another example, which you may have heard, refers to people who have asked to be buried alive, only to emerge as large as life when unearthed weeks later. There is a scientific explanation for this. In the heart, blood is pumped from the atria to the ventricles, and from there into the arteries. There is a valve between the atrium and the ventricle, which opens and closes like a door. By ordering the valve of the heart and the heart muscles to slow down, these people can induce a state of hibernation and stay buried for weeks. Such experiments have been carefully observed by skeptical scientists. Another example is the baffling case of islanders in the South Pacific who practice walking on scorching hot stones in bare feet, without incurring the slightest burn.

In these instances of intentional control, we cannot but recognize that the upper nerve center is controlling the lower nerve center.

This shows that the consciousness of the LNC is of the same quality as that of the UNC, except that the former is hidden (subconscious), whereas the latter is apparent. In other words, there is no essential difference between intentional control and reflex control, since in both cases consciousness is the subject. This is a key point for verifying the existence of protoconsciousness.

Accordingly, there are various levels of consciousness, or life, in man. The higher the position in the brain, the more precise and clear the consciousness becomes. As explained before, life is a manifestation of God's *Sung Sang*. It can manifest itself in various levels—such as the level of a single cell or the level of man's cerebral cortex, which manifests God's *Sung Sang* to the highest degree.

That a cell can respond to stimuli points to consciousness within it. Though on a small scale, the cell does carry out cybernetic activities. The consciousness (life) of the lower nerve center is of a slightly higher dimension than that of individual cells, tissues, and organs; the LNC, in fact, stores, judges, and integrates information from the cells, tissues, and organs. This means that the prototypes that reflect the inner environment—that is, the prototypes before one's experiences with the outside world—seem to be stored in the LNC, especially in the limbic system.

The limbic system is said to be directly related to instincts and animal-like emotions. Information from the cerebral cortex may also be stored here. Emotion and instinct are closely related to memory. Although a memory center appears to exist in the temporal lobe—as discussed above—information from experiences is said to be stored in the area centering in and around the archicortex (hippocampal formation). Accordingly, this area has the functions of recording, retaining, and recalling information.

The upper memory storage center of the archicortex is connected with many lower centers—such as the hypothalamus, midbrain, hindbrain, and spinal cord. All of them can be said to form the memory system. The various bits of information are stored as prototypes in their appropriate positions. Prototypes acquired from the external environment as well as those acquired through reflex processes are stored in this way. As explained before, these prototypes can be recalled to the consciousness of the cerebral cortex to be collated with outer information, as part of the process of developing new cognitions.

C. TRANSMISSION OF INFORMATION

Why don't messages stop when they come to the tip of a neuron (nerve fiber)? The sending tip (telodendria) of a sensory neuron leads to the receiving tip (dendrite) of a neuron in the central nervous system. There is, however, a gap (synapse) between them, which is filled with a fluid; the information has to be transmitted across this gap. The fluid is not only in the synaptic gap, but surrounds the nerve fiber.

The transmission of information through the axon (long, cord-like part) of a nerve fiber is an electrical process. The nerve fiber is enveloped by a membrane which in its resting state is polarized: the outside has a positive charge, while the inside has a negative charge. When the information is passing through the fiber, the polarization vanishes (depolarization). The area of depolarization (the impulse) moves along the fiber. While the impulse is passing, the outside of the membrane is negatively charged, but it reverts to its positive state after the impulse passes.

This negative wave reaches the tip of the fiber, and the impulse (information) is transmitted across the gap filled with fluid, which includes chemical substances, such as potassium, sodium, chlorine, phosphate, and special enzymes. With the aid of enzymes, conveyers (acetylcholine, adrenaline, etc.) are formed at the tip of the nerve fiber. These chemical substances move across the fluid and stimulate the tip (dendrite) of the next fiber, in which the same negative wave appears. The transmission process across the gap (synapse) is purely chemical.

The process of depolarization, though not yet fully understood, is, however, known to be related to the movement of potassium and sodium ions in and out (penetration or permeation) of the membrane. The membrane appears to have selectivity with regard to the permeation of ions; enzymes seem to be connected with this activity.

The discrimination of impulses occurs to a certain degree at the connecting point of the peripheral nerves with the central nerves; a decision is made whether they should be sent directly to effectors in a reflex arc, or should be carried to the brain. This means that conscious action (selection by the consciousness) is at the root of the physiochemical process, controlling both the electrical processes in the fiber (axon) and the chemical processes across the synapse. This understanding is based on the Unification Principle, which says that every *Hyung Sang* process is necessarily accompanied by a *Sung*

Sang process.

This completes my explanation of the existence of the protoconsciousness of the cell, with its protoimages and images of form, as well as its connection with the consciousness of the cerebral cortex.

D. SPIRITUAL COGNITION

The Unification Principle says that the spirit-man receives vitality elements from the physical body and gives living spirit-elements to the physical body. I think that both are spiritual elements and are like refined electricity; among the various physical processes in our body, electrical processes are the most refined. Based on the statement that the spiritual senses develop on the basis of the physical body, we can quite easily link an underlying spiritual function with the electrical flow in the nerve fibers. It may be helpful to think that the spirit-man has nerve fibers that work in correspondence with, and in a similar fashion as, the nerve fibers of the physical body.*

In some cases, spirit-men other than one's own may help in one's cognition. Spiritual influence can be exerted in all three stages of cognition—i.e., in the perceptual stage, the understanding stage, and the rational stage. Cognition with spiritual accompaniment is finer and faster than ordinary cognition.

IV. CRITIQUE OF THE EPISTEMOLOGIES OF KANT AND MARX
A. CRITIQUE OF KANT

The first problem in Kant's epistemology is related to his explanation of 'a priori forms', which is partially right and partially wrong, from the Unification Thought viewpoint. He considers the subjective thinking form (category), but fails to include the objective existing form. Kant said that time and space are a thinking form; in actuality, they are also an existing form. Two successive phenomena are not just cognized with the thinking forms of time and space; they are indeed caused within actual time and space in the objective world. With regard to plurality (*Vielheit*), it is not that we just happen to see things in great numbers; a great number of things

---

*This describes the action of living spirit elements at the basic level, from spirit-body to physical body. See *Divine Principle*, Part I, ch. 1, VI, 3, (2) for the higher effects of living spirit-elements.

Critique of the Epistemologies of Kant and Marx

actually do exist.

The second problem is related with the *thing-in-itself (Ding-an-sich)*. Kant says that the thing-in-itself can in no way be cognized. In the Unification Thought view, however, thing-in-itself corresponds to *Sung Sang;* we can understand the *Sung Sang* of something by observing its *Hyung Sang,* since the two are inseparable, and the *Hyung Sang* resembles and expresses the *Sung Sang.*

The third problem is that of *imagination (Einbildungskraft),* which is said to unite the forms of intuition and the forms of synthesis, either consciously or unconsciously. According to Unification Epistemology, cognition is reached by the give-and-take action between the prototype (image) of the subject and the image of the object. In other words, in the mind, give-and-take action appears between the prototype and the image of the object. This means that we collate the two images to see if they coincide. The mind, or consciousness, does the collating; consciousness, therefore, is necessary in cognition. Kant's position that unity between intuition forms and understanding forms occur without consciousness cannot, therefore, be considered correct.

Finally, Kant said that God and spirit cannot be objects of cognition, claiming we do not, and cannot, know that God exists, but simply postulate His existence. How strange it is to postulate a non-existing God! If we are to postulate God and deepen our faith, God must really exist and not be a mere figment of imagination. Unification Thought says we can experience the Heart of God and cognize Him, for we have spiritual senses.

B. CRITIQUE OF MARX

Since Marxist epistemology is based on dialectical materialism, our critique is directed to the materialistic view that mind (spirit) is the product of the brain (matter). This view is based on the observation that brain damage or paralysis of brain cells by alcohol leads to insanity, loss of memory, etc.; at the same time, recovery of the brain brings about the recovery of the mind.

This conclusion is not necessarily logical. In a radio set, for example, if something goes wrong with it, no sound will come out; if it is repaired, the sound returns. From this, however, we cannot conclude that the voice is the product of the radio. The radio simply intercepts electromagnetic waves broadcast from the radio station and transforms them into sound. We can liken the brain to a radio set, or to an extremely sophisticated transceiver.

In Unification Thought, mental activity is understood as the synthesis of two give-and-take actions: first, that between the spirit-mind and the physical mind; second, that between mind and brain. Consequently, we can easily understand that brain damage prevents the give-and-take between mind and brain, leading to confusion in the mind. From this point of view we can also understand that abnormal mental activity may occur due to a big shock, deep grief, or sudden astonishment, even if the brain is in perfect condition.

The first problem in the materialistic view is that, physiologically, a product cannot dominate its parent body. Bile, for example, secreted by the liver, can never control the liver. Urine does not control its producer, the kidney. Gastric juice can digest rice, bread, meat—even the stomachs of other animals—but never the walls of the stomach by which it was secreted, except in the case of gastric ulcers, a pathological condition. It is a physiological law that the product cannot control its producer. Consequently, if mind (spirit) were a product of the brain, then it would never be able to control the brain—according to this physiological law. But Marxists are actually saying that the mind *can* control the brain, when they maintain that man verifies cognition through practice (without probing the meaning of "practice"). Practice is accomplished according to a purpose and a plan, which are, in fact, formed in the mind. In practice, therefore, the mind sets the brain in motion and moves the body and limbs: a product controls its parent body.

If spirit were the product of the brain—the parent body—we would have another problem. Just as in the case of saliva, which is secreted by the salivary gland, a product is always separated from its parent body and is independent of it. Thus, if spirit were produced by the brain, it should also be separated from, and independent of, the brain. Such a "floating" spirit, of course, would pose a serious problem to materialists, who emphatically deny the existence of spiritual beings. This is another contradiction of the Marxist philosophy.

In the Unification Thought view, mental activities come about through the give-and-take action between mind and brain. Although mind and brain interpenetrate, they are actually different, for mind (spirit-mind) leaves the physical body upon a person's death. Mind, therefore, is not a product of the brain; its origin is the cosmic consciousness, which is the manifestation of God's *Sung Sang*.

5 LOGIC

Logic is the study of laws and forms of thinking. Formal logic, started by Aristotle, dealt with universal laws and forms of thinking, which are variously different in content, while dialectical logic, especially that proposed by Hegel and Marx, dealt with the laws and forms of the development of nature and thinking.

It is my intention in this chapter to discuss and critique the various systems of logic and to present Unification logic, which is a system of logic derived from the Unification Principle.

I. TRADITIONAL LOGIC
A. FORMAL LOGIC
1. Basic Principles of Thinking

The basic laws of valid thinking, in traditional formal logic, are four principles, as follows:
1. The principle of identity.
2. The principle of contradiction.
3. The principle of excluded middle.
4. The principle of sufficient reason.

The principle of identity, which is expressed in the form "A is A", corresponds to the identity-maintaining character of the existing being in Unification Thought. The principle of contradiction, which is expressed in the form "A is not non-A", is a negative way of expressing the (affirmative) principle of identity, as we can see by comparing the two propositions: "A is a flower", and "A is not a non-flower". These are supposedly the basic laws by which man thinks.

The principle of excluded middle, saying that "A is either B or non-B", is the principle of alternative judgments, which we often use in thinking.

The principle of sufficient reason established by Leibniz says that all thinking has a reason, and there is no thinking without a reason. When applied to phenomena, we get the proposition, "Every phenomenon has a cause"; in other words, we get the law of cause and effect. Thus, reason (grounds) and conclusion in the thinking process correspond to cause and effect in the natural world. There are many other laws and principles, but they are derived from the four principles stated above, according to traditional logic.

2. Concept

Concept is a representation of the common properties abstracted from a group of individuals. A concept may be "generic" or "specific". Let us think about the series, "living being, animal, vertebrate, mammal, etc." Living beings have life. Besides life, animals have a sensory system (instinct), and vertebrates have also a backbone. Besides having life, instinct, and backbone, mammals are lactational. Finally, man has all these attributes as well as reason. The attributes that each concept contains are called *connotation* (intension). The class of things to which a concept is applicable is called *extension*. As examples of extension, 'living being' includes plants and animals; 'animal' includes vertebrates and invertebrates; 'vertebrate' includes reptiles and mammals; 'mammal' includes anthropoid apes and men; 'man' includes Peter, Mary, James, and so on.

Of two concepts, the one with broader connotation and narrower extension is called the *specific concept* (subordinate concept), whereas the one with narrower connotation and broader extension is called *generic concept* (superordinate concept). The concept 'man', for example, is specific, and the concept 'mammal' is generic, comparatively speaking. Similarly, the concepts of 'vertebrate', 'coelenterate', and 'echinoderm' are specific, when compared with the concept of 'animal'. Furthermore, even the concepts of 'animal' and 'plant' are specific, when compared with the concept of 'living being'.

Following along these lines, we reach the highest generic concept, which is 'existence'. Under this concept we have 'matter' and 'spirit'. 'Matter' is the highest concept in natural science, which usually deals solely with material processes and existence. Under the concept of 'matter', we have 'living being' and 'inorganic matter'. Under 'living being', we have 'animal' and 'plant', and so forth.

The highest generic concept is called *category*. Each philosopher has his own category, according to his system of thought. Aristotle, Kant, and Marx, for instance, have their own categories. Unification Thought, also, has its own category, based on the concepts of Quadruple Base and give-and-take action. (See Ch. 4, "Epistemology.")

3. Judgment

Judgment is the determination of the relationship between two concepts. A judgment consists of subject, predicate and copula, which brings the subject and the predicate into a relationship. When it is expressed with language, a judgment is called a proposition. There are many forms in judgment. Kant has four of them: the forms of quantity, quality, relation, and modality. Each of these forms has three components, making twelve judgment forms, which are often quoted as representative forms of formal logic.

4. Inference

Inference is a way of thinking with which a new judgment (conclusion) is drawn from known judgments (premises). The main forms of inference are *mediate inference*, which has more than two premises, and *immediate inference*, which has only one premise. A syllogism is a type of mediate inference that contains two premises, as we can see in the following example:
1. All men die
2. Socrates is a man
3. Therefore Socrates will die

This is a three-staged process: (1) the major premise (which contains the predicate of the conclusion); (2) the minor premise (which contains the subject of the conclusion); and (3) the conclusion.

Immediate inference, however, has only one premise, from which the conclusion is directly derived. From the premise, "All Koreans are honest," one can conclude directly that "Some Koreans are honest."

Another kind of inference is *analogical inference*. Suppose 'A' and 'B' have the elements a, b, c, d, and e. 'A' has also the element 'f'; thus, by analogical inference we say that 'B', also, may have 'f'. Let us suppose that 'A' represents the earth and 'B', another planet. Both contain 'a' (atmosphere), 'b' (existence of water), 'c', 'd', and 'e'. Let us further suppose that 'f' is the existence of living things. Here, we can analogically infer that, since the earth supports living things, quite possibly so does the other planet.

B. DIALECTICAL LOGIC
1. The Dialectic of Hegel

Hegel's *Science of Logic* has the reputation of being difficult to grasp. Unlike other logical systems, Hegel's logic involves the world of God before the creation of the universe, describing the nature of God's thinking during the Creation process.*

The essence of his logic can be found in the form Being-Nothing -Becoming *(Sein-Nichts-Werden)*, and Being-Essence-Notion *(Sein-Wesen-Begriff)*. The Notion *(Begriff)* finally becomes Idea *(Idee)* in its development. He explained this form as being the process of *affirmation-negation-negation of the negation*, or thesis-antithesis-synthesis. His theory is developed in the Doctrine of Being, the Doctrine of Essence, and the Doctrine of Notion, his three broad divisions of logic. It is difficult to understand the meaning of his Being-Nothing-Becoming (as presented in the Logic of Being). Hegel's own explanation of it is vague, and scholars interpret it in different ways. Briefly stated, my best understanding of what he means is as follows:

Hegel regards God as Logos (Word), and he explains the world as having been formed from Logos in the same way as explained in St. John's Gospel. He tries to clarify how the word has developed into the world. For him, the world is not the created thing, but things developed from Logos (Idea). What was Logos like before being developed? How did it develop to become all things? He answers these questions through his 'dialectic'. God (Logos) first thinks of Being *(Sein)*. The 'Being' that exists in the beginning has no restrictions—i.e. no content or form; it is indeterminate and contentless *(Bestimmungs-und-Inhaltslosigkeit)*. It is called *pure Being (reines Sein)*.

This Being, then, is actually Nothing, which means, not complete emptiness, but something without a definite character or form. It has the *possibility* of assuming certain determinations; when it does, through the unity or synthesis of Being and Nothing, it will be a developed form of Being with content, the Becoming *(Werden)*,

---

*In his "Science of Logic," Hegel says, "This content shows forth God as He is in His eternal essence before the creation of nature and of a finite spirit." *(The Philosophy of Hegel*, edited by Carl J. Friedrich, New York: The Modern Library, 1953, p. 186).

which is neither Being nor Nothing, but Being that has passed through Nothing. This may be the true meaning of his saying that Being is denied by Nothing to become a new being, or Becoming, giving rise to another developing process (dialectical process).

The new starting point, also, is Being, but not in the same sense as Being in the process of Being-Nothing-Becoming; it is actually the very Becoming of that process. The new dialectical process is *Being-Essence-Notion (Idea)*. Essence is the eternal, unchangeable aspect of Being, and Notion (Idea) is formed by the synthesis of Being and Essence. The Notion (Idea) here is not an abstract and static representation, like the concept in formal logic or in Kant's logic, but a concrete and self-developing one.

This is Hegel's Being-Nothing-Becoming and Being-Essence-Notion (Idea), a form that can be regarded as God's thinking process before Creation. How do we know this? Simply by observing that man's thinking develops in a similar way in recognizing something. Man's thinking proceeds from the cognition of mere being to the cognition of essence and then to that of the idea. Initially, for example, man recognizes a flower only phenomenally, then he recognizes the essence of the flower, and then the idea of the flower is formed in our thinking, when the phenomenal attributes of the flower (color, shape, aroma, etc.) and the essence of a flower are united.

An idea is originally what is thought in mind, so it can't have the ability of thinking. But in systemizing his theory of Logic, Hegel seems to have dealt with God's thinking only as the self-development of Idea. This point remains an aporia of his logic. Owing to this, philosophers find it difficult to understand the real meaning of his dialectic.

Many philosophers have tried to explain Being-Nothing-Becoming. One explanation is like this: imagine ice to be Being and heat to be Nothing (the negation, or antithesis of ice). When the ice is united with heat, it becomes water. Nothing (heat) is the motive, or mediator, for Being (ice) to develop into Becoming (water). According to another explanation, Being is like the day, Nothing is like the night, and Becoming is like the morning.

According to T. Takechi, Nothing is not 'nothing of the being', but *not-Being*. If reason is Being, matter will be Nothing, since matter is not reason (or spirit). This matter is not visible matter, but has the potential of taking visible form and shape. What reason has thought will be realized (as Becoming) by the interaction between reason (Being) and matter (not-Being). Scholars have set forth different explanations of Hegel's views, first because he considered the Logos, or Idea, to be the same as God Himself; and also, because he failed to present an adequate explanation of his concept of Nothing.

According to Hegel, the Idea formed in the world of God manifests itself as Nature in the 'form of otherness' *(die Form des Anders-Sein)*; in other words, Nature is the opposite, the antithesis of Idea (thesis). So, if logic is considered to be the thesis, philosophy of Nature must be the antithesis. From Nature appears man—a spiritual being. The estranged Idea in Nature regains itself in man. Accordingly, the philosophy of Spirit cannot but be a synthesis in his dialectical system of philosophy. Finally, in the philosophy of Spirit, Idea develops to become the Absolute Spirit—in other words, it returns to 'Being' (God Himself), in a developed state. The process of development in Nature and in Spirit is also thesis-antithesis-synthesis, the dialectical process.

The natural world develops in three stages: the stage of Mechanics *(Mechanik)*, the stage of Physics *(Physik)*, and the stage of Organics *(Organik)*. This, however, is not the development of the natural world itself, but the process of realizing the Idea *(Idee)*. In other words, the natural world develops according to the development of the Idea. First, the Idea of force appeared; next, the Idea of physical phenomena originated; finally, the Idea of living organisms came to appear. In correspondence with the development of Idea, nature itself develops; nature, therefore, is considered as Idea in the 'form of otherness'.

Finally, man, a spiritual being, appeared. There are three kinds of spirit: subjective spirit *(Subjektiver Geist)*, objective spirit *(Objektiver Geist)*, and Absolute Spirit *(Absoluter Geist)*. The subjective spirit is the spirit of an individual man. The objective spirit is the objectified spirit, or socialized spirit, which goes beyond the scope of an individual; it develops through the stages of right *(Recht)*, morality *(Moralität)*, and social ethics *(Sittlichkeit)*.

Right is an elementary form of relationship among persons, where persons are considered as individuals, not as citizens of a state. By respecting other persons' rights, one attains harmony with the universal will. Morality represents the duties that the universal will establishes as limitations to the individual will. The relation between right and morality is as that between subjective and objective; morality itself, however, is also quite subjective. Finally, social ethics appears for all men to obey. Thus, the objectified spirit undergoes the development of right, morality, and social ethics.

The first stage of social ethics is the family. If the members of a family are united in love, both love and liberty will be alive in that family. When the family increases to become a civil society, however, it will be confused, due to egoistic desires of man; both love and liberty will be restricted. The state, then, appears as the synthesis of the family and the civil society. This process of development is that of thesis, antithesis, and synthesis.

For Hegel, mankind's hope lies in the establishment of a rational state, in which the Absolute Spirit (Logos, Idea) is fully realized. Men could live a vigorous life of love and liberty in such a state, since it would be controlled and ordered by the law of Reason. History is the process of the development of the Idea toward such a State.

What is the Absolute Spirit? Its first stage appears in man's art; its second stage, in religion; and its third and highest stage, in philosophy. The Idea regains itself when it becomes philosophy. The purpose of the development of the Idea is to go back to the Absolute Spirit (in its developed form), passing through man, going through the stages of right, morality, social ethics (family, civil society, state), art, religion, and philosophy. When this is accomplished, the process of development is completed. Here we have touched upon a weak point in Hegel's philosophy: there is no more development when the Idea becomes Absolute Spirit again. In a rough sketch, this is the dialectic of Hegel's logic.

2. The Dialectic of Marx

Marx said Hegel's dialectic stood on its head, and that his own stood on its feet. Hegel's dialectic is idealistic; it says that natural things are not material, but are the Idea robed in the clothes of matter. Thus, natural things are nothing but a means of expressing the Idea externally.

Marx, however, maintains that matter—which has contradiction within itself—is the objective existence; the 'Idea' is nothing but a reflection of matter in man's brain. The 'Idea' does not exist objectively; this notion is no more than a figment of Hegel's imagination, Marx holds. Material development itself follows the process of thesis-antithesis-synthesis. Marx's dialectic is, therefore, materialistic, while Hegel's is idealistic. Along the lines of materialistic dialectic, a communistic system of logic has been developed by the followers of Marx. It is called 'dialectical logic', and one of its characteristics is its opposition to the principle of contradiction of formal logic. It says that the principle of contradiction is wrong, on the grounds that the change and development characteristic of all things imply that things contain negation in themselves. Accordingly, the proposition "A is not non-A" should be changed to "A is non-A (i.e., A is not A), as well as A is A." (See Section 3 of this chapter.)

C. SYMBOLIC LOGIC

Symbolic logic, or mathematical logic, is the study of methods of correct judgment through the use of mathematical symbols. It is a development of formal logic, but maintains that intuitive thinking, used in formal logic, lacks mathematical precision. The form and method of expression of a philosophical system—however great—must be carefully scrutinized in order for any existing faults to be disclosed. How can we disclose faults in expression? Symbolic logicians argue that correctness of expression can be examined by reducing everything to algebraic expression and then performing mathematical calculations on them. Symbolic logic, then, is actually symbolized formal logic.

As an example of the symbolization propositions are represented by p, q, r.... The negative of p is represented by $\sim$p; 'p and q' is represented by 'p•q'; 'p or q' is represented by 'p v q'; 'if p, then q' is represented by 'p ⊃ q'. Any complex inference can be expressed by the simple use of these algebraic symbols.

D. TRANSCENDENTAL LOGIC

Transcendental logic refers chiefly to Kant's logic. According to Kant—as introduced in "Epistemology" in this book—thinking necessarily takes on certain kinds of forms (category). These are thinking forms *(Denkformen)* or understanding forms *(Verstandformen)*. The thinking form itself is empty, unless it is filled with content *(Inhalt)*, the sensible qualities of the object. Kant says, "thinking apart from contents is emptiness, and intuition without concepts is blindness." In other words, man's thinking is senseless apart from the cognition of the object. Accordingly, Kant's transcendental logic is sometimes called "Epistemological logic."

II. UNIFICATION LOGIC
A. BASIC STANDPOINT
1. The Starting Point and Direction of Thought

The traditional logics, as we have explained, emphasize the laws and forms of thinking. Unification logic, however, begins by considering the starting point of thinking and then discusses laws and forms.

Man's existence is generally thought to be fortuitous. By the time we become aware of our own existence, we are already living and do not know why. As Heidegger says, it seems as though we are meaninglessly thrown out into the world *(Geworfenheit)* by somebody unknown. Our thinking, also, seems to be fortuitous and not necessary. Why do we think? This question is answered easily: we think in order to live. But what does it mean to live? This is related to the purpose of life. If man is a "creature," he was created with a purpose. The Unification Principle asserts that man was created according to the Purpose of Creation and thus has purpose in life (as, for example, a watch has the purpose of telling time). According to the Unification Principle, man is given two purposes: the purpose for the individual and the purpose for the whole. In the fulfillment of his dual purposes lies the meaning of his life.

It is for these two purposes that we think. Thinking should be conducted not for its own sake, but for the sake of practice, which has purpose and direction. Primarily, such thinking (original thinking) is based on the purpose for the whole and has the direction of realizing this purpose; secondarily, it is based on the purpose for the individual and has the direction of realizing this purpose. God has endowed us with the ability to think in order for us to accomplish these purposes and to follow these directions—in other words, in order for us to love one another, not to hurt or destroy one another or our environment. Man's thinking was originally a kind of creative power, the power of *practice*. These are the lines along which logic should be established.

2. The Standard of Thinking

In Unification Thought, logic originates in the Original Image, as do Ontology and Epistemology. In order for any theory concerning the phenomenal world to be exact and true, it must take into account the Original Image—i.e., the starting point of Creation.

This is the basic standpoint of this thought.

It is generally thought that we are free to think about anything and to let our thoughts go as we please, since reason has freedom. Our thinking, however, should not deviate from the direction of the realization of the Purpose of Creation. Then, where does the standard for this direction come from? It comes from the logical structure of the Original Image.

3. Interrelated Fields

Not only man's logical structure, but also his cognitive structure, as well as the ontological structure of all beings, have their origins in the structure of the Original Image. Man's practice on nature—that is, his domination of it, previously explained in the "Theory of the Original Image" as the process of forming the outer quadruple base—is also patterned after the structure of the Original Image. Thus, the logical structure, cognitive structure, existing structure, and the practicing structure (in all the practicing fields, such as education and industry), are naturally interrelated. This is fundamental to Unification Logic.

B. THE LOGICAL STRUCTURE OF THE ORIGINAL IMAGE

The structure of the Original Image that is most related to logic and thinking are the Inner Developing Quadruple Base. (Fig. 21) The functions of the Inner *Sung Sang* are intellect, emotion, and will. Intellect is related to sensibility, understanding, and reason; emotion to feelings; and will to the desire to do something. These three functions are interconnected: there are emotion and will in intellect, intellect and will in emotion, and intellect and emotion in will. We think of them separately for the sake of convenience; in fact they are united. An intellectual action is one in which the intellectual aspect of the mind appears most strongly, even though the other functions are involved as well. Modern psychology emphasizes the interconnectedness and inseparability of these three functions.

The Inner *Hyung Sang* contains ideas and concepts. Ideas are the concrete image of an individual being, such as a certain kind of fish, a dog, or a cow; concepts are images of common elements abstracted from ideas, such as 'animal' and 'plant'. Concept, here, is not the same as Hegel's notion *(Begriff)*, but has the usual meaning of concept, such as the one used in the dispute about universals *(Universalienstreit)* in the Middle Ages. Besides ideas and concepts, the Inner *Hyung Sang* contains also original law and mathematical principle.

Fig. 21 The Inner Developing Quadruple Base

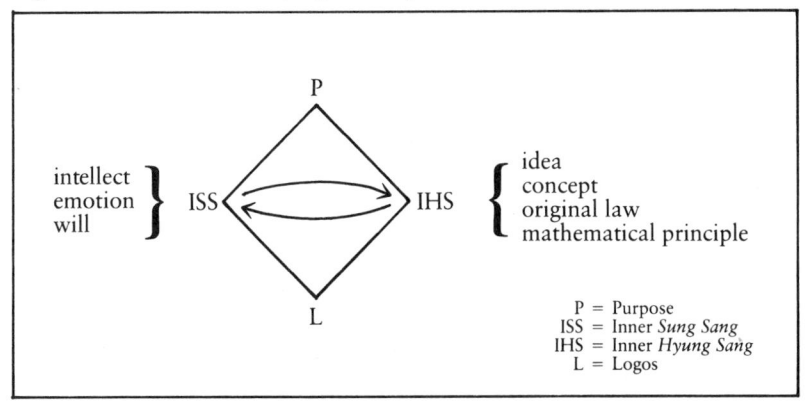

```
                    P
       intellect  ⎫        ⎧ idea
       emotion   ⎬ ISS ⇄ IHS ⎨ concept
       will      ⎭        ⎩ original law
                                mathematical principle
                    L
                              P   = Purpose
                              ISS = Inner Sung Sang
                              IHS = Inner Hyung Sang
                              L   = Logos
```

The Inner *Sung Sang* and Inner *Hyung Sang* engage in give-and-take action centering on Purpose. The result is Logos, or reason-law. Thus, a quadruple base is formed, called the Inner Developing Quadruple Base. The relative importance of reason and law (original law) vary, however, between the logos of man and the logos of animals and plants.

Purpose comes from Heart. Both the Inner *Sung Sang* and the Inner *Hyung Sang* begin to work in the direction of realizing the Purpose. This means that our thinking, also, is based on purpose; in other words, it has direction. The thinking of God is for realizing the Purpose of Creation, which is to realize joy through loving man and all creation, that is, through making them rejoice. Our thinking, also, should be for realizing the Purpose of Creation—in other words, it should be based on Heart, or love.

Because man is fallen, he does not think in this direction; rather, he has come to have evil ideas and evil concepts. As long as we live in a non-principled world, it is difficult for us to think in accordance with the Purpose of Creation, for give-and-take action with evil men easily brings about evil thinking. Sometime in the future, when the ideal world is free of evil persons, our thinking will naturally be in the direction of the Purpose of Creation, based on Heart, without any special teaching or effort. Many religious leaders have urged us not to think evil thoughts. They have not, however, clarified what the standard of thinking should be. In the Original Image, Logos is formed through the give-and-take action between Inner *Sung Sang* and Inner *Hyung Sang* centering on the Purpose of Creation established by Heart. This structure of Logos gives us the original standard of our thinking.

Logos engages in give-and-take action with the *Hyung Sang* (Original *Hyung Sang*), forming the Outer Developing Quadruple Base. This is the so-called *two-staged structure of creation* or in short, the *two-staged structure*. Logos, or the Inner Developing Quadruple Base, is closely related to the Outer Quadruple Base. Our thinking, therefore, should not stop at the inner quadruple base, but should develop outwards, forming the outer quadruple base. In other words, thinking is originally for practice.

C. THE TWO STAGES IN THE PROCESS OF THINKING AND THE FORMATION OF QUADRUPLE BASES

There are three stages of cognition: the perceptual stage, the understanding stage, and the rational stage. Since perceptual-stage cognition is regarded as a window through which the information coming in from outside is passively received, it can be called direct cognition. In the understanding and rational stages, however, the process of thinking takes place. In the understanding stage, thinking is influenced by sense-impressions from outside; not so in the rational stage. Thinking is an active participant in these last two stages, which form quadruple bases similar to those of the Original Image. (Fig. 22)

Kant's epistemology, also, ascribes a three-stage process to cognition. In the perceptual stage, sense-impressions (content) are united with forms of intuition. In the understanding stage, the content, which is already united with forms of intuition, is united also with thinking forms. In the rational stage, thinking takes place freely, through the work of reason.

In Hegel, we find three stages of cognition as well. He considers the perceptual-stage cognition as thesis, the understanding-stage cognition as antithesis, and the rational-stage cognition as synthesis. In the rational stage, cognition, or thinking, proceeds first with negative reason and then with affirmative reason to reach the perfect cognition, or thinking.

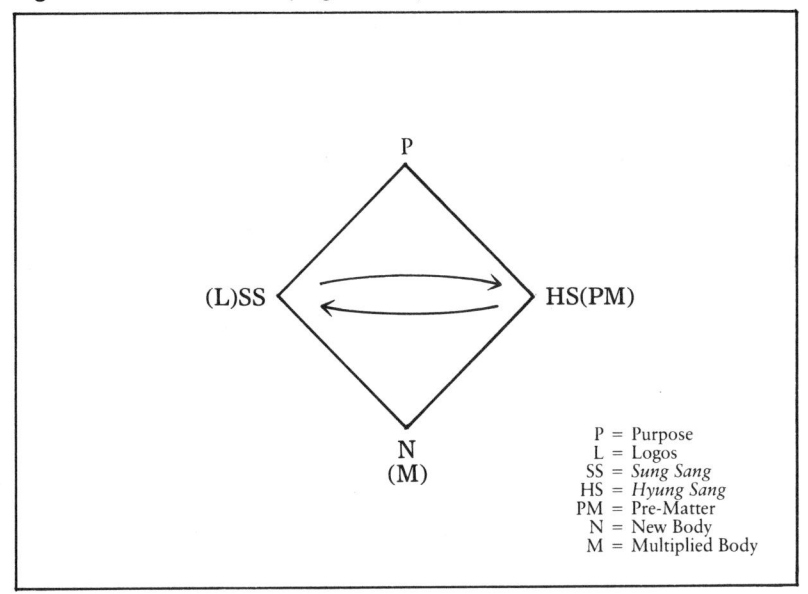

Fig. 22 The Outer Developing Quadruple Base

```
              P

   (L)SS  ⇄  HS(PM)

              N
             (M)
```

P = Purpose
L = Logos
SS = *Sung Sang*
HS = *Hyung Sang*
PM = Pre-Matter
N = New Body
M = Multiplied Body

In communism, the first stage is the perceptual stage, or the stage of sense-impressions, where the sensible qualities of an outside object are reflected in the brain. The second stage is the rational stage, where judgment and inference take place. The third stage is the practice stage, where rational knowledge is examined by practice.

In Unification Thought, both cognition and thinking are carried out through the establishment of quadruple bases. In terms of cerebral physiology, perceptual-stage cognition is carried out in the sensory areas of the cerebral cortex; understanding-stage cognition, in the parieto-temporo-preoccipital (PTP) association area; and rational-stage cognition, in the frontal association area. (See chapter 4, "Epistemology.")

The PTP association area has countless nerve cells. Each nerve cell is connected, directly or indirectly, to fourteen billion other cells in the cerebral cortex, just as a telephone is connected virtually to millions of other telephones throughout the world. Just as we can talk with anyone in the world by telephone, any kind of information (prototypes) can be freely shared, through give-and-take action, among the nerve cells. In this way, quadruple bases for thinking and for cognition can be easily formed.

In the understanding stage, thinking is restrained by its involvement with sense-impressions (content) from the outer world. In this stage, the content from the outside and the prototype from the inside are collated to complete a cognition; in other words, a completing quadruple base is formed as a cognitive structure. In the rational stage, however, thinking is performed freely, using information obtained from the understanding stage, but not restrained by anything from the outside. Accordingly, thinking is developed in this stage. Development of thinking refers to successive fragmentary instances of thinking. Saying that thinking develops is the same as saying that new instances of thinking appear one after another. In this case, each instance of thinking forms its own *completing quadruple base*. The completing quadruple base, although it is developing while it is formed, is identity-maintaining after it has been formed, that is, after a thought is completed. In the rational stage, therefore, the process of thinking is developing and at the same time it has the identity-maintaining aspect.

Let us depict this figuratively. A guest comes to the reception room of a mansion and requests to speak with the owner. A servant announces him to the owner and is told to show the guest to the drawing room. The guest and the host meet in the drawing room and talk, but the host cannot think at random, because his thinking is restrained by the talking of his guest. When the conversation ends, the host retires to his private chamber, where he thinks, reads, paints, sleeps, and does as he likes. The reception room corresponds to the sensory centers of the brain; the drawing room, to the PTP association area, where understanding-stage thinking is carried out; and the private chamber, to the frontal lobe, where unrestrained, rational-stage thinking takes place.

In rational-stage thinking, the logos (plan) is formed by the give-and-take action between the Inner *Sung Sang* and Inner *Hyung Sang*. The thinking process may be terminated with the attainment of a conclusion (logos), which is called a first-stage conclusion. Sometimes this conclusion is used, along with other ideas, to make up the Inner *Hyung Sang* of a second-stage quadruple base, giving rise to a second-stage conclusion (logos 2). The thinking process may be completed here, or may be indefinitely extended over numerous other stages, in spiral development, figuratively speaking. (Fig. 23)

Unification Logic

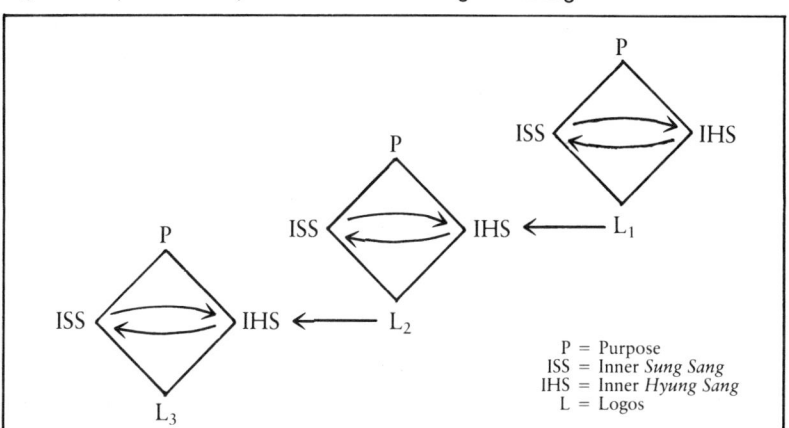

Fig. 23 Spiral Development in Rational-Stage Thinking

P = Purpose
ISS = Inner *Sung Sang*
IHS = Inner *Hyung Sang*
L = Logos

D. THE BASIC FORMS OF THINKING

An understanding-stage cognition, or thinking, is realized by the give-and-take action between sense-impressions and prototypes —i.e., by the formation of a reciprocal relationship between them, centering on purpose. A prototype consists of protoimages and images of form in the protoconsciousness (the consciousness on the cellular level). A protoimage is the image of a single cell, or of many cells; an image of form is that of the existing form of a single cell, or that of relationship between cells—such as Subject and Object, *Sung Sang* and *Hyung Sang*, and Position and Settlement. The images of form become the thinking forms in cognition and in thinking.

Since the lower nerve center knows the normal stage of *Sung Sang* and *Hyung Sang* of the cecum, for example, in the case of appendicitis it immediately knows the change through the information from the appendix and takes appropriate measures to relieve the inflammation. (It is similar to a watchmaker being able to repair a broken watch because he knows its normal state.)

The Positivity and Negativity of bodily functions are seen in such systems as the Autonomic Nervous System, whose sympathetic and parasympathetic nerves are often antagonistic in function— i.e., one is accelerating and the other is restraining. When the function of the stomach muscles, for instance, is over-strengthened, gastric cramp may appear; when it is too weak for a long time, gastroptosis may occur. The lower nerve center, knowing all the information concerning the activities of the stomach muscles, regulates their functioning. If the regulation is disturbed, disorders, such as cramps and ptosis, come to appear. It can do this because it has the sense of positivity and negativity. Cells of the lower central nervous system have information on the arteries and veins, which exist in a subject-object relationship. Of course, the cells do not know the concepts of *Sung Sang* and *Hyung Sang*, subject and object, etc., but they have an awareness of these correlative relationships. Thus, when the relationship is disturbed, the lower central nerve cells try to respond to the disturbance promptly.

Cells know neither the concept of time nor of space, but they have a sense of time (that something is lasting) and a sense of space (position and direction). White corpuscles, for instance, move accurately to an inflamed part of the body; the semicircular canals of the ear, knowing direction, enable us to maintain our balance through the central nervous system.

'Infinity' and 'finiteness' are philosophical concepts, but each nerve cell has the sense of infinity and finiteness. Infinity in living things means the durability of the actions of cells, tissues, organs, etc. Finiteness refers to the limitation of the span of life. Nerve cells have the awareness of such durability and limitation.

Perceived Images, which consist of protoimages and images of form, are considered to be stored in the spinal cord, hindbrain and the limbic system to become prototypes. The lower central nerves maintain normal bodily conditions by using this information in a feedback system, a process which our consciousness (cerebral cortex) is unaware of. Perceived images, also, influence our conscious thinking. Figuratively speaking, thinking can be compared to a soccer game: even though the players seem to be running and kicking at random, in fact their motions and actions are regulated by soccer rules. Similarly, our thinking is influenced by the perceived images. We cannot think about outside sensations in the cerebral cortex independently of the protoimage and image of form, which come from the lower nerve center. That our thinking is regulated by the image of form is the same as saying that we have *thinking forms*.

Unification Thought identifies ten basic thinking forms (though there may be more), which are established from the concepts of give-and-take action and the quadruple bases. Many forms and concepts of the category established by other philosophers correspond to the thinking forms in Unification Thought. "Essence and phenomenon," for example, correspond to *"Sung Sang and Hyung Sang."*

I have divided the Unification Thought thinking forms into two groups, the first consisting of the ten basic forms (first category), and the second consisting of those forms derived from the first (second category). The first category is already shown in chapter 4, "Epistemology." The second category, which is not limited in number and contains the traditionally used concepts, is as follows.

1. quality and quantity
2. content and form
3. essence and phenomenon
4. cause and effect
5. totality and individuality
6. abstract and concrete
7. substance and attribute

Someone may wonder why we have used such concepts as 'Sung Sang and Hyung Sang' instead of 'essence and phenomena' and 'content and form', or why we have used such purely new concepts as 'existence and force', 'relation and affinity', and so on as concepts in our category (first category).

Without Quadruple Base, C-B-H action, and give-and-take action, we would no longer have the Unification Principle. Since these are fundamental concepts, our category must be based upon them. As a new system of thought, Unification Thought naturally gives rise to new concepts. A category can be looked upon as a signboard for the system of thought; it is natural, therefore, for the Unification Thought category to be new as well.

Marx's philosophy has a category that is characteristic of Marx; Kant's and Hegel's philosophies do so also. Similarly, the first category of Unification Thought, which comprises ten thinking forms, is uniquely characteristic of Unification Thought.

E. THE BASIC LAW OF THINKING

Formal logic has given us two fundamental principles (the principles of identity and contradiction) and two more, derived from them (the principles of excluded middle and sufficient reason). In Unification Thought the most fundamental principle is the *principle, or law, of give-and-take action,* or in short, the *give-and-take law,* or *coaction law.**

I began this section by explaining that the Quadruple Bases in the Original Image are the origin and standard of our thinking. These Quadruple Bases are established by give-and-take action; accordingly, the basic law of thinking, upon which the principle of identity and the principle of contradiction and all other laws stand, is the give-and-take law. (See item G. below.)

In formal logic, logical terms, such as "be," "be not," "and," "or," and "if...then..."—play as important a role as that of bone structure in the body, because without them, a proposition cannot be established and inferences cannot be made. In Unification Thought, a proposition or an inference containing such logical terms is dealt with as an instance of collation-type (contrast-type) give-and-take action, for logical terms are viewed as means of establishing relationships between concepts or between propositions.

The laws of thinking, which are expressed through the use of logical terms, are all based on the give-and-take law. A representative deductive inference, syllogism, which is expressed in the form "*if* [A (major premise) *and* B (minor premise)], *then* C (conclusion)," is subject to the give-and-take law.

Let me explain this in the following example.
1. All men die
2. Socrates is a man
3. Therefore, Socrates will die

In this example, we want to know what will become of Socrates in the future; this is the purpose in our thinking. Next, the two propositions ("all men die" and "Socrates is a man") are compared, or collated. The first proposition, the major premise, is the subjective proposition; the second one, the minor premise, is the objective proposition. By collating them through the correlative give-and-take law, we find that the range of the major premise is broader than, and

---

*When we fight with words against the dialectic based on communist philosophy, the terms with which we fight need to be concise and sharply anti-dialectical. The term 'give-and-take action' is the best weapon to overcome the term 'dialectic', but its expression does not seem to be concise enough. So, I have created the new terms 'coaction' (noun) and 'coactic' (adjective) with the same meaning as 'give-and-take action', and I would like to use the new terms in combination with 'give-and-take action', especially in criticizing communistic philosophy. Accordingly, the law of give-and-take action can be expressed as 'coaction law'; similarly, the term 'give-and-take unitism' can be expressed as 'coactic unitism'.

Unification Logic

includes that of, the minor premise; in other words, Socrates belongs to 'man', and therefore, will die. (Fig. 24)

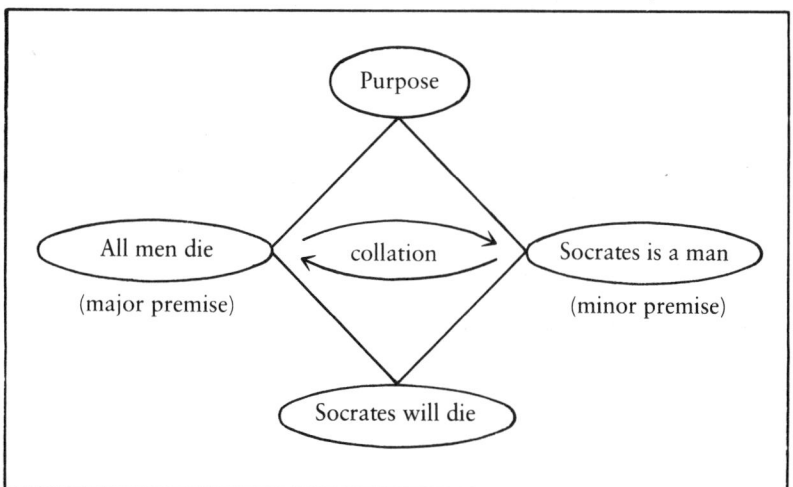

Fig. 24 Collation-Type Give-and-Take Action between Two Propositions

```
                        Purpose
                          /\
                         /  \
                        /    \
           All men die  ←collation→  Socrates is a man
                        \    /
           (major premise)  (minor premise)
                         \  /
                          \/
                     Socrates will die
```

Even a single proposition, such as "Man is mortal", is based on the give-and-take law. The subject "man" and the predicative adjective "mortal" are connected by the logical term "is". One concludes that "man is mortal" by comparing "man" and "mortal", according to the give-and-take law.

We can conclude that "Some Koreans are honest," if the proposition "All Koreans are honest" is true. This is immediate inference, in which the conclusion can be directly derived from a single premise. Immediate inference is actually an abbreviated kind of syllogism (mediate inference). In the example above, the minor premise "some people are Korean" is omitted. Thus, even immediate inference is based on the give-and-take law. In fact, so is the premise "All Koreans are honest," which is the result of comparing 'All Koreans' and 'honest' through the give-and-take law. We can similarly show that inductive inferences, also, are based on the give-and-take law.

By the way, if our thinking is subject to laws, do we have any freedom of thought? Yes we do. As stated before, Logos is formed by the give-and-take action of the Inner *Sung Sang* and Inner *Hyung Sang*. The element of reason in the Inner *Sung Sang* has freedom, whereas the element of law in the Inner *Hyung Sang* is predetermined. What kind of freedom, then, does reason have? There are numerous concepts and ideas in the Inner *Hyung Sang;* reason can freely select any of them in order to form a Logos, even though the purpose has been decided beforehand.

Man has countless concepts and ideas, acquired from life-experiences, and he can select any of them in thinking or making a plan. He can exercise his freedom without violating the law. In other words, he can freely perform give-and-take action in thinking.

III. A CRITIQUE OF TRADITIONAL LOGIC
A. FORMAL LOGIC

Though we approve its basic laws, still we find something lacking in the foundation of formal logic. All beings carry out give-and-take action within themselves in order to exist. Between man and the rest of creation, there are two kinds of give-and-take action. First, man takes an interest in all things (concern), and they return information (cognition) to him; second, man works on all things (practice) and they return information (cognition) to him. The former give-and-take action forms the cognitive structure (cognitive quadruple base); the latter, the dominating structure (dominating quadruple base). In addition, there is give-and-take action in the mind of man, forming the logical structure (logical quadruple base), and in each creation, forming the existing structure (existing quadruple base), both among men and among created beings. These structures are closely connected to one another.

This means that man's logical structure is not independent or isolated; rather, it is related to other structures. One cannot think normally apart from the cognitive and dominating structures. In other words, man's thinking is performed in cognizing as well as in practicing. (Fig. 25) The formal logic itself has only dealt with the logical structure without paying attention to other structures.

Of course further study about judgment forms and inference forms is necessary, but these matters should be entrusted to logicians.

B. SYMBOLIC LOGIC

Precision in thinking and expressing thoughts is a goal worth striving for, so we accept symbolic logic as such. The full range of human communication, however, encompasses more than mere

A Critique of Traditional Logic

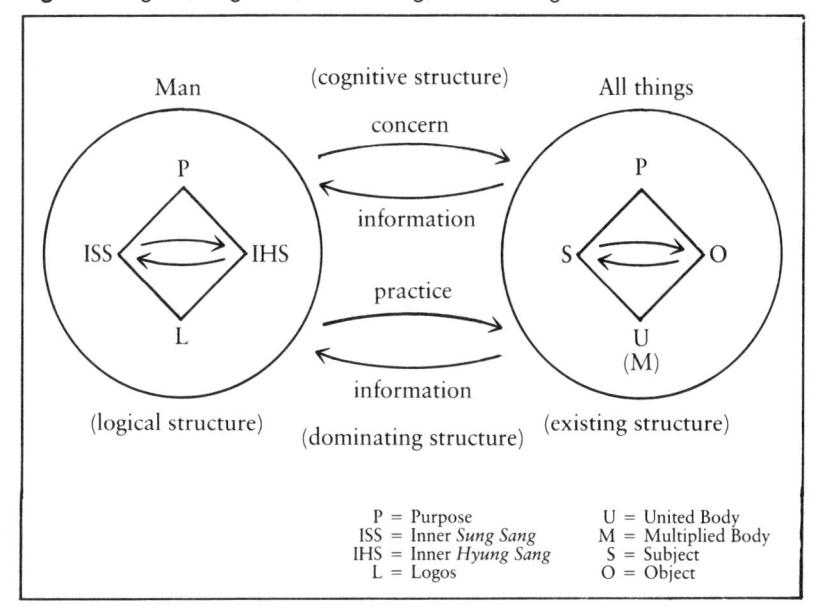

Fig. 25 Logical, Cognitive, Dominating, and Existing Structures

```
        Man          (cognitive structure)      All things
                          concern
              P                                       P
                         ──────▶
        ISS ◆ IHS        information          S ◆ O
              L          ◀──────                      U
                          practice                   (M)
                         ──────▶
                         ◀──────
                         information
      (logical structure) (dominating structure) (existing structure)

              P = Purpose              U = United Body
              ISS = Inner Sung Sang    M = Multiplied Body
              IHS = Inner Hyung Sang   S = Subject
              L = Logos                O = Object
```

mathematical accuracy in the use of language, as shown below.

Logos is formed through the give-and-take action between the Inner *Sung Sang* and Inner *Hyung Sang*. Since the Inner *Hyung Sang* contains original laws and mathematical principles, all created beings (created through the Logos) have these laws and principles. Scientists have conducted research on these principles and have been able to send men to the moon as a result of their discoveries.

Man, also, has mathematical principles, not only in his physical body, but also in his language. By making use of these principles, even if unconsciously, he thinks and speaks accurately and correctly. These principles come from the Inner *Hyung Sang* of God, and reason comes from the Inner *Sung Sang* of God. But the motive (center) of the give-and-take action between them is the Heart behind Purpose. Heart, therefore, is in the highest position. This means that man is not only a being of logos (reason, law), but also a being of pathos, (heart, love, emotion). By stressing only mathematical accuracy, the emotional factor cannot be conveyed. Thinking itself is for practice, which requires give-and-take action (cooperation) with others, and this can only take place if thoughts are communicated to others. But, if the thinking language is totally transformed into mathematical symbols, the emotional content of thinking will disappear and the flow of communication will be impaired.

For instance, if someone shouts, "Fire!" we do not know from the word itself whether he means, "This is a fire," or "There is a fire burning now," or something else. We can understand the meaning, however, because there is an emotional factor in his expression. Here, the question of grammatical accuracy (essential in symbolic logic) is actually unimportant, for "Fire!" is an emotional utterance, not a rational one. We use emotional utterances especially in cases of emergency, and they are understood immediately (intuitively).

Since man is the union of logos and pathos, our language has both an intellectual and an emotional aspect. If we root out all emotional utterances, we are rooting out a part of our humanness. In fact, people whose language is often inaccurate may actually be more warm-hearted than those whose language is always precise.

Kant's language and behavior, for instance, were reputed to be consistent and accurate. People could set their watches by him, for he always passed by the same place at the same time every day. Similarly, there is a rigor to his philosophy, and we feel constrained by it. We need not be so pedantic. Jesus' words in the Bible were sometimes not logical, yet we consider them to be true, because they were accompanied by God's love. We cannot but say that symbolic logic is one-sided, because it disregards the factor of pathos in normal language.

C. HEGEL'S LOGIC

Hegel considered Logos to be God, making the created (Logos) the Creator (God). In Unification Thought, Logos is the Multiplied (New) Body formed through the give-and-take action between Inner *Sung Sang* and Inner *Hyung Sang*, centering on Purpose. By making Logos the starting point of his logic, he lost the purposive element in his philosophy; consequently, he was drawn to making serious errors.

The Unification Principle explains that development is realized through the give-and-take action between correlative elements. Nothing is produced by a single element. But Hegel had no correlative element in Reason (Logos), which is considered to be thesis, so he had to give it an antithesis. Consequently, the dialectical process of thesis-antithesis-synthesis became purposeless and purely mechanical.

The thesis (Being) is supposed to proceed to the antithesis

A Critique of Traditional Logic

(Nothing), but since this antithesis is nothing, it does not substantially exist. In this way, the thesis, denied by the antithesis, cannot but turn into thesis again. This is the synthesis. The synthesis, therefore, necessarily returns to a stage similar to what it was before. Thus, Hegel's logic is actually a returning, or completing, system; in his philosophy development cannot continue eternally, but is destined to end sooner or later. This point was criticized by Marx and Engels.

According to Unification Thought, development is realized by the harmonious give-and-take action between subject and object, centering on purpose. In Hegel's philosophy, however, the thesis and antithesis oppose each other. This assertion gave rise to the philosophy of struggle. Hegel's philosophy lacks any theoretical basis for love. By making Reason (Logos) equal to God, he excluded the aspect of God's love.

Hegel said nature is the estranged Idea (God). If so, we have a kind of pantheism, in which we can see Logos (God) in nature. This could be understood also as the assertion "nature is God, therefore God is no more than nature." Such an assertion can lead to materialism; in fact, some have said that Hegel's pantheistic tendency was largely responsible for Marx's materialism.

According to Hegel, the appearance of nature is a stepping stone for the appearance of man. Idea manifesting itself first as nature and then as man, finally returns to Idea (after realizing itself completely), or the Absolute Spirit. Nature becomes irrelevant after man appears. It can be compared to scaffolding, which is needed while a building (man) is being made, but becomes unnecessary after its completion. In Hegel, nature need not be useful to man's life. In Unification Thought, however, nature is man's object, both for his joy and for his dominion.

In Hegel's view, the history of mankind is an account of man's puppet-like manipulation by Reason. This is called the *trick of reason (List der Vernunft)*. If this is true, what becomes of man's contribution to history? What should man live for, and why should he work hard, if he is only being used? There is no need or incentive for making effort; since there is no room for man's own portion of responsibility. In the Unification Thought view, the progress of human history has been greatly affected by man's success or failure in the accomplishment of his portion of responsibility. (See chapter 10, "Theory of History.")

Yet Hegel was ready to go to war to defend Prussia, his rational state. (Apparently the Absolute Spirit does not refrain from going to war.) Why should we believe in God anyway? Such problems in Hegel's view of history have arisen from his making Logos equal to God and his considering the progress of history the self-realization of Logos (Idea).

There is one more thing to be pointed out. Hegel's philosophy may look like a philosophy of development; actually, it is not. Hegel believed that Prussia was to be the rational state appearing at the consummation of history. History need not develop any longer. His philosophy, therefore, was destined to die with the disappearance of Prussia.

The position of Logos in Hegel's philosophy corresponds to that of the Original Image in Unification Thought. His dialectic within the Logos corresponds to the give-and-take action within the Original Image. Hegel's thesis-antithesis-synthesis corresponds to *Chung-Boon-Hap*. Hegel's 'antithesis' corresponds to *Hyung Sang* (pre-matter). What Hegel intended to accomplish through the 'completing dialectic' is accomplished by the dynamic give-and-take action and static give-and-take action of Unification Thought. What Hegel understands by 'nature' corresponds, though symbolically, to the understanding of the Original Image through 'all things' in Unification Thought. Finally, Hegel's pantheistic tendency is surpassed by the Pan-Divine-Image Theory of Unification Thought.

D. MATERIALISTIC DIALECTIC

The idealistic dialectic, as demonstrated above, has many problems, but the materialistic dialectic has even more. The first problem concerns the starting point of materialistic dialectic, and the second one concerns its view on the principle of contradiction of formal logic.

First, about the starting point of materialistic dialectic. Hegel starts with the Logos, but Marx has no starting point, unless matter is considered that. Marx used Hegel's dialectic after taking away the starting point—i.e., Logos.

If matter is the starting point, then natural laws must be considered as attributes of matter. Even admitting this, we cannot say that laws are matter itself. Matter is supposed to have no definite laws originally, since it consists of atoms, or more precisely, of elementary particles, which are supposed to have originated from energy without any kind of restriction or law. But matter consists of atoms, which have a certain structure, with atomic weight, atomic numbers, atomic shell, atomic value, etc. We know that there are many kinds of atoms, each of which has a different structure and character. The atomic structure (thus, the atomic character) has an influence upon chemical and physical laws (i.e., natural laws). How can atoms come to have such different structures and laws? In other words, how did matter come to have such attributes as laws, character, etc.? This question cannot be solved by materialism. Therefore, the materialistic dialectic, as a law of development, clearly lacks a definite starting point for its theory of dialectic development.

Second, I would like to criticize the view of the materialistic dialectic on the principle of contradiction of formal logic. The principle of identity says that "A is A," and the principle of contradiction says that "A is not non-A." These two principles have the same meaning, only differing in expression. But the communist dialectic says that "A is A and at the same time is non-A." Communists say that development is not possible if A is only A, but is possible if A is not only A, but simultaneously is non-A.

They say that a hen's egg must be a non-egg as well as an egg in order for it to develop into a chicken. The non-egg, or negation of the egg, is supposed to be the embryo. The antinomic conclusion, "an egg is a non-egg as well as an egg", is against the principle of contradiction. Credit for its formulation should go to Hegel, who said that a notion cannot develop unless it has a negative element (negation of the notion) within itself.

What does the proposition, "An egg is a non-egg as well as an egg" mean? In this case, non-egg means the negation of the egg—that is, the embryo. Accordingly, this proposition can be changed to "An egg is an embryo as well as an egg." We know that an egg consists of four elements: the white, the yolk, the shell, and the embryo. So, to say that an egg is a non-egg (embryo) is the same as saying that the four elements equal one element, or the total equals one of its parts. This proposition is quite false; it is not a logical statement.

In the Unification Thought view, development takes place without contradicting either the principle of identity or the principle of contradiction. I explained before that the logical structure originates from the dynamic structure of the Original Image, or the Developing Quadruple Bases; still we should remember that the Developing Quadruple Bases cannot be separated from the Identity-Maintaining Quadruple Bases. Accordingly, thinking, besides being dynamic, has also an identity-maintaining aspect.

The result of the copulation (give-and-take action centering on the purpose of producing progeny) of a cock and a hen is a fertilized egg. This is the first-stage dynamic quadruple base. In this process the principles of laying eggs and of mating male and female remain unchanged. This is the identity-maintaining aspect.

The two main constituents of an egg are the embryo and the other contents (the yolk and the white). When these two elements enter into dynamic give-and-take action centering on purpose, the egg becomes a chicken. This is the second-stage dynamic quadruple base. In the first-stage dynamic quadruple base, through which an egg is laid, the egg is simply an egg; in the second stage, however, it becomes a chicken. The developing (dynamic) quadruple bases, then, have an identity-maintaining aspect. When an egg is laid, it is an egg only, and not simultaneously an egg and a non-egg; when it becomes a chicken, in the second stage, it is a chicken only, and not simultaneously a chicken and a non-chicken. A chicken is not born by the struggle between egg and non-egg, but it is born purely from an egg through the give-and-take action between correlative elements within it.

Understanding-stage thinking (or cognition) is predominantly identity-maintaining, since it becomes complete, to a certain extent, with the collation of the inner prototype and the outer sense-impressions. Rational-stage thinking, however, is predominantly developing, since rational thinking is a continuously and infinitely developing process. Yet it has also a completing (i.e., identity-maintaining) aspect, because rational thinking is carried out step by step, and at each step, thinking is completed to some extent. Unification Thought, then, recognizes both the principle of identity and the principle of contradiction, as it recognizes the identity-maintaining aspect of every being.

In 1950, Stalin published his book *Marxism and Problems of Linguistics*, where he stated that formal logic should be accepted even in communist society. Before that, there was a heated discussion among scholars in U.S.S.R. concerning formal logic. Some scholars maintained that the forms and laws of formal logic should be aban-

A Critique of Traditional Logic

doned, since they belong to the superstructure and have class characteristics; others maintained that they should be accepted, since any proposition would become invalid if the principle of identity and the principle of contradiction were denied. Then, Stalin concluded that formal logic does not belong to the superstructure and has no class characteristics and, therefore, should be accepted.

Aside from the question whether logic belongs to the superstructure or not, this fact shows that the materialistic dialectic could not but approve of the unchanging aspect in the process of development (of thinking), without being able to carry out the dialectical principle that states that everything is not in the state of immutability, but constantly changes and develops. This implies a modification, or strictly speaking a collapse, of the materialistic dialectic. To put it another way, this fact shows that Unification Thought—which stresses the unity of identity-maintenance and development and the unity of unchangeability and changeability in all things—is right.

In conclusion, I would like to present a diagrammatic comparison of Unification Logic, formal logic, materialistic dialectical logic, and transcendental logic. (Fig. 26)

Fig. 26 A Comparative View of Unification Logic, Formal Logic, Materialistic Dialetical Logic, and Transcendental Logic

	UNIFICATION LOGIC	FORMAL LOGIC	MATERIALISTIC DIALECTICAL LOGIC	TRANSCENDENTAL LOGIC
thinking form	objective & subjective	subjective	objective	subjective
content of thinking	objective & subjective		objective	objective
law of thinking	give-and-take law	principle of identity, principle of contradiction	dialectic	transcendental method
basis of thinking	structure of the Original Image (logical structure)			
characteristics	collation	formalism	reflection	synthesis

6 AXIOLOGY

I. NECESSITY OF AXIOLOGY

Let me explain first why axiology is necessary.

A. IN ORDER TO PREPARE FOR THE FUTURE SOCIETY

The confusion in today's world has largely been caused by the decay of our sense of values. We urgently need a new view of value (Axiology), if we are to change this fallen world into the future, original world. First, the future world will be a sincere society, in which the value of trueness* is realized. The falsehood and hypocrisy that prevail in today's world should be eradicated through the new view of value. Second, the future world will be an ethical society, in which the value of goodness is realized. Someone may object that in this ethical society one's freedom will be restrained. This is not so, however. Up to now, people have pursued the freedom to acquire things and to enjoy human rights, but even in today's free and democratic world, people are suffering from anxiety and despair. They have not attained true freedom. Unification Principle says there is no freedom apart from the Principle—i.e., the norms to realize God's love on earth through the family base. Accordingly, the freedom lost because of the human Fall is not the freedom to acquire things or enjoy rights, but the freedom to love; in other words, it is freedom within the Principle. Principle actually means ethics; thus,

---

*Traditionally, in dealing with values, the aspects of truth, goodness, and beauty are cited. I think, however, that "truth" seems primarily to imply "true knowledge" or "true principles." In Unification Thought, therefore, I will use the term "trueness," instead of "truth," when referring to the value or state of being true.

the future society can also be referred to as an ethical society. Third, the future world will be an artistic society, in which the value of beauty is realized. A new view of value is necessary for establishing such a society.

A new view of man will be established based on the new view of value. The man of the future world will be a person who lives for others (man for others), based on the life for God. He will live a *life of attendance*—that is, a life of service to God and to others.

B. IN ORDER TO SAVE THE WORLD FROM CONFUSION

Today, the traditional views of value are generally declining. As a result, the world abounds with corruption, social crimes, and struggle. Unless the world is saved from this state of confusion—through the establishment of a new view of value—communism cannot be prevented from invading the free world, for this materialistic ideology best thrives where people lack a firm view of value.

C. IN ORDER TO UNIFY ALL TRADITIONAL CULTURES

Cultures are established upon the foundation of a religious view or a system of thought. The Hellenistic culture, for instance, was based on polytheism, which was the Hellenistic religion; the European culture was based on Christianity; other cultures follow a similar pattern. Religions and systems of thought are based on a view of value. Accordingly, in order to unify traditional cultures, we need a new view of value that can embrace and unify all the traditional views of value. Specifically, the new view of value must be able to unify *love* in Christianity, with *benevolence* in Confucianism and *mercy* in Buddhism, as well as the various virtues included in those three. (See sec. VII, B of this chapter.)

II. AXIOLOGY AND THE MEANING OF VALUE

Axiology is the philosophy of value; it deals with problems of the definition, essence, and judgment of value.

Immanuel Kant clearly separated the realms of being (realm of *Sein*) and of value (realm of *Sollen*) by distinguishing fact from value. Because of Kant, "value" has come to be considered a philosophical field of enquiry; by the end of the 19th century, it had come well into the domain of philosophy.

Essentially, value is the nature of the object that gives joy to the subject (man) by satisfying his desire. Man has two kinds of desires: one is his *physical desire* regarding food, clothing, shelter, etc.; the other is his *spiritual desire* regarding knowledge, art, moral life, etc. Physical desires can be fulfilled through material values (*Hyung Sang* values), such as commodities; spiritual desires, on the other hand, can be fulfilled through the spiritual values (*Sung Sang* values) of trueness, beauty, goodness, and love. In this chapter I deal with spiritual value.

At this point, I would like to clarify the difference between "fact" and "value." The characteristic of "fact" lies in the *objectivity* of the judgment; the characteristics of "value," in the *subjectivity* of the judgment. When I look at a flower, for example, and say, "This is a flower," I am expressing a judgment of fact; if, however, I say, "This flower is beautiful," I am stating a judgment of value. The judgment of value of trueness, goodness, and beauty takes place when there is intellectual, volitional, and emotional stimulation; here, the role of emotion is central. By contrast, objective judgments of fact are chiefly intellectual phenomena, with no significant emotional stimulation. Emotion and intellect, of course, cannot really be separated; what we are describing here is a matter of emphasis. When a person's emotions are positively stimulated by an object, that object can be said to have value for him. An object that does not significantly stimulate a person's emotions has no value for him.

When the object of judgment is a person, he stands in a position actively to create value for the subject. Here the problem of how to display value arises: how does one convey trueness? How does one display beauty? And how does one behave according to the standard of goodness?

Axiology, therefore, is a philosophical field directly connected with man's cultural and social life.

III. THE THEORETICAL FOUNDATION OF AXIOLOGY

A discussion of value, according to Unification Thought, must begin with the discussion of man; for man is the center of the universe, and all problems have their starting point in him.

First, man has both *Sung Sang* and *Hyung Sang* aspects.

Consequently, he has also two aspects of desire—that is, the *Sung Sang* (spiritual) desire, concerning the values of trueness, goodness, beauty, and love; and the *Hyung Sang* (material) desire, concerning the values of food, clothing, shelter, and sex. Man's physical mind, the locus of his physical desire, is always connected with his spirit-mind, the locus of his spiritual desire; thus, there is a spiritual component even in his physical desire. For instance, man sees beauty and goodness in food; at the same time his desire to eat should always be connected with (and be supportive of) his desire to realize a life of love.

Second, as explained in "Ontology," man is a substantial object of God as well as the subject of dominion over the whole creation. As the substantial object of God, man is in the position to give joy to God; this he does by realizing the values of trueness, goodness, and beauty.

God is the Original Being, transcending and embracing all visible and invisible beings. He is the whole of all wholes. Man, therefore, has been endowed with the purpose for the whole, feeling a constant impulse to do something for an ever greater whole—to work for his family, his clan, his race, his nation, or the world. Accordingly, man becomes interested in how to act *(Sollen)* in order to benefit his family, clan, race, etc. Kant's categorical imperatives, or oughts, originate from the purpose for the whole.

As the subject of creation, man has the purpose of dominating the creation with love; besides, he also seeks to appreciate the values of trueness, goodness, and beauty—which come from the creation—thereby obtaining joy. This is the purpose for the individual.

From these dual purposes—for the whole and for the individual —come two kinds of desire: one, the desire to *realize value* (which impels us to realize value before God and the whole) and the other, the desire to *seek value* (which motivates us to seek joy through finding the values of trueness, goodness, and beauty in creation).

A purpose is meaningless unless it is being actualized. God endowed man with everything he needs to attain the Purpose of Creation; yet He left it up to man's own free will whether or not to actually complete it. In other words, man cannot achieve the Purpose of Creation merely by remaining as he was when he was created; he must grow spiritually in order fully to resemble God.

As man grows, he tends to actualize his purpose (Purpose of Creation); for this he needs motivation, or volitional impulse (founded on Heart). This motivation, or impulse, with which he was endowed at the time of his creation, is the desire to *realize value* (purpose for the whole) and the desire to *seek value* (purpose for the individual).

Though man is not the only created being with purpose, yet he is the only one who must actualize his purpose through his own desire. In other words, he is the only one who has the desire for value as a means to achieve the Purpose of Creation. Inorganic materials follow laws; plants have life functions; animals have instinct. None of them, however, have any conscious desire for value as a means to attain their purposes. In addition to laws, autonomy, and instinct—which are also found in other created beings—man has the desires both to realize and to seek value. By fulfilling these desires, he accomplishes his purpose.

The foundation for these desires is his impulse for growth in order to complete the Purpose of Creation. This is the ultimate foundation for Axiology in Unification Thought.

IV. TYPES OF VALUE
A. TRUENESS, GOODNESS, AND BEAUTY

Man has *Hyung Sang* desire to fulfill his physical life through food, clothing, shelter, sex, etc. The purpose of Creation, however, cannot be accomplished by the mere fulfillment of this desire; actually, *Hyung Sang* desires exist only to satisfy the physical man, who in turn, exists solely to support the spirit-man during the earthly lifetime. The desire that is directly connected with the Purpose of Creation (i.e., to give joy to God as His object of love) is the *Sung Sang* desire for trueness, goodness, and beauty. These three kinds of values correspond to the three functions of man's mind, or the three aspects of man's personality—intellect, will, and emotion. These values are necessary in order for man to actualize joy.

1. Trueness. Man has an internal desire to live in accordance with truth, to teach truth, to become a true being himself, and so on. This is the desire to realize trueness. In addition, he has an intellectual desire to search for and uncover the aspects of trueness within his world.

2. Goodness. Man has a desire to realize goodness, which he uses to guide himself in leading a good life, in forming a good family, and so on, for the sake of God and the whole. Moreover, he has the desire to find goodness in the world around him.

3. **Beauty.** The realization of beauty is another of man's desires. Through his conduct, his creative activity, his lifestyle, and so on, he wishes to offer beauty to those around him and to God. He also has the desire to seek beauty in the world around him.

Communism considers as having the values of trueness, goodness, and beauty only those things that help the proletariat in their revolutionary struggle against the bourgeoisie. Obviously, this is an extremely narrow view of value, in which value is made into nothing more than a political tool.

B. LOVE

Love has an inseparable relationship to the values of trueness, goodness, and beauty. Trueness, goodness, and beauty are values that the object returns to the subject; they are values of the object, primarily. Love, on the other hand, is the emotional force that the subject directs toward the object. With love, God endows man with the purpose of life. Similarly, parents give their children the purpose of their lives, or the reason for their lives. Thus, the object has the purpose or goal of realizing the values of trueness, goodness, and beauty, and also the standard by which to measure the degree of their realization. When the object displays value according to this purpose, the subject receives joy, and his love for the object increases. Furthermore, when man is in the position of object, his motivation in offering value to the subject, according to this purpose, should be love. A person may even act in complete oblivion of trueness, goodness, and beauty, but if his deeds are motivated by love, they will be received by his subject as containing trueness, goodness, and beauty.

Furthermore, if you (as subject) look upon a person's actions with love, you will tend to find trueness, goodness, and beauty in them, because of your love—even though the actions themselves may not have been intended with the idea of value. Thus, we can say that *love is the source of trueness, goodness, and beauty.*

Since the guidelines for behavior based on love are determined by ethics, value is inseparably connected with ethics. (See ch. 8, "Ethics.")

C. HOLINESS

Since man fell away from God's love, lost trueness, goodness, and beauty, and became self-centered, he has sought "holiness," considering it a value in itself.

The original world, however, is a world of love; this means that trueness, goodness, and beauty themselves are holy. Unification Thought, therefore, deals with values as they should exist in the original world, where everything is holy. Reverend Sun Myung Moon said in a speech on his sixtieth birthday, "To be holy is to be natural. A bird singing is holy; a butterfly flying is holy; the wind blowing and the typhoon attacking are holy; the thunder roaring is holy." "Holiness," therefore, is not considered a value in the same sense as trueness, goodness, and beauty are values.

V. THE ESSENCE OF VALUE

The concept of value includes two aspects: the actual and the essential. The essential aspect of value comprises the inner factors of an object, which make that object contain value—i.e., a certain character of the object that fulfills the subject's desire for value. The actual aspect of value, on the other hand, refers to value as actually expressed in the relationship between subject and object. For example, when a person looks at an object (thing or action) and feels joy from it, the contents of the actual joy are the actual value. They are actual trueness, goodness, and beauty. The essence of value consists of the following two factors.

A. PURPOSE OF CREATION

The first factor is the Purpose of Creation. Every existing being has been created with a purpose. With the exception of man, God's purpose for each creation is automatically realized. A flower can directly please man with its beauty, as can a bird with its song. By contrast, man must realize his purpose (purpose for the whole and purpose for the individual) with his own free will and responsibility. We cannot say, therefore, that man is able directly to realize his Purpose of Creation without taking initiative and making effort.

Every created being has its Purpose of Creation, which is one of the factors of the essence of value. The purpose that man has given to an artifically created object (such as a work of art) can also be included here. An existing being without a purpose is worthless.

B. GIVE-AND-TAKE HARMONY BETWEEN CORRELATIVE ELEMENTS

The second factor is the harmony of the give-and-take action, (give-and-take harmony), between its correlative elements of *Sung Sang* and *Hyung Sang*, positivity and negativity, principal element and subordinate element. The give-and-take harmony between these correlative elements is carried out centering on the purpose of creation, whether it be in natural or in artificial beings. For example, man's supreme purpose is to work in accordance with the will of God (the whole) and to return joy to Him. Leading a good life through the harmonious give-and-take action between one's spirit-mind and physical mind, and leading a harmonious and peaceful life through give-and-take action with others will equal the necessary factors for realizing the essence of value; this will be perceived by God as joy (actual value). Accordingly, when the subject faces an object that has a purpose as well as a harmonious give-and-take action within itself, he will have an actual experience of the values of trueness, goodness, and beauty.

Flowers, for example have the *Sung Sang* purpose of pleasing man with their beauty. Centering on this purpose, harmonious give-and-take action between the correlative elements in their *Hyung Sang* takes place. The correlative elements in the *Hyung Sang* imply differences—such as those of length, breadth, height, movement, and color. The unified harmony of these differences (give-and-take harmony) produces beauty.

Beauty can be found in observing a blue sky, for instance, through which white clouds are moving, or flowers which have bees or butterflies flying around them. The blue sky and the flowers are motionless, but the movements of the clouds, the bees, and the butterflies brings harmony. The greater the number of differences that are harmonized, the greater the beauty. Of course, nature is beautiful in itself; yet, when man—the subject—is in nature, its beauty is enhanced, because new harmony comes to appear centering on him.

VI. DETERMINING ACTUAL VALUE AND THE STANDARD OF VALUE
A. DETERMINING ACTUAL VALUE

Even though an object may have a purpose of creation and

give-and-take harmony between its correlative elements, still it cannot realize actual value by itself. Actual value is determined by the judgment of the subject in the process of the give-and-take action that takes place between the subject and the object. The value of the object is determined through a judgment, and judgment can only be carried out by the subject; the participation of a subject, therefore, is a prerequisite for determining actual value.

In order for give-and-take action between a subject (observer) and an object (observed) to take place, the subject should have the desire to seek value from the object, and at the same time both the subject-conditions and the object-conditions should resemble each other. The *Sung Sang* of the subject must first resemble the *Sung Sang* of the object. The subject's way of thinking, view of life, individuality, interests, hobbies, ideas, education, etc., should find like elements in the object's *Sung Sang*. In this context, the object's *Sung Sang* refers to the creator's *Sung Sang*—purpose of creation, way of thinking, individuality, etc. —which lies behind the object (in a work of art, for instance).

The harmony between the correlative elements (*Sung Sang* and *Hyung Sang*, etc.) in the object and the harmony between these elements in the subject should resemble each other. This is a prerequisite for the give-and-take action between the subject and the object. Often the subject (man) observes an object and adds new meaning to it, by creatively projecting his way of thinking, view of life, individuality, etc., into it. The nature and intensity of value, therefore, depends on the subject. This type of projection is called "subjective action."

A poet, for instance, may see the moon differently from how a scientist would see it. (The moon often looks sad to a man who is sad himself.) The subjective factor is important in the determination of value. In fact, subjective action in the appreciation of beauty can be regarded as a kind of creation (as explained in "Theory of Art").

The process of actualizing value is not a simple passive reflection of the object onto man's consciousness, but requires man's subjective, active process of cognition. The importance of our subjective input can be clearly perceived when we observe historical relics, such as the ruins of old cities and the remains of ancient civilizations: through understanding their historical background, we can appreciate their significance more deeply. (Fig. 27)

Fig. 27 Determining Actual Value

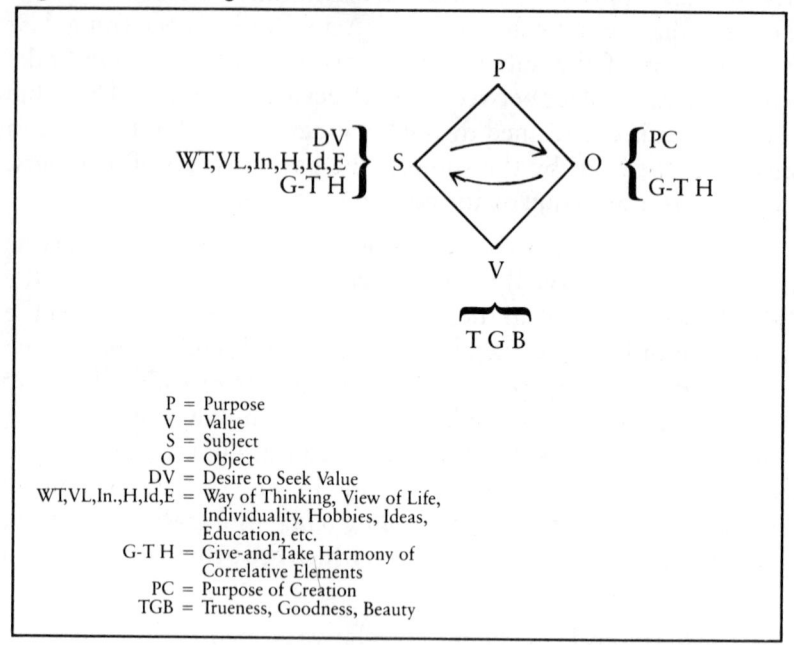

$$\left. \begin{array}{c} DV \\ WT, VL, In, H, Id, E \\ G\text{-}T\ H \end{array} \right\} S \diamondsuit O \left\{ \begin{array}{c} PC \\ G\text{-}T\ H \end{array} \right.$$

(with P at top, V at bottom of diamond; TGB braced under V)

P = Purpose
V = Value
S = Subject
O = Object
DV = Desire to Seek Value
WT, VL, In., H, Id, E = Way of Thinking, View of Life, Individuality, Hobbies, Ideas, Education, etc.
G-T H = Give-and-Take Harmony of Correlative Elements
PC = Purpose of Creation
TGB = Trueness, Goodness, Beauty

Goodness is determined in the same way as beauty. As the Bible says, "The Kingdom of God is in the midst of you" (Luke 17:21); we can see more goodness and even tolerate the shortcomings of others, when love fills our spirit. If the way of thinking and feeling of the subject is reformed, the object will gain new meaning.

In summary both the object and subject conditions are involved in determining actual value; the subjective factor, however, is more decisive.

B. THE STANDARD OF VALUE

What is the standard for determining value? As already mentioned, the subject factor plays an important role in determining actual value. Since there are both universal and individual aspects in the subject, the standard for determining value is the complete union of the universal and the individual.

At this point, I would like to discuss relative and absolute values. A value is considered relative, or temporary, when both the subject-conditions and the object-conditions are relative. Then, how can we acquire an eternal, absolute value? The first aspect to be considered is that of the absoluteness of God's Purpose of Creation for man and the rest of creation. God created man and all things (especially man) in order to receive joy from them, by seeing them express the values of trueness, goodness, and beauty and by seeing them love one another.

The purpose of man, therefore, comprises (a) the purpose for the whole—that is, to please God and the whole (mankind, nation, society, family, which represent God to him) by realizing the values of trueness, goodness, and beauty; (b) the purpose for the individual—that is, to be joyful himself, by seeking values from persons and other created beings around him. Accordingly, God gave man the desires to *realize* and to *seek* value. These are the *original* desires of man to seek and to realize value. The purpose of other created beings, on the other hand, is to please man. God's Purpose of Creation is absolute; thus, the purpose of the existence of man and other created beings, also, is absolute.

Another aspect to be considered is the harmony of correlative elements in man and in the rest of creation. If the correlative elements of a created being are in a harmonious relationship of subject and object centering on the Purpose of Creation (thus reflecting the absolute harmony of God's dual characteristics), the harmony of these elements, also, becomes absolute.

Based on these two conditions (Purpose of Creation and harmony of correlative elements), man seeks as well as realizes absolute value. In order to meet such conditions, man, first of all, must complete his personality by fully understanding God's Purpose of Creation for himself and by achieving complete harmony within himself (through a harmonious give-and-take action between his spirit-mind and physical mind). Furthermore, he must perceive God's Purpose of Creation for humans and the rest of creation. Finally, he must perceive the harmony between the correlative elements within those objects. When all these conditions are fulfilled, and man conducts harmonious give-and-take action with other persons and all creation, the values he seeks and realizes, according to his original desires to seek and to realize values, become absolute.

Man's personality can be completed only when his Heart becomes one with God's Heart (love). Furthermore, the Purpose of Creation of man is based on love; man, in fact, must love God and the whole, realizing and offering values to them (purpose for the whole) and must love persons and other created beings, seeking values from them (purpose for the individual). In other words, absolute values are sought and realized on the basis of absolute love—that is, God's love.

In the fallen world, man is ignorant of the Purpose of Creation of everything, including himself. As a result, he no longer has the *original* desire with which he was endowed at the creation. Moreover, he does not realize the complete harmony within himself (harmony of spirit-mind and physical mind), nor complete harmony with other persons and the creation. Thus, the value he seeks and realizes cannot be absolute, even when his object possesses an absolute condition.

In becoming one with God, Jesus fulfilled the Purpose of Creation, establishing complete harmony. He gave humankind everything for their salvation, even to the extent of allowing himself to be crucified, establishing perfect give-and-take action with God. The value realized by Jesus was absolute. Every person has the possibility of realizing absolute values, since all of us have latent original human nature, given to us by absolute God.

VII. VALUES IN TODAY'S WORLD

In the modern world distrust abounds among humans. In many cases, people distrust their government; workers, their managers; students, their teachers; children, their parents; wives, their husbands; husbands, their wives, and so forth. It seems that there is nobody one can trust but oneself; as a result, people have become defensive and self-centered. With nothing to trust and no one to believe in, people have become unable to judge good and evil, right and wrong—as crime figures indicate.

Why have the traditional views of value collapsed? The first cause is today's materialistic, amoral, and value-neglecting education system. People's view of life has traditionally been based on religion, but religion is excluded from curricula in today's schools. The understanding of value has, consequently, diminished. Second, communists have been working to destroy the view of value that forms the basis for human relationships in the free world, as part of their world communization strategy. Through their philosophy of class struggle, communists have been trying to foment distrust between government and people, managers and workers, nation and nation, and so forth. Third, atheists, such as Nietzsche, Sartre, and Bertrand Russell, have, through their influence, added more value-neglecting thinking to the decline of values. Fourth, religions of the world today have lost their leadership of the human spirit. Consequently, religious values have come to be belittled.

A. WEAKNESS IN TRADITIONAL VIEWS OF VALUE

Humanistic thought says man has reason and love and is different from animals, claiming that his individuality should, therefore, be respected. But since this thought does not clarify why man is different from animals and what the absolute distinction is, its view lacks persuasive power. In fact, many different views of life have been advanced from amongst its ranks, such as the view of man as intellectual *(homo sapiens)*; man as a manufacturer and developer of techniques *(homo faber)*; man as a religious person, who lives depending on some mysterious force *(homo religiosus)*; man as related to economic matters, and who thinks that money is most important *(homo economicus)*; man as a free individual, who feels liberty is of paramount importance *(homo liberalis)*, etc. Each assertion is different. Communists attack those who have humanistic views of value, calling upon them to abandon such self-centered views of life and to engage in reforming society and the world. These accusations are difficult to refute, and many people give in to them.

Christianity teaches real social virtues, such as that we should love our fellow man, should love our enemies, should treat others as we would have them treat us, and so on. The most important of all the virtues of Christianity is love: "Knowledge puffs up, but love builds up." (I Corinthians 8:1). The foundation of Christian love is God, but God was denied by Nietzsche, Feuerbach, Marx, Russell, Sartre, and many others. Christianity has been unable to reply to their charges effectively, and so many people have become atheists. Communism is attacking the Christian view of value, by saying that only class love is true love and by denying God and absolute love.

In Confucianism, also, there are virtues, such as the three bonds (三綱); the five moral rules (五倫) between lord and vassal, father and son, husband and wife, old and young, and between friends; and the five cardinal virtues (五德)—benevolence, justice, politeness, wisdom, and fidelity. The foundation of these virtues is *jên* (仁 = benevolence), and the foundation of *jên* is heaven (天). But, what is heaven? Is it the sky? The concept of heaven is not very persuasive to modern man, and Confucian virtues have lost a great deal of their power. They are often denounced by communists as remains of the feudal age.

The great virtue in Buddhism is mercy (慈悲). Buddhism says that in order for man to be liberated from suffering he must perceive that original human nature is eternal, but mundane material life is transient. He must train himself to abandon his attachment to material things and to escape from ignorance (無明). Only then can he achieve Buddhahood and practice mercy. Communists attack these ideas, saying the cause of evil is not man's ignorance, but the class contradictions in society, and that Buddhism is an escape from reality. Buddhists cannot overcome such criticisms.

B. THE ESTABLISHMENT OF A NEW VIEW OF VALUE

The crisis of traditional views of value cannot be resolved with a relative view of value. If a new view of value is to revive and unite these traditional views—thus resolving the confusion of today's society—it must be absolute. An absolute view of value should be based on absolute love, as stated above.

The main point of the teachings of all religions is the practice of love. The virtues of Christianity are based on love; the virtues of Confucianism are based on benevolence; and the virtues of Buddhism are based on mercy. Here, "benevolence" in Confucianism and "mercy" in Buddhism can be looked upon as corresponding to "love" in Christianity, even though they are not completely identical; they can, therefore, be included in the concept of love. Nevertheless, if the origin of love is not clarified, love cannot have absoluteness. In other words, the existence of the absolute God should be confirmed, in order to prove the existence of absolute love.

Jesus taught us God's love, but he did not teach us clearly how God's love is to be realized on earth or why God created man and the universe. In fact, he said, "I have yet many things to say to you, but you cannot bear them now." (John 16:25) In other words, Jesus did not make clear the Purpose of Creation, and neither did Saints Augustine and Thomas Aquinas clarify these matters. Christianity, therefore, was unable to answer questions, such as why is God the creator? Why is God love? Why should we love one another? This is a weak point not only in Christianity but also in other religions, and atheists could easily attack this point. Feuerbach, for example—as I have explained in "Theory of the Original Image"—asserted that

God did not create man, but man created God. He said man objectified his essence of genius—such as love, reason, and will—and called it God. Even if God is omnipotent and omniscient, there is no reason for God to create, since He can remain silent if He chooses to do so. Such atheistic assertions were possible only because the reason why God created man and the universe—the Purpose of Creation—had not been made clear; in other words, the necessary relationship between God and creation had not been clearly explained.

Unification Thought explains that God's most essential attribute is Heart—that is, the emotional impulse to seek joy through love. This impulse is difficult to restrain. We can understand the existence of such an impulse through our daily experiences: whether man or woman, young or old, and regardless of occupation, every person lives and works for joy. This means that man has an unrestrainable impulse to seek joy. Furthermore, there must be an object before the subject is able to love and become joyful. In other words, the subject can be joyful only when he has an object of love. Accordingly, God's impulse to seek joy cannot but become the impulse to create objects of love. God could not remain silent; He could not but create man and creation for His joy. Through understanding God in this way, we can perceive more clearly the reason for saying that God is love and that God's love is absolute. Man is created in the direct image of God; originally, he has a quality of love that resembles that of God's love. Accordingly, man should love his neighbors.

Traditional views of value, as well as the virtues connected with them, are becoming powerless to motivate modern man. They are actually quite vague; besides, they seem to have nothing to do with one another. Unification Principle, however, has clarified God's Heart, the basis for a view of value that can embrace and unify all the traditional views of value. This implies that the Unification Principle can protect Christianity, Confucianism, Buddhism, and so on, from the attacks of atheists, and at the same time, give new life to these traditional religions.

Theological, philosophical, and historical foundations should be established for setting up this new view of value. To establish the theological foundation means to explain the Heart of God and the Purpose of Creation, making it clear that all traditional views of value, or virtues, come from God's love, and were intended directly or indirectly, as a means to realize the Purpose of Creation.

To establish the philosophical foundation means to apply the law of creation (the cosmic law, or Heavenly Way) to human life, in order to prove that all human virtues are no more than the application of the cosmic law to human conduct. In other words, the very cosmic law is the standard of the view of value of human life. This foundation has already been explained in Ontology.

To establish the historical foundation means to demonstrate that the Heavenly Way has been in operation throughout history. Mencius (孟子) said that he who obeys the Heavenly Way prospers, but he who disobeys it perishes. Men of power have often persecuted religions, through which God's providence has been carried out; the powerful have passed, but the persecuted religions have remained until today. Numerous righteous men and saints have been persecuted and martyred by men of powerful position, but their teachings and deeds have remained for posterity, while their powerful persecutors have perished. This proves the operation of the Heavenly Way in history—in other words, the absoluteness of the Heavenly Way. This will be the historical foundation for the view of value. This foundation is explained in the Principle of Restoration in the Unification Principle and will be discussed in Chapter Ten, "Theory of History."

The Unification view of value has such foundations. It is our hope that, through this new view of value, traditional views of value may be reinvigorated and unified.

7 THEORY OF EDUCATION

Why do we need a new theory of Education? First, we must prepare ourselves for the future world, which is a world of sincerity, without falsehood or hypocrisy. Second, we must save today's education from its present state of confusion. Since there is no such thing as an established ideal of education, a large number of teachers and educators today have lost their sense of direction in their educational activities. To an alarming degree, the duties of teachers and students are being neglected, and the dignity of teachers has deteriorated. Numerous schools have become a kind of market place for selling and buying knowledge and technique; universities are sometimes made into hotbeds for riots and political demonstrations. Moreover, existing theories of education have not availed against such problems. Third, we must overcome the communist theory of education. Communists—especially Lenin—look upon education in democratic society as bourgeois education, favoring a policy of obscurantism, while teachers in democratic society work only for the sake of the bourgeoisie. Lenin said that schools in capitalist society are no more than tools in the hands of the ruling class. In communist societies, they say, education should be a tool for the proletariat. Unless we can prevail over such ideas, it will be difficult to establish the original society we hope to see.

I. FUNDAMENTALS OF EDUCATION

Two basic points make up the fundamentals of the Unification theory of education. First, God created everything to resemble Him; it was a creation of resemblance, or similarity. Second, a certain period of time is necessary for the growth of created beings.

As explained in "Theory of the Original Human Nature," man was created resembling God directly—i.e., resembling God's Divine Image and Divine Character. The Divine Image is *Sung Sang* and *Hyung Sang*, Positivity and Negativity, and Individual Image; the Divine Character is Heart, Creativity, and Logos. In God, *Sung Sang* and *Hyung Sang* are engaged in harmonious give-and-take action centering on Heart. Man's *Sung Sang* (spirit-mind) and *Hyung Sang* (physical mind) should enter into give-and-take action centered on Heart, to form a perfect union. Man should resemble the perfection of God. Jesus said, "You, therefore, must be perfect, as your heavenly Father is perfect." (Matt. 5:48) Man's spirit-mind strives for spiritual value, whereas his physical mind is concerned with physical life. As the spirit-mind is in the subjective position, man should strive primarily for the perfection of his character through spiritual value.

Second, man should exhibit God's multiplication, which is the harmonious union of positivity and negativity. Just as Adam and Eve were created as the result of this harmonious union, centering on Heart; husband and wife should similarly unite and bear children, forming a family filled with love.

Finally, man must resemble God's nature of dominion, or His Creativity. God created man and all things with love and intended to dominate them with love. Man, in turn, has been given creativity by God so that he, also, can create and dominate things with love. Man dominates things through manifesting his creativity.

To dominate does not mean merely to manage or control; it implies the use of creativity, which can be applied in a large number of ways. Farmers, for instance, cultivate their crops creatively, thinking up new ideas to increase the productivity of their fields. This is dominion over land. In factories, workers use machines to convert raw materials into different products. This is dominion over material and machines. In commerce, one cannot prosper without new and creative ideas. Fishermen exercise dominion over the sea; lumberjacks, over mountains and trees. In short, farming, manufacturing, commerce, fishing, forestry, and so forth, are manifestations of dominion, and each one of them requires creativity.

Thus, to resemble God is to resemble His perfection, His multiplication, and His nature of dominion. In other words, it is to resemble the give-and-take action between His *Sung Sang* and

Hyung Sang and that between His Positivity and Negativity. It is also to resemble His Creativity.

Positivity and negativity do not function independently of Logos (reason-law). Accordingly, the give-and-take action between husband and wife, must, likewise, be based on Logos. In other words, their principled responsibility, either as a husband or as a wife, is determined by Logos, or reason-law.

The unity of man and woman is not merely biological; it is the unity of Logos. Resembling God's multiplication, therefore, refers to resembling not only His harmony of Positivity and Negativity, but also His Logos. That man has been created to resemble God does not mean that he does so completely at the moment of birth; he must first grow up to be an adult. In order to grow, he needs a certain period of time. If man were not corporeal, conceivably he might resemble God immediately upon being created; but he does have a physical body and is subject to the restrictions of time and space.

A flower does not suddenly bloom soon after the seed is sown; it needs time, as well as water and fertilizer. After spring and summer have passed, and autumn comes, the flower we have been waiting for finally appears.

Likewise, even if God longs for the appearance of a man who is a substantial object fully resembling Him, such an individual cannot appear immediately. He needs to grow first. In order to become perfect, he must grow through the three stages of formation, growth, and completion. Through the growth process, he comes to resemble God's character completely—that is, His level of Heart, His Logos, and His Creativity. Only when this is achieved will God feel true joy through man, for the first time.

The giving of the three blessings (to be fruitful and multiply... and have dominion: Gen. 1:28) actually means the direction to grow and become like God. The promise of the second blessing (to multiply), for example, does not mean that someone can marry immediately. Through this promise, God encourages man to grow, that he might marry, reaching the stage of individual perfection. The giving of the three great blessings was, in fact, the promise of the three blessings; in order actually to receive them, man had to grow first.

God created man and gave him these commandments. Because God's commandment is absolute, these commandments are still valid today, even though man has fallen. Consequently, man has tried— consciously or unconsciously—to grow spiritually, to relate to the opposite sex, and to dominate the creation.

One of man's desires, for instance, is to grow through acquiring knowledge. As a result, he goes to elementary school, junior high school, senior high school, and the university. By contrast, animals have no such desire. They do not wish to grow by learning, but merely live according to the *autonomy of the principle,* or according to instinct. All that is needed for their growth is sufficiency in external conditions and opportunity, such as availability of food. No significant novelty may be required, from generation to generation.

Why does man try to learn and experience a great variety of things? It is because God originally commanded him to grow, and thus become perfect, to multiply and to dominate all the creation; and these commandments are still valid. Deep down in his subconsciousness, man has the desire to follow these commandments.

Without desire, the three blessings cannot be realized; so God gave man desire, in order for him to attain the blessings. Desire itself is not evil; it is evil only when its direction is wrong. The desire to accomplish the three great blessings of God is good. This is why man somehow always seeks to realize the three great blessings.

He wishes to grow in personality, through acquiring knowledge, experiencing beauty, doing goodness, giving love, etc. He wishes to form a good family by marrying a good partner and by having good children. He wishes to dominate all the creation and to relate to other persons.

Even if he tried, man could never suppress these desires, because the commandments given by God for the fulfillment of the three great blessings are still valid. We call these absolute orders the supreme commandments.

Man has to grow by accomplishing his own portion of responsibility. His body grows naturally through the *autonomy and dominion of the principle;* here, all he needs is heat, air, food, water, and exercise. But when God ordered man to "be fruitful," He was referring, not to the growth of the physical man, but to that of the spirit-man. In order for the spirit-man to grow, man's spirit-mind must make a reciprocal relationship with his physical mind, centering on heart, thus resembling the harmonious give-and-take action of the *Sung Sang* and *Hyung Sang* of God. In order to accomplish this, man's heart should resemble God's Heart. The growth of the spirit-man refers, not to its increase in height or size, but to its ripening.

An apple, for instance, is green and sour before it ripens. Since man fell, he has been like an unripened apple, even though his physical man becomes adult. If he had not fallen, he would have fully matured when he became adult. Fallen man, however, grows only physically; he does not become ripe in personality or spirit; neither does his heart resemble God's Heart.

The English translation of the Bible says that God told man to 'be fruitful'. To be fruitful means to ripen and to bear fruit. In the Japanese translation, man is told to 'multiply', but I think that this is not the original meaning. The Korean translation uses the word 'grow', and I think this is more correct. The word 'fruitful' implies also 'multiply' or 'produce much', but in the English version, 'be fruitful' is immediately followed by 'and multiply'. I think this means that 'be fruitful' should be interpreted as 'bear fruit', or 'ripen'. It actually means that one's personality, or spirit-man, should mature. It is impossible for a personality to become perfect merely through the autonomy of the principle. Even if one's body becomes bigger, one's spiritual state does not mature only through autonomy. In order for personality growth to take place, man must fulfill his portion of responsibility, given to him by God.

Man's portion of responsibility means that he must make effort with creativity, freely using his own wisdom and will; it is man's portion of responsibility to judge, decide, plan, and act by himself. Even if he is tempted by Satan, he must overcome the temptation. Because of fallen nature, however, temptation tends to return again and again, for Satan persistently tempts man. In order always to reject temptation, fallen man must grow through steadfast faith and a deep yearning for God.

Although God cannot intervene in man's portion of responsibility, He encourages man to fulfill it. In the case of Moses, for example, when he had to endure hardships over a long period of time, God granted the Israelites the gift of manna and quail. In the same way, if we overcome trials when we are growing, God will grant us similar gifts, as long as that does not interfere with our portion of responsibility. God intended to bless Adam and Eve when they had grown, but for that to have happened, they had to fufill their own portion of responsibility. Adam and Eve could not have had their portion of responsibility lightened or reduced in any way.

Does this mean that the children of Adam and Eve would have had to fulfill a portion of responsibility as great as that of their parents? No, it does not. Children do not need to be troubled to the same extent by the trials and temptations their parents had to overcome. And if temptations come, they need only ask their parents what to do, and then follow their instructions. By obeying the directions and teachings of their parents, they can grow. Originally, then, the children's portion of responsibility is chiefly to obey their parents.

What I have said is not only true for the first Adam, but also for the second Adam and the third Adam. The disciples who followed Jesus (the second Adam) did not have to suffer in the same way as he did. If they had obediently followed Jesus' commandments, all their burdens of indemnity would have been reduced by his prayer and efforts. They would have grown simply by passing through mild suffering.

The third Adam, the Lord of the Second Advent, must indemnify heavy burdens of six thousand years of fallen history, so he has to suffer greatly. His followers, however, have only to obey his directions obediently to be restored to the original *principled* state.

The growth of Adam and Eve, mankind's ancestors, represented not only their own growth, but also that of all mankind, their descendants. If Adam and Eve had completed their growth, thus becoming perfect, they would have shown that all mankind could be perfect. In other words, their perfection would have been an assurance of the possibility of their descendants' perfection. The children of Adam and Eve would have naturally become perfect by obeying their parents.

It is here that the matter of parental guidance, instruction, and supervision of children arises, as well as the need for children to obey their parents. The parents' guidance of their children is what is actually meant by the word "education." Children cannot carry out their portion of responsibility unless they are guided. Education is the pre-condition for children to accomplish their portion of responsibility. Here lies the starting point of Unification Education.

In general, education is carried out in school, because the diversification and greater complexity of human life have specialized the contents of education. In other words, parental guidance and instruction have been partly entrusted to school teachers, owing to the greater complexity of the contents of what needs to be taught. School education, therefore is essentially a specialized form of family education. Thus, the position of teachers is essentially equivalent to that of parents.

II. METHOD OF EDUCATION

The basis of our theory of education is man's resemblance to God and the existence of a period of growth. To resemble God fully means to resemble His perfection, multiplication, and dominion. First, we should resemble God's perfection by perfecting our individuality. Second, we should resemble the multiplication of God by qualifying ourselves to live as a couple and form a harmonious family. Third, we should resemble the dominion of God by perfecting our ability to dominate all things. These three qualifications correspond to the three great blessings.

Having mentioned the above, we can now have a clearer understanding of the idea of Unification Education. First, the idea of education for the perfection of individuality—the first blessing—is to educate children so that they may perfect themselves as individuals. Furthermore, the idea of education for the multiplication of children—the second blessing—is to educate children so that they may have the ability to establish a perfect family, in which parental love, conjugal love, and children's love are fully realized. Finally, the idea of education for the dominion over all things—the third blessing—is to educate children so that they may come to love each other and dominate all things with God's love.

What kind of educational methods are we going to employ to reach these fundamental goals? For the perfection of individuality, the education of heart is necessary; for the perfection of the family, the education of norm, (or the education of standards of conduct) is necessary; and for the perfection of dominion, the education of dominion (or the education of abilities for dominion) is necessary. I would like to explain these points one by one.

A. THE EDUCATION OF HEART

The education of heart must produce men of personality, who love persons and things as God loves them. One cannot be such a person unless one's heart fully resembles God's Heart. This means that children and students must be guided to experience the Heart of God.

The concept of God's Heart must first be demonstrated theoretically and then shown in practice. This kind of education can best be carried out by parents who themselves have grown up and fulfilled their portion of responsibility. Ideally, the teacher should be a "husband-and-wife" team, because God's Heart can best be expressed through their unity.

Because of practical problems, however, such a situation is rare; conditions are far from being ideal. Nevertheless the teacher's responsibility remains to teach his or her children (pupils) the Heart of God as a parent. He or she must convey the Heart of God as it is expressed in the following three historical situations: during the creation, at the Fall of man, and during the providence of restoration.

Before He created His children (Adam and Eve), God spent a long time creating the universe. During that time, He was not at all troubled, for He knew that in the end His substantial objects of joy—that is, man and woman—would appear. Time spent in hope and expectation seems to pass quickly.

Finally, Adam and Eve were created. God's joy at that time must have been beyond all description. If a man were in God's position, he would have danced and sung with exhilarating joy. God's joy must have been a thousand times—ten thousand times—greater; it was the joy from the fulfillment of His long-cherished hope and expectation. The Heart during the creation, therefore, can be called "the Heart of expectation."

But Adam and Eve fell—that is, died spiritually. The Heart of God at that time became the very opposite of joy. When betrayed, infinite joy turns into infinite sorrow. God's sorrow was a thousand times—ten thousand times—greater than the sorrow a man feels at the loss of a loved one. We can say, therefore, that the Heart at the Fall of man is "the Heart of grief and sorrow."

Parents feel pain-stricken when they lose a child. Even if the child's death may have been expected—because of terminal illness, for instance— still their sorrow is beyond description. In these cases, some parents just won't give up hope that the child may recover. When the child actually dies, they feel immense sorrow, in spite of having had plenty of warning beforehand.

God's sorrow at the time of Jesus' death on the cross was indescribable. It was the second time God had felt such sorrow, during the course of human history. When the Messiah comes again, the same thing will happen. Although the Third Adam will not die without accomplishing his mission, nonetheless he will receive an incredible amount of persecution—and this will be yet another reason for God to feel grief and sorrow.

God could have created a new Adam and Eve if He had wished, since He is omniscient and omnipotent; but if He had done so, abandoning Adam and Eve, everything He had done before would have become meaningless; He would have lost His dignity and contradicted His own principles. For this reason, God has worked to restore fallen man. But it has been a very painful path. He has continuously suffered throughout all six thousand years of human history—a piteous God. The Heart of God during the providence of restoration, therefore, can be called "the Heart of pain and suffering."

In Adam's family, God watched with great expectation as Cain and Abel made their offerings. But Cain and Abel were unable to fulfill their portion of responsibility. God's Heart was shattered, and He had to leave them, lonesomely and tragically. He had to surrender Adam's family to the claims of Satan, and had no one with whom to walk the course of restoration. God has been searching for a co-worker on earth ever since. The world that God had created with so much expectation became Satan's possession. Everyone turned their backs on Him. There was not one house in which He could abide; not one square foot of land upon which He could stand; not one heart He could enter. Rejected like a beggar, God searched for a co-worker.

Finally, He found Noah. God's joy at that moment was intense. To His regret, however, right away He had to give a very strict order to Noah: to build an ark, under very difficult conditions. Noah accepted His commandment and built the ark over a period of one hundred and twenty years, keeping steadfast faith in God and overcoming numerous hardships. God walked with Noah every step of the way and suffered together with him.

God is a God of Heart; He can never remain aloof in heaven, looking down indifferently while men suffer on earth. Christianity has generally emphasized the transcendence of God, yet God's pain because of man's suffering is greater than the suffering man himself has experienced.

Though, strictly speaking, Noah did not have the qualification of son of God, he was, nevertheless, God's servant—a righteous man who had devoted everything to God. God suffered in the position of a servant together with Noah; what a miserable and pitiable existence! When Ham, Noah's second son failed to fulfill his portion of responsibility, God was put in the position of having to hand over Noah's family to Satan. With tearful, heart-rending sadness, He had to leave Noah's family.

Four hundred years later God found Abraham. The most serious moment in Abraham's course was when he offered Isaac, his only son—born when Abraham was a hundred years old—as a sacrifice. Abraham's heart felt incredible pain, as he struggled about whether to let the boy live, in accordance with human ethics, or whether to offer him, as God's providence had demanded. He would probably have preferred to offer himself instead, but finally he made up his mind to obey God's command. His journey toward the mountain in Moriah, where the sacrifice was to take place, must not have been an easy one. The three-day journey must have seemed like thirty days. At that time, also, God was not just observing from a distance; it grieved Him to see such a righteous man suffer because of His stern command.

Abraham's decision to sacrifice his beloved son established the same condition as if he had actually done it. As a result, God stopped him from killing Isaac and gave him a ram to sacrifice instead. As the God of love, He suffered even more than Abraham.

God walked in the same way with Jacob, with Moses, and with Jesus. The sight of Jesus on the cross was too much for God to bear. He could not watch, nor could he liberate His beloved and only son. How painful! He felt as if He had been pierced with hundreds of nails.

During the past two thousand years, God has suffered along with all the numerous martyrs. At the Second Advent, the Lord's course will be even more miserable, and God's pain even greater.

Teaching children God's painful and suffering Heart during the providence of restoration can be done in a variety of ways: through words, through pictures, through audio-visual aids, etc. It can be taught also by presenting a serious expression, by shedding tears, and by introducing the biographies of famous persons that were loyal to Heaven. The time will come when the education of heart will be carried out through the mass media—television, radio, newspapers, magazines, etc. Surely, this age will witness the emergence of men and women of personality, who can truly express the Heart of God.

B. THE EDUCATION OF NORM

The relationship between husband and wife is by no means a mere biological union of a man and a woman. Men and women are the substantial objects of God, created by Logos; their union is the harmony of positivity and negativity based on Logos (reason-law). There are certain norms, therefore, that a man must observe in his conduct as a man, and a woman must observe in her conduct as a woman; in addition, there are norms for the perfection of the family. Everyone must learn these norms from early childhood and must incorporate them in their conduct, in order for love to be realized.

The *education of norm*—also referred to as the education of standards of conduct—starts at home, practically as soon as a child is born. A child must be taught certain manners and customs, first at home, then both at home and in school. When a man fully understands and practices the *principled duty* of a man, and a woman fully understands and practices the *principled duty* of a woman, the *education of norm* has been completed.

The norms for individual conduct are called morality; these include honesty, righteousness, temperance, self-control, endurance, and so on. As a member of a family, the person must likewise keep certain standards. These are filial piety toward one's parents, conjugal love, parental love for children, and love among siblings. Taken together, these standards, or norms, are called "Ethics." When an individual has come fully to embody the norms of ethical conduct within a family, he will be able to maintain the same standard of conduct in carrying out whatever responsibility he may be given in society.

At the base of ethical conduct, however, there must be the practice of love, for without love norms are nothing but rules and regulations that one can easily ignore. This explains why injustice, corruption, and scandal often plague fallen society.

Those who have received a complete *education of norm* and

fully embody the ethical norms learned at home and in school could never become unjust or corrupt. Morever, when they are ready to settle down as a husband or a wife, they will make a wonderful family.

C. THE EDUCATION OF DOMINION

The *education of dominion*, which means the education of abilities for dominion, is necessary for perfecting man's creativity and dominion. Creativity refers to the ability to make new things and to develop new ideas; dominion refers to the ability of the subject to dominate* the object (whether it be a thing or a human being). These two abilities are like the two sides of a coin.

Man is naturally endowed with dominion and creativity; yet, in order to develop them, he needs to practice and make effort. A potential musical genius, for instance, cannot develop unless he is taught how to play his instrument or how to sing and spends countless hours practicing. Only through developing his intellectual abilities and technical skills will he be able to express his creativity fully. This is an instance of what is meant by *education of dominion*.

In order for man to perfect his dominion and creativity, he needs also to be in good health and in good physical fitness. Accordingly, he must receive physical education through gymnastics, sports, etc. The *education of dominion*, therefore, comprises three general areas: intellectual education, technical education, and physical education.

Only when accompanied by *education of heart* and *education of norm* can the *education of dominion* be perfected. Today, however, the *education of heart* and of *norm* are sadly being neglected. Intellectual , technical, and physical education have developed greatly; moral and ethical education, however, are given very little attention; though officially part of educational curricula, they generally exist in name only and have become of little import.

Teaching a child technical skills without any *education of heart* or of *norm* is like giving him a sharp knife and not telling him what it should be used for. Though science has developed greatly, it has, nonetheless, been unable to solve problems such as pollution and

---

*In Unification Thought, 'to dominate' means 'to rule', 'to control', 'to deal with', and 'to love'.

the lack of resources. The reason is that science today is generally devoid of a system of values, since it has not been developed on the basis of heart and ethical norms.

In conclusion, the *education of heart, of norm* and of *dominion* must form a trinity; within such a structure, the *education of dominion* should be carried out on the foundation of the other two.

D. THE IDEAL IMAGE OF MAN

Because of the human Fall, numerous ways of thinking about man, or images of man, have appeared. In communist philosophy, for example, man is portrayed as a militant being, since the atheistic ideology of dialectical materialism is militant. Christianity, on the other hand, has its own characteristic way of looking at man, as does Buddhism, and so forth. In sum, the image of man changes according to the various religions and systems of thought.

Let us suppose for a moment that man did not fall. What kind of person would he be? In other words, what would be the ideal image of man if no Fall had occurred? According to Unification Thought, one can perceive the ideal image of man simply by applying the fundamentals of education described above.

The first aspect of the ideal image of man is that of a *man of personality*. As discussed above, personality is moulded by the education of heart. Ordinary society seems to lack a concrete definition of ideal personality. It is vaguely connected with knowledge, character, health, etc. In Unification Thought, however, the central element of personality is heart; in other words, an individual can be considered as a *man of personality* only to the extent that his heart resembles the Heart of God. Though important, intelligence and physical qualities are not enough to constitute a perfect personality. In fact, a person with only those characteristics, and lacking heart, would actually rank behind a handicapped, ailing, or non-intellectual individual with a high standard of heart. If a man receives education of heart, and his heart becomes fully united with the Heart of God, then he can be called a *man of personality*.

Another aspect of the ideal image of man is that of a *good citizen*. A citizen is a member of a state or nation, and the Heavenly Kingdom is really one nation. Good citizens are good family members and good members of society; moreover, they love their country.

They have been educated to live according to ethical norms and can faithfully fulfill any responsibility assigned to them in society.

The final major aspect of the ideal image of man is that of *genius*. This aspect is based on the education of dominion, described above, by which man can develop his creativity. Man is given creativity by Heaven, from birth; in fact, 'genius' (天才 in Chinese characters), means 'Heavenly talent'. If someone develops his creativity to the full, he may be called a *genius*. Though some people are born crippled or intellectually handicapped, everyone, nonetheless, has the capacity to become a *genius*, because, originally, everyone is given boundless creativity.

Everyone is endowed with his or her own individual creativity or talents. Some people have musical talents, others, mathematical creativity; some have political ability, others, business management ability. If you develop your creativity, you, too, can become a *genius:* a musical genius, a mathematical genius, a political genius, or a genius in whatever field suits your individuality. Fallen man, however, cannot develop his creativity to the full. He is inhibited due to a deficiency in, or a total absence of, his education of heart and of norm.

Let us suppose there is a child with a talent for music. He is sent to music school and practices very hard playing the piano. At home, however, his parents do not get along well and are constantly scolding him. His home atmosphere is confused, and he is confused, too. At school, his heart is troubled and scarred; he cannot practice well; when he plays the piano, his fingers just won't move as he wishes, and he feels discouraged. Certainly, he has creative talents, yet he cannot become a *genius*, because his situation does not allow him to develop to the full.

If the education of dominion were based upon the education of heart—in other words, if it were carried out in an atmosphere of love—children would always be able to learn with satisfaction and joy, thus developing their creative talents. In reality, only one in a hundred or in a thousand individuals approaches the level of a true *genius*, while the rest have just an average ability, or even less. This is the situation in fallen society.

If any one of the three types of education is missing, a *genius* cannot appear; we need all three types. Whoever receives them becomes a *man of personality,* a *good citizen,* and a *genius*. This is the ideal image of a man who has been properly educated according to the three types of education.

When people are perfected through these three types of education, they will be blessed in marriage by God. In fact, the theory of education I have been describing—derived from the Unification Principle and the teachings of the Reverend Sun Myung Moon—could be succinctly described as a method for educating people so as to enable them to realize the three great blessings and to come to resemble God.

E. THE GOAL OF EDUCATION

In a nutshell, the goal of education is to unite people's heart, thought, and action. Because of the Fall, man's heart lost its direction, and people have largely become self-centered. Though there is heart and love in fallen society, yet their manifestation has become extremely limited, often taking contradictory directions. The different directions of people's hearts have given rise to the different directions in their thoughts, actions, and way of life. Conflict and confusion have been the inevitable result. People seek gain for their own country, at the expense of other countries, and self-gain, at the expense of others. In such a world, true peace can never be realized.

In order to realize true peace, we must turn our hearts, our thoughts, and our actions in one direction, with one goal—God. Individuals, families, societies, races, and nations all must turn to God. The unity of our hearts, thoughts, and actions will then be realized. The world will progress in one direction.

When people all over the world give their children this kind of education, their hearts, thoughts, and actions will be united with God. Mankind will become one family—brothers and sisters serving the same God, and realizing an eternal worldwide peace. The aim of Unification Education is to create such a world.

F. UNITY AND INDIVIDUALITY IN EDUCATION

In Unification Pedagogics, the education of heart and the education of norm constitute the foundation of education. These aspects of education, therefore, will be carried out transcending nation, race, occupation, etc. The education of dominion consists of intellectual education, technical education, and physical education. Students may choose from among the numerous areas of studies, according to their individuality and temperament. Some will choose politics; others, economics; others, natural science, etc. From the standpoint of Unification Thought, however, politics, economics, natural science, law, art, medicine, etc., are all within the realm of the education of dominion. The education of heart and of norm can be called *education of unity*, whereas the education of dominion can be called *education of individuality*. On the basis of the education of heart and of norm, unity of heart, unity of thought, and unity of action—the three elements of the Unification of cultures—can be expected.

8 ETHICS

As explained in "Axiology," the society we hope to build in the future will be a sincere, ethical, and artistic society. It will come about, not automatically, but with our effort, under God's guidance. The theory that will enable us to build the new ethical society is referred to as *New Ethics*.

In an ethical society, people will lead the *life of attendance* to God, centering on the True Parents of mankind. (See *Divine Principle*, part I, Ch. VII, Sec. IV, 2.) All aspects of social, cultural, and economic life will be based on the life of attendance, and all mankind will form a united family.

Another characteristic is that in the ethical society the spirit-world and the physical world will come closely to cooperate with each other, since man will become a mediator between the two worlds. Moreover, the ethical society is a society of eternal love. Love is the emotional impulse to give to others and to become united with them. In love there can be found eternal joy, eternal freshness, eternal longing, and eternal yearning. In order to bring about such a society, the existing views on ethics should be criticized and supplemented by a new theory of ethics.

I. UNIFICATION ETHICS
A. THE FOUNDATION OF UNIFICATION ETHICS

Unification Ethics is derived from the Unification Principle and other teachings of the Reverend Sun Myung Moon, as are other chapters of the present book. Its foundation includes four main points:

1) God is the God of Heart
2) God is the subject of love, trueness, goodness, and beauty
3) God's love is realized through a family quadruple base as

three kinds of *divisional love:* parental love, conjugal love, and children's love

4) Each position in the family quadruple base faces three objective positions.

With regard to the fourth point, each position can assume a subject-position, thus fulfilling the *three objective purposes.* The father, for example, has duties to the grandparents (who stand in the central position in the family quadruple base), to his wife, and to his children. The mother has duties to the grandparents, to her husband, and to her children. A child has duties to his grandparents, to his father, and to his mother. These are the three objective purposes.

B. ETHICS AND MORALITY

Ethics and morality are usually viewed as almost identical. The distinction Unification Thought makes is that ethics is the standard of conduct for family life, whereas morality is the internal standard of conduct for individual life. There are certain standards of conduct required of a man, whether he belongs to a company, plays sports, or in fact, whatever he may do and wherever he may happen to be. Man's standard of conduct for family life is called *ethics.*

Morality, on the other hand, is the standard of conduct for an individual based on his internal conscience, or *Sollen* ("ought"). Ontologically, man is both an individual truth body and a connected body.* The standard of conduct that man should observe as an individual truth body is morality; the standard of conduct he should observe as a connected body is ethics.

Morality is related to the fulfillment of the first blessing (perfection of personality) given to man by God; ethics is related to the fulfillment of the second blessing (perfection of the family). In the Unification Thought view, morality consists of the formation of the original human nature: the united body of *Sung Sang* and *Hyung Sang,* which is realized through the harmonious give-and-take action between spirit-mind and physical mind.

Traditionally, especially in ancient Greek philosophy, morality also has been considered as the attainment of inner harmony. For example, Plato's virtues of temperance, courage, wisdom, and justice

---

*Every being has a dual purpose and forms an internal quadruple base and an external quadruple base. Viewed as such, it is called a "connected body." (See "Ontology.")

are related to inner harmony, which is attained by controlling the irrational aspects with reason. Since I have already discussed the united body of *Sung Sang* and *Hyung Sang* in "Theory of Original Human Nature," I will not deal with morality here.

We should consider also the fulfillment of the third blessing—the perfection of dominion. The third blessing refers, not only to dominion over creation, but also to abilities such as statesmanship and business management. In the Unification Thought view, the standard of conduct necessary for realizing the third blessing is nothing but an extension and application of the standard of conduct in family life—i.e., ethics. When these ethical standards are applied to business, they become *business ethics;* when applied to a nation, they become *national ethics*. The same standards can be applied also to man's dominion over creation (especially parents' standard of conduct toward their children).

C. THE QUADRUPLE BASE AND ETHICS

The standard of conduct for a family represents a practical way to actualize love among family members. *Ethics* can be defined as a method of realizing love in a proper direction. A family is formed by the relationships of parents and children, and husband and wife. When parents love their children, when husband and wife love each other, and when children love their parents, their conduct cannot but be an expression of love. Here, the parents will express love to their children even while scolding them.

A family is where man can actualize the love of God. In order to resemble God, people must love one another. In God, *Sung Sang* and *Hyung Sang* as well as Positivity and Negativity maintain harmonious give-and-take action centering on Heart. The nature of God is harmony; those who want to resemble God must enter into harmonious give-and-take action with one another, thus actualizing love. Within such a family, God can find true joy.

As already mentioned, God is absolute and without form, while man lives in time and space and needs, therefore, to grow in order to actualize God's love. The kind of love man experiences in a family changes as he grows. When young, a man actualizes love from the position of a child; this is *children's love*. The love he actualizes when he grows up and marries is *conjugal love;* when he becomes a parent, he actualizes *parental love*. Children's, conjugal, and parental love are the three basic forms of love. These, however, can be further subdivided into father's love, mother's love, elder brother's love, younger brother's love, elder sister's love, younger sister's love, and so forth. Each type differs from the others. Even a child's love toward his parents, as well as the parents' love toward their child, changes in nature as the child grows through the various stages of life from infancy to adulthood, and also as the parents themselves grow. Conjugal love, also, changes, as husband and wife grow.

While on earth, all of us should experience these kinds of love through family life. Otherwise, we will never be able to feel true joy in the spirit world. If someone has actually experienced God's love totally on the earth, he will be able to enjoy a life of love eternally in the spirit-world. Without such experiences, however, he will not be able to understand why other people are so happy loving each other; he will always feel lonely in the spirit-world.

The Unification Principle says that the spirit-man grows in the "soil" of the physical man. Spiritual development, therefore, can only take place on the foundation of the physical body. Accordingly, while he still has his physical body, man needs to love other persons and God by actualizing love within the family. Through realizing love, his spirit-man will grow, and he will attain eternal joy. Since no one on earth has ever fully achieved such a standard of love, no one has actually been totally happy in the spirit-world. Accordingly, spirit-men tend to remain earth-bound, seeking to attain vicarious experiences of these kinds of love through people living on earth.

In the fallen world, also, there are parental love, conjugal love, and children's love, but in general, they are not based on God's love. In other words, they are not the three basic kinds of divisional love that God intended to be manifested in the family. If parental love had manifested God's love, it would have been several times—tens of times—broader and deeper than the parental love we know in the world today. The same can be said of conjugal and children's love.

But for the human Fall, we would certainly have experienced these kinds of love on earth and in Heaven. In that case, no man could have ever fallen, because the God-centered divisional love is supreme, and no other love would have been able to break up the relationships based upon it. Fallen man, however, has never been able to build such families; accordingly, people are easily drawn to anyone who loves them.

Each divisional love has its own direction. Parental love is directed downwards toward the children; children's love is directed upwards toward the parents; conjugal love has a horizontal direction. Love should not remain only in the mind, but should be expressed in real actions. When parents love their children, for example, they express their love through concrete actions, such as providing food, clothing, shelter, and education.

Each type of love needs a different form of expression. Parents need to use warm-hearted words to their children, even when scolding them; if scolded lovingly, children will not be damaged in any way. On the other hand, children should be polite and respectful toward their parents. They should not say, for instance, "Hurry up, Father! Sit down here and eat!" This would be impolite, however dutiful the child might be. There must be a certain standard of conduct, and the child should be more polite, using such words as, "Father, please come here and have something to eat." There are different positions at the table. A child should not sit at the head of the table and say, "Hey, Father, look sharp and sit down!" because he would be reversing the father-child position. It is important that children respect their parents and use suitable words and actions to show their respect. Husband and wife, also, must follow a certain standard of conduct in their mutual relationship.

Thus, there are rules to be followed in each position, but they are not hard to follow since they are based on love. Actually, it is a joy to follow these rules. When a child wants to make his parents happy but doesn't know how, he will gladly try to find out how to do it. Standards (norms) of conduct, therefore, do not restrict man's freedom at all.

Since there is little heart or love in the fallen world, people feel restricted when they have to act according to duty. When the standard of conduct is based on love, there is no such feeling of restriction. When parents tell their children to do something, the children will be happy to obey, because they know how deep their parents' love is.

To those educated in this way it will become second nature—almost like a reflex action—to observe the standards of conduct, not only in the family, but also in school, at work, or even in executing the laws of a nation. When in the spirit world, such persons will easily keep the heavenly laws and standards. Indeed, if one becomes accustomed to keeping family standards, one can easily keep the proper standards wherever one may go.

The ideal family represents the fulfillment of God's ideal for the creation and the place where His love is realized. Family ethics are the foundation for all ethics, such as business and national ethics. The numerous labor problems in capitalist society, for example, can be solved, if family ethics are applied to the economic world. The relationship between the president of a firm, for instance, and his employees should be like that between a parent and his children; the relationships among workers, like those among brothers and sisters.

The idea that the president of a business organization should reap most of the profit is wrong. In order to create a family-like atmosphere, the president must have the heart of a parent. Parents exist for the whole family and want their children to earn money as well. The president should think of his employees as his own children or his own brothers and sisters, taking responsibility for them as if they were members of his family. His attitude should be that he is earning money, not primarily for himself, but for them.

There will be no need, then, for employees to strike in order to take money away from the president. They will try to cooperate with him, as if he were their parent or older brother, assisting him in the development of the company. In this way, they will really have something to live and work for. They may even say, "I have enough to eat, you don't need to give me a big salary." The president, however, may say in reply, "No! With prices as high as they are, your salary can't be enough. You need more money to take care of your family." As the president and employees enter into a close give-and-take relationship, the company prospers.

If this ethical system is expanded to the national level, it means that the President or Prime Minister of a nation will love the people as if they were members of his own family, thinking of them whether awake or asleep. As the people respect and support him as a parent, a harmonious atmosphere is created, and the nation develops.

D. ETHICS, ORDER, AND THE HEAVENLY WAY
1. Ethics and Order

Love has different directions, depending upon the relative positions of the subject and the object within the family quadruple base. Without position and order, there is no direction, and love cannot be expressed. Ethical standards, therefore, deal with the order of love. Accordingly, ethics can be briefly defined as the establishment of order.

The main cause of today's collapse of traditional views of value comes from the restlessness and collapse of order in the world. The starting point of the collapse of order in the world lies in the family. The order between parents and children, husband and wife, older brother or sister and younger brother or sister has become neglected, and all members of the family have become leveled horizontally.

The collapse of the order of love is closely connected with today's disorder in sexual love. Sexual love should be for the realization of God's second blessing—the establishment of a family centered on God's love—but today many people have no such idea. In addition, mass communication scatters sexual stimulation and promotes immorality and free sex. The collapse of the order of sexual love necessarily leads to the collapse of order in the family, society, and world.

The disorder of sexual love originates from the Fall of the first human ancestors, Adam and Eve, as revealed by the Unification Principle. Accordingly, the Fall of man is the original cause of confusion in the world. God has sent saints to restore order in the family, society, nation, and world by establishing religions. Today, however, people are deviating from these various kinds of order, under the name of liberalism, democracy, and so forth. Accordingly, there is an urgent need to establish *New Ethics*, which is the ethics of order and, at the same time, of love.

2. Ethics and the Heavenly Way

The family system is a microcosm, or an integration of the whole universe. The ethical standard within the family, therefore, can be looked upon as the contracted, or integrated cosmic law. In other words, ethics is the cosmic law, or the Heavenly Way.

Accordingly, there are both vertical and horizontal kinds of order in the family, as there are in the cosmos. The relationships among grandparents, parents, children, and grandchildren are the vertical order; and the relationships between husband and wife, older brother or sister and younger brother or sister are the horizontal order. There must be standards of conduct suitable to each of these kinds of order. They correspond to the vertical view of value and the horizontal view of value, as explained in "Ontology."

E. ORDER AND EQUALITY

The concepts of *order* and *equality* are often thought of as antinomic, so that if order is brought into force, equality suffers, and vice versa. It is argued that order—even for the purpose of ending confusion—will necessarily destroy equality. In communist societies, order is comparatively well established, but human nature and individuality have generally been trampled on; no true equality can be found there. In democratic societies, equality and freedom are highly prized; on the other hand, confusion abounds. Looking at the world today, therefore, it does seem that when order comes to the fore, equality suffers; and when equality is given priority, order is brushed aside.

We need to reconsider the meaning of equality. The French Revolution and the American War of Independence were fought to gain democracy; democratic systems have been maintained until today in the hope of realizing equality. True equality, nonetheless, has never been realized in democratic societies.

Democracy in ancient Greece meant democracy for the ruling class; slaves had few rights as human beings. Even today, the law provides only nominal equality. All adults have the right to vote, for example, but this right is exploited by the wealthy and influential. True equality is not bought with money or controlled by power. The communists accuse capitalist societies, saying, "Equality and freedom for whom? Freedom only for the rich and powerful? What kind of freedom or rights do workers enjoy?" There is some truth in these accusations.

There is no historical precedent for a truly democratic society. In spite of this, man has continued to strive for it. The concept of democracy is based on the principle of equality of rights, that people are born equal and that the nation is governed by the people. The American Declaration of Independence states that man is born equal before God. Man continues to strive for—but has yet to realize—true equality.

Although laws emphasize equality, I think there are few persons that will sincerely maintain that all people are actually equal. Biologists, psychologists, and sociologists tell us that all people are different from one another, physically—in build and constitution—and psychologically. Furthermore, we are different in age, sex, occupation, and rank, and in this sense there is no equality either.

We know that rights, being accompanied by duty, differ according to position, and there is no position without rights. Originally, equality as a democratic principle meant the equality of rights to protect one's life, wealth and freedom. But there is a problem here: who determines the compass of the rights of an individual? How is it determined? Obviously, determining the compass of exercising rights depends chiefly on the subjective views of each person. For instance: if "A" and "B" are two individuals, A may regard B's conduct as infringing on his fundamental rights; on the other hand, B may likewise regard A's conduct as infringing on his fundamental rights. By the same token, there may be overemphasis on human rights, resulting in conflict with authorities. Things get out of control, confusion results, and peace is impossible. So, the idea of equality of rights fundamentally contradicts itself, and the demand for equality of rights is impossible to realize.

Then, can equality ever be realized? Yes, it can. The desire for equality is from the original mind. What is the equality that the original mind desires? It is not the equality of rights that it actually wants, but the equality of love. Since man has been robbed of his rights for so long, he seeks to secure them, and is willing to fight or even die for them. Nevertheless, it would be a mistake to think that equality of rights is what man is really after. Undoubtedly he needs rights, yet the equality he seeks is, not of rights, but of love.

It is because there is no love that man has been oppressed, alienated, and ignored. If man is fully loved and loves fully, he has no reason to complain. In our original mind, we think, "I want to be understood and loved by my superiors; if I were, I would respect them." The subject should dominate the object with love, and the object should respect the subject who loves him. Because the subject has so often dominated, not with love, but with power or reason, the object has had reasons to complain.

Thus, what man wants is not actually equality of rights, but of love. Man suffers when he is alienated or ignored; he wants his individuality to be recognized and understood. He wants to be loved. Equality of love means equality of joy and satisfaction; when a man truly loves and is loved, he feels true joy. Though everyone is expected to maintain his own position, yet they feel joy and satisfaction in that particular position.

An older brother, for instance, has his own position; a younger brother has his; older and younger sisters have their own positions;

and the husband and wife have their positions as spouses and as parents. Everyone, however, should feel great joy in their respective positions. This is true equality, which means equality of satisfaction—not that everyone has the same position, but that everyone is fully satisfied in whatever position he or she may have.

The equality of love can be expressed as the equality of personality, because parents would value the personality of their children, and children, that of their parents. True equality, therefore, is equality of love, personality, joy, and happiness.

Love is expressed in a certain direction, which, in turn, presupposes position and order. Without order, therefore, there can be no equality of love. Thus, order and equality, which appeared to be antinomic, are actually inseparable from each other, because there is true equality in true order. The conclusion of Unification Ethics is that when true order is established, true equality will be realized.

Today's democratic societies are going in the wrong direction in their search for equal rights. Democracy should pursue the equality of love. The task to actualize true equality, however, cannot be left to politicians. In order to revive democracy and realize true equality, sincerely religious and ethical people should undertake the responsibility and appeal to people all over the world to love one another and practice love in their daily lives. Only in this way will true democracy be realized.

During the past two hundred years, democracy has spread all over the world, and it has made comparatively sound development. This is because it has been supported by the Christian spirit of love, which made up for various faults in democratic systems. Today, however, Christianity has almost lost its vitality, and its spirit of love has declined. Christianity has become paralyzed in its role of supporting democracy. Accordingly, democracy is beginning to show its essential contradictions. These contradictions have appeared because democracy has tried to realize equal rights, which can never be realized.

True ethics is both the ethics of order and that of love. When the Principles of family ethics are extended to a society and a nation, they will become social ethics and national ethics. Then true equality will be realized in a society and a nation. Thus, in Unification Thought the problem of order and equality is solved through love. True democracy is the democracy of love, which is the ideal of the heavenly family.

II. A CRITIQUE OF TRADITIONAL VIEWS OF GOODNESS
A. BENTHAM'S VIEW OF GOODNESS

While the Pope and the Church amassed great power and wealth in the Middle Ages, the rights and needs of the people came to be ignored. The Renaissance and Reformation developed, in reaction to that situation. The morality and ethics of the Middle Ages were to "keep God's commandments," but with the Renaissance and Reformation, questions like, "Is it good to keep God's commandments?" "Has man become happy by keeping them?" "Don't the commandments make man unhappy?" were asked. Views of value with man as their center developed, and one of them was Bentham's *Utilitarianism*. Bentham thought that man lives for happiness—but that happiness is material happiness. He said that there is true joy in material prosperity—eating good food, wearing good clothes, and living in a good house, and goodness is to work for the happiness of the greatest number of people. Goodness is judged, he asserted, by "the greatest happiness for the greatest number of people."

I do not mean that Bentham did not consider spiritual happiness at all, but he did not distinguish between spiritual happiness and material happiness, and it seems that he mainly dealt with material happiness in his view of goodness.

With regard to people living in developed countries, such as the U.S.A. and Japan, though materially prosperous, can they, nevertheless, be called happy in the true sense? In those countries we still find anxiety, crime, misery, and confusion, showing that happiness cannot be realized only through material prosperity.

Unification Thought agrees that there is goodness in happiness, but the method of achieving happiness is different. Happiness does not lie in seeking material prosperity, but in love. In love one gives first, and then takes. In giving, therefore, is true happiness to be found. Happiness is not something of the *Hyung Sang*, but of the *Sung Sang*. This is a very important point.

Many people are lapsing into materialistic ways, and since we have been blindly seeking material prosperity, we have caused a serious shortage of natural resources. A movement to conserve these resources has finally begun, but we should have used them correctly from the beginning. If we had awakened a couple of decades ago, and taken corrective measures, we would not have the problems we have today.

Although we recognize that Bentham's utilitarian movement contributed to the British social welfare system, utilitarianism is no longer important, because it was not effective in solving man's fundamental problems.

So, true goodness is to "live for others." In other words, it is the conduct of loving the family, society, nation, and mankind. Moreover, true happiness can be found in living this way. When the energy man uses to pursue material prosperity is used to realize love, a beautiful world can be built.

B. KANT'S VIEW OF GOODNESS

According to Kant, goodness is the conduct based upon the "categorical imperative" *(Kategorischer Imperativ)*—that is, the command from within man, the command of conscience.

Conduct based upon the categorical imperative is unconditional. If one acts in order to achieve a certain purpose, such as winning praise or financial profit, it is conditional behavior and not goodness. Goodness is acting unconditionally, without thinking of the potential gain.

To be honest unconditionally, in accordance with the categorical imperative "be honest," is goodness. Kant says that even if someone is honest, but has the purpose of gaining the admiration of others because of his honesty, it is not true honesty. A categorical imperative is an unconditional order, while a conditional order is a *hypothetical imperative (Hypothetischer Imperativ)*. When someone is suffering, our conscience says "Help him!" so we go and help. The one who is helped may thank us, of course, and may even pay us for our help, but because we have helped him without thinking of the reward, it is goodness. This is an example of acting in accordance with the categorical imperative.

Where does this categorical imperative come from? Kant says it is an order issued by practical reason. To what is this order issued? To the will *(Wille)*. When the will receives the order to "do good" from practical reason, it is called *good will (guter Wille)*. Good will determines conduct, and such conduct is goodness.

What is practical reason? The mind has three functions: intellect, emotion, and will. The ability to reason comes from one's intellect; with it we can think deeply and perceive the truth. Also, with reason we determine our course of action or our way of life. Kant called the reason that perceives truth *pure reason (reine Vernunft)*, or *theoretical reason (theoretische Vernunft)*, and that which determines how we should live or act *practical reason (praktische Vernunft.)*

Practical reason orders the will to do something and also determines the way to do it—the direction of the action. The will makes the decision to act in that direction. The will that makes decisions in accordance with practical reason is good will. When practical reason gives the order to "be honest," for example, the will determines a concrete action, such as apologizing to others.

So, Kant's view of goodness is to behave unconditionally according to the orders of practical reason, but there are several problems in this view. First, how can we judge the results of our actions? Kant separated pure reason and practical reason. So our behavior has nothing to do with pure reason, which perceives truth and makes judgments (because it is only practical reason that determines our actions). But as pure reason is not involved in our actions, we can only motivate our actions, not judge their results.

Kant's view implies that if the motivation is good, the actions themselves are good. But what if someone is made unhappy by our actions? For example, suppose someone looks very pitiful and seems to need help, and my practical reason orders me to help him. I speak to him and take him to a hospital, because he is in pain. He may be somewhat annoyed, however, thinking, "I don't need your help, I can go by myself." On the other hand, I feel satisfied, because I have acted as my practical reason has ordered. This might happen, if pure reason does not play a part in judging the results of our actions. So, Kant's categorical imperative attached importance only to motivation.

Second, reason is, by itself, very cold. Someone who has developed only his reason sees many defects and few good points in others. He is always watching others and examining whether their actions are in accord with his standard of judgment or not. Not only does he watch others, but he feels that others, also, watch him. His own conscience, or practical reason, watches him, others watch him, and he watches others. It is a world of observation, just like a military outfit. There is no real warmth where people are just watching one another. Knowing that they must act in goodness as the categorical imperative directs, they feel cramped and cold.

Kant's view of goodness is similar to the Law of the Old Testament. At that time, people believed in God, and, knowing that they should obey God, kept the Law unconditionally. The Law of the Old Testament was given by God, but in the case of Kant, the standard of action, called "maxim," is legislated by practical reason. But if man should unconditionally obey the maxim, just because of practical reason within him, he will feel distressed and will finally be unable to obey. With this view of goodness, we cannot establish true ethics, because ethics must be something that everyone is willing to practice.

Why did Kant's ethics become so much like laws? Because he did not understand Heart. Heart (love), which comes from God, originally lies behind reason and is more essential than reason. Reason by itself does not issue orders; it is love and Heart that cause it to do so. There is motivation in orders, and that is Heart. Because of Heart, reason tells the will to "do good."

Within motivation itself there is Heart and one feels warmth because Heart lies behind the orders of reason. Because of this, one is always willing to forgive others. If someone uses only reason, he may not forgive others when they make mistakes. But if he has Heart, he must forgive them.

We can understand that there is Heart behind reason if we think of the process of creation in the Original Image. In the beginning, centering on Heart (purpose), the Inner *Sung Sang* and Inner *Hyung Sang* engaged in give-and-take action to form the Logos, and creation took place according to Logos. In other words, before God's creation began, there was Heart, and with Heart as the motivation, creation came into being.

It is the same with man. With Heart as the motivation, reason enters into give-and-take action with ideas and laws. Plans are produced, and actions take place according to those plans. So, reason itself cannot directly motivate actions. Since Heart (love) is the motivation, there is always purpose and direction in actions. In other words, in creation or action, purpose is necessarily formed from Heart. Kant, disregarding purpose and direction, called the action that follows a categorical imperative goodness. But good actions must be motivated by love, and there can be no love without a purpose and direction. So, the action of love, having purpose and direction, is goodness.

⑨ THEORY OF ART

Art is a treasured element of mankind's cultural heritage. In this chapter, we will clarify our attitude toward it. As you probably know, communists value their theory of art highly, because for them art is an efficient means for achieving revolution. Lenin said that all aspects of art—including literature—must be coherent with, and subject to, the policies of the Communist Party. Stalin said that artists are the engineers to reform and reconstruct men's minds. The communist theory of art is called *Socialist Realism*, whose aim is to ensure that the content of art and the method of creating it meet with Party policies. When we look at the history of revolutions, we can see how important a role artistic activities have played in them.

When I was young, there was a great deal of artistic activity conducted by the communists. They would often put on plays in a house they rented in the countryside. They had two favorite themes: one was about the Japanese occupation of Korea; the other, about the way landowners and capitalists harshly treated peasants and laborers. The effect was the same as openly publicizing their theories. Even now they still make use of different cultural groups—seemingly without any ideological purpose—under the pretext of improving cultural exchange. (These cultural groups are readily accepted in the free world, which stresses the freedom of artistic expression and has no standard or theory with which to distinguish true from manipulative art.) I cannot deny my fear that the engineers referred to by Stalin might indeed reform men's minds. Clearly, we need a theory of art to oppose such manipulation.

Reverend Sun Myung Moon has begun artistic activities with the "Little Angels" group in order to inspire people to give joy to God. It is not good for art to be used for political contrivance; true art can never be made into a tool of politics, for true art is that which pleases God and man. Another reason why a theory of art is necessary is that when society is restored to its original state, it will be an artistic society, where the Purpose of Creation is completely realized. In that society, people will love one another; for that reason, they will want to dance, sing, and engage in various kinds of artistic activities. In the ideal society, economic problems will be solved; as a result, artistic activities will come to the fore. To those leaders who are trying to build such a society a theory of art is indispensible.

If it is our aim to construct a new culture, we must pay attention to art, for art is the essence of culture. First, we must protect the cultural heritage we already have. This heritage includes architecture, sculpture, music, painting, industrial design, and so on. Communism aims at destroying our cultural heritage. Of course, they act as if they were trying to protect art; yet they appreciate art, not for its own sake, but merely as something to be used for the purpose of publicity. They see no significance in a piece of art that has no propaganda-value. Those who are not well-informed have the impression that communism is protecting our traditional cultural heritage, but this is a fanciful notion.

When we consider such things, we feel responsible not only to inherit our own culture, but to keep it alive, and on this foundation, to develop a new culture. This new culture will come about through the integration of the best elements within the cultures of various nations and racial groups. So, keeping our national cultural heritage is a *sine qua non* for building a new culture.

I have developed the Unification theory of art deductively from the teachings and Unification Principle of Rev. Sun Myung Moon, making almost no reference to the traditional theories of art. Rev. Moon himself has a highly developed artistic sense, which I would like to make known through this theory. Based on this new theory, we must play a central role in constructing a new culture.

I. WHAT IS ART?

Generally speaking, intellect is related to philosophy; will, to morality and ethics; and emotion, to art. So, art is the emotional activity of creating and appreciating beauty. The purpose of art is to produce joy. In other words, the purpose of creating and appreciating beauty is for people to be joyful. Therefore, in Unification

Thought view, art is "the activity of creating joy through the creation and appreciation of beauty." As explained below, appreciation is a form of creation; accordingly, we can simply say that art is "the activity of creating joy through creating beauty."

Other scholars define it in various ways. Sir Herbert Read, for instance, said that "art is an attempt to create pleasing forms,"* which is a view similar to that of Unification Thought.

II. JOY AND RESEMBLANCE IN ART

What is joy? I would like to discuss this point philosophically. The Principle of Creation contains many philosophical points that most people fail to notice when they first read it. The concept of joy comes from the Principle of Creation, and this is an important element in establishing our theory of art. The section in the Principle of Creation entitled "Object of Goodness for the Joy of God," is related to the creation of works of art. The Principle of Creation says:

> Joy comes when we have an object, whether invisible or visible, in which our own character and form are reflected and developed, thus enabling us to feel our own character and form through the stimulation derived from the object.
>
> For example, man feels joy as a creator only when he has an object; that is, when he sees the product of his work, whether it be a painting or a sculpture, in which his plan is substantiated. In this way, he is able to feel his own character and form objectively through the stimulation derived from the product of his work.†

A plan—which belongs to the invisible *Sung Sang*—is substantiated (objectified) to form a work of art. Works of art, therefore, are objectified plans. The artist's joy comes when he feels his *Sung Sang* and *Hyung Sang* as objectified forms, or as reflected objects standing in a position relative to him, through the stimulation from the object (work of art). In other words, when the subject and object resemble each other, the object stimulates the emotion of the subject; at that moment, beauty is appreciated and the experience of joy comes about.

Odebrecht said that joy is the feeling produced when one's personality is released from all pressures. What does this mean?

---

*Herbert Read, *The Meaning of Art* (Faber & Faber, London, 1968), p. 18.
†*Divine Principle*, 2nd ed. (HSA-UWC, New York, 1973) p. 42.

Man usually feels that his mind is oppressed by something, sometimes by his own conscience. When he is released from this pressure, he has a feeling of liberation. Odebrecht called this feeling joy. I think there is some truth in Odebrecht's interpretation.

This reminds me of the effect of alcohol on a drinking person—even though I am aware of the essential difference involved. When someone drinks, the cerebral cortex, especially the frontal lobe, becomes dulled with the effect of the alcohol. As a result, he feels a sense of release, as if the pangs of his conscience had suddenly vanished; he sings and dances happily. What happens in the experience of art is quite different, of course, yet there is a point of similarity: in art, also, one can feel released, through the experience of losing oneself in the fascination of beauty—a kind of catharsis. An example of this would be the experience of joy and release one may feel when watching a fine performance of a play.

A. RESEMBLANCE AND PROTOTYPE

Resemblance is the precondition not only in epistemology and logic, but also in the artistic experience of joy and beauty. When there is resemblance, collation follows and cognition takes place. The same resemblance brings about cognition in some cases, beauty in others. How can this be explained? The concept of resemblance is based on the fact that man is the integration of the whole universe. He is a microcosm, or a contracted body, of the cosmos. Accordingly, the cosmos can be looked upon as the expanded body of man. This is why the subject (man), and the object (other created beings) resemble each other. If the resemblance were limited merely to *Hyung Sang* aspects, however, the experience of joy would not occur. Some elements of *Sung Sang*, also, must resemble, corresponding to the resembling *Hyung Sang* elements. In the subject, this is the so-called "prototype" mentioned in Epistemology. When the object (precisely speaking, the object's image) and the prototype resemble each other, collation is performed and joy can come about. (See Epistemology, Section 3)

The collation of subject and object elements is accomplished through the give-and-take action between them. In the case of cognition, the give-and-take action is intellectual; in the case of art (when one feels beauty), it is emotional. Actually, intellect, emotion, and will are not independent of one another. It is just that in art, emotion is stronger than the other two. Deciding which of the three functions is more active is sometimes a problem. In appreciation, even though emotion plays the major role, it is always accompanied by intellect. Thus appreciation is accompanied by cognition. (Fig. 28)

Fig. 28 Appreciation and Cognition through Give-and-Take Action between Subject and Object

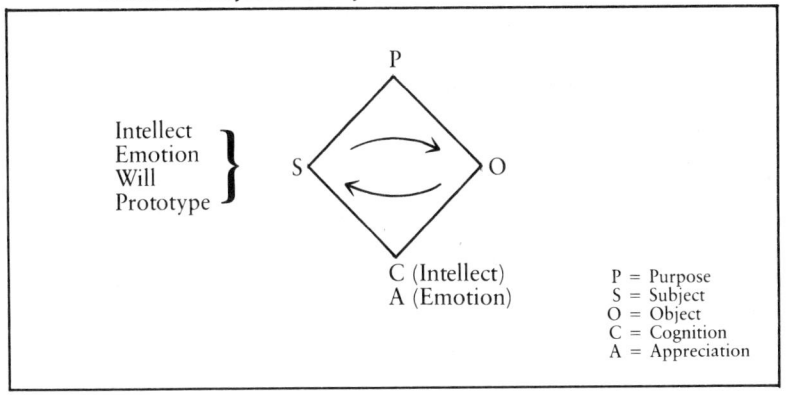

P = Purpose
S = Subject
O = Object
C = Cognition
A = Appreciation

B. *SUNG SANG* RESEMBLANCE

Sung Sang resemblance means that the *Sung Sang* of the subject and that of the object resemble each other. The more they resemble each other, the greater the appreciation of beauty.

Let us take Millet's painting *The Angelus* as an example. First, Millet must have had a *motive* (purpose) in painting, for no work of art can be produced without a motive. Millet's motive might have been his desire to paint his impression of faithful peasants in a farming village. Then, too, the artist needed a *theme,* or a way to express the motive. In choosing a theme he had to decide, for instance, whether to make the church bell or the married couple the most prominent feature, which may have been difficult to decide. Finally, Millet needed a *plan,* or concrete details, such as where to put the church, where to place the married couple, and which colors to use. The motive, the theme, and the plan are part of the *Sung Sang* aspect of a work of art.

When we appreciate works of art, we need also to consider the painter's way of thinking. To appreciate Millet's works, for instance, we need to find out more about him as a person by reading his biography or by inquiring about him.

From 1830 (the July Revolution) to 1871 (the Paris Commune) there was a revolutionary atmosphere in France; it is said, however, that due to his aversion to the prevailing atmosphere of violence, Millet moved to a quiet farming village, where he painted farmers who were pure in heart. By learning about Millet's background, we can understand his mind more fully and feel closer to him; this will lead to a deeper understanding of his painting.

If we are to appreciate Millet's works even more deeply, we need to know more about his motive, theme, plan, and way of thinking at the time he created his works. In this way, more *Sung Sang* relationships of resemblance between us and the work of art will be formed, and greater beauty will become manifest.

C. *HYUNG SANG* RESEMBLANCE TO THE *SUNG SANG* OF A WORK OF ART

The resemblance between the *Hyung Sang* and the *Sung Sang* of a work of art is also a necessary factor for the appreciator's joy. In *The Angelus,* for example, physical conditions—such as lines, shapes, form, mass (thickness of paint), size, light, and shade are all part of the *Hyung Sang* aspect. These must be in harmony with one another; besides, they must be a good expression of Millet's motive, theme, and plan (i.e., the *Sung Sang* aspect). When the *Hyung Sang* and the *Sung Sang* of the work are in harmony, the appreciator can feel beauty in the work. (Fig. 29)

Fig. 29 *Sung Sang* Resemblance and *Hyung Sang* Resemblance to *Sung Sang*

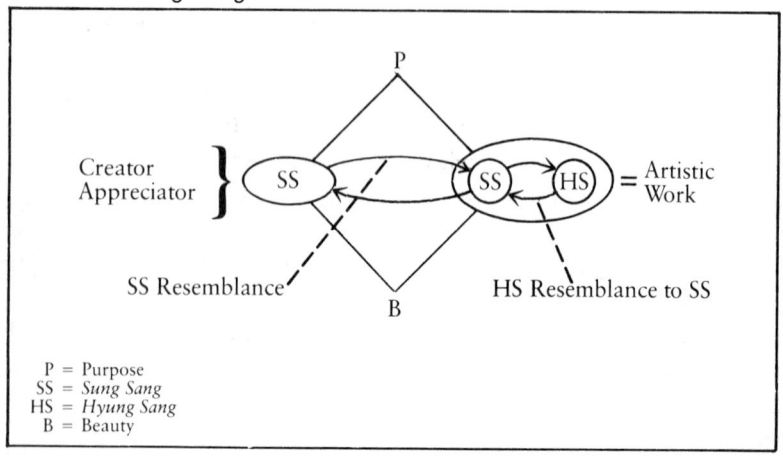

P = Purpose
SS = *Sung Sang*
HS = *Hyung Sang*
B = Beauty

III. WHAT IS BEAUTY?
A. DEFINITION OF BEAUTY

There have been a number of theories of art, and almost all of them have been concerned with beauty itself. The Unification Principle defines love as "an emotional force that the subject gives to the object," and beauty as "an emotional force that the object returns to the subject." Both love and beauty are emotional elements (emotional forces); these two elements, however, are not always equal. In some cases, they are the same; in others, they are not. According to Rev. Moon, in human relationships there can be love both from the subject and from the object, and beauty both from the subject and from the object. The emotional force that the subject gives to the object is always a conscious force. If the object is a person, he or she may love the subject, too; but if it is a "thing," it cannot do this, because it does not have a conscious emotional force. Whether the object is a person or a thing, it still gives emotional elements to the subject. These elements may be called *emotional stimulation*. Therefore, we can define beauty as "the emotional stimulation that the object gives to the subject."

Some people may object to the term "emotional stimulation," pointing out that, though people have emotions, things do not. Still, it is appropriate to use this term, because emotion is something subjective. Even when the stimulation coming from the object is only physical, the subject can receive it, not just physically, but also emotionally. On the other hand, even if the object is a person who is consciously giving emotion to the subject, still the subject does not necessarily have to receive it emotionally. When he does not, stimulation does not occur. A lot depends, therefore, on the subjective element.

Sir Herbert Read said that beauty is something that gives us a pleasant feeling. Cho Yo Han, a Korean scholar, said that beauty is a quality of the object that satisfies the (subject's) desire for the spirit of beauty.

Kant, on the other hand, said that to feel beauty is to judge *(beurteilen)* the subjective purposiveness *(subjective Zweckmässigkeit)* of an object *(Gegenstand)* by the emotion *(Gefühl)* of pleasantness *(Lust)* and unpleasantness *(Unlust)*. Kant called this kind of judgment "taste judgment" *(Geschmacksurteil)*. For Kant, therefore, the feeling of beauty can be called the feeling of joy coming from the subjective purposiveness of an object. I will give an example of what he means. Let us imagine a tree coming into flower. What is the purpose of the flower? According to Kant, the flower itself actually has no purpose, but since man has a desire to seek beauty, he looks at it subjectively as if it had the purpose of expressing beauty. In other words, he objectifies his subjective purposiveness in the object, and judges the objectified purposiveness (with an emotion of pleasantness) as beauty. To Kant, therefore, the object of beauty is the object with *"purposiveness without purpose" (Zweckmässigkeit ohne Zweck)*.

Kant said that there are two kinds of beauty: grace *(Anmut, Grazie)* and sublimity *(Erhabene)*. Grace is something that generally gives us pleasure. Sublimity, on the other hand, seems not to give any feeling of pleasure; it does, however, stimulate our sense of beauty, conveying such feelings as wonder *(Staunen)*, solemnity, reverence *(Erfurcht)*, and awe. We sometimes experience the indescribable wonder of nature, or feel deep reverence toward a certain great man. Along the same lines, E. Burke, also, distinguished between the beauty that gives man pleasure and the beauty that inspires wonder, such as the one felt when facing something greater than human dimensions.

More theoretically, beauty can be defined also as "the object's value felt as emotional stimulation," for beauty is the object's value and is, at the same time, an emotional stimulation. The object's value is not limited to beauty; goodness and trueness, also, are values of an object. Moreover, not only beauty gives man joy; knowing the truth and learning of persons of goodness, also, can bring joy. So, beauty is the object's value grasped emotionally. If the stimulus coming from the object is grasped volitionally, it becomes goodness; if grasped intellectually, trueness. I will deal with this point in more detail at the end of this section.

B. THE DETERMINATION OF BEAUTY

How can we decide on whether or not something is beautiful? The Unification Principle says:

> The original value of an individual body is not latent in itself as an absolute. It is determined by the reciprocal relationship between the purpose of the individual body (as a particular kind of object centered on God's ideal of creation) and the desire of man (as the subject) to pursue the original value of the object. Accordingly, in order for an object to realize the original value of its creation, it

must unite with man through give and take action, thus forming the original four position foundation by becoming the third object to God.*

This is the fundamental way to determine original value (beauty). Specifically, how is the beauty of anything determined? How, for example, is the beauty of a flower determined? The Unification Principle explains it as follows:

> [The original beauty of a flower] is determined when God's purpose in creating the flower and man's spontaneous desire to pursue the flower's beauty are in accord with each other—when man's God-centered desire to find its beauty is fulfilled by the emotional stimulation he receives from the flower. This brings him perfect joy. In this way, the beauty of the flower will become absolute when the joy which man feels from the flower is perfectly centered upon the purpose of creation.
> Man's desire to pursue the beauty of creation is the desire to feel his own character and form objectively. When God's purpose of creating the flower and man's desire to pursue its value are found to be in accord, the subject and object form a state of harmonious oneness.†

The essential points concerning the determination of beauty are found in these passages.

I would like to explain philosophically how beauty may be determined. In general terms, beauty is determined through the give-and-take action between subject and object. Beauty is not something that "exists," but something that is "felt." A fact "exists," but value can only be "felt." Value is felt by the subject when there is a relationship between the subject and the object. Beauty, therefore, does not exist objectively; it is obtained by the reciprocal give-and-take action between the subject and the object. That does not mean that there is nothing in the object; it must contain something that can give rise to the emotional feeling of beauty. This is actually the essence of value within the object. As explained in "Axiology," the essence of value consists of (1) purpose of creation (plus theme and plan, in a work or art); (2) the harmony of *Sung Sang* and *Hyung Sang*, and that of correlative elements within *Hyung Sang* (such as the harmony of lines, shapes, colors, shades of light, masses, and the harmony expressed in space and time).

---

*Ibid, p. 46.
†Ibid., p. 47.

What requisites, then, should the subject have in order to be able to appreciate beauty? First, he should have the desire to seek value (beauty) from the work or art; furthermore, he should have a certain standard of way of thinking, view of life, individuality, education, interests, hobbies, ideas, etc., in order to understand and make resemblance with the *Sung Sang* of the work of art; finally, he should have the harmony of spirit-mind and physical mind and the harmony of the *Hyung Sang* elements.

In judging actual beauty, the subject's activeness and concern—which work on the basis of his desire to seek value—are also important. The subject can creatively add his own way of thinking, individuality, ideas, and so on, to the work of art. Accordingly, in the very process of appreciating beauty, an appreciator can, to some extent, create beauty as well. This is called *subjective action*.

Kant said that the judgment of beauty is a subjective judgment of how much the object is in accordance with the appreciator's purpose. The feeling of pleasantness, in this judgment, is beauty. Since Kant went little further than to recognize that man requires God, he could not say that all beings were created with a purpose. Accordingly, for Kant, objects such as flowers and birds do not have a purpose to exist. Man, the subject, gives the purpose to them, and the judgment of how much the object lives up to this purpose is the judgment of beauty. Unification Thought agrees with Kant's view in that beauty is judged subjectively; yet it also recognizes objective purpose, which Kant did not. As all works of art were created according to a certain purpose, so, also, were all created beings. There is harmony in nature because there is purpose. Man's emotions are stimulated when he perceives this harmony, and a feeling of beauty is generated.

The judgment of beauty is subjective. It is always accompanied by *subjective action*—that is, the inevitable addition of subjective elements to the judgment of beauty. In judging beauty, the appreciator tries to unite with the work. By creating a resemblance to the work of art, he can appreciate it much more deeply.

Lipps refers to this with the concept of *empathy (Einfühlung)*, which means *feeling into* or projecting oneself into, the form of the work of art. When someone is crying, we only need to see his tears and look at the expression on his face to realize he is sad. He does not have to say anything. Since we have had the experience of crying when we were sad, we can understand his sorrow by feeling how we would feel if we were in his place.

Empathy corresponds to subjective action in Unification Thought. An actor sometimes pretends to weep, even though he is not at all sad. Special make-up techniques give him the appearance of crying real tears. The audience sympathizes with him and also starts to cry. We can say that the actor has tricked the audience through empathy.

An incident that happened in 1945 may be given as an illustration of how empathy works. At that time, F.D. Roosevelt had just died, and a photograph of Stalin, crying, appeared in the newspapers. One journalist said, "Stalin's eyes are crying, but his mouth is laughing." I, also, felt that perhaps he was just acting. Though he was probably pleased, yet he could not openly display his satisfaction, because he was afraid of what the American people might think. So, he pretended to cry. He was able to make his eyes look sad, but did not manage as well with his mouth. Stalin, also, may have made use of empathy.

Empathy, here, corresponds to "subjective action" in Unification Thought. Subjective action means that subjectivity is projected upon the object.

C. THE CAUSE OF THE FEELING OF BEAUTY —HARMONY

A work of art contains various elements that can give emotional stimulation to man and can, therefore, be perceived as beauty. What, exactly, is the basis for emotional stimulation in man? It is the perception of harmony in the object. Through perceiving harmony, man can have emotional stimulation and thus obtain the experience of beauty. Accordingly, when the physical elements of a work of art, such as lines, shapes, and colors, are well balanced and harmonized with one another, we can perceive them as beauty and can derive joy and satisfaction from them.

Man can feel this harmony because he himself is originally a harmonious being. Just as the cosmos is a harmonious system, the physical body of man is a harmonious system; in other words, the various elements within his body are in harmony among themselves. Though man has fallen into a sinful state, his mind and body also have a tendency to be in harmony. In this sense, man, originally, is God's best work of art. Thus, man (the appreciator) can resemble works of art by his own inner harmony. Conversely, if he is not in a harmonious state, he cannot understand the real beauty of a work of art when he sees it. When we appreciate works of art, therefore, we must empty our mind of mundane thoughts and be very calm. When we purify our minds and maintain a harmonious state, we can easily experience beauty from a work of art. This is called *contemplation*. At the moment of contemplation, the appreciator, who is in a state of harmony, forms a common base with the artistic work, and beauty is experienced.

H. Read said, "The work of art has an imaginary point of reference (analogous to a center of gravity) and around the point the lines, surfaces, and masses are distributed in such a way that they *rest* in perfect equilibrium. The structural aim of all these modes is harmony, and harmony is the satisfaction of our sense of beauty."* Henri Matisse said, "A work of art implies a harmony of everything together."† Paul Cézanne said that verisimilitude matters little and the harmony of form and color is the essential for great art.‡ The opinions of these artists and philosophers concur with the conclusion drawn from the Unification Principle—that is, when harmony is achieved, a great work of art is produced.

There are two kinds of harmony: harmony in space and harmony in time. Painting, architecture, sculpture, handicrafts, calligraphy, and so on, are examples of harmony in space. In Greece we can find great spatial harmony in the ancient buildings and sculptures. Celadon porcelain (bluish green porcelain) made during the Koryo Dynasty in Korea, is one of the most famous examples of such harmony in space as far as handicrafts are concerned. Novels, poems, music, and so on, are examples of harmony in time; these forms of art express beauty through a passage of time. Whichever of the two kinds of harmony a work may express (dancing expresses both), harmony is what makes it beautiful.

D. THE RELATIONSHIP BETWEEN BEAUTY AND GENERAL VALUES

Value usually refers to trueness, goodness, and beauty. Suppose there is an object and that it gives a certain stimulation to the subject. When that subject (a man) grasps an object's stimulation with his intellect, it is called trueness. Man desires to obtain not only

---

*Herbert Read, *The Meaning of Art*, p. 35.
†Ibid., p. 264.
‡Ibid., p. 200.

information, but also trueness. There can be falseness in information, but no falseness in trueness. In this case, man wishes to know trueness rather than mere information, and the stimulation from the object is now trueness. Scientists, also, study in order to obtain trueness, if possible, not just information and knowledge.

When the same stimulation is grasped by man's will, it becomes goodness. Even things that have no will—such as plants and minerals—can be viewed as good, when grasped by will.

God created the universe, and on the sixth day He proclaimed everything as good. Since the universe was just as God had intended it to be, it was *good*. He appreciated it with His will; had God appreciated it with His intellect, He might have said, "It is true." On the other hand, if He had appreciated it with His emotion, He might have said, "It is beautiful." Depending on the way a man appreciates the same object, it becomes either true, good, or beautiful. Value, then as mentioned before, is appreciated differently according to which one of the three functions of the mind—intellect, will, or emotion—is emphasized. In this sense, value is decided upon by the reciprocal relationship between the subject and the object.

So far, the subjective element has been emphasized; nevertheless, there must be a latent (potential) element of beauty within the object itself. This element, when perceived by man, can give him the emotional stimulation that may result in the experience of beauty. A flower, for instance, has no active emotional function, but it can give stimulation. Since man receives the stimulation emotionally, it is the same as saying that emotion has come from the flower. Accordingly, we can say that beauty is produced by an emotional stimulation coming from the object.

IV. TYPES OF BEAUTY

Beauty is determined by the give-and-take action between a subject (man) and object, centering on purpose. There are numerous kinds of objects, such as flowers, birds, mountains, and rivers; Accordingly, numerous kinds of beauty can be perceived. Furthermore, the same object displays different kinds of beauty when perceived by different subjects. Flowers, for example, are perceived by a poet differently from the way they are perceived either by a scientist or by an artist. When considering the varieties of quadruple bases, this diversity is inevitable. (Fig. 30)

Fig. 30 Varieties of Beauty

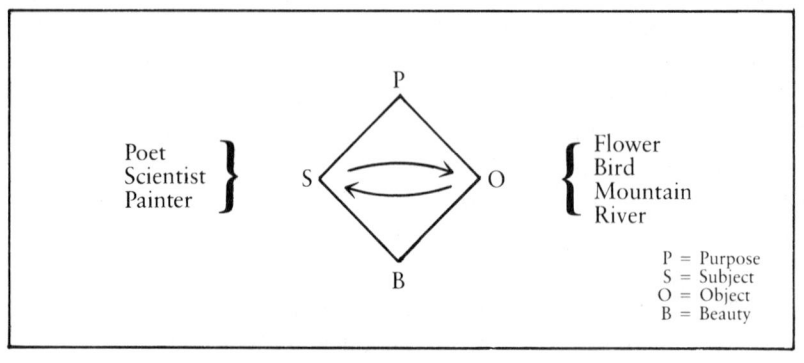

Poet, Scientist, Painter } S

Flower, Bird, Mountain, River

P = Purpose
S = Subject
O = Object
B = Beauty

A. KANT'S CLASSIFICATION OF THE TYPES OF BEAUTY

Kant recognized two kinds of beauty: "grace" *(Grazie)* and "sublimity" *(Erhabene)*. Grace can be subdivided into "free beauty" *(freie Schönheit)*, "appendant beauty" *(anhängende Schönheit)* and "pure beauty" *(Reinschöne)*. Free beauty is unrestricted, whereas appendant beauty is slightly restricted. Suppose there is a great variety of clothes, but only a few items that suit me. I consider those that suit me as especially beautiful, but the kind of beauty I see in them is dependent upon the restrictions of my limited purpose; hence, it is called appendant beauty. Pure beauty is that which contains moral elements, such as the beauty expressed in religious paintings. Sublimity is that which we feel when we see something great; it is a feeling of solemnity, awe, and reverence. In other theories of art one finds also "comic beauty" and "tragic beauty." An example of "tragic beauty" would be a soldier going to the front line, risking his life for the sake of his nation.

Kant, as well as other theorists, was actually unable to set forth a solid philosophical standard for classifying beauty. Scholars generally make subjective classifications, based on their own experiences. A philosophical basis for classifying beauty, however, is necessary; this can be derived from the Unification Principle, as shown below.

B. THE UNIFICATION THOUGHT VIEW OF THE TYPES OF BEAUTY

In the Unification Principle, beauty and love are inseparable. There is no beauty apart from love. When considering the types of beauty, therefore, we need, first of all, to think about the types of love. Take parental love, for example. The more parents love their children, the more beautiful the children become. The relationship between love and beauty is reciprocal. When the subject loves the object, the love of the subject is perceived by the object as beauty. Reversely, when the object gives beauty to the subject, the object's motive (starting point) should be love.* What types of love are there? There are three types of love in the Unification Principle: parental love, conjugal love, and children's love. Then, what concretely are the types of beauty corresponding to the three types of love? I would like to clarify this question by explaining love more deeply.

Parental love is either paternal or maternal. When parents love their children, their love is perceived emotionally by the children as beauty. I visited a certain family some time ago, and asked the children, "Whom do you like best, your father or your mother?" They answered, "We like both." "But whom do you like best?" I insisted. One child answered, "Father"; and another said, "Mother." To like someone is to feel that he or she is beautiful. The children felt that their parents were beautiful because the parents gave them love.

Paternal love becomes paternal beauty for the children. Fathers do not always give their children tender, warm love. When the children are disobedient, fathers may punish, or scold, or frown at them. Although children may feel bad at that moment, they are usually thankful later. Strictness, also, can be an expression of love. Not only spring-like warmth, but also autumn- or winter-like strictness are expressions of the same love. This kind of love, also, may be felt as beauty by children. This may be called sublime beauty.

Suppose a child makes a mistake and comes home fearing he is going to be scolded, but his father forgives him saying, "That's all right." The child feels a certain kind of paternal beauty at that moment. It could be called beauty of generosity, which seems as wide as the ocean. In receiving various kinds of love from their father, children experience various kinds of beauty.

When we see the ocean, or majestic mountains, or a waterfall that cascades over a high cliff, we feel a kind of awesome beauty. Where does this feeling come from? This type of beauty in nature is

---

*Accordingly, the relationship of love and beauty is that of inner and outer, and so the types of beauty can be said to correspond to the types of love.

a modified extension of the paternal beauty we felt in our childhood.

Many people lose their father at a young age, but can still experience paternal love indirectly, through older relatives or friends, through teachers at school, or even through watching movies and television programs. I once saw a television drama in which a scientist and his son were kidnapped. Someone came to the rescue, but surprisingly enough, the child did not want to be rescued. He preferred to stay with the kidnapper because he was receiving more love from him than he had ever received from his father. The man who came to rescue them, however, treated the child also with love and kindness. So, he finally allowed himself to be rescued. That particular child had not received love from his father; yet he was able to experience paternal love from someone else. Children, therefore, can experience paternal love and paternal beauty, either directly, from the father, or indirectly, from another person.

Maternal love is different from paternal love. A mother is gentle, kind, and peaceful. Children perceive maternal love as what may be called peaceful beauty or graceful beauty. We may feel such beauty when we see, for instance, a statue of the Virgin Mary. After we have experienced such maternal beauty, we may feel it transformed into the peaceful beauty of the natural world.

With regard to conjugal love, a husband's love for his wife is felt by her as masculine beauty; her love for him is felt by him as feminine beauty. Since everyone has a different character, there are a great number of different kinds of masculine and feminine beauty— among persons as well as in nature. Though there are cases in which the husband has an effeminate character, yet the wife can still experience masculine beauty, by observing it in other men. Reversely, there are cases in which the wife has a masculine character; here, also, the husband can still experience feminine beauty, by observing it in other women, through reading novels, watching plays and movies, and so forth.

What is children's beauty? Children with a loving heart look beautiful to their parents. The original nature of a child is to make the parents happy. They do that through little things, such as showing their parents something they have painted or drawn, or making them laugh, or romping cheerfully about. This is children's love; parents see it as charmingly beautiful. Sometimes children show their parents actions and gestures that are ludicrous and comical. This is "comical beauty." As children grow, the beauty they express changes.

Once we have experienced children's beauty, we can begin to perceive such beauty all around us. For example, young animals—such as baby chicks—are lovely; flower buds, also, are delicately beautiful. These things are extensions of children's beauty. In a family, the father sees the beauty of his children differently from the way the mother does. Similarly, a man and a woman probably see different aspects of the beauty of nature. In the family there is yet another kind of beauty, which comes from love among brothers and sisters; it is a kind of children's beauty. The extension of such beauty can be found in nature as well. Our experience of beauty, therefore, is an extension of our experience of paternal, maternal, conjugal, and children's beauty. Since there are as many such kinds of beauty as there are individuals, there are innumerable kinds of beauty.

In summary, the types of beauty correspond to the types of love. Parental love is felt as parental beauty (paternal and maternal beauty); conjugal love, as conjugal beauty (masculine and feminine beauty); and children's love, as children's beauty (including brothers' and sisters' beauty). These three kinds of love are God's love expressed divisionally through the basis of the family. Accordingly, beauty, as well as love, originates in God. This is the philosophical basis for the different types of beauty.

V. THE DUAL ASPECTS OF ARTISTIC ACTIVITY AND THE DUAL ASPECTS OF PURPOSE AND DESIRE

Now I would like to discuss the philosophical basis for the activities of creation and appreciation. Looking at the world of artistic expression today, we have reason to be concerned. When people create and appreciate art, do they always have a truly aesthetic attitude? Can the activity of creation be totally separated from that of appreciation, and vice-versa? Why is creation necessary? Why is appreciation necessary? Are creation and appreciation compatible? These are a few of the many questions that require the establishment of a true philosophical foundation for art. The purpose of this section is (1) to show how the fundamental truth of the universe relates to creative activity; (2) to establish a solid philosophical foundation for artistic expression; and (3) to help creative persons find the right direction for developing their creative talents.

As mentioned before, the Principles set forth here are based on the teachings of Rev. Sun Myung Moon, especially the Unification Principle. The section in the Principle entitled "Purpose of Creation" explains the reason why the universe was brought into being. God created man and all of creation in order to obtain joy from them; each created being has two purposes: the purpose for the whole and the purpose for the individual. In man's case, the purpose for the whole is to give joy to God and to the whole (i.e., mankind, nation, society, and family, which represent God to him).

But God cannot be happy if man is sorrowful. When man is happy, God, also, can be happy. Man is created to be happy; this is the purpose for the individual. He wants to be happy not only by pleasing God and the whole, but also by seeking value from his objects—that is, creation and the persons in the object position to him. He should put the purpose for the whole first, and the purpose for the individual second. Some artists have a sense of mission in their work because they are unconsciously aware of this purpose for the whole. In the ideal world, all artists will have a similar sense of mission.

In order to achieve these two purposes, one must have will and desire. God, therefore, has given man the desires to *realize value* and to *seek value*, in order to achieve the purpose for the whole and the purpose for the individual. The desire to achieve the purpose for the whole is the desire to realize the values of trueness, goodness, and beauty. Man tries to serve the whole by living truthfully, by doing good deeds, and by creating beauty for others and for God. The desire to achieve the purpose for the individual is the desire to receive joy through obtaining values from one's objects.

On one hand, man creates things with the desire to realize value, by which he tends to fulfill the purpose for the whole (man as a creator); on the other hand, he appreciates created things with his desire to seek value through which he tends to fulfill the purpose for the individual (man as an appreciator). Of course, man himself is pleased when he creates something, yet his primary purpose should be to please others with his creative works; this is from his desire to *realize* value. Furthermore, man feels joy by looking at the natural world, by admiring paintings, or by reading literature; this comes from his desire to *seek* value. We have always known that these kinds of desire exist, but perhaps have not clearly understood the reason why. This has now been explained.

VI. REQUISITES FOR CREATIVE ACTIVITY
A. SUBJECT REQUISITES (ARTIST)
1. The Establishment of Motive, Theme, and Plan

The first requisite is that the subject (artist) must have a purpose for engaging in creative activity. Just as the universe has the Purpose of Creation, so the work of art should have the artist's own purpose of creation, which is the *motive*. Rodin, for example, was inspired by Dante's "Inferno" to design *The Gate of Hell*. He wished to create a figure of a poet overlooking the scenes of hell, meditating on the pain of hell fire and pondering upon what kind of life man should lead on earth. This is the motive for his sculpturing *The Thinker* in *The Gate of Hell*.

An artist, then, sets up a theme based on the motive. Rodin's theme is a thinking individual. After determining the theme, he still had to decide on how to express it. Would it be a sitting or a standing figure? Perhaps it was only after deep consideration that he decided to sculpt a sitting figure, with its back bent. This is the *plan*. With a concrete plan, he was ready to begin his work of art.

Millet, also, first established a plan for *The Angelus*, as do all artists in creating their works of art. The plan corresponds to Logos in the Creation process. The process through which an artist forms a plan for his work of art corresponds to the process of the development of the Logos within the Original Image. In the case of painting, the plan must include all aspects of the work—color, form, size, etc.

In abstract art, the theme of a work may not be readily apparent, as there is no attempt on the part of the artist to represent anything in the natural world. Instead, the theme is hidden, and it may be necessary to analyze the artist's motive and plan quite thoroughly in order to discover it. The title of the work itself may be a helpful clue in this direction.

The motive, or the purpose of creation, is established by heart, the emotional impulse. An artist's way of thinking, individuality, interests, view of life, ideas, educations and so on are engaged in making a plan. Accordingly, both an artist's emotional element and an intellectual element are involved in the creation of a work of art.

Tolstoy said that art is the activity of transmitting the *feeling* of the creator. H. Read made an amendment to it and said, "The real function of art is to express *feeling* and transmit *understanding*."*

---

*Herbert Read, *The Meaning of Art*, p. 266.

They have expressed ideas along similar lines to the Unification Theory of Art.

2. The Attitude of the Artist (Object-Consciousness)

Now that the reason why artists have creativity (to achieve the purpose for the whole, through creation, and the purpose for the individual, through appreciation) has been clarified, we can also come to understand the attitude an artist should have in creating a work of art. This attitude may be called *object-consciousness*.

First, it should be an attitude of comforting the Heart of God, who has been sad throughout history. In other words, the artist's creative works should be centered on God. Art is the activity of creating joy; its first requisite is that of being comforting to God. God, an artist Himself, endowed man with His creativity so that man, also, could create works of art. God created man and the universe in order to receive joy from them; accordingly, man's first concern should be to please God. Owing to the Fall, however, artists, as a rule, have not thought of pleasing God in their creative activity. This is a sad thing for God indeed. Throughout history, God has endeavored to establish the Kingdom of Heaven on earth. He gave man creativity so that man might play an important part in building the Kingdom. Because of the Fall, however, numerous artists have not believed in God, which has been a cause of grief for Him. Artists, therefore, must endeavor to comfort the historically sad God.

Second, the artist should comfort Jesus and the saints, who were persecuted by fallen people. To comfort them, now in the spirit-world, is to comfort God, who sent them to people on earth in order to realize the Kingdom of Heaven.

Third, the artist should record and publicize the good, virtuous, and righteous deeds that are being performed now or were performed in the past. Innumerable good deeds have been done, but most of them have been disregarded by sinful man. Actually, a great number of righteous men were miserably persecuted, not only in the past, but also in the present. Such good deeds are surely still being performed. Artists, therefore, should attempt to portray them in their works; by doing so, they will be cooperating with the providence of God and helping to counter the tendency of today's mass media to publicize only man's evil deeds.

Fourth, the artist should proclaim the coming of the ideal

world, having firm confidence in the future. Without such an attitude, his works will not be as beautiful as they possibly could be. In the Renaissance, for instance, artists usually displayed a great deal of hope and idealism—which many of them derived from a strong faith in Christ.

Fifth, artists should try to give glory to God by depicting the wonders of nature. God created nature in order for man to have joy upon seeing it. Because of the Fall, man has been unable to really see beauty in nature. If he had perfected his personality through completing the first blessing—thus becoming the perfected object of God—man would have been able to see the brilliant and wondrous side of nature. Flowers, trees, rivers, etc., would have looked exquisitely beautiful. Nature is the manifestation of God's attributes; artists, therefore, should portray nature so as to manifest God's mysterious, profound, and wondrous attributes, giving Him glory and returning deep thanks to Him for bringing nature into existence.

Good works of art are created only if the artist has a fundamental attitude of serving the whole and pleasing others. Undoubtedly, a lot of fine works of art created during the Renaissance have this object-consciousness. Actually, a great number of artists of that period were pious people. Raphael, for instance, made use of religious themes in a large number of works; Michelangelo did likewise and produced famous works, such as *The Last Judgment*. They painted those works of art in order to give glory to Jesus and to God, as well as to help the development of Christianity. This is *object-consciousness*. For this reason, I think they received a great deal of cooperation from the spirit-world. The highest form of object-consciousness is to wish to offer glory to God, the supreme Subject.

3. Individuality

Man is a being with individuality, created resembling a particular Individual Image in God; individuality, therefore, is an essential characteristic of the original human nature, as explained in "Theory of Original Human Nature." Accordingly, in the creation of a work of art the individuality of the artist should be expressed, since the work is a manifestation of the artist himself. Man's purpose includes the free display of his individuality, in order to please God; this is especially true of artistic activity. Artists should fully display their God-given individuality, so as to please God and mankind. Thus, even though maintaining an object-consciousness, artists can, nevertheless, express their own unique personality and ideas.

B. OBJECT REQUISITES (WORK OF ART)

The harmony between the *Sung Sang* and *Hyung Sang* elements is the most important requisite for the object. By *Sung Sang* elements I mean the motive, theme, and plan; by *Hyung Sang* elements, such things as shapes, lines, and material elements. In Rodin's *The Thinker,* for instance, *Hyung Sang* elements would be such things as the head, the back, the chest, the curved lines, and the material element (bronze). Collation should take place between the *Hyung Sang* elements and the motive, theme, and plan. Of course, the *Hyung Sang* elements themselves should all harmonize with one another to create a well-harmonized whole.

When the artist sees harmony between the *Sung Sang* and the *Hyung Sang* elements, as well as among the various elements within the *Hyung Sang,* he experiences beauty and joy. This is because the harmony of the elements within the object (work of art) resembles the harmony of *Sung Sang* and *Hyung Sang* and the elements within the *Hyung Sang,* of the artist himself.*

The terms "content" and "form" are often used in art. In this context, content corresponds to motive, theme, and plan *(Sung Sang* elements); and form, to the material elements *(Hyung Sang* elements). The harmony of *Sung Sang* and *Hyung Sang* elements, therefore, can be expressed also as *harmony of content and form.* As mentioned above, artists have various viewpoints about art; yet many of them agree that balance and harmony are the most important characteristics of a fine work of art.

C. THE TECHNIQUE AND METHOD OF CREATION
1. Technique

Technique corresponds to the skill in expressing beauty according to the two-stage structure of creation. The two-stage structure means, first, that the Logos is formed through the give-and-take action between the Inner *Sung Sang* and Inner *Hyung Sang* centering on purpose, and second, that an art work is created through

---

*In the next section of this chapter I will discuss what takes place in the process of appreciation.

give-and-take action between the Logos and *Hyung Sang*, centering on purpose. We have, therefore, an inner quadruple base and an outer quadruple base. Whenever creative activity—such as manufacturing in a factory, the ploughing of fields by farmers, or research by scholars—takes place, skill is always applied, according to this two-stage structure of creation.

Since there is Purpose within the two-stage structure of the Original Image, purpose is necessary in the creation of an art work as well. Why are motive, theme, and plan necessary? Because they were also necessary for God. In the created world, all phenomena, except those originating from the Fall, came from the Original Image. When God created the universe, He had an irrepressible impulse to create an object of joy. This was His motive for creating the universe. Then what should He create? He decided to create man in His likeness. This was His theme, the idea of man. Then he pondered upon where to put the head, eyes, legs, internal organs, and so forth. This was the plan, or Logos. Finally, He created an actual man through give-and-take action between His plan, or *Sung Sang* elements, and the appropriate *Hyung Sang* elements.

Man is God's masterpiece. God gave man the ability to create his own object of joy by giving him even His Creativity. Probably God would have said to man, "Have motivation as I have, have your own themes, and create." A true artist uses all the creative powers at his command to create a work of art, because that is what God did in creating man. Since man is made in the likeness of God, he has an irresistible impulse to conduct his creative activities following a pattern similar to that established by God.

2. Formation of the Outer Quadruple Base

Technique, in the context of creative activity, refers specifically to the skill to form the outer quadruple base (i.e, the second stage of the two-stage structure of creation).

In the formation of the quadruple base, materials are necessary. There are two kinds of materials: *subject-matter* and *medium*. The subject-matter corresponds to the theme and is referred to as the *Sung Sang* material; the medium corresponds to physical materials employed and is referred to as *Hyung Sang* material. The formation of the outer quadruple base means the preparation of *Hyung Sang* materials to actualize the plan.

An author uses his experiences, imagination, or actual events as his subject-matter. A sculptor sometimes uses a model as his subject-matter; he needs marble, or wood, or some other material, as well as tools. A painter needs paint materials, brushes, canvas, an easel, and so forth. These physical materials are the medium *(Hyung Sang* material) in the second stage of two-stage structure of creation.

Furthermore, the quality and quantity of physical materials must be decided upon: how much marble to use, how hard it should be, what kind of gloss it should have, etc. (Rodin's works, for example, have considerable gloss.) As we can see, the artist must take into account a large number of factors when choosing his materials. This is the preparation of the *Hyung Sang*.

To create the actual object of art, an artist must perform give-and-take action between the plan *(Sung Sang)* and the medium *Hyung Sang)*. For example: in painting, the artist performs give-and-take action with brushes and other materials, while following a plan.* In order to carry out this give-and-take action harmoniously, artists need to develop skills—which means that they need art education. (Fig. 31)

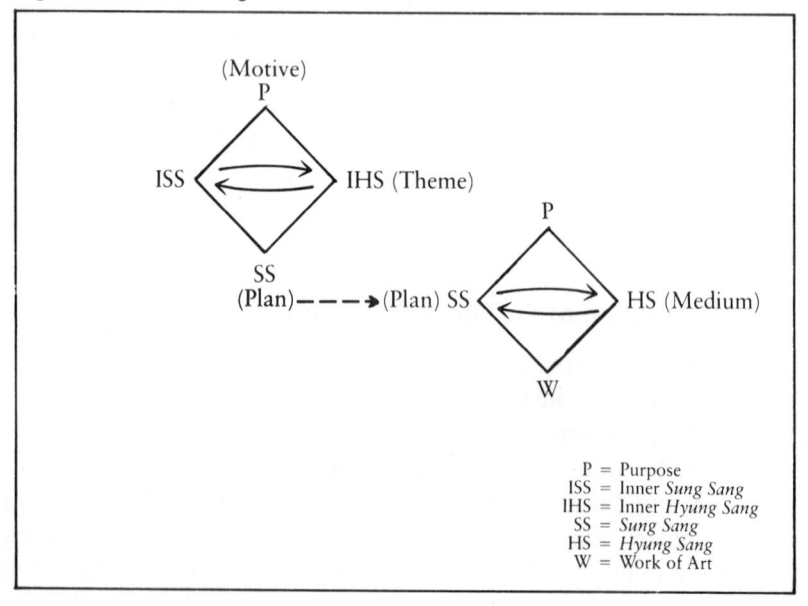

Fig. 31 The Two-Stage Structure in the Creation of a Work of Art

P = Purpose
ISS = Inner *Sung Sang*
IHS = Inner *Hyung Sang*
SS = *Sung Sang*
HS = *Hyung Sang*
W = Work of Art

---

*This type of give-and-take action, which occurs between a conscious party (the artist) and an unconscious one (paint, brush, etc.), will be further discussed in "Methodology."

3. Method

Method is the way of realizing the two-stage structure of creation. The first stage is when the Inner *Sung Sang* and Inner *Hyung Sang*, centering on the purpose, engage in give-and-take action. Variety comes about if any of the three factors—that is, purpose, Inner *Sung Sang*, or Inner *Hyung Sang*—is changed. Of course, if the *Hyung Sang* (medium) of the second stage is changed, the work will vary also.

Suppose we decide to paint a certain autumn scene. One person might paint the red leaves of a maple tree; another, a lonely scene of trees without leaves. The Inner *Hyung Sang* (theme) varies, depending on the artist. Even though the theme is the same, the substance of each picture is different, influenced by the individuality, or style (which is related to the Inner *Sung Sang*), of the artist.

Artistic expression, therefore, can vary endlessly, according to the artist's individuality. If, for instance, other sculptors had been assigned the task of creating a statue similar to Rodin's *The Thinker*, each statue would have been different. Nevertheless, different kinds of artistic expression often share common characteristics, and thus may be classified under various *styles*. I would like to say a few words in explanation of the main styles and their characteristics.

(a) **Realism.** Realism is usually called 'actualism' in philosophy. Realists try to express the object photographically, with precision and vividness of detail. Realist art tends to be intellectual, real, and objective.

(b) **Idealism.** Artists of idealism do not paint things as they appear, but select only those elements that suit their motive or theme. In painting a man, for example, they paint an idealized man, one worthy of respect, who may be, however, a vulgar person in real life. Many works of art in the Renaissance are examples of Idealism. Tolstoy and Lee Kwang-Soo, for instance, may be called idealists.

(c) **Expressionism.** Expressionists try to manifest their own views about life, as well as their thoughts, ideas, and emotions, through artistic works. They express what is in their minds, rather than objects as they appear to the eyes. Thus their style has a tendency to be subjective. The works of Van Gogh and Edward Munch are examples of Expressionism.

(d) **Classicism.** Classical art was popular in the seventeenth and eighteenth centuries. Classical artists respected the arts of the ancient Greeks and Romans and tried to continue in the same style.

Classicism respects intellect, universality, harmony, and completion—and attaches great importance to form.

(e) **Romanticism.** Romantic art, popular during the eighteenth and nineteenth centuries, was just the opposite of Classicism. Romanticists expressed man's dreams of an ideal. Passionate love between man and woman is a common theme, and the term 'romantic', used today to refer to this love relationship, comes from Romanticism. Artists attached more importance to content than to form. A representative writer of this period is Byron. Shakespeare's *Hamlet* and Goethe's *Faust*, also, are examples of Romantic style.

(f) **Symbolism.** Symbolism, a movement that began in France at the end of the nineteenth century in reaction to the rigidity of naturalism and realism, expresses subjective feeling (emotion) in symbols, rather than depicting objects as they appear. Lyricism in poetry belongs to symbolism.

(g) **Impressionism.** The impressionist movement in fine art, at the end of the nineteenth century, sought to convey the brightness of a fleeting impression of a scene through the use of points of primary colors. Instead of depicting the natural colors of things, impressionist painters allowed the observer's eyes to mix the colors on the canvas and thus form the color of the objects depicted in the painting. In this way, impressionist paintings create an impression of freshness and life. In literature, impressionists portray a subjective and sensuous impression of things in the natural world. Monet, Pissaro, and Sisley are representative impressionist painters.

Other styles, such as Cubism, Fauvism, and Surrealism have developed in the twentieth century, but I will not deal with them here. From the styles mentioned, we can see that if the methods of expressing something are different, the same theme will be expressed in a different manner. Why do the various styles appear? Philosophically, it can be said that when the four factors—that is, purpose, Inner *Sung Sang,* Inner *Hyung Sang,* and *Hyung Sang*—change according to the artist, the result (here, the work of art) cannot but change as well. This is the reason for the appearance of the different schools of artistic style.

VII. REQUISITES FOR APPRECIATION

Art has a close connection with ethics, since love and beauty are complementary. Ethics refers to the practice of love, while art is the creation of beauty. The practice of love is realized on the basis of the harmony between the spirit-mind and the physical mind. The spirit-mind seeks to attain the values of trueness, goodness, and beauty; the physical mind pursues physical things, such as food, clothing, and shelter. The two minds have a subject-object relationship. Thus, the first requisite for appreciation is a harmonious relationship between the spirit-mind and the physical mind of the appreciator. In other words, the appreciator must lead an ethical life, approaching art with a pure mind, free from mundane trivialities.

Upon this foundation, the appreciator must also have his own way of thinking, individuality, interests, hobbies, view of life, ideas, education, and so on. He needs a basic understanding of culture in order to understand art in any real depth. Of course, even if he knows nothing about it, he may still feel beauty, but not very deeply. In addition, his interests and hobbies should be congruent with the work of art; if they are not, it will be difficult for him to feel beauty, since appreciation involves the aspect of creativity. Heart and love, which are prerequisites for artistic activity, should be considered as well; these qualities will enable the appreciator to be emotionally stimulated by the right kind of atmosphere. In fact, art galleries are so constructed as to provide a conducive atmosphere for the appreciator, for one cannot easily appreciate art in a crowded or noisy environment.

Another requisite is that the subject should have a healthy physical body *(Hyung Sang)*. Though he need not have unusual strength, he should, at least, have sound optic and auditory nerves in order to judge beauty, for he appreciates a work of art with his eyes and ears. It is very difficult fully to appreciate a work of art—no matter how splendid it may be—if one's physical capabilities are impaired. Beauty is determined through harmonious give-and-take action between the work and the appreciator. The appreciator will be able to enjoy art only to the extent that he has these requisites for appreciation.

As I have said before, creation and appreciation are not entirely different. Creation is closely related to will, and appreciation, to intellect, but both activities are performed centering on emotion. Will and intellect cannot be separated, so there is appreciation in creation, and creation in appreciation. A painter feels beauty by appreciating the picture while he is in the act of painting it. In appreciating the object, the appreciator modifies it into something more beautiful, by adding his own subjectivity to it, which is a kind of creation. Thus, creation and appreciation are divided, in this explanation, only for the sake of convenience.

The one who appreciates works of art must have *Sung Sang* requisites, as explained above. At the same time, he must understand the *Sung Sang* aspect of the creator. The artistic work can best be understood when the *Sung Sang* aspect of the appreciator and the *Sung Sang* aspect of the work of art are united. Beauty does not appear without resemblance. Since the appreciator has harmony within himself, he may feel the beauty of a work immediately upon seeing it; if he wants to feel beauty more deeply, however, he needs to understand the *Sung Sang* aspect of its creator.

Once created, a work of art cannot be transformed to be the way the appreciator wants it to be because it has already been completed. In order for harmony and unity to come about between the *Sung Sang* aspect of the appreciator and the *Sung Sang* aspect of the work, the appreciator himself must endeavor to attain a closer resemblance to the work. That's why it becomes necessary to understand the creator's way of thinking, planning, etc.

The subjective action already explained in this chapter is also significant in the appreciation of a work of art. An appreciator creatively adds his own way of thinking, individuality, ideas, and so on, to the work of art, in order to establish a closer resemblance between the work and himself.

VIII. UNITY IN ART

Artistic activity is, in a word, activity of unification. Art is the unity of various correlative activities and elements in creating beauty. There are several kinds of unity, which can be classified as follows.

A. *Unity of Creation and Appreciation.* Creative activity and the activity of appreciation in art should be carried out in unity. I have explained this already.

B. *Unity of Content and Form.* When the content, of the *Sung Sang* elements of motive, theme, plan, etc. are in accord with the form, or the *Hyung Sang* elements of line, form, color etc., a fine work of art is produced. Thus, content and form should be one.

C. *Unity of Universality and Individuality.* An artist himself is the unity of universality and individuality. He can be a Japanese and, at the same time an individual named Takahashi. As a Japanese, he has characteristics common to Japanese people in general—including customs and language—and, at the same time, his own individuality. If he paints a picture, and if the style of painting in Japan tends toward romanticism, for example, he will probably paint in a romantic style; within this style, however, he will express his own individuality and character. Universality and individuality, therefore, are united in his person, as well as in his work.

Japanese art has been influenced by other cultures in different periods of history. Greek artistic influence, for example, appears to have entered Japan by way of India, China, and Korea. Greek art was internationally influential, and so corresponds to universality. After entering Japan, it was integrated with indigenous art; thus, we can say that Japanese art, also, is a unity of universality and individuality.

The relationship between the unified culture and national cultures will be important in the future. Communism says that destruction is inevitable when constructing something new, which means that old traditions would have to be annihilated upon global communization. If that were God's way, He would have destroyed mankind after the Fall and created a new Adam. We know, however, that He could never have done such a thing. On the contrary, He has worked to restore them and to build a new world based on the Principle. In the same way, we will create a new culture by preserving existing cultures and restoring them.

The basis for the unity of universality and individuality, according to the Unification Principle, is that one of God's own attributes is the unity of the Universal Image and the Individual Image. Thus, every created being, also, is the unity of universal and individual images. Because man's way of creating a work of art resembles the way God Himself creates, universality and individuality appear also in man's works of art.

D. *Unity of Eternity and Temporality. Historicalness* is another word for eternity in a work of art, and *actualness* is another word for temporality. The unity of eternity and temporality can be seen in Millet's *The Angelus*. The church and the scene of the people praying represent the eternal (historical) aspects of the painting; the countryside and the landscape—which are peculiar to a certain period and region—represent the temporal (actual) aspects. Their clothes, also, can be seen as part of the painting's actualness or temporality. In this way, historicalness and actualness are united in

The Angelus.

Let's take another example. Suppose there is a vase with beautiful roses arranged in it. The unity of eternity and temporality is also expressed there. The beauty of roses is unchanging, and the form of a rose is the same now as it was in the past and will be in the future. On the other hand, the unique arrangement of the roses, as well as the vase that contains them, are peculiar to the present time and may be seen as the aspects of actualness, or temporality. Thus seen, the vase and the roses are an example of the unity of eternity and temporality. When we realize this, we can appreciate their beauty even more deeply.

IX. ART AND ETHICS

Creation and appreciation are activities of dominion. If man had not fallen he would have grown through the three stages of formation, growth, and completion and would have been given authority of dominion by God. To grow is to perfect one's individuality, and to perfect one's individuality means to become fully united with the Heart of God, or to perfect one's personality. In other words, it is to become an ethical person by experiencing God's love. Such a man is given the right of dominion. True dominion is dominion through love. For this reason, the practical activity of art is inseparably connected with ethics.

Even fallen men have known this and, to a certain extent, have attempted to acquire this ethical aspect of personality. Since, however, they had little philosophical understanding of why artists, also, should be ethical, they sometimes became discouraged. When in financial difficulties, they would often brush aside their ethical principles and produce works that could be sold easily. Man is to be given the authority of dominion after having grown through the formation, growth, and completion stages. Only when artists understand this in detail will they seriously endeavor to become truly ethical.

Numerous artists have dealt with themes of love in their novels, plays, movies, and other art forms, but very rarely were the artists themselves persons of high ethical standards. In fact, a great number of them spent their lives wantonly. Oscar Wilde, for instance, a well-known writer of the nineteenth century, was a typical case: he pursued immoral love and was put in prison for violating the law.

In the Unification Principle view, the kind of love mundane artists have usually portrayed is not God's love, but fallen love—

that is, the fallen love of the archangel, who deceived Eve, as well as the fallen love of Eve, who deceived Adam. As a rule, artists have done nothing but modify and embellish fallen love—though some of them have sincerely tried to express original human nature and original love.

Accordingly, artistic beauty has been expressed on the basis of fallen love, not of true love, or God's love. Only when artists realize God's love in their lives—that is, when they realize the unity of art and ethics—will they be able to create a true work of art.

X. CRITIQUE OF SOCIALIST REALISM

Socialist realism in the communist theory of art stresses expressing things as they really are. Communists say that artists in the capitalist society will not express contradictions within capitalism, but will only express its good qualities, idealizing them. They are, therefore, idealists and romanticists. Socialist realism demands that artists express the conflict between capitalists and laborers, or the miserable lives of laborers and farmers. Socialist realism asserts also that an artist should create in order to help realize a socialist society; that is, he should help to incite public antipathy toward the capitalist society, and lead people toward the socialist ideal.

Lenin said that all literary men should commit themselves to the Party. Stalin said that artists are the engineers who reconstruct men's minds. Gorky, a Russian proletarian writer who was awarded the Stalin prize, said that a writer is a teacher of the proletariat, and that an artist is a gravedigger who buries capitalism, as well as a midwife who helps give birth to socialism. Proletarian art is well and truly under the control of the Communist Party.

Although modern communist art pretends to depict man's original nature, in fact it does not. The communist philosophy of art can never change, because it is based on communist ideology. Under communist regimes, some artists may express divergent views of art, but they are not considered as being representative of the proletariat.

According to historical materialism, art, being a part of social life, is supposed to belong to the superstructure. Since the superstructure is based upon a foundation, it changes when the foundation changes. Communist theory claims that it is the duty of the newly built superstructure to nourish and protect the development of the new foundation and help destroy the old foundation. The foundation consists of the production relations—i.e., the social system. Socialist art, therefore, should contribute to the preservation and development of this newly established social system.

This assertion is based on the materialist idea that spirit comes from matter. The communist theory of art, also, is based on this idea; as long as communists have this idea, art will be a tool for realizing a communist society. It is a lie to say that their art is for the protection of democracy. If they wanted to protect democracy honestly from the bottom of their hearts, they would have to announce that they are giving up the whole of communistic thought, because the principle of democracy can never be produced from communistic materialism and the dialectic. They would have to confirm publicly that their theories of "dialectical materialism," "historical materialism," and other theories based on Marx's *Capital, Communist Manifesto,* etc., are all quite mistaken. But then they would also have to do away with the name "Communist Party," because when they have given up their whole system of thought, the name "Communist Party" becomes devoid of meaning.

Pasternak took part in the Russian Revolution, putting much hope in communism. He later realized he was wrong, and it was then that he wrote *Dr. Zhivago*. The communists criticized him severely, calling him "a bourgeois writer," and a "reactionary element." Although he received a Nobel Prize from the free world, he and his work were criticized by the communist world as being evil and ugly, obviously from completely different standards of value.

H.E. Read criticized the Soviet Union, saying that it is wrong to compel someone to create a work of art in support of a certain dogma. G. Mittal, in India, said that Communism is the major enemy of man's freedom of thought. Ehrenburg, who once received the Stalin prize for Peace, later regretted accepting it. He criticized the writing of one of his friends, which depicted a girl in a textile factory, saying that the girl described in the book was like a machine, with no personality. It is true that people in the Soviet society are regimented and have very narrow scopes within which to develop their individuality.

André Gide wrote the famous *Return from the U.S.S.R.*, after his trip to the Soviet Union. He observed that wherever he went people would give him the same answers to his questions. This showed him that their freedom was restricted. We cannot accept that Soviet art is the honest expression of an individual's heart.

I would like to criticize Soviet art from the standpoint of the

Unification Principle. In one of his books, Marx admits that he found some difficulties in his theory. In his words,

> The difficulty we are confronted with is not, however, that of understanding how Greek art and epic poetry are associated with certain forms of social development. The difficulty is that they still give us aesthetic pleasure and are in certain respects regarded as a standard and unattainable ideal.*

According to Marx, therefore, art is a part of the superstructure and develops on the basis of the economic foundation. So, the superstructure, theoretically, can never remain, after the foundation has been changed. Throughout the two thousand years since the Greek downfall, however, the foundation (social system) has changed several times, whereas some elements of the superstructure (for example, interest in art) did not change. This is the difficulty to which Marx refers; it is counterevidence to his theory of history.

He said that Greek mythology—such as Homer's epic poems *Iliad* and *Odyssey*—can still be aesthetically pleasing to persons living today. According to his historical materialism, the superstructure, including our interest in Greek art, should have vanished completely by now, since the foundation of Greece was completely destroyed long ago. Nevertheless, our interest in Greek mythology remains.

This means that his philosophy, including his theory of art, is wrong. His consideration that art belongs to the superstructure, which is built on an economic foundation, is quite mistaken. He cannot but be mistaken, because his theory is based upon materialism, which asserts that spirit comes from matter. The shortcomings of this notion have already been pointed out in other parts of this book. His theory of art loses its credibility with the loss of the credibility of materialism and the dialectic.

Seen from the standpoint of the Unification Principle, human history has been the history of struggles between good and evil, because of the Fall. The goal is the ideal world, the Kingdom of God. Human history is the history of restoration. Although man has not been conscious of it, God has been working through man's conscience to lead history in the direction of righteousness, goodness, and love.

We can regard the Trojan War, for instance, as the struggle

---

*Marx, *A Contribution to the Critique of Political Economy,* Progress Publishers, Moscow, 1977), p. 217.

between good and evil. In the *Odyssey,* Odysseus found, upon returning home, that his wife had been faithful to him during his ten-year absence after the Trojan War. Several men had attempted to seduce her and to take her away, but she remained chaste to the last. This is a story of righteousness. In making the effort to remain faithful to her husband, she went in the direction of restoration. We unconsciously know that God's providence has continued in every period of history, and feel joy to hear stories of faithfulness that are in accord with it. Although Lenin banned the works of Pushkin, Dostoevsky, Tolstoy, and others, factory workmen read them in secret. Why do they read them? Stories about people who walked the way of restoration and suffered a great deal in pursuing trueness appeal to man's heart. These books contain such stories.

10 THEORY OF HISTORY

INTRODUCTION

What has the future in store for mankind? Is there hope for better times? Should we simply give up and wait for the final destruction of the world? Such are the questions of people today, especially the young.

Although a great number of scholars have expounded their views on the future, none of these views has proved very satisfactory. The only view that has been widely accepted among young people is that of historical materialism, proposed by Marxists. There are two main reasons why communism has spread to all corners of the earth and is attracting so many intellectuals: first, communism offers a view of history; and second, it presents a new ideal for mankind's future.

If we want to go beyond historical materialism, we must have a new and better view of history. The Unification view of history, I believe, has these characteristics. A lot of people have studied the chapter on the "Providence of Restoration" in the Unification Principle, but perhaps many have not fully understood its importance. Accordingly, I have tried to organize this chapter into a system of thought; through this systematization I hope the full significance of the Unification view of history can be perceived.

In my student days, I found myself leaning very much toward communism; later, however, I gave it up, for I felt that its answers were not satisfactory and could not really solve life's problems. After that, I became restless for a while, because I had no new view of history to take its place. Communists are convinced that global communization is the key to solving all the problems mankind faces in the world today. When I abandoned communism, I felt I had to find a new vision for the future, but I didn't even know whether that was possible or not. Since joining the Unification Church, however, my feeling of unrest has disappeared; I have steadfast confidence in this new view of history.

We will not see a communist world in the future, but instead, the ideal world of God's creation. It will be a world governed in accordance with cosmic principles; society will be as one great family, filled with God's love. The significance of our view of history is its ability to give young people who have lost hope a new ideal for the future.

Because Christianity has not presented a convincing view of history, communism has been able to spread all over the world in the last one hundred and twenty years. Christians view history—in a nutshell—as the history of the providence of God, at the end of which Christ will come again, and God will judge the world in order to establish His Kingdom. One can accept such a view as a canon of faith, but it is difficult to accept it as a scientific proposition. God, the judge, sits up in Heaven, rewarding the good and punishing the wicked as He sees fit; He can intervene whenever and wherever He chooses. There seem to be no laws.

The Christian view of history does not offer any theories or laws with regard to God's providence in the world; consequently, it is not easily accepted as a subject of study among other subjects in school curricula. Since history belongs to the field of social sciences, a historical view can be taught as a social science only if it contains theories and laws related to historical development.

We live in an age when science is considered omnipotent. In order to survive today, theories must be empirical and theoretical, as well as presenting concrete formulae. Just as natural science is based upon laws, social sciences—such as economics, politics and jurisprudence—must also be backed up by laws.

Light, for instance, obeys the law of refraction; gases obey Boyle's law and Charles's law; the heavenly bodies follow Newton's law of universal gravitation. All the natural sciences are based on laws; hence, they have authority. Theoretically, where there are no laws there is no authority.

It is reasonable to expect that historical events have also developed according to certain laws—and young people want to learn them. They are fascinated by the possibility of the existence of historical laws, and thus are attracted to historical materialism, which claims to know these laws.

Christianity has been unable to defend itself against the onslaught of the communist ideology. Needless to say, it has also been unable to attack the communist "heresy." The communists maintain that there are materialistic and dialectical laws in history, and they scorn Christians for failing to produce any laws to back up their beliefs.

Historical materialism states that just as spirit is produced from matter, so economics provides the material base in history from which "spirit" arises. Spirit refers to ideology, such as political, philosophical, religious, and moral ideas; these constitute the *superstructure* of society; they are based upon and determined by economy, which is the *infrastructure* of society.

Historical materalism claims that history has developed because economy has developed (or more precisely, the *relations of production* have developed in accordance with the development of the *productive forces;* then, in accordance with the development of the relations of production, the superstructure develops). From the primitive communal society came the slave society, the feudal society, and then the capitalist society. The material conditions of life (productive forces and relations of production) are the determining factor for the ideological development. This is a law of history. The historical view that the economic development precedes that of ideology is nothing but the application of this materialistic view to history.

According to dialectical materialism, development is the result of struggle. Everything contains opposites, which struggle against each other, thus bringing about development. In the same way, history has developed through struggles between two opposing classes. At first glance, this way of thinking seems to be very reasonable, so much so that Christians themselves are becoming convinced of it in great numbers. The Christian ranks have been sadly depleted of intellectuals; Russia and Eastern European nations, once Christian, are now ruled by communism. The Christian forces in those countries have been reduced to a pitiful state. It is the intention of the Unification Church and Unification Thought not only to defend Christianity against the communist ideology, but also to counteract and neutralize that ideology by showing its errors, and then present a better counterproposal. Communism is doomed to lose its ground.

Because God is the God of principle and laws, He not only

created the universe according to laws, but also has been carrying out His providence according to laws. Indeed there were laws in history, and they are described in the "Principle of Restoration."

The laws of historical materialism are not real laws, because they are subjective. Laws must be objective. The sun, for instance, rises in the east and sets in the west, whether we like it or not; this is "objective." Historical laws should also be objective, transcendent, and independent of the human will. The laws of historical materialism, however, cannot be found in history; in other words, actual examples of the laws of historical materialism cannot be identified in any age of history. They are pseudo-laws, fabricated subjectively only to support class struggle and violent revolution. They cannot be called objective laws.

These various assertions will be substantiated when I explain the Unification view of history; first, however, I would like to introduce a representative selection of views of history of past historians.

I. TRADITIONAL VIEWS OF HISTORY
A. THE CYCLIC VIEW

The cyclic view of history originates from Greece. It says that history does not have any specific direction or goal, but repeats itself in circular motion. Its recurring cycles explain the repetitive rise and fall of civilizations. Men and nations prosper if they are lucky, but decline if they are unlucky. Prosperity and decline are guided by the invisible hand of fate. (Accordingly, this view may be called the fatalistic view of history; representative historians holding this view are Herodotus and Thucydides.) As this view does not clarify where man came from or what his purpose is, those who uphold it can hardly have any real hope for a secure and prosperous future.

B. THE PROVIDENTIAL VIEW

St. Augustine, in his book *The City of God*, sets forth this view of history around the time of the fall of the Roman Empire, in the fifth century A.D. He was the first influential thinker to develop a systematic philosophical explanation of God's providence. He said there is a beginning and an end to human history; in other words, history has direction. It develops in a straight line, from the beginning till it reaches its goal. Compared with the cyclic one, this view of history is quite progressive; nevertheless, it is still rather vague.

At the end of the world—according to this view—the Messiah will come; Satan will be bound; Christ will reign for one thousand years. After this, the eternal Kingdom will be established. What the eternal Kingdom is and how it will be formed, however, are not clear from Augustine's writings, perhaps because the Bible itself does not clarify these points. Though St. Augustine's views on the providence of God may have been rather vague, nevertheless they had tremendous influence in Christian theology and led Christianity through the Middle Ages.

C. THE PROGRESSIVE VIEW (SPIRITUAL VIEW)

The modern era began with a reaction against the rigidly God-centered Middle Ages, in which everything was interpreted with God as the standard. Since the people of the Middle Ages had only a vague understanding of God, numerous problems arose. The clergy, headed by the Pope, oppressed the people and ignored human individuality.

In reaction to such circumstances, humanism—a man-centered ideology—appeared, as part of the movement of the Renaissance. The Reformation—a religiously-oriented movement—occurred at about the same time. Based on humanism, the medieval view of history was challenged and then replaced by a new view, according to which technological and social developments continue as long as the human spirit and reason continue to develop. This is the progressive, or spiritual, view of history.

In recent times, science has been making rapid progress. Man has come to believe that he can do anything by himself, through the simple use of reason. The providential help of God, considered essential in the Middle Ages, has largely been dismissed as unnecessary. The various views of history presented in this period differ among themselves, of course, but they generally agree on this one point that the development of history is caused and explained by the development of the human spirit and reason. Representatives of this view are Vico, Voltaire, Condorcet, Kant, Herder, Lessing, and Hegel.

Specifically with regard to Hegel, there are scholars who set him apart from the others. He had a spiritual view of history, and the spirit to which he referred was the absolute spirit, or Logos—that is,

God.* The absolute spirit manifests itself in the visible form of nature, which then develops to form man. Man, therefore, is a manifestation of the absolute spirit. Consequently, what makes history develop is not man, but the absolute spirit (world spirit) working through man.

D. THE REVOLUTIONARY VIEW

The revolutionary view of history came after the progressive view. This is the historical materialism of Marx. According to this theory, history develops on the basis of the material conditions—that is, productive forces and relations of production. Productive forces are tools, skills, knowledge, experience, and techniques by which man obtains the necessities of life. Relations of production are the social relationships of human beings viewed in the light of the means of production.

At certain points in economic development, the relations of production become a hindrance to the progress of productive forces. Productive forces, however, cannot be stopped; relations of production must be broken down; in other words, the old social system must be destroyed and a new one built. The outcome of the struggle between productive forces and relations of production is revolution.

The ruling class, it is held, desperately tries to maintain the established relations of production, whereas the ruled class wishes to see the productive forces continue their development. Their struggle, therefore, actually means the struggle between the rulers and the ruled. This is how historical materialism explains social change and development. Societies develop, not by the work of the human spirit or reason—as the progressive view had said—but by economic, or material forces.

Historical materialism may sound true, but a careful scrutiny of its foundations and assumptions will show it actually is false. This brings to mind the circumstances of the Human Fall at the Garden of Eden. Satan, also, approached Eve with words that seemed to be true but actually were false. He tempted her by saying, "When you eat of the fruit of the tree of the knowledge of good and evil your eyes will be opened." The consequences of the Fall show that those

---

*Hegel frequently used the terms 'Logos', 'absolute spirit,' 'idea' *(Begriff)*, and 'spirit,' instead of the word 'God'.

words were totally false. In a similar way, communists present and interpret social phenomena in any way that will suit their needs, cloaking their theories with a scientific garb and luring a great number of persons into their ranks.

Communists say that productive forces and relations of production are material things, but we insist that they are more than just material. Through the "Theory of the Original Image" and "Ontology," I have shown that every existence and phenomenon has the dual characteristics of *Sung Sang* and *Hyung Sang*. Productive Forces and Relations of Production, therefore, have these dual characteristics also. This is easily shown. Technology has both material and spiritual aspects: laborers have to learn technical skills, which can never be learned without knowledge—and knowledge is a spiritual reality. At the same time, the necessary physical strength is a material power; so, productive forces have both spiritual and material aspects. The same can be said with regard to relations of production; they are human relations, which should be centered on ethical and spiritual values.

Man develops economy in order to satisfy his desire to live a more comfortable life. Economy, therefore, exists solely because of man's desires. Since desire is essentially spiritual, even economy has both physical and spiritual aspects. (See "Axiology," section 2) The reason is that all things are created as individual truth bodies—that is, in the image of God. Since God has the dual characteristics of *Sung Sang* and *Hyung Sang*, all things must likewise have these dual characteristics. The assertion, therefore, that economy is only material is a one-sided and tendentious fallacy, as is the ensuing view of the development of history.

The spiritual aspect, or *Sung Sang*, is the subject; the material aspect, or *Hyung Sang*, is the object. Accordingly, we can say that the causal power for the development of history originates from a spiritual element, that is human desire, and not from a material element. Even though spirit may be the subject and the most important element, matter, nevertheless, must be included as well, for without it there can be no productive forces. Both elements need to enter into a give-and-take relationship in order for history to develop. The Unification view is neither a spiritual view nor a materialistic view of history. This does not mean, however, that it is a composite view. Our view is founded on the Original Image, which is the United Body of *Sung Sang* and *Hyung Sang*, as is man.

Consequently, it is the Unification view that *Sung Sang* and *Hyung Sang*—or spirit and matter—have worked jointly to bring about the development of history.

Out of all the historical views, that of historical materialism is being most strongly disseminated in the world today, in spite of its inconsistencies. Its propagators declare with confidence that the communist society will surely come in the future, so it has gained a large following, especially among the young.

E. THE PHILOSOPHY-OF-LIFE VIEW

The progressive view had become too inclined toward rationalism, disregarding the emotional and real aspects of human life. On the other hand, the revolutionary view had dealt with man as a being subordinate to material forces and laws, disregarding man's subjectivity and his ability to rule over material things and laws. After that, a new view appeared, taking positions different from those of the above two views. That was the view based on the Philosophy of Life, which dealt with history as the growth process of life, as the unity of emotion, intellect, and will, and as an expression of the direct experience of life. Dilthey, Bergson, and Simmel are representatives of the philosophy-of-life view of history.

This view, also, contains a blind spot. The suffering, pain, and unhappiness in human history are occurrences that inevitably take place during the growth process of life, according to this view. Accordingly, there is no real hope to liberate mankind from pain and anxiety.

F. THE CULTURAL VIEW

Until the present, the term 'history' had usually been used to refer to the record of a people's or of a country's past. Most historians have concentrated on political and national histories; world history is considered to be a mere synthesis of these histories.

Arnold Toynbee, on the other hand, saw history from the standpoint of culture. If we are to study human history, we cannot study each nation as a separate entity. American history, for instance, cannot be studied separately from British history, for those who pioneered the United States were British. British history, on the other hand, must be viewed in the larger context of European history, especially Italian history. This, in turn, must be viewed in the context of Greek history, and so on.

The history of any one country, Toynbee maintains, is connected with that of other countries. For this reason, a study of history should have a world-wide perspective; its themes should be about civilizations or cultures, rather than national events. When we study the history of the Far East, for example, we should regard Japan, Korea, and China as originating from the same culture, and study them from this perspective. This approach is called the civilization view of history, or cultural view of history.

Here I wish briefly to outline Toynbee's view of history. Since modern times, few historians (theologians aside) have dared to believe in St. Augustine's providential view of history. Toynbee, however, introduced the idea of God's providence in his theories, making, therefore, a very significant contribution.

Toynbee questioned the validity of traditional theories concerning the birth of civilizations. One of them says that civilizations developed along the valleys of large rivers, such as the Nile, Tigris, Euphrates, Indus, and Yellow rivers. According to most historians, this happened because of the physical advantages of those regions, especially their fertility due to silt accumulation from seasonal flooding. People were naturally attracted to settle there and to begin farming. In order to irrigate their crops they developed technology and constructed dams. They also had to learn how to prevent or control floods, which could wash away everything they worked for. This is one way to explain the birth of civilizations. Other historians, however, have a different theory. In their view, certain races just naturally had the talents and ability required to develop a civilization, whereas other races did not.

Toynbee found weaknesses in these traditional theories. The rivers around which civilizations developed are not the only ones in the world that have special environmental conditions. Other rivers, such as the Mississippi and the Yangtze rivers have equally good environmental conditions; yet, no great civilizations rose up around them.

Toynbee formulated his new theory about the birth of civilizations based upon an idea he found in Goethe's *Faust*. He took a hint from the "Prologue in Heaven." Three archangels and Mephistopheles come before God, and the three archangels praise the perfectness and greatness of God's creation. Afterwards, Mephistopheles criticizes God's creation of humankind. Then, God mentions a righteous man named Faust. So Mephistopheles asks God for permission to corrupt Faust and lead him into betraying God. Permission is granted. Mephistopheles goes out and joyfully begins his destructive work. He goes into the body of Faust and corrupts him, making him drink heavily and spend his time uselessly. Mephistopheles is happy with what he has done, because he thinks that he has managed to destroy the work of God, who is supposed to be omniscient and omnipotent.

Eventually, however, Faust repents, leaves his evil ways, and returns to God. The Heavenly Kingdom, which was supposedly lost, is recovered. Seeing this, Mephistopheles feels vexed. He realizes that God has actualy been using him. God's creation was so perfect that He had nothing to do after completing it. He had been bored and wanted some stimulation; when Mephistopheles asked permission to destroy the world, God willingly gave it to him. After he had destroyed the world, God came along and recovered it. He was happy to do it, because it was something more to be achieved.

In this story, Toynbee says that Mephistopheles, or Satan, had challenged God, and He had responded to the challenge. This is the origin of Toynbee's concept of *challenge* and *response*. He said that civilizations emerge from man's response to a challenge, such as the flooding of a river. In order to respond to the challenge of the flooding of a river, for instance, God works through man to develop technology and build dams and irrigation systems.

A civilization, therefore, starts as a response to a challenge. If it fails to meet the challenge, it perishes; if it succeeds, however, it begins to grow. This is how God has been working to make civilizations develop. Through the process of challenge and response, history is moving toward the formation of God's Kingdom, but Toynbee is unsure that it can be established on earth.

Tonybee views civilizations as having a life span similar to that of humans. He divided it into five stages: birth, growth, breakdown, disintegration, and death. Whenever a civilization emerges as a response to a challenge, a *creative minority* appears to lead the masses and to set an example for them to follow. After the civilization becomes stable and prosperous, problems may appear, as the creative minority tends to become corrupt. (In this stage it is known as the *dominant minority*.) Because of their power and position, they no longer think of the masses, but turn into a greedy and selfish ruling minority. Such cases can be found in nations all over the world.

When this happens, those who are discontented begin to organize themselves. There is a group of discontented people within the state (the internal proletariat) and a group of discontented people outside the state (the external proletariat). The word 'proletariat' here has a meaning that differs from the one given to it by Marx. In Marxism, proletariat refers to unpropertied people, or the labor class; in Toynbee's theory, it refers to those who are discontented with the age in which they are living and feel alienated from it.

As discontentment grows, the dominant minority strengthens its military control within the state in order to prevent an internal uprising, while attacking neighboring states with the intention of expanding its own territory into a *universal state*. Though large in territory, the state is already beginning to erode and get out of control from within.

At the disintegration stage, the internal proletariat turns to spiritual values, forming a religious group that ultimately seeks love and compassion. This higher religion, which Toynbee calls the *universal church,* keeps the civilization alive by preserving a germ of life through the difficult period between the dissolution of one civilization and the genesis of another. At the same time, militant groups form to oppose the state from outside. Here three forces come into conflict: the ruling minority, the religious groups, and the militant groups. As a result, this universal state, which by now possesses a very large territory, becomes unable to function, and thus perishes. The Roman Empire is an example of this situation. Even though its territory covered all the area around the Mediterranean Sea and beyond, it became ungovernable. Christianity rose as a protest to its internal corruption; rebellions took place in the provinces; and the empire fell with the invasion of the Germanic tribes.

Toynbee writes in *A Study of History* that today's western civilization is in the stage of disintegration. He maintains, however, that if the leaders take responsibility to make great effort, western civilization can be saved, and a universal state—literally worldwide—can be established.

Today's Christians, it is held, should not deny communism completely; rather, they should learn from its good points. Since the monopolistic capitalist system has numerous deficiencies, we should combine the economic system of socialism with the liberal and humanistic views of capitalism in order to establish a new universal government. If leaders fulfill their responsibility by carrying out such a plan, our civilization can be revived, but he is not completely certain of this. He feels that the political and spiritual unification of the world may not necessarily be achieved by a western agency. He maintains, however, that a truly universal state, based upon a higher religion must come about soon, if mankind is to survive at all. This, Toynbee believes, is the only alternative to self-destruction.

This is a brief outline of Toynbee's view of history; through it we can see he had a certain understanding of the providence of God. The problem with his view is that it is rather pessimistic and fails to give young people any concrete hope for the future. This is one of the reasons why his ideas are no longer widely supported in the world today. Nevertheless, we can say Toynbee's view has fulfilled a mission similar to that of John the Baptist, in the sense that it has prepared the way for a new view of history based on the providence of God—the Unification Theory of History.

Introducing an awareness of God's providence into his theory of history was a great step forward; from the point of view of God's providence, this cannot but be regarded as Toynbee's major achievement. Just as other historians have accepted Toynbee's idea of God's providence in history, so will they soon accept the Unification view of history, including it in their lectures in schools, as part of social science.

G. COMPARATIVE ANALYSIS OF THE PROVIDENTIAL VIEW AND THE REVOLUTIONARY VIEW

Communism has spread all over the world, overwhelming Western Christian countries. The reason—without exaggeration—is that the revolutionary view of history has been more persuasive than the providential view of history. The revolutionary view is more persuasive because it is the completion-stage thought on the Satanic side. Accordingly, a new view of history on the Heavenly side should be established in order to overcome the revolutionary view. Before presenting such a view—that is, the Unification view of History—I think it would be useful to know why the providential view has been defeated by the revolutionary view, in spite of being on the Heavenly side.*

---

*The providential view presented here is based on St. Augustine's ideas. Though other Christian thinkers hold similar views, I have adopted St. Augustine's view as being the most fundamental among them.

1. The Beginning of History

The providential view says that human history began with the Fall of man; it started, therefore, as sinful history. The Fall was caused by the first human ancestors' eating the fruit of the Tree of the Knowledge of Good and Evil. But most people, even Christians, think this explanation is no more than a myth. This view, therefore, is not persuasive today.

On the other hand, the revolutionary view maintains that human history started from the primitive communal society. Furthermore, it says the development of the productive forces divided society into classes: the ruling class and the ruled class. This view, which is supported by Lewis H. Morgan's Theory of Ancient Society, seems more persuasive—especially to intellectuals—than the providential view.

2. The Motive Power of Development

In the Providential View, God's Providence is considered the motive power of development in history. It has not made clear, however, what kinds of laws have worked in history. God rewards the good and punishes the evil, according to His providence. This explanation is only a matter of belief; it is difficult for intellectuals to accept it today.

The revolutionary view, on the other hand, says the motive power consists of the productive forces. According to the development of the productive forces, human society has changed from the classless, primitive communal society to the *class society*—first to slave society; next, to feudal society; then to capitalist society; and finally to the classless communist society, through socialism. In this view, the development of history is material and proceeds in accordance with material laws. The revolutionary view seems scientific, while the providential view does not.

3. Opponents and Struggle

According to the providential view, there has been struggle between those who belong to the City of God and those who belong to the City of the World. Behind those people, good angels, led by Michael, and evil angels, led by Satan (the Dragon) have been struggling, and the Dragon will be cast out on earth in the Last Days.

(Revelation 12:7-9)

On the other hand, the revolutionary view says history has developed through the struggle between the ruling class—which owns the productive instruments—and the ruled class, which has only the labor force. The providential view is considered today as an imaginative story, and a matter of belief; by contrast, the revolutionary view seems quite congruent with modern man's perception of the world.

4. Events at the End of History

The providential view holds that, at his second coming, Christ will come down from the clouds and will judge good and evil, giving eternal glory to those who belong to the City of God and eternal damnation to those who belong to the City of the World. This is the Last Judgment. But this, also, is considered only a matter of belief; besides, there are numerous interpretations of what will take place in the Last Judgment, depending on various theologians; this view, therefore, is not persuasive. On the other hand, the revolutionary view claims that at the end of history revolution will occur to exterminate class society. The last class society is capitalist society. Violent revolution and the dictatorship of the proletariat are justified in this view. Here, too, the revolutionary view seems more convincing than the providential view.

5. The Ending of History

In the providential view, the ending of history is the ending of the sinful world, but it is not clear how the end will come or what will actually happen. On the other hand, in the revolutionary view, the ending of history is the ending of class society—that is, the ending of capitalist society. It says that the gap between the rich and the poor, or the ruling and the ruled, has now come to the peak, and this is the symptom of the final day of capitalism. Here, again, the revolutionary view is more concrete and more convincing than the providential view.

6. The New World after the End of History

According to the providential view, the *millennium* will come after the end of sinful history, and Christ will reign on earth for a thousand years; those who participate in the first resurrection shall reign with Christ. (Revelation 20:1-7) But it is not clear what resurrection means or what the millennium is like. By contrast, in the revolutionary view, the ideal of the communist society, which will come after the end of class society, is concrete and realistic, even if it is something difficult to put into practice, as history has shown.

In conclusion, the revolutionary view appears more reasonable, more logical, and more convincing than the providential view; consequently, a large number of intellectuals have been attracted to it. Under such circumstances, the free world, which is based on Christianity, will be unable to stop the expansion of communism. Here lies the necessity for the appearance, on the Heavenly side, of a new view of history that can overcome the revolutionary view, supplementing and revitalizing the providential view.

According to the Unification Principle, the evil side (Satan) imitates the ideal of the Heavenly side in advance. The revolutionary view of history is, therefore, the evil view established by Satan in anticipation of the appearance of the new Heavenly view. In other words, when the Heavenly view appears, it will set forth a new view of history that can overcome the revolutionary view. Undoubtedly, the Unification view of history contains such requisites.

II. THE UNIFICATION VIEW OF HISTORY
A. FUNDAMENTAL POINTS

Basically, the Unification View cannot be classified under the cyclic, providential (i.e., Augustinian), progressive, philosophy-of-life, materialistic, or cultural view. What kind of view is it, then? It is a view based on the premise that human history contains the three aspects of "history of sin," "history of re-creation," and "history of restoration."

First, human history is the history of sin. It is not normal history, or principled history, because it derives from the Fall of man. We cannot apply the laws of development observed in nature to human history directly, because in nature there is no sin, whereas in human history there is. Conversely, the laws that our research may discover as applicable to human history do not necessarily coincide with the laws of nature; they may be similar, but not identical. Since human history has been marred by sin, there must be different laws to explain its transition from one stage to another.

Second, human history is the history of re-creation. Because of the human Fall, creation became imperfect, lost its connection with

God, and came under the dominion of Satan. Man and society, therefore, need to be made perfect; in other words, they need to be re-created.

Third, human history is the history of restoration. It is not just "providential history," as St. Augustine said; it is the history of the "providence of restoration," through which man and the world are to be restored. Unification Thought, therefore, clarifies the nature of God's providence.

B. THE ORIGIN, DIRECTION, AND GOAL OF HISTORY

There is an origin and a direction in history. The Christian providential view of history believes that history has an origin; other thinkers do so as well. Jaspers, for instance, said that the origin of historical development was man's creation by God, not his Fall. If this were the case, then human history would have proceeded in a natural way. If the history we have seen is natural, and has been carried out by original man, what an imperfect creation on God's part! The Unification Thought view, however, is different; it places the origin of historical development at the Fall of man, not at his creation.

Human history, according to Jaspers, began long before cultural history, back in the prehistoric past, when man's fires lit up the caves he lived in. (Jaspers calls this the Promethean Age.) According to the Unification point of view, however, history began from the Fall of the first human ancestors. Here a question might be asked with regard to the number of the first human ancestors: were they one couple or many couples? Many people today believe in the pluralistic view, according to which there were several original couples (Cro-Magnon man, Java man, Peking Man, etc.); but we hold the monistic view and maintain that the original human ancestors were just one couple—Adam and Eve. (See *Divine Principle*, especially Part I, Chapters 1 and 2.)

The goal of history, therefore, is the realization of God's ideal world of creation. This is the ideal that every person cherishes, because it was once promised to us by God and then lost as a consequence of the human Fall. For this reason, every person has continuously sought the ideal world (though unconsciously at times), and God has done likewise.

The origin and goal of history, therefore, are definite. Moreover, we do not feel that history will end upon reaching its goal. On the contrary, since the purpose of history is to restore mankind and the original world, when this is done mankind will lead a sinless life here on earth, by living according to God's ideal of creation. Here the Unification view is quite clear, as opposed to Augustine's view, for example, which says that at the end-time the earth will be incinerated and God will make a new heaven and a new earth.

Whether or not there is an origin and a goal in history has been a problem hard enough to solve; aside from this, the issue of how to achieve that goal has been a major concern. These questions generate a great deal of controversy among historians, who take definite positions against one another, according to their various interpretations.

For Marx, the origin of history is the primitive communal society. Though he does not speak about the end of the world as such, he does, nevertheless, say that the goal of history is the realization of the communist society. After this goal has been reached, Marx does not speak clearly about the fate of the communist society.

According to Marxism, not only the origin of history and its goal, but also the process through which this goal is to be realized, have been previously determined. From the primitive communal society, to the slave society, to the feudal society, to the capitalist society, to the socialist society, and finally to the communist society—the developmental stages of history are already determined. This view is known as *determinism*.

On the other hand, the view that the origin, goal, and process of history are not determined is known as *indeterminism*. Toynbee's view is an acknowledged example of indeterminism. Though he says that every civilization follows the pattern of birth, growth, breakdown, disintegration, and death, yet if man fulfills his responsibility and responds to the challenge, a supposedly doomed nation can be revived.

Toynbee maintains that God's goal is to establish His Kingdom, but no one knows how soon that will be realized, for it depends on how man responds to the challenges he must face. This can also be called *theory of free will*, as it asserts that history develops according to man's free will.

The Unification view of history seems to be both deterministic and indeterministic. It is deterministic in asserting that history has an origin and a goal (to be reached in definite stages); on the other hand, it is indeterministic in asserting that the attainment of the goal partially depends on the ability of the various providential figures to fulfill their portion of responsibility. In other words, whether the course of history moves directly toward the goal, or makes a detour, or is prolonged is not determined. Noah's family for instance, failed to complete its portion of responsibility in the Old Testament period. Had they been successful, the Messiah would have been able to come shortly thereafter. Since failure occurred in numerous other instances in the providential history, the attainment of the goal of history has been delayed for six thousand years (according to the symbolic numbers of the Bible).

The goal of history, therefore, is determined; the process to reach it, however, is not. This is a unique view, which must be expressed by a new term. I would like to offer the term *theory of responsibility,* or *responsibilism.*

Indeed, whenever a new thought appears, new terms are coined to express its nuances and are eventually integrated into common usage. Now, for instance, we use the expression "law of give-and-take action" and "correlative elements", rather than "dialectic" and "opposing elements." Time will show that the Marxian terms will pass away, and the Unification ones will replace them.

C. THE LAWS OF HISTORY

Communists have continually denounced the Christian view of history, saying that it has no laws. They are confident that they have defeated it, and that the Christian view of history can never again be reconstructed. Contrary to their expectations, the Unification view of history has appeared. They have been surprised and horrified to learn that a new view of history has appeared and that it contains history's true laws. There are two general categories of laws in history: the laws of creation and the laws of restoration.

1. The Laws of Creation

The first laws we can observe in history are the laws of creation. The reason why the laws of creation have been applied in history is that history has been the history of re-creation. God applied certain laws when He created the universe, and He applies the same laws to the history of re-creation.

If I were to single out the most important of these laws, they would be the following six: the law of correlativity, the law of give-and-take action, the law of the dominion of the center, the law of completion through three stages, the law of the period of the number six, and the law of responsibility.

(a) The Law of Correlativity

The correlativity of subjective and objective elements is the first pre-requisite for progress in history, whether it be religious, cultural, political, economic, or scientific progress. The correlative elements in history refer (1) to *Sung Sang* and *Hyung Sang*, such as spiritual culture and material culture, and man and environment; and (2) to principal individual (individuals) and subordinate individual (individuals)—such as king and subjects, government and people, and managers and laborers. I would like to explain this law, giving an example of correlativity of *Sung Sang* and *Hyung Sang* in history.

One time I spoke with a Korean professor who specialized in political history. He realized, though not clearly, that there seem to be laws that vertically penetrate human history. He called this a *vertical axis,* but he said he was unable to understand the essence of it. I explained to him that from the standpoint of the Unification Principle this is the law of correlativity. I went on to explain that just as God is the United Body of *Sung Sang* and *Hyung Sang,* so is man. History also has both *Sung Sang* and *Hyung Sang* aspects, just as man does.

As an application of this law, we can see that central history is divided into two currents. With the providential purpose of restoring man's spirit, Hebraism, the *Sung Sang* current, entered the Roman Empire and absorbed part of it to become the Christian civilization, which went on to lead the West during the period of the Middle Ages. It continued through the modern age and finally became the western democratic civilization of today.

Hellenism, the *Hyung Sang* current, providentially had its primary purpose in restoring the environment of man. The Hellenistic civilization also entered the Roman Empire and formed the Roman civilization. After the western Roman civilization perished, it was preserved in the Byzantine culture centered on Constantinople and the Saracen civilization of the Middle East. It appeared again in Italy at the end of the Middle Ages and gave impetus to the Renaissance. It continued as the thought of the Enlightenment via British empiricism (Locke and others) and French materialism. In the form of the

Enlightenment it caused the French Revolution; from there it appeared as socialism, and finally as communism.

The confrontation between democracy and communism can be seen as the confrontation between Hebraism and Hellenism. This is the vertical axis of history, the central axis; all else is peripheral history.

We can make such an assertion because we know the laws of God's creation. Everything in the universe exists with the correlativities of *Sung Sang* and *Hyung Sang,* positivity and negativity, principal element and subordinate element, reflecting the correlativity of God's *Sung Sang* and *Hyung Sang,* and Positivity and Negativity. Since history has been the record of fallen man's deeds, it resembles fallen man. In fallen man, the *Sung Sang* (spirit) and the *Hyung Sang* (body) are separated, though not completely. So, the spiritual and physical senses of fallen man are not in harmony; men on earth, therefore, do not have a clear understanding of the spiritual world. The senses are separated, but the correlativity itself is not gone. History, therefore, follows a pattern similar to that of fallen man. Consequently, Hebraism and Hellenism, which originally should have developed together in history, have actually been developing separately, influencing each other occasionally.

(b) The Law of Give-and-Take Action

For any development to occur, give-and-take action must take place between subject and object. The law of give-and-take action, therefore, cannot be separated from the law of correlativity. They are like the two sides of a coin. For example, government and people must cooperate in harmonious give-and-take action in order for a harmonious society to be formed and to develop.

Give-and-take action is a prerequisite for invention. Watt, for instance, invented the steam engine, but he did not do it all by himself. He cooperated with a lot of people, who helped make his invention possible. When someone works to develop technology or to put it to practical use, harmonious give-and-take action must take place between laborers, technicians, machines, and so forth.

The cause of the steady development of history is found in the law of give-and-take action. The harmonious give-and-take action between the correlative (not opposing) subject and object elements gives rise to development.

Marxists insist that both nature and society develop through struggle between opposing elements. Admittedly, there have been numerous struggles during the course of human history, but Marxists recognize only one kind of struggle—that between classes. They claim that history has developed because of class struggle. According to Unification Thought, however, the basis of the numerous conflicts in history has not been struggles between classes, but struggles between good and evil. I stated before that development comes about only through give-and-take action and has nothing to do with struggle. Then, what role does struggle play in history? Has it facilitated the development of history or has it hindered it? I will discuss this point in more detail later in this chapter, under the topic of "the basic laws of historical change."

Whether man is fallen or not, development is brought about only through give-and-take action. Although the society in which we live is non-principled, there remain some aspects of it that are principled in external appearance. It is a non-principled society with a principled appearance. It is a Satanic society that looks like a principled one. The direction in which it is going, however, is quite different from that of the principled society; yet even in the fallen society some aspects of principled give-and-take action can be found.

In conclusion, it is our assertion that the development of history has been realized in accordance with the principle of harmonious give-and-take action.

(c) **The Law of the Dominion of the Center**

Whenever give-and-take action between subject and object takes place, the subject always takes the position of center. This is considered as one of the laws of creation. I stated in the section, "The Existing Mode of the Existing Being," that all created beings are involved in circular motion. This, however, can only take place if there is a center—that is, a subject—as well as an object that revolves around it.

In the quadruple base, the Heart (or purpose) and the United Body do not directly take part in circular motion. It is the subject and the object that do so. Purpose—the center of the quadruple base—is actually within the subject. Accordingly, the object revolves centering on the subject; in other words, it is controlled by the subject. The earth, for instance, revolves around the sun; we say, therefore, that the earth is controlled by the sun. The same law applies in the providential history. God first prepares a suitable social environment, and then selects a central person to control it and to move His providence to a higher stage. This is the law of the dominion of the center.

Japan, for example, was in a state of great confusion at the close of the Tokugawa era; some new figures appeared and brought about the Meiji Reformation. Korea, also, was in a state of confusion just before the May 16th Revolution; new leaders appeared and led the people into a new era.

Since it is one of God's Principles, during a period of confusion, to raise up a central figure that can gain control over the environment, Satan imitates this method and does the same thing. At the time of the Bolshevik Revolution, for example, Lenin emerged and became the central person, controlling the situation and pulling the whole country in his direction. This is another example of the law of the dominion of center.

Which is more important, the central figure or the environment? Communists say that the environment is more important, based on their materialistic ideology, which claims that spirit is a product of matter and that man is just a product of the environment. Man's spiritual value is secondary in this system. They say that when the environment becomes confused and suitable for a revolution, the needed revolutionary leaders will naturally appear. They feel, therefore, that environment is fundamentally more important than leaders. Unification Thought differs from the communist view. Although both the central figure and the environment are considered important and necessary, Unification Thought stresses the role of the central figure (subject), rather than that of the environment, since it recognizes the law of the dominion of center.

Every time a central person was unable to fulfill his portion of responsibility, providential history was prolonged. This means there is only one central person in each stage of the providence. If it had not been for Moses (or a Moses-like figure), would the Israelites have been able to leave Egypt and enter Canaan? No, they would not. Likewise, if it had not been for Lenin (or a Lenin-like figure), the Bolshevik Revolution would not have been successful.

Not just anyone can become a central person; God selects someone who has the proper personality, knowledge, leadership ability, and other essential qualities. (Satan, who hinders the providence of God, chooses his central figures in the same way.) Even if

Trotsky had possessed the leadership qualities that Lenin had, it would have been very difficult for him to carry out a successful revolution, for he thought it necessary to bring about world revolution first, before a revolution in Russia could be successful. If he had led the Russian Revolution, it would probably have ended in failure. Similarly, the Chinese Revolution was successful primarily due to its leadership—that of Mao Tse-tung. It would not have been successful with only Liu Shao-chi and Chou En-lai.

Though the central figure is very important, yet there can be no subject without an object. Consequently, God raises up a particular central person only after He has prepared a suitable environment. This person is the only one who can meet the necessary conditions; he is the only one who can be relied upon. In the Old Testament age, for instance, God gave Noah's family a mission, but they failed. After that, there was no other family that God could use immediately; thus, providential history was prolonged. Although there are various reasons for the prolongation of providential history until today, the main reason is that at crucial points the central persons have failed, and there was no one else to succeed them.

Should we direct our energies into reforming the environment, or should we try to reform man first? In Marx's opinion, the environment is more important; thus, he tried to change it. We, however, feel that we should first work to reform the human spirit.

Communists say verbally that the environment is of greater importance; in actuality, however, they carry out very extensive education programs to develop their leaders, showing that they, also, know that man is more important than the environment, and unconsciously recognize the law of the dominion of the center. They say that leaders will naturally arise from the environment, after they have put society into confusion (just as spirit comes from matter), yet they make a great effort to train people in the communist ideology.

If a great leader appears and fulfills his responsibility, he can mold the environment and move it into the proper direction. No matter how hard the general populace struggles to find a way out of social confusion, unless a leader appears to take charge, no improvement will be made.

Most young communists in the free world have been taught that to assert the importance of leaders is bourgeoisie mentality. In a free country, they oppose the appearance of leaders in principle and in action, for this reason; another reason is that the emergence of a great leader might work against their revolutionary fomentations. By contrast, we assert the law of the dominion of the center.

(d) The Law of Completion Through Three Stages

All things should be perfected after passing through the three stages of growth—that is, formation, growth, and completion. The providence of restoration, also, passes through three stages, but cannot be prolonged beyond this. Failure in the formation stage carries with it a prolongation of providential history and leads to the growth stage. Failure in the growth stage causes another prolongation and leads to the completion stage. Once in the completion stage, the providence must necessarily succeed.

In the providence for restoring a family, both Adam's family and Noah's family failed. Abraham's family, therefore, had necessarily to succeed. Since Abraham made a mistake, God had to call his son Isaac and then Jacob, whose victory could be taken as Abraham's victory. This explains why, to this day, the Jews call God "the God of Abraham, the God of Isaac, and the God of Jacob." The three patriarchs are as one.

Similarly, the third Adam must necessarily fulfill the purpose of the providence of restoration. If he fails in one direction, he must succeed in another. In Jesus' case, he had only one possible course; when the people failed to accept him, he had nowhere to go.

Just as God works His providence through three stages, Satan's movement, also, develops through three stages. Furthermore, just as on God's side there is the "law of completion through three stages," on Satan's side we find its counterpart, the "law of inevitable failure through three stages." Communism is the third stage of a movement whose first stage is humanism (Renaissance), and whose second stage was the Enlightenment. Consequently, the fall of communism is inevitable. Moreover, since communism—an atheistic thought—persecutes Christianity, it is bound to fail, just as God's providence in its third stage is bound to succeed.

The Roman Empire reigned with its *Pax Romana* for two hundred years. It seemed so strong, and nobody thought it would ever fall, though some people recognized certain signs of decay. Constantine the Great, who officially recognized Christianity, and Theodosius I, who declared Christianity the state religion, were believed to be God-instated emperors. Why, then, did God allow the empire to fall? Because, though they were God-instated, nevertheless they exploited Christianity for their own gain.

Clearly, the time in which a non-principled nation appears to be most prosperous is the time closest to its end. Communism, which has extended its power throughout the world (as the completion stage of the powers opposing God), is destined to fail.

(e) The Law of the Period of the Number Six

According to Genesis, God commanded that there be light on the first day, and there was light. On the second day, He created the firmament and separated the waters above and below it. On the third day, He separated the earth and the sea and created plants on the earth. On the fourth day, He created the sun, moon, and stars; on the fifth, animals; and on the sixth day, He created man (Adam and Eve). We can see, therefore, that Adam was created with the period of the number six. This period of the number six applies also to the providence of re-creation. Accordingly, God had to start a new providence six centuries before sending Jesus (Second Adam).

The Greek civilization emerged about the sixth century B.C., with the providential purpose primarily to develop man's environment and to form a basis on which to accept the Messiah. The Greeks developed science, art, mathematics, politics, philosophy, and other fields of knowledge to a high degree.

On the other hand, God also prepared the hearts of men to receive Jesus. In the East, He sent Confucius, Mencius, and Lao-tzu, around the sixth century B.C., to show men how to live conscientiously. The purpose of all this preparation was for people to accept —not to reject—Jesus, six centuries later.

In India, Gautama Buddha appeared about six centuries before Christ in order to turn the minds of the Indian people toward goodness. At that time, Brahmanism had developed a rigid and discriminatory caste system. The lowest class comprised the Sudras, or manual laborers (who, incidentally, were the indigenous natives); these were followed by the Vaisyas, who were merchants, tradesmen, and farmers. Then came the Kshatriyas who were formed of warriors, rulers, and royalty; on top of these there were the Brahmins, or the priestly class. These distinctions were extremely rigid; inter-caste marriage was strictly prohibited. Members of different castes were forbidden even to eat meals together.

With such class consciousness, they would have been unable to receive Jesus, who was to teach that we ought to love every person equally, just as the sun shines on all without discrimination. Accordingly, Buddha appeared and taught that every person, regardless of class, partakes of the Buddha nature—thus advocating the equality of all humans.

Six centuries before Christ, the Israelites were taken into exile in Babylon. The leadership had fallen into faithlessness, and the value of the temple could no longer be upheld. In order to renew the Jewish faith, God allowed them to be taken to an unknown land, where they had to work hard until they became repentant. Many prophets—such as Jeremiah and later, Malachi—attempted to lead the people back to a faithful life. At the same time, Democritus, Socrates, Plato, Aristotle, and other scholars appeared in Greece, and the Greek civilization developed to a high degree.

Around the sixth century B.C., therefore, great leaders appeared both in the East and in the West, though there was no actual contact between them. This is the period that Jaspers calls the *Axial Era*. What is the significance of it? Historians are still pondering this question. Actually, all of these leaders appeared about the same time in order to lay a foundation to receive the Messiah. According to the law of the period of the number six, God worked to re-create the spirit of man by sending intellectual and spiritual leaders six centuries before He sent the Messiah.

A similar providence was carried out in preparation for the Second Coming of the Messiah. The Renaissance and the Reformation, which began around the fourteenth century and were in full swing by the sixteenth century, marked the beginning of this preparation.

The purpose of the Renaissance was to prepare a suitable environment for the coming of the Messiah. It was to bring back that high level of material civilization in Europe, which had existed in the times of the Greek and Roman Empires, but had withered away after Jesus' crucifixion. Thus, the civilization initiated by the Renaissance started out as an imitation of the Greek civilization, and then developed along a materialistic path. Partly, it was a reaction to medieval Christianity, which had neglected the restoration of man's environment. This can be called the *Hyung Sang culture*.

A reformation of Christianity was also necessary to restore man's spiritual life. The leaders of the church at the end of the

Middle Ages had become corrupt and trampled upon the fundamental rights of man. The Christian practices of that age were somewhat similar to the discriminatory practices of Brahmanism referred to before. God, therefore, brought about a democratic movement in religion—the Reformation. Christianity itself had to go through this reformation in order to be prepared for the Second Coming of the Messiah.

The remark could be made that few spiritual leaders like the ones who appeared around the sixth century B.C. arose at the time of the Reformation. The reason is that such leaders did not have to appear again. There was no need, for instance, for Confucius to come again; the people only had to put into practice what he had already taught. The same applies to Buddha. The teachings of the religious leaders of the past were still valid; they only had to be practiced. Actually, those teachings should have been fulfilled and unified by Jesus, but he was unable to do that, because of the crucifixion. The world is still waiting for his return. Confucianism and Buddhism have been waiting for more than two thousand years for the fulfillment of their religious teachings. Likewise, Islam, founded by Mohammed in the Middle East in the sixth century, has been waiting for this time.

God has kept the religions of the world alive in order to prepare man to accept the Messiah. When the Messiah comes, all these religions should recognize him and complete their missions by accepting his teachings and following him.

Confucianists will accept the Messiah from the Confucian standpoint; Buddhist, from the Buddhist standpoint. All religions will become one by centering on the Word of God as revealed by the Messiah. The Word of God revealed by the Messiah is broad enough to encompass the various aspects of all religions. Confucianists will say that the Word brought by the Messiah is the same as the teachings of Confucianism; Buddhists will see it as identical to the teachings of Buddhism, and so forth.

All the existing religions today have lost their ability to guide mankind, as traditional values are increasingly being discarded. God is preparing man to accept the Word of the Messiah.

The law of the period of the number six has been guiding history—it transcends the thoughts of man. It can, therefore, be called a transcendent, or objective law.

(f) The Law of Responsibility

When man fulfills his responsibility, God's will, expressed through the providence of restoration, is realized; when man fails to do so, the attainment of the goal of history is postponed. Responsibility is given to each providential figure; he must carry it out with his own wisdom, creativity, and effort. Unfortunately, almost all the providential figures in the past have been unable to carry out their responsibilities. Restoration history, therefore, has been prolonged until now.

For example, if John the Baptist, the priests, the scribes, and other leaders of Jesus' day had carried out their responsibilities, Jesus would not have been crucified. The Kingdom of God would have been realized at that time.

Marxist determinism claims that slave society must turn into feudal society, and feudal society into capitalist society. But if the people at the time of the Roman Empire (which Marx calls a slave society) had carried out their responsibility, the seeds of the Kingdom could have been sown then.

If Marx had lived at the time of Jesus, he would have had to say that communist society (the "kingdom of heaven" on the communist side) could not be realized for another two thousand years, until after the slave society of the Roman Empire had faded and passed into feudal society, and this had passed into capitalist society, which would then have to be overthrown by violent revolution. Thus placed in perspective, we can see how ridiculous such ideas would have been; they would actually have hindered the development of history. Definitely, if only man had done his part, the Kingdom of Heaven could have been realized at the time of Jesus. It was not God's desire for the providence to be prolonged or for man's suffering to continue. People were not aware, however, that they had such a responsibility. The law of responsibility exists independently of man's will; it is a transcendent, or objective law.

To abide by the law of responsibility was originally that which Adam had to do in his period of growth. God's creation would be perfected after Adam perfected himself by accomplishing his responsibility. The law of responsibility, therefore, is also one of the laws of creation and applies to all ages. Adam's responsibility (as the representative of all mankind) has been transmitted to the providential figures in the history of restoration, especially to the second Adam and the third Adam.

2. The Laws of Restoration

Through the providence of restoration, God has been continuously working to restore fallen man back to his original position. As He is a God of law and principle, He carried out His providence of restoration not in a haphazard way, but by observing definite laws. The most important of these laws are as follows: (a) the law of indemnity; (b) the law of separation; (c) the law of the restoration of the number four; (d) the law of the conditioned providence; (e) the law of the false preceding the true; (f) the law of the horizontal reappearance of the vertical; and (g) the law of synchronous providence.

(a) The Law of Indemnity

How is fallen man to be restored to his original state? First, he must establish the *foundation of faith,* by setting up certain conditions; then, the *foundation of substance,* by obeying the providential figure of his age. By doing so, he will lay the *foundation to receive the Messiah* (see "Introduction to the Providence of Restoration" in the Unification Principle). All this is known as *restoration through indemnity.*

In opposition to God's will, however, people usually persecute the providential person, instead of uniting with him. Numerous providential figures have been martyred in their mission—such as Jesus, the best example, as well as other righteous persons and prophets. The law of indemnity, therefore, refers to a life of persecution, tribulation, and sacrifice for the restoration of mankind.

The providential figures of restoration history could not but walk the course of indemnity in order to save sinners. The law of indemnity could be described also as the *law of affliction.* Not only the individuals that stood as God's representatives, but also families, tribes, and nations on the Heavenly side have had to walk a difficult path. Through the law of indemnity, the reason for the suffering of righteous persons all throughout history can be clarified for the first time. When fallen men set up conditions of faith, it is difficult for them to avoid the persecution, abuse, and misunderstanding of persons around them. Accordingly, even when ordinary conscientious persons (not necessarily providential individuals) try to go the way of true faith, they are always afflicted with problems. This is also because of the law of indemnity; God can use these indemnity conditions gradually to restore the fallen world.

(b) The Law of Separation

This law goes together with the law of indemnity. In order to restore our fallen society, God selects certain figures as His representatives in certain ages—such as Noah, Abraham, Jacob, and Moses. God chose representatives not only from among the Israelites, but also from among the people of many other nations. From among the Israelites, God chose those with the strongest faith; from among the people of other nations—which at times did not even believe in God—He chose those who were righteous and closest to His ways. That is how the law of separation works, by which God is separating the good world from the evil world.

After God chooses His representatives and separates them from the evil world by this law, He does not allow them to lead a quiet life; He makes them fight against evil, not with weapons, but with His Word. While teaching the Word of God and instructing people on how to live according to God's will, they are often brutally attacked by evil people. The base of goodness, however, sooner or later wins and expands. Throughout history, therefore, we always see good families struggling against evil families, good clans against evil clans, and good nations against evil nations.

This sheds a different light on the communists' claim that significant struggles throughout history have been caused by class struggles; according to Unification Thought, they have actually been caused by struggles between good and evil. History is full of examples of struggles not involving class struggles. The Persian War, the Phoenician War, the Hundred Years' War, the Prussian-Austrian War, the Prussian-French War, and the Russian-Turkish War—these were all racial or national struggles. On the other hand, the Spanish War, the Seven Years' War, the Crimean War, World Wars I and II—these were wars involving alliances. Furthermore, the Huguenot War, the Crusades, the Thirty Years' War, and the Puritan Revolution were religious wars.

Of course, a few struggles in history were class struggles—such as the French Revolution and the Farmers' War in Germany. But even in these cases, we can regard the opposing classes as representing good and evil sides. Obviously, the terms 'good' and 'evil' are used here in a relative way. In a struggle between two opposing groups, though neither side may be called 'good' in the absolute sense, nevertheless one side is usually closer to God's will and providence than the other.

Whenever there is a struggle between good and evil, the evil side always attacks first. In the Korean War, it was North Korea who attacked first; based on this principle, we can say that North Korea was on the evil side. In all struggles in history, the good side retaliates against the attacks of the evil side and sooner or later wins victory. The good side tries to subdue its opponent with words and with love; the evil side, however, usually brings out physical weapons and provokes a physical battle. By observing who initiates violence, therefore, we can often find out which one is the evil side.

Once good and evil have been separated, good is referred to as Abel, and evil as Cain—based on the situation of Adam's family, in which Abel represented good, and Cain represented evil. In today's world, the communist block represents Cain, while the free world represents Abel. In order to be successful and obtain victory over the communist block, the leaders of the free world—the Abel side—must fully understand and be obedient to God's will. If they fail to do this, then the free world will suffer greatly at the hands of the communist power, just as the Israelites of the Old Testament suffered at the hands of the Gentiles.

(c) **The Law of the Restoration of the Number Four**

Fallen man has lost the original quadruple base. Adam and Eve should have become husband and wife centering on God; they should have given birth to sinless children, to form the family quadruple base centered on God. Because of the Fall, however, they formed the quadruple base centering on Satan. Consequently, the goal of history has been to restore the lost quadruple base centered on God—that is, to restore the number four. This was Jesus' mission as the Second Adam; tragically, he was crucified before being able fully to accomplish his mission. The responsibility to restore the quadruple base now lies with the Lord of the Second Advent.

Providential history is the history of restoring the quadruple base. It has been a tremendous task. In order to establish the God-centered family quadruple base, God must send the Messiah, for whom careful preparation is to be made. We can say that the four thousand years until the arrival of Jesus were no more than a preparatory period to receive the Messiah. Just as a runway must be prepared before an airplane can land, the period of the number four must be prepared before the Messiah can arrive. In order to lay this foundation, God has been working to restore the number four. The restoration of the number four is, therefore, the conditional restoration of the quadruple base. Hence, God carried out the providence of Noah's flood with the number forty. The period of four hundred years after the failure of Noah's family until the providence of Abraham is also an example of the providence of restoring the number four.

Even after God restores the period of the number four (by waiting forty years, or four hundred years), Satan tries to take it back again by destroying the *foundation of faith* which should be set up after that period. If Satan succeeds, God will continue to restore the period over and over again by the providence of the number four. This is the reason the numbers four, forty, and four hundred appear so often in history. Arnold Toynbee is one of the few historians who noticed this. He mentioned four centuries of conflict and disunity before the establishment of order and unity, without making clear the reason for the appearance of such a period.

For example, the time period between the outbreak of the Peloponnesian War in 431 B.C. until the establishment of *Pax Augusta* in 31 B.C. was precisely four centuries. In China, likewise, it was four centuries from the time the Second Han Dynasty split into three nations until the reunification under the T'ang Dynasty. In Japan, also, there were four centuries of disunity from the Kamakura period until the unification of Japan by Hideyoshi. These are examples cited in *A Study of History* and *Civilization on Trial* by Arnold Toynbee.

In addition to these examples, the Japanese occupied and ruled Korea for forty years, from the signing of the Eul Sa Treaty in 1905—when Korea gave up her rights to conduct independent foreign relations—until Korea's release from the Japanese domination in 1945.

These are examples of the application of the law of the restoration of the number four.

(d) The Law of Conditioned Providence

The final purpose of God's providence is to send the Messiah. In order to do this, God prepared the Israelites during the Old Testament Age. One of the things they had to do was to fulfill the requirements of the law of conditioned providence.

The law of conditioned providence means the establishment,

through the work of the providence, of an act or event that is actually significant and, at the same time, symbolizes the content of an act or event that will happen in the future, conditioning or determining—though not entirely—the content of the future act or event. Accordingly, the content and the direction of an act or event in restoration history—especially at the time of the coming of the Messiah—have been determined, to some extent, by the way the previous act or event was performed in history.

The things centering on the ark of Noah, for instance, effected the judgment of sinners at that time, while also foreshadowing acts and events that would take place at the coming of Jesus. The flood judgment symbolized the future judgment to be carried out by Jesus. Noah sent out a dove from the ark three times; it came back after the first and second times, but did not return after the third time. This was a warning about future events, foreshadowing matters relating to man's portion of responsibility upon the arrival of the Messiah. The first dove, which went back to the ark, symbolized the first Adam, who failed to realize God's ideal on earth. The second dove, which went back to the ark with an olive leaf in its beak, symbolized the second Adam, Jesus. The story about the second dove signifies that, if the faith of the people were not sufficient, Jesus would not be able to remain on earth; he would do so only if there was enough faith. The third dove, which did not go back to the ark, symbolized the third Adam, the Lord of the Second Coming. The story about the third dove signifies that, when Christ comes again, he will be able to realize God's ideal of creation on earth without fail.

The providence centering on the tabernacle, at the time of Moses, was the providence to strengthen the belief of the Israelites; at the same time, it foreshadowed the responsibility or mission of the Israelites at the coming of Jesus. The two tablets of stone that Moses brought down from Mount Sinai, on which the Ten Commandments were written, symbolized Jesus and the Holy Spirit. The tabernacle symbolized the Messiah; later, the temple was built as an image of the Messiah. Through these, God administered strict training to the Israelites. This is an instance of the application of the Law of Conditioned Providence; by learning how to attend God through serving and honoring the tabernacle and the temple, the Israelites were actually preparing themselves to attend the Messiah when he came.

Another example is the act of striking the rock twice by Moses.

The rock symbolized Jesus; striking it twice was a condition that enabled Satan to claim the body of Jesus. If Moses had struck the rock only once—in other words, if he had maintained his heart of faithful attendance to God—perhaps Jesus would not have had to die. The reason is that, even if the Israelites became faithless toward Jesus, God would have been able to call others to take their place, by believing in, and attending Jesus. Thus, God could have prevented Satan from invading Jesus' body.

We can see, therefore, that a conditioned providence at a certain point in time can have great influence upon the work of the providence at a later time. In Noah's case, if he had understood the significance of what he was doing from the point of view of conditioned providence, his family might not have failed. If he had gathered his three sons and made them agree that, even if one of them violated God's providence, he himself was not to be blamed, that would have become a condition for him to attain success in his mission. In this case, if Ham failed, Noah could have put another son in his place.

Numerous providential persons failed to accomplish their responsibility due to the lack of understanding of the significance of their actions and circumstances in the light of the law of conditioned providence. Moses did not actually know whether to hit the rock once or twice. If he had been completely faithful to Heaven, however, he would have found out intuitively that the rock was not to be hit twice. Because of his anger, caused by the constant grumbling of the Israelites, he hit the rock twice—with tragic consequences. We can learn from this that leaders must take care not to express their anger in a self-centered way.

(e) The Law of the False Preceding the True

Before the true Messiah comes, a messiah-like figure on the Satanic side will appear. Likewise, before the true Heavenly Kingdom comes, a false heavenly kingdom will appear.

Satan, who was originally a good archangel created by God, believes that he can build an ideal world without God's help. God has had no choice but to allow him to try, for Satan has been the ruler of the created world since the fall of man. Satan has a lot more knowledge than fallen man, because he helped God to create the universe. God's desire is for his most beloved children to create the Heavenly Kingdom on earth, but Satan wants to do that by himself.

God, therefore, has been carrying out the providence after Satan has attempted to do it his own way.

Before Jesus came, Julius Caesar appeared as the head of the Roman Empire. Caesar stood in the position of messiah on the Satanic side. Together with Emperor Antonius he created *Pax Romana* and united a huge area centering on the Mediterranean. It was an intercontinental state, which developed the highest culture the world had ever seen. It was a false heavenly kingdom, preceding the true unified world that should have been created through the messianic work of Jesus.

In our own time, Stalin appeared as the false messiah, preceding the Second Coming of the True Messiah. He tried to create a unified world based on communism and managed to unite the communist parties of the world, centering on his country's communist party (Comintern).

Stalin's death in 1953 signaled the end of the mission of the false messiah and the formal beginning of the mission of the Messiah of the Second Advent. The mission of Jesus is to be inherited by the Lord of the Second Advent. Communism appeared as the false thought, proposed by the false messiah; this heralds the coming of the true thought, which is brought to the world by the true Messiah. Similarly, the formation of the unified communist front heralds the appearance of a unified world on the side of good. Based upon the law of the false preceding the true, we can know that the time for these things to happen is at hand.

Before starting his world-level mission, the Messiah will first appear in a certain nation. Consequently, before the Messiah comes, a messiah-like figure on the side of evil must appear in that nation and proclaim himself to be the parent of the people. This person is none other than Kim Il Sung, of North Korea. He is instructing his people to call him their "honorable parent." Nowhere in the communist ideology is the word "parent" used to describe a communist leader; why, then, does Kim Il Sung, a communist leader, expect his people to call him their parent? Though he may be unaware of it, he is doing this in compliance with the law of the false preceding the true.

(f) **The Law of the Horizontal Reappearance of the Vertical**

In this context, 'vertical' refers to historical time, while 'horizontal' refers to the actual world. Accordingly, this law means that events that took place in the past will recur at the present time. Through studying the principle of restoration we can understand the significance of the events and the missions given to the central figures of the Old Testament period, such as Noah, Abraham, Jacob, and Moses. The missions carried out by those people are now being repeated (on the world-wide level), because they were never fully completed before.

Noah's family failed to complete their mission, leaving their indemnity condition unfulfilled. The same applies to Abraham. Consequently, most of the major problems of restoration history remain unsolved. God, therefore, works the providence to make these events and figures reappear, so that the past unfulfilled indemnity conditions can be completely solved. Of course, the events of the present time will not be exactly the same as the ones of the past; neither will the required conditions be exactly identical to those of the past. Nevertheless, in each case the principle is repeated. Certainly, God will not cause a great flood today—as He did at the time of Noah—yet He does ask providential persons to go through the same types of trials as Noah had to go through. Another example of the application of this law is that the ancient conflicts between the Israelites and the gentiles have reappeared today as conflicts between Israel and the Arabic nations.

The last days are prophetically depicted as days of chaos, turmoil, and uncertainty. These are the phenomena of the reappearance of historical events that have been left unsolved in the providential history. These unsolved matters cannot be allowed to remain so; if they do, the providence of restoration will not be completed, and the sinful history of man will not terminate.

How, then, will these historical problems be completely solved? This is only possible with the Second Advent. When people accept and follow the instructions of the Messiah, all the complex global problems will be solved. Furthermore, the six thousand years of sinful history will end completely. When all the historical problems are solved by the Messiah, God will be able to consider these last six thousands years as sinless history, because God's long-cherished desire has always been to forget mankind's sad and sinful history and to receive joy forever, by loving us as His true children.

(g) The Law of Synchronous Periods

When in the course of providential history there is an event that delays it, God repeats the providence, by arranging for a similar event to occur, in a similar period of time, and with similar persons. The providence that took two thousand years from the time of Abraham until the arrival of Jesus was left unfulfilled because of Jesus' crucifixion. God, therefore, began a similar providence right after the death of Jesus.

The period of persecution of the Christians under the Roman Empire is similar to the period of slavery the Israelites had to go through in Egypt. The Christian patriarchal period corresponds to the Old Testament period of the Judges. The Christian Empire (the Frankish Empire, started by Charlemagne) corresponds to the United Kingdom (founded by Saul). The period of the divided kingdom of East (East Frankish Empire) and West (West Frankish Empire) corresponds to that of the divided kingdom of North (Israel) and South (Judah). The papal captivity and return (1309-1377) corresponds to the Jewish captivity and return. Finally, the period of preparation for the Second Coming, starting from the Reformation led by Martin Luther, Calvin, and others, corresponds to the period of preparation for the coming of Christ, which began at the time of Malachi. After this period of preparation, the Messiah will be able to come. These are the six stages of the religious synchronous providence.*

There is also the synchronous political and economic providence, which has four stages: the Old Testament (Israelite) clan society, feudal society, monarchic society, and democratic-type society. Politically, these have been synchronized, in the A.D. era, with the early church society, the feudal society, the absolute monarchic society, and the Christian democratic society; and economically, with the slave-society, the manor system (feudalism), capitalism, and democratic socialism.

D. BASIC LAWS OF HISTORICAL CHANGE
1. Development and Give-and-Take Law; Turning and Repulsion Law

Marxism has rightly asserted that human history has devel-

---

*The term 'synchronous' connotes the idea that even though the new providence chronologically is at a time in history different from that of the old one, from the point of view of Restoration History they are identical. This makes the period of time itself identical, or synchronous, when viewed from Restoration History.

oped according to certain laws. Nevertheless, the Marxist law of development—that is, the development by class struggle—is not right. In the Unification Thought view of history, the development of history is the result of give-and-take actions between subject and object; in other words, development takes place according to the give-and-take law. Politics, economics, and culture have developed through the harmonious give-and-take action between individual and individual, between group (or individual) and group, between person and things, and among things. Examples: the relationships between government and citizens, manager and laborers, worker and machine, machine and machine; all of these are relationships of subject and object. This is called the *Law of Give-and-Take Action*, or briefly, the *Give-and-Take Law*.

Give-and-take action is always carried out between subject (+) and object (-), not between subject (+) and subject (+). The action between subject and subject is repulsive—that is, they refuse to unite and, actually, repel each other. The reason for their mutual repulsion is that this very action causes a strengthening of the give-and-take action between subject and object. The action of repulsion usually works invisibly in the natural world; it works latently, supporting the give-and-take action between subject and object. This law can also be applied to history. The repelling force between the two subjects appears in the form of struggle between good and evil. In history the actions of repulsion appear visibly.*

Adam and Eve should have become one through give-and-take action in their respective positions of subject and object. The archangel, however, appeared and, leaving his own position, became Eve's subject and controlled her. There was only one person in the object-position—Eve; consequently, both Adam and the archangel stood in the subject-position.

This situation is unprincipled, because, although there can be two or more objects centering on one subject, there can never be two subjects for one object. For example, there are many planets revolving around the sun; in an atom, many electrons orbit one nucleus; but it is impossible for a single object to revolve around two subjects,

---

*Why is this repulsion law applied to history? It is because, by God's providence, the leader (subject) of the good side is separated from the sinful world, being prepared to confront the leader (subject) of the evil side. In nature, therefore, the law of repulsion is concurrent with the give-and-take law; in history, it is concurrent with the separation law.

either in celestial relationships or in atoms. The situation of having two subjects for one object, however, has appeared because of man's Fall. Such a relationship is unprincipled and cannot last; either Adam or the archangel has to forfeit his subject-position. Since Adam fell through Eve's temptation, the result was that Satan remained as the only subject. Thus, the principled relationship of one subject and one object was manifested in pseudo-form—that is, centered on Satan.

This is the way human history came to be sinful history. God began working immediately to overcome the evil subject, by selecting a good subject to oppose him. By using the law of separation, God has called people from the sinful world to confront and win victory over the evil subject in order to advance His providence. In fact, the history of the last six thousand years has been the history of struggle between the subject on the good (Abel) side and the subject on the evil (Cain) side.

Struggles, therefore, are a manifestation of the repulsion between subject and subject—not between subject and object. The only possible relationship between subject and object is that of give-and-take action, not struggle.

Satan is loath to give up his sovereignty. When the leader on the side of good (good subject) first appears, there is bound to occur a struggle between him and the leader on the side of evil (evil subject). This struggle, which can be either ideological or physical, will result in the eventual victory of the good side over the evil side—at least in the long run. After all these things have taken place, it remains to be seen whether the good leader will maintain the attitude of a good subject over the people, or will become corrupt himself. If he does become corrupt—thus becoming a leader on the evil side—then he himself will have to face a struggle with another new leader, who will have gained popular support through give-and-take action with the people. Thus, the process is repeated.

If development comes about through give-and-take action and has nothing to do with struggle, then what is the significance of struggle? Through the process explained above, struggle plays the role of turning the direction of history toward goodness. Whenever the good side wins, history turns somewhat toward the direction of goodness. In this way, restoration has been making slow but steady progress, with the degree of goodness determining the degree of restoration.

Once the direction is changed, give-and-take action takes place and development occurs. This process may be compared to what takes place when a car is about to turn. The engine moves the car forward; the brake and the steering wheel are used for changing direction. The engine can be likened to give-and-take action, and applying the brake and steering wheel can be likened to the struggle between good and evil. Thus, the fact that the direction of history can be turned through the struggle between good and evil can be viewed as an application of the *law of repulsion* or *repulsion law*.

God separated Abel, Noah, Abraham, and other providential persons, from the sinful world. He has even called persons that were not among the elect to be leaders on the side of good and guide mankind out of darkness, according to the law of separation.

Struggle, however is not a requisite in restoration history. Though a certain leader errs and causes dissatisfaction among his people, he may, nevertheless, perceive the will of God and change his policies, thus eliminating the need for struggle. In this case, the direction of history will be turned to the good side without struggle. If struggle does occur, it is always between two subjects, one of whom is comparatively closer to God's will than the other.

Strictly speaking, therefore, it is not correct to say that historical struggles are struggles between the ruling and the ruled. During the Bolshevik Revolution, for instance, not all the Russian people supported Lenin. He appeared as a new leader, speaking out for the Russian people, whose living conditions had been very miserable. Like Marx and indeed most communist leaders, Lenin was from the intellectual class, not from the working or farming class. Knowledge is one of the prerequisites of a leader. Lenin stood as subject to a part of the ruled class (the masses) and through give-and-take action with them, he gained power. At that time, however, there was a group of people that supported Kerensky's provisional government; these wanted to solve the problems in a relatively good manner. The struggle that occurred, then, was a struggle between two leaders, both of whom had the support from a group of loyal followers. It was a struggle between two subjects—i.e., Kerensky and Lenin.

Struggle does not bring about historical development, but hinders it. Whether it be a revolution, a war, or a riot, once it begins, every kind of give-and-take action is hindered, chaos spreads, and development is interrupted.

Here the objection may be raised with regard to the tremendous scientific and technological progress that was made during war times in the past. The United States, for example, developed the pilotless plane during the Vietnam War. Nevertheless, can we actually say that this plane was developed through the process of struggle? No! Though the Vietnam War was the impetus for this invention, nevertheless the plane itself was not invented at the battlefront. On the contrary, it was the result of the cooperation between scientists, technicians, workers, and others, who worked at a place very distant from the war zone. The pilotless plane, therefore, was made through harmonious give-and-take action, not through struggle.

War may be one of the occasions suggesting the impetus for scientific development; it is not, however, the only one, and certainly, not an essential factor. The airplane, for instance, was invented to carry persons and transport goods; it was a great step forward for mankind. A pilotless plane, on the other hand, constructed to carry bombs, cannot be called a positive contribution to humanity, and if scientists had used the techniques they developed to construct the pilotless plane for peaceful purposes, they might have made more progress than they have. It is of paramount importance to develop technology that can be used to serve mankind in times of peace.

Wars have caused unbelievable destruction and wastage of natural resources, human lives, cultural resources, etc. Only when wars are over does development begin again. The Russian economy took a ten-year step backwards after the Bolshevik Revolution broke out. It took the Russians until 1927 to bring their economy back to the pre-revolution level. Though struggle does retard historical development, nonetheless we should remember that when the good side wins, the direction of history is changed to one of comparative goodness. A motorist must apply the brakes and turn the steering wheel if he wants to make a change in direction. Similarly, society's development has to be restrained, or even stopped (through struggle), before socio-historical change can occur.

In conclusion, socio-historical development can only occur according to the *law of give-and-take action;* on the other hand, the turnings in historical direction come about according to the *law of repulsion*. Definitely, history does not develop through dialectic struggle (Fig. 32)

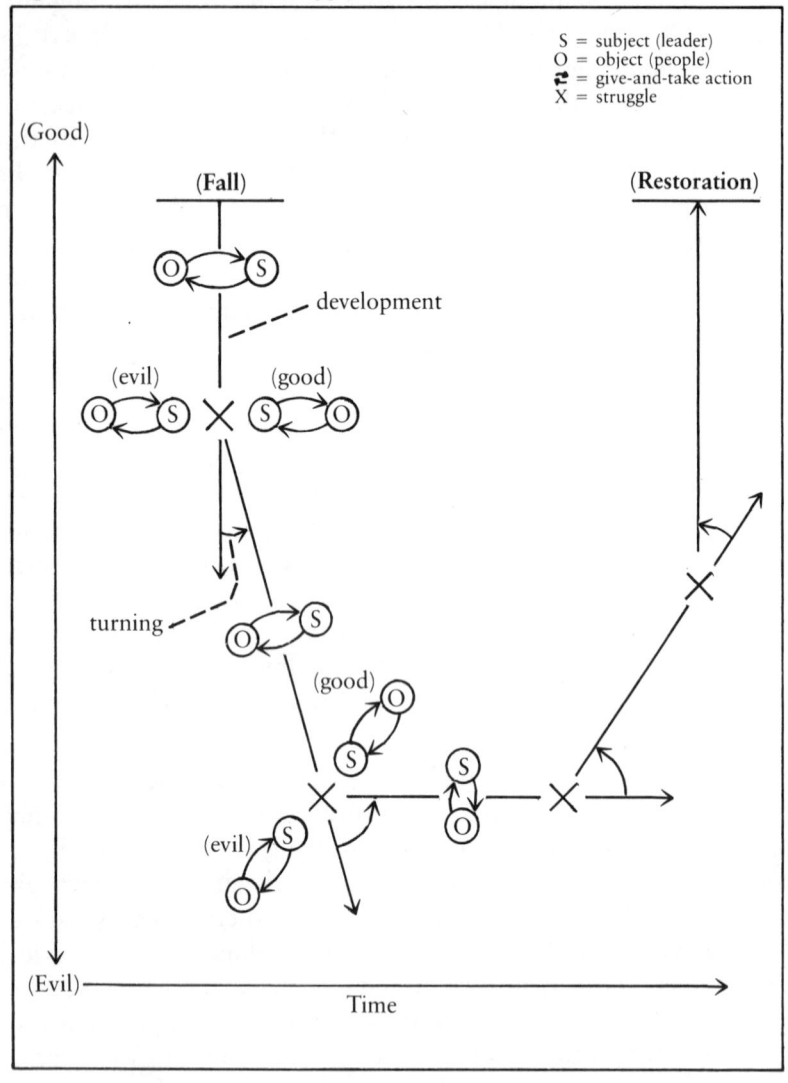

Fig. 32 History and the Struggle between Good and Evil

S = subject (leader)
O = object (people)
⇄ = give-and-take action
X = struggle

2. The Law of Willed Action

History has developed through the give-and-take action between subject and object—that is, between man and his fellow men, between man and nature, and between man and his social environment. Here, let us discuss the aspect of give-and-take action between man and the natural and social environment.

Marx described productive forces and relations of productions only within the materialistic framework. Since in his view spirit comes from matter, he maintained also that the various forms of ideas (which are nothing but spirit applied to social phenomena) are derived from the relations of production (which are material). The Unification View of History, however, maintains that the productive forces and the relations of production themselves are the result of give-and-take relationships between man and nature and between man and the social environment, to say nothing of relationships between man and man. Stone implements, for instance, the primary tools during the stone age, were made through the give-and-take action between man's desire and the stone (matter). The steam engine was the product of give-and-take action between Watt's inventive desire and the socio-material conditions of his time. The Russian Revolution, establishing new relations of production, was brought about through give-and-take action between the revolutionary desires of the leaders—foremost of whom was Lenin—and the social environment of Russia at that time.

Thus, the development of human society needs both man's will and socio-material conditions—that is, the *Sung Sang* element and the *Hyung Sang* element. This assertion is based on the Unification Principle view that development is a multiplication that is brought about by the give-and-take action between *Sung Sang* and *Hyung Sang*, in which *Sung Sang* plays the dominating and central role in relation to *Hyung Sang*. Accordingly, in the development of history, man's will has played a decisive role when compared to socio-material conditions—the opposite conclusion to that arrived at by the historical materialistic view.

E. CULTURAL HISTORY

Human history is cultural history. The world that God originally intended to create was a world rich in cultural splendor. If it were not for the Fall of man, human history would have been the account of how the original culture (the Unified Culture, or the Moderate-Harmonious Civilization*) had prospered. As we know, however, history has displayed a continuous rise and fall of non-principled civilizations.

---

*'Moderate-Harmonious Civilization' denotes a civilization that is harmonious in its various elements and, at the same time, moderate— i.e., neither excessive nor insufficient— both in quality and in quantity, centered on the cosmic principle.

God always begins with one, whether it be in the creation process or in providential history. God did not create Adam and Eve at the same time. He first created Adam as the subject, and then Eve, as the object. Adam and Eve were later supposed to form a family and raise up good children. The providence of restoration, also, began with one. God chose one family, that of Abraham, before forming a clan and a nation—the Israelites.

In the same way, God does not bring salvation to all people at the same time. He first chooses one nation as His elect and sends the Messiah to that nation to save it first; then, by extending the sphere of salvation, He works to save all mankind. Knowing this, we can distinguish the *central history*, by focusing on God's chosen people, and the *peripheral history*, that is, the history of all other peoples.

Culturally, there is a *central history of culture* and a *peripheral history of culture*. Within the central history of culture we can also distinguish *Sung Sang* culture and *Hyung Sang* culture, the former being the culture stemming from Hebraism, and the latter being the culture stemming from Hellenism.

Let us first investigate the flow of Hellenism, the *Hyung Sang* culture. Developed in Greece, Hellenism was then inherited by the Roman Empire, as its culture. After the fall of the Roman Empire, Hellenism was preserved in Constantinople and in the Islamic civilization. In modern times, it entered Europe again during the Renaissance and stimulated the development of science and the arts.

The time following Galileo and Newton, from the seventeenth to the eighteenth centuries, saw the appearance of the rationalists on the continent (such as Descartes, Spinoza, and Leibniz), and the empiricists in Britain (such as Bacon, Hobbes, and Locke). From this line appeared the French philosophers of the Enlightenment, including, Voltaire, Rousseau, and Montesquieu. This led to the French Revolution.

Around the time of the French Revolution, socialist thought was developed by men such as Saint-Simon, Fourier, Owen, and Blanqui. Succeeding these men came Marx, then Kautsky, Bernstein, Plekhanov, and finally Lenin. Communism was imported to Russia by Plekhanov, and eventually the Communist Revolution took place under the leadership of Lenin. Russian influence then spread eastwards.

Now, let us look at Hebraism—the civilization and the thought of the Jewish people since the time of Abraham. Hebraism entered the Roman Empire from Israel, influenced the Roman civilization, and entered Germany after the fall of Rome. After shaping the Christian civilization, it ruled Europe. The Reformation in the 16th century brought about the appearance of Protestantism, and the Puritan Revolution occurred in England. Christianity also influenced the Industrial Revolution; in fact, it is the spiritual backbone of the modern Western civilization. Protestantism was brought to America on the Mayflower. After that, America succeeded Europe in developing Western civilization. From America and from Great Britain, Western civilization—which is of Hebraistic descent—also spread to the Far East, both in the scientific and in the religious fields.

Tracing Hellenism backwards, we find that the Greek civilization came from the Aegean civilization, which originated chiefly from the Egyptian civilization. The Egyptian civilization came from the Hamatic tribes.

On the other hand, Hebraism was born out of the Babylonian civilization, which originated from the Accadian civilization. The Accadian civilization was born out of the Sumerian civilization, as a result of the influence exerted by the Semites on the Sumerian civilization.

Incidentally, where did the Hamites and the Semites come from? Even today historians have been unable to give us a concrete answer to this question, so we have only the Bible to shed light on our inquiry. According to the Bible, Noah's son Ham is the father of the Hamites, and his brother Shem, the father of the Semites.

According to the Principle of Restoration, Noah's family was supposed to restore the failure of Adam's family, in which both Cain and Abel offered sacrifices, but were not able to accomplish God's will. After a lapse of 1600 years, Noah's family was chosen. Ham, the second son, was established by God in the position of Abel, and Shem, the first son, in the position of Cain. Ham, however, failed his mission, and his son was cursed by Noah. After that, from the point of view of results, the positions of Ham and Shem were reversed: Ham came to have the position of Cain, and Shem the position of Abel. From among the descendants of Shem came Abraham. The descendants of Shem came to be in the historical position of Abel; the descendants of Ham, in the historical position of Cain.

Christianity grew out of Hebraism, the *Sung Sang* civilization. The *Hyung Sang* civilization is the Greek civilization. These two civilizations should have been united at the time of the Roman

Empire; their unification, however, was postponed, because Jesus—the center of unification—was crucified.

We can ultimately regard human history as having been prolonged until today in order to restore the offerings of Cain and Abel. God's will was for the Romans, who were in the position of Cain, to unite with the Israelites, who—had they accepted Jesus—would have been in the position of Abel, in order to restore through indemnity the failure of Cain and Abel and thus lay the foundation for the Kingdom of Heaven. Today, once again, communism and democracy should unite with the Messianic providence to restore through indemnity the original failure and realize the Unified or Moderate-Harmonious Civilization. (Fig. 33)

As was mentioned before, both of these streams have spread to the Far East. Their confrontation is most pronounced on the Korean Peninsula, which, therefore, becomes the providential focal point for their unification and the birthplace of the new culture. North Korea is well known for its espousal of communist doctrine whereas South Korea has become famous for the extraordinary growth of Christianity there.

Whether Christian democracy can fulfill its responsibility or not is at the moment a matter of grave concern. As Toynbee pointed out, Marxism is an accusation against the shortcomings of Christianity. It appeared with the intention of liberating poor majorities, such as laborers and farmers, but is now trampling down human rights, restricting freedom, and suppressing true values.

At the time of the Industrial Revolution, Christians should have practiced Christian love, denouncing the greed of capitalists and the exploitative inhumanity of the industrialists, as well as resisting the influence of those who had begun to worship material things. However, numerous Christians turned a blind eye toward the greed of the bourgeoisie, and Christianity more often than not supported the exploitation. Calvinism—especially its doctrine of Predestination—was a wonderful aid in legitimizing these activities.

Consequently, Marx regarded both capitalists and Christians as one and the same—that is, as enemies of the workers. There were other reasons for Marx's opposition to Christianity—such as his father's conversion, Jewish problems, his suspicion of Hegel, oppression by the Prussian government—but I will not go into detail on these points here.

The very fact that communism exists is proof of Christianity's

The Unification View of History

Fig. 33 The Streams of Hebraism and Hellenism
(This diagram is designed to show the essence of the two cultural streams. It does not show all the interrelationships of each age).

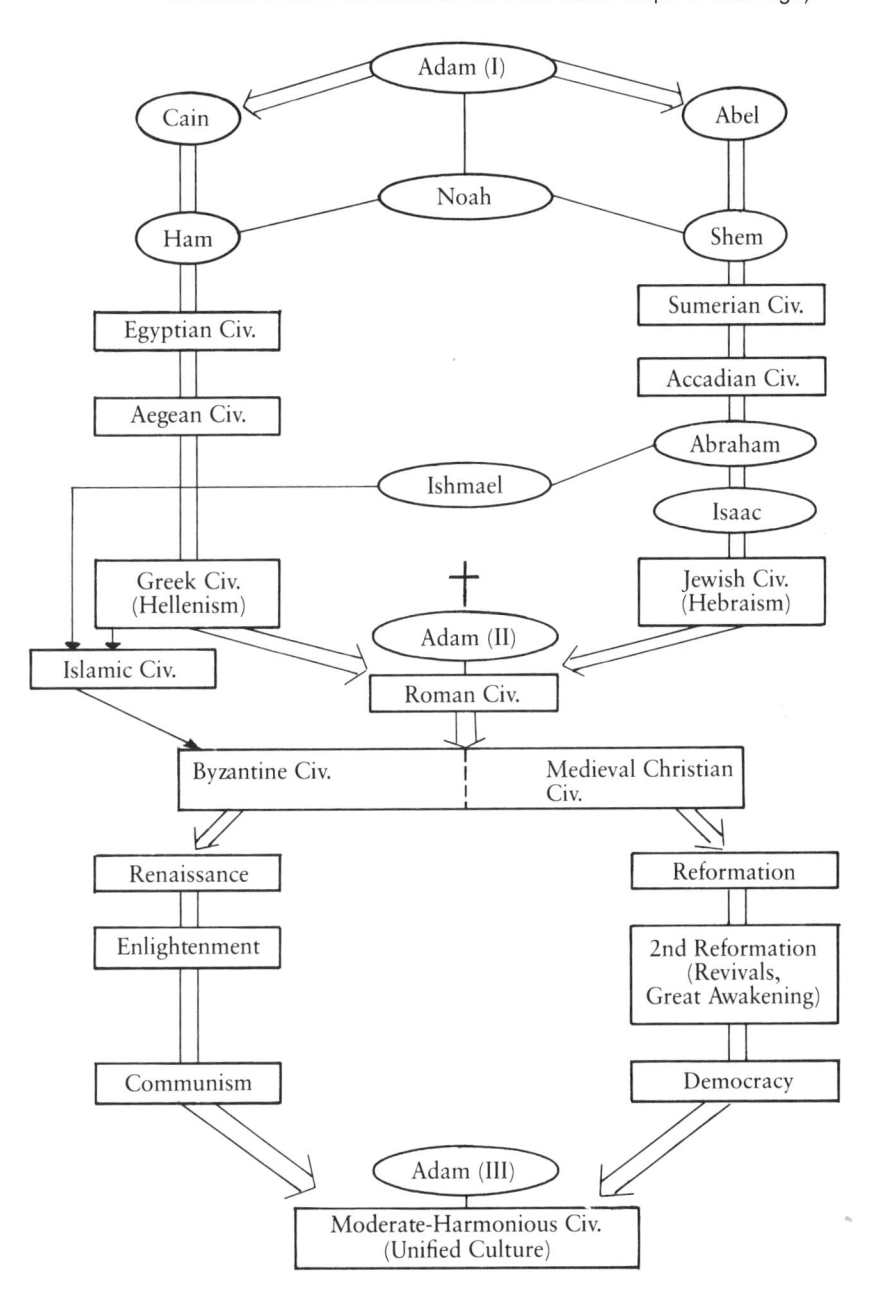

failure. Christianity has lost the power, the sense of duty, and the sense of responsibility that it needs in order to overcome communism and to offer young people a higher ideal.

The Unification Church is taking on that responsibility. It seeks to awaken Christians throughout the world and to overcome communism with its message, thus reconciling the long divided *Sung Sang* and *Hyung Sang* cultures. This is the stream of the central providential and cultural history.

11 METHODOLOGY

Man lives in a complex world, amidst complex phenomena, both natural and social. In order to find a way to live in the most advantageous fashion in this world, he needs understanding—that is, correct knowledge and correct cognition. But how should he go about obtaining it? What methods should he use in his search for truth? These questions lead us to the subject of this chapter: methodology.

Scientists develop methodologies for their respective fields; every philosophical system, also, has a characteristic methodology. Marxism, for example, developed materialistic dialectics, claiming that it is the law of development of nature, society and man's thinking.

What place does methodology have in Unification Thought? It is at the very base of it. Through methodology, certain fundamentals of the Unification Thought view are established. The problem of how things should exist and should relate among themselves; how man thinks; how he should dominate the creation; how he goes about finding the truth, and so on, are all questions to which Unification Methodology addresses itself.

In this chapter we will, first, investigate a few of the most representative approaches set forth in the history of philosophy; next, we will compare them with Unification Methodology; finally, and as a result of this process, we hope to clarify our viewpoint on these important issues.

I. HISTORICAL APPROACHES
A. HERACLITUS (c535-c475 B.C.) —THE DIALECTIC (DYNAMIC METHOD)

Heraclitus, a Greek philosopher, is sometimes called the father of the dialectic. He considered *archē* (original substance) to be "fire." All natural things, he asserted, are changing in a process of constant mutation. As one person is born, another dies. Everything is changing because of struggle.

In his methodology, Heraclitus was chiefly concerned with the problem of how nature exists and develops. Though he recognized harmony in nature, Heraclitus, nevertheless, advocated a concept akin to the dialectic, since, in his view, struggle is the cause of development in nature. His method can be called *dynamic method,* since he tried to catch the dynamic aspect of things.

B. ZENO OF ELEA (c490-c430 B.C.) —THE DIALECTIC (STATIC METHOD)

Zeno is usually called Zeno of Elea to be distinguished from Zeno of Citium (c336-c265 B.C.), the founder of Stoicism. Zeno of Elea supported Parmenides (the founder of the Eleatic school of philosophy) in opposing Heraclitus' view that everything is changing. They argued that everything that really exists is unchangeable, being neither born nor destroyed. Existing beings seem to move, but actually do not; they seem to be born and destroyed, but actually are not; they seem to change, but are in fact unchangeable.

Zeno sophistically demonstrates this with his famous "Paradox of the Flying Arrow." An arrow flies from point A to point C. In doing so, it passes through point B. When it passes through point B, however, it stops there. There are actually infinite such points between A and C, so the arrow must continuously be at repose. Even though the arrow is seemingly moving, in fact it is not moving, but is stationary.

Zeno gives another illustration, the story about "Achilles and the Tortoise." Achilles, hero of the Trojan War, was very fleet-footed, but could not outstrip a tortoise. Letting it get a head start, he ran to the place where it had been when he started, but it was no longer there. Seeing it ahead of him, he ran to that place, but again it had gone a little further. Each time he reached the point where it was before, it had gone a little further. The tortoise, finally, won the race. This story, also, is very sophistic.

Marxism has a ready answer for the puzzle of the arrow: it is moving, and is at the same time stationary. If an arrow is stationary at any point, it is always stationary, and if it is not (i.e. if it does not exist at any point), there is no movement at all. Such an impasse can only be resolved by the dialectic, i.e. by the unity of repose and motion, Marxists hold. This is more sophisticated sophistry than Zeno ever managed to produce.

Time and space exist in a correlative interaction, just like *Sung Sang* and *Hung Sang*. One cannot exist without the other. Movement, therefore, cannot exist without time and space. Assuming that time is T, and distance (space) is S, we can say that the velocity of a movement $V = S/T$. If we think, here, of such a point as has no space (i.e. S equals zero), time T necessarily becomes zero, and the equation becomes meaningless.

Accordingly, in the discussion of an arrow's going through a point, we must consider a point which has definite space, however small it may be, since a mathematical point which has position but no size, does not exist in the physical world, but only in the world of thought. It is fallacious to combine an abstract point with actual motion.

The movement of a substantial being should be examined within a definite time and space. Then we can conclude that the flying arrow is moving at a point, since it moves through an infinitesimal space in an infinitesimal time. It is neither stationary at a point as Zeno asserts, nor stationary and moving as Marxism asserts.

As for "Achilles and the Tortoise", Zeno reaches such a sophistic conclusion, because his discussion is limited to space only, neglecting time.

Zeno's method was considered dialectical by Aristotle. It is called idealistic dialectic, or subjective dialectic. To Zeno, the dialectic was a debating device; he persuaded others by pointing out the contradictions in their arguments.

But, it is important that we do see an unchanging, or eternal, aspect in every being. There is, therefore, some validity in Zeno's speculation. We may call his approach the *static method*.

C. SOCRATES (469-399 B.C.)
—THE DIALECTIC (DIALOGIC METHOD)

Socrates deplored the fact that the sophists of his day prospered by confusing people's minds. The Sophists said that, even if nature has objectivity and necessity, human problems are relativistic, so there is no objective truth in human society. Truth depends on time, place and man. Truth may be untruth; it is a matter of expediency.

In the midst of a confused society, Socrates maintained that people must talk to each other with sincere hearts. Sophists pretended to know much, but knew nothing. "Know thyself!" he said. We cannot arrive at an ultimate, universal truth until we recognize that we really know nothing and begin to engage in earnest and sincere dialogue with one another.

D. PLATO (427-347 B.C.)—THE DIALECTIC (CLASSIFICATION OF IDEA)

Plato's method is dialectical. His dialectic is the method of connecting Ideas to form a hierarchy of Ideas—that is, the method of dividing the world of Ideas.

Plato maintained that what really exists is Ideas, the physical world being made up of shadows of Ideas. Ideas develop into substantial entities. In the world of Ideas there is no disorder, but a hierarchy, or stratified structure. In the same way that numerous cells are gathered to form the structure of man, numerous Ideas are gathered to form the hierarchy of Ideas. Just as scientists acquire knowledge about the physical world by analysis and synthesis, we can do likewise with the world of Ideas, by applying the dialectical method.

In the hierarchy of Ideas, the Idea of Good occupies the highest position (instead of God). The development of the universe has purpose—that is, the purpose of reaching goodness. Plato was the first thinker with a teleological cosmology.

E. ARISTOTLE (384-322 B.C.) —THE DEDUCTIVE METHOD

The deductive method of Aristotle remained unchallenged for almost two thousand years. This method starts with a universal truth and then tries to arrive at concrete conclusions by analyzing this truth. The deductive method can be seen in the following example of a syllogism: (i) All men die; (ii) Socrates is a man; (iii) Therefore Socrates will die. Another example is (i) All beings with mass respond to gravity; (ii) An apple has mass; (iii) Therefore an apple responds to gravity (i.e., will fall to the ground from a tree). This may seem quite obvious, but it illustrates that the deductive method is used as a means to ascertain concrete facts from universal truths. There is a lot of truth in it, so it has been universally recognized.

In the Middle Ages, theology reigned supreme. That God created all things was the universal truth. All beings were His creatures. All things and phenomena were explained from the universal truth that God created the whole of nature and humans. The deductive method was a useful aid for theological arguments, so it did not undergo any alterations, but remained unchallenged all through that period.

F. BACON (1561-1626)—THE INDUCTIVE METHOD

The Renaissance was the beginning of scientific development, and a challenge to dogmatic deductivism. Francis Bacon maintained that the only way to gain new knowledge from nature is through experimentation and observation, and that it is impossible to obtain it through speculation, i.e. through the deductive method. If I already know for certain that all men are mortal, for instance, then when I say that an individual will die I am not stating anything new; this is not new knowledge, but an obvious fact.

Bacon maintained that we should throw away prejudices in order to gain true knowledge and insights. He called these prejudices that we all harbor *Idola* (Idols), of which we have four types: Idols of the Tribe, Idols of the Cave, Idols of the Market Place, and Idols of the Theater.

The Idols of the Tribe are the prejudices of the human species; illusions of the senses, and the tendency to personify things. Because of this, people once thought that when a rock fell over a cliff, some great manlike power might have pushed it.

The Idols of the Cave are the prejudices which come from individual customs, opinions and education. This is the attitude of judging everything based on one's own narrow view of life.

The Idols of the Market Place are the prejudices which come from the inaccuracy of the words men use in daily life. They sometimes use words which indicate things that do not exist at all.

The Idols of the Theater are the prejudices of authority. People are apt to believe blindly the various philosophical treatises which represent worlds of their own creation; i.e. theaters.

Bacon asserted that, after taking away such Idols, we should make observations and experiments on nature, and obtain by abstraction the general concept of the things. This is the theory of induction.

G. DESCARTES (1596-1650)
—THE METHODICAL DOUBT

After he had doubted all things, René Descartes realized that what he could not doubt was that he was thinking. Reason, or thinking, finally became a surety for him, so he maintained that reason is the only subject of cognition in which we can believe. Methodical doubt is to seek to obtain truth by doubting all things, especially experiences. From this method came rationalism.

Descartes doubted the certainty of all existence, except the fact that he was thinking. He went on with his thinking, and decided that what is clear and distinct in thinking is certain, because God guarantees it. We can only say this, however, if we accept that God exists. Does God exist? Descartes said that man knows the idea of God naturally (a priori), and that the idea of the perfect Being, the idea of God, cannot come from the imperfect being, man, therefore God exists.

I think that it is not unreasonable to say, "I think, therefore I am" *(cogito, ergo sum)*, because there is no one who doesn't think, but to assert that God exists from the above reasoning is dogmatic, for not all people think of God, and among those who do, there are endless disagreements about what or who God is. The rationalism, in which experiences are considered unimportant, fell into dogmatic metaphysics when it came to Wolff through Leibnitz.

H. HUME (1711-1776)
—IDEALISTIC EMPIRICISM

When empiricism came to David Hume, it turned into skepticism. The knowledge obtained from scientific observations seem to be true, but may not actually be so. Suppose we see a flash of lightning and hear a peal of thunder a few seconds later. Light and sound are completely different. We see light with our eyes, and hear sounds with our ears. Nonetheless, we think that the sequence is causal, because one comes before, and the other follows it. But how about a cock crowing just before dawn? Can we say that the sun rises because the cock crows? Of course not!

We can only say that the relationship between lightning and thunder—like that between the cock and sunrise—is one of before and after. To say that the relationship is causal is to insert our own subjectivity into the judgment, a mistake we often make.

There is also the matter of "substance" *(substantia, ousia)*. We should not assume that the substance of a flower exists. We do not feel the flower itself, but only experience its color, shape, aroma, etc. With our eyes, we see its color and shape; with our nose, we smell its aroma; with our hands, we touch its softness. Only the perceptions (impressions and ideas) coming from these sensations actually exist; existence is nothing but a bundle, or collection, of perceptions. We cannot, therefore, say that the substance of a flower—or of anything—exists in reality. Starting with empiricism, Hume became skeptical, for he doubted the existence of objective beings which are independent of the subject and are the source of experience.

I. KANT (1724-1804)
—THE TRANSCENDENTAL METHOD

Immanuel Kant wanted to unite rationalism and empiricism, since both have good points. He said that both reason and experience (subject and object) are necessary for cognition, since *forms of intuition* and *forms of synthesis* come from the subject, whereas sense-impressions come from the object.

The attributes of an object reach our senses in the form of sense-impressions (content), yet this is not enough for us to recognize the object. We need 'forms of synthesis', or 'thinking forms', in order to reach the judgment, "This is such and such." These thinking forms exist a priori. There are twelve thinking forms. One of these is causality. Because of this form, we can judge whether or not two successive events have a causal relationship. In an electrical storm, for instance, the sensible qualities are light (from the lightning) and sound (from the thunder). Because we use our causal thinking form, we understand light to be the cause and sound to be the effect.

Besides these thinking forms, we need also forms of intuition: space and time. When we see an object, we always see it through the forms of space and time. It seems, therefore, that all things exist in space and time.

Kant's attempt at unifying rationalism and empiricism into a new way of understanding cognition was an effort to overcome the then prevailing skepticism and dogmatism in the philosophical world. We have forms of intuition and forms of synthesis inside us congenitally, or a priori; yet the sense-impressions—such as color, shape, aroma—actually come from the outside.

With his transcendental method, Kant tried to make it clear how an experience can become an objective cognition. So, in the *Critique of Pure Reason,* he maintained that *a priori* forms are necessary in man's cognition.

J. HEGEL (1770-1831)
—THE IDEALISTIC DIALECTIC

Most idealists begin with God and explain the phenomenal world deductively. Hegel's theory is deductive, too. Hegel, however, in *The Phenomenology of Mind* tries to grasp the Absolute epistemologically, starting from sense-consciousness and reaching absolute knowledge, through self-consciousness and reason. Then, he explains deductively how the absolute knowledge, or Logos, develops into the world in the *Science of Logic.*

Perhaps Hegel questioned why Almighty God created all things, why He did not keep silent eternally. Thus, He developed the concept of Being-Nothing-Becoming. The thinking of God starts from Being, which is pure Being without any determination or feature. Accordingly, Being is at the same time Nothing. For example, we consider that an eraser has weight, shape, and color, but, said Hegel, if we remove its contents we have to say that it merely exists. It exists as indetermination *(Bestimmungslosigkeit)* and emptiness *(Leerheit).* This is the same as Nothing. I think that Hegel's establishment of Being is quite arbitrary.

He explains that, the thesis, Being, and antithesis, Nothing, are in contradiction, and the unity or synthesis of Being and Nothing is Becoming *(Dasein).* Becoming is the Being which has overcome Nothing. Being becomes Nothing once and then once again becomes Being, only this time it is an enriched Being. The enriched Being then develops into the new dialectical process, Being-Essence-Notion (Idea), which has already been explained in Chapter 5 Logic.

This explanation is very difficult to understand. The reason, I think, is that Hegel did not treat what is true as truth, but wanted to pass something untrue for truth, using complicated logic to do it. Isn't it enough for us to call an eraser 'eraser'? The starting point of Hegel's dialectic is unreliable, so it is natural that it was difficult to develop his logic. It seems somewhat forced.

I will explain his dialectic a little more concretely. The notion

(Begriff) develops through the three stages of thesis-antithesis-synthesis. Consider a hen. The notion of 'hen' exists in God before the actual hen exists. Next, there appears a notion that denies the hen—the notion of 'egg.' Finally, the notion of 'chicken' comes to deny egg. The initial notion, therefore, has developed through the three stages of thesis, antithesis, and synthesis, or hen, egg, and chicken. Thus, actual hens, eggs, and chickens come to appear.

According to Hegel, nature is what the Idea has developed into in the form of otherness. This is a kind of pantheism, the view that all things are the materialization of the Logos (God) and can be regarded alternately either as God or as matter. Clearly, it is easy to edge into materialism from here; pantheism, therefore, can become the foundation for pan-materialism.

For Hegel, thinking (Logos) develops through the three stages of thesis-antithesis-synthesis, accordingly the phenomenal world develops similarly through the three stages. Therefore, Hegel's dialectical method is the way of thinking and at the same time the way of development of the world.

K. MARXISM
—THE MATERIALISTIC DIALECTIC

Marx and Engels constructed the materialistic dialectic by turning Hegel's idealistic dialectic upside down from the standpoint of materialism. It is the science of nature, human society and thought.*

Although both Hegel's idealistic and Marx's materialistic dialectic are those of contradiction—a thing or a state which contains its negation, there is no mention of real struggle in Hegel's dialectic, in which inseparability and correlativity are stressed, except in an explanatory note†, while the real struggle becomes essential in Marx's dialectic.

The fundamental laws of the materialistc dialectic, according to Engels are: (1) the law of transformation of quantity into quality, (2) the law of the unity and struggle of opposites and (3) the law of negation of negation.

The first law states that qualitative changes occur only through quantitative changes, and that the quantitative change suddenly

---

*Engels, *Anti-Dühring*, Progress Publishers, Moscow 1969, p. 169.
†Hegel, *Hegel's Science of Logic*, trans. by A.V. Miller, (London: George Allen & Unwin Ltd., 1969), p. 435-438.

brings about a qualitative change at a certain point. The second law states that everything has contradictory elements (opposites), which oppose each other and at the same time cannot be separated from each other, i.e. in the relationship of unity, and that motion and development are caused by the struggle of opposites. The third law states that, in the development of things, the negation of a state leads to a new state and further negation leads to the restoration of the original state, which is not, however, the same as the original state but is the original state in a developed form.

Among these three laws, the most fundamental law of the materialistic dialectic is the law of the unity and struggle of opposites, or the law of contradiction. In fact, Lenin considered it the most fundamental law of the materialistic dialectic. He stated that the unity of opposites is conditional and relative, while their struggle is absolute, and that everything develops through the struggle of opposites. Accordingly, in the final analysis, "the struggle of opposites" is the core of the materialistic dialectic.

L. HUSSERL (1859-1938)
—THE PHENOMENOLOGICAL METHOD

Edmund Husserl said we must understand things as precisely as we do in mathematics. Mathematical precision is the first characteristic of Husserl's philosophy.

Cognition has three stages. The first is that of seeing things as they are. "To the fact itself" *(zu der Sachen selbst)* was Husserl's motto. When we see a flower, we should not think "Oh, this is the beautiful flower I have been dreaming of." We must take away our subjectivity and see it objectively. In this stage of cognition we see the "fact" *(Tatsache)*, which is purely objective. During this stage we must have a *natural attitude (natürliche Einstellung)*.

A flower, however, is always changing. First it is a bud, then a bloom, and finally it withers and dies. We cannot really say we understand a flower if we do not understand its essence—i.e., what is unchanging in it and what makes it as it is. The change from seeing the actual flower to seeing its essence is called *formal reduction (eidetische Reduktion)*.

The cognition of essence, called *ideation (Ideation, Wesensanschauung)*, is made by *free variation (freie Variation)*, a process in which the subject freely changes individual beings and finds what is universal in them. The essence of a flower, for example, is obtained, first, by thinking about variety freely (free variation), such as a rose, a tulip, a bud, and a withered flower; then, by taking that which is unchanging and common to all of them.

The final stage of cognition is that which deals with *pure phenomena (reines Phänomen)*. Even if there is a phenomenally existing flower, the essence of it is shaped in our consciousness; we must, therefore, consider consciousness, if we want to have correct cognition.

If we exclude (bracket, *einklammern*) the actual object and essence of it by the method of *suspension of judgment (Epoche)*, the field of consciousness comes to be the remainder *(Residuum)*. This remainder is called *the phenomenological remainder (das phänomenologische Residuum)*. This is actually *pure consciousness (reiner Bewußtsein)*. Such a procedure is called *transcendental reduction (transzendentale Reduktion)*. The two methods of reduction, formal and transcendental, are together called *phenomenological reduction (phänomenologische Reduktion)*. The attitude of seeing the pure consciousness by phenomenological reduction is called *phenomenological attitude (phänomenologische Einstellung)*.

In the study of consciousness, it becomes clear that consciousness consists of *noesis* and *noema*. *Noesis* is the functional part (thinking part), and *noema* is the objective part (thought part). True phenomenological cognition is the understanding and cognition of this structure consisting of *noesis* and *noema*.

Some people manage to reach the second stage of cognition, but Husserl wants to enter the stage of pure consciousness. He tried to describe man's consciousness in a strict way. Natural science observes and records facts, trying to eliminate all subjectivity. Ontology considers the essence of the object, and how it exists. The fundamental ontology, which was later developed by Heidegger, however, considers pure consciousness or pure experience.

M. THE ANALYTIC METHOD

Many thinkers have emphasized the study of actual facts in their quest for truth; analytic philosophers, however, tell us that philosophers need not concern themselves with the study of them. Why not? Because we should leave that up to scientists—physicists, biologists, astronomers, botanists, zoologists, and so on; they are the ones who should study actual facts.

Philosophy, science, and all of man's systems of truth are written in words. First and foremost, therefore, we must study and examine words, to see whether or not they are correctly used. Philosophers have established gigantic philosophical systems; yet, if we analyze the words they used, we can find a great number of false expressions. Besides, if we exclude as meaningless that which is not provable or which is ambiguous, a lot of these philosophical systems are doomed to collapse.

Analytic philosophy is positivistic and empirical in every point, largely excluding from its investigation that which man cannot, or does not, experience. So, it considers God as unnecessary for philosophy. Analytic philosophers algebraize words in order to analyze them, since they can acquire mathematical precision by doing so. This, then, is a method for correcting man's thinking, rather than a method for pursuing truth.

In this section I have outlined the methodologies of representative philosophical systems. Having done this, I would like to introduce Unification Methodology.

II. UNIFICATION METHODOLOGY —THE GIVE-AND-TAKE LAW

Unification Methodology is based on the Unification Principle, and may also be considered as a methodology that has unified traditional methodologies. The basic law of Unification Methodology is the law of give-and-take action, or briefly, the give-and-take law.

A. KINDS OF GIVE-AND-TAKE ACTION

Give-and-take action is the foundation both of the Quadruple Bases and of the Origin-Separation-Union Action or *Chung-Boon-Hap* (C-B-H) Action. The Quadruple Bases represent the structure of the attributes of God; the C-B-H action, on the other hand, describes the process of forming the Quadruple Bases from the perspective of time. The Quadruple Bases consist of Heart (Purpose), Subject, Object, and United Body. When seen from the time perspective, we find that Heart (Purpose) is first; next, Subject and Object conduct give-and-take action; finally, they become one in the United Body. This process is called *Chung-Boon-Hap* Action. (Fig. 34)

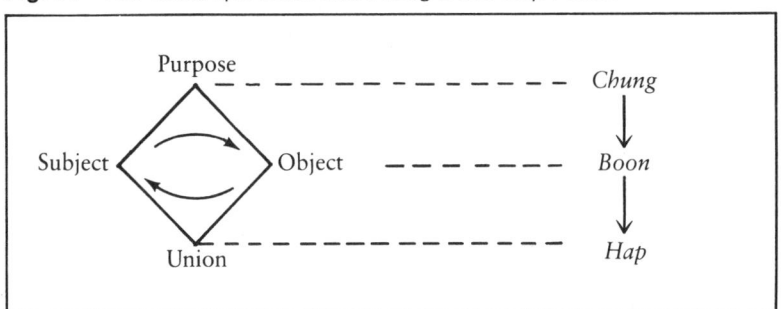

Fig. 34 The Quadruple Base and *Chung-Boon-Hap* Action

```
        Purpose
           /\  _____    Chung
          /  \                       ↓
Subject  <    > Object   _ _ _ _ _  Boon
          \  /                       ↓
           \/  _____    Hap
         Union
```

Boon, in the C-B-H action, represents two separate elements in the world of creation relating between themselves as subject and object. These separate elements are not to be understood as divided parts of *Chung*. *Chung*, in fact, is purpose established by Heart, and the two elements, centering on *Chung*, enter into give-and-take action to become *Hap* (United Body). Of course, God is not a divided being. In God, *Boon* means not two divided elements, but two relative attributes of the one God. These relative attributes engage in the give-and-take action centering on *Chung* to become *Hap*. The meaning of *Chung*, in the *Chung-Boon-Hap* of Unification Thought, then, is different from that of 'thesis,' in the thesis-antithesis-synthesis of Hegel and Marx.

As explained in "Theory of Original Image," there are four kinds of Quadruple Bases: Identity-Maintaining, Developing, Inner, and Outer. These derive from the four kinds of give-and-take action—that is, the Identity-Maintaining Give-and-Take Action, the Developing Give-and-Take Action, The Inner Give-and-Take Action, and the Outer Give-and-Take Action.

1. Identity-Maintaining and Developing Give-and-Take Actions

Everything in the natural world has an unchanging, identity-maintaining aspect. Although the universe is always moving and changing, its shape is relatively unchanging. A galaxy revolves, maintaining its shape of a convex lens. Our solar system revolves around the center of our galaxy (a nuclear system of fixed stars), taking two hundred and fifty million years for one revolution; its shape is always elliptical, and it is always at roughly the same distance from the center of the galaxy. Similarly, the nine planets including the earth in our solar system orbit the sun, maintaining their relative positions and shapes.

Nations come and go, since they are not built by God; yet a few of their aspects do not change, even in the non-principled world. The principle of ruling and ruled (in whatever form of national government), is one such example. In the family, the relationship between parents and children has an unchanging, eternal aspect. Every individual has a few characteristics that do not change during his life. In the human body, cells change with body metabolism, yet each part of the body maintains its function and position. With regard to water, whether it be in the form of liquid, steam, or ice, the molecular structure of H_2O is unchanging.

The origin of all these identity-maintaining functions is God, the Cause of the phenomenal world, for one of God's attributes is eternity, or unchangeability.

According to the Unification Principle, when a subject and object enter into give-and-take action, all power necessary for its existence, action, and multiplication is generated. Multiplication in the Unification Principle means development and generation; action means movement and change. The multiplication and action of all things are caused by the developing give-and-take actions.

All things develop and change; in the short-term, however, development appears to be a phenomenon characteristic only of living beings. The main factors that initiate development are autonomy and dominion. Autonomy refers to the spontaneity of life, dominion refers to its nature of influencing other beings. Autonomy and dominion are actually different expressions of the function of life; the former applies to the individual truth-body aspect of a living being; the latter, to the connected-body aspect.

In our discussion of development, I will limit my explanation largely to the aspect of autonomy. When a being has autonomy, it develops and grows. Autonomy is an expression of life; it is a kind of latent consciousness, or latent will. From man down to single-celled organisms, all living things have consciousness. God's *Sung Sang* can be fully expressed in man's consciousness, whereas in the consciousness of lower forms of life, only the abilities to grow, to replicate, to respond to stimuli, etc., are expressed. The millions of cells in the body, also, have consciousness (autonomy), and each cell controls itself to a certain extent.

Since autonomy is latent consciousness (or latent will), it has purpose. A living being grows and develops according to this purpose. Development, therefore, has direction. If we sow apple seeds, apple trees will sprout up and eventually bear fruit. The apple seed already has in itself the plan of an apple, and the direction of its growth is to develop into an apple-bearing tree.

Development is the result of the give-and-take action between subject and object in a living being, as for example, between an embryo and albumen in a seed, but in actual fact, not only living beings exhibit the quality of development. The whole universe may be looked upon as a living organism which has developed and expanded over a period of billions of years. The development and expansion of the universe is the process of Creation. As a part of this process, the earth has developed from a gaseous to a molten state, and then to a solid state, with the subsequent appearance of plants, animals, and man.

God's creation process begins from oneness. All things develop from a simple state to a complex one, from a lower state to a higher one, and from old to new. The complexity of the countless heavenly bodies has arisen from a relatively simple state. Though complex and developed, the heavenly bodies, nevertheless, maintain correlative positions and relationships in the process of expansion; they have developed, keeping their identity.

2. Inner Give-and-Take Action and Outer Give-and-Take Action

The give-and-take action between a man's spirit-mind and physical mind is an example of inner give-and-take action, since it makes an inner quadruple base; whereas the give-and-take action between persons (e.g., husband and wife) is outer give-and-take action, since it forms an outer quadruple base. (Fig. 35)

Every existing being engages both in the inner give-and-take action and the outer give-and-take action, but it should be noted that these are relative, not absolute concepts. In the Great Macrocosm, there is the spirit-world and the physical world. Relatively speaking, give-and-take action within the physical world can be seen as inner give-and-take action; in this case, the give-and-take action between the physical world and the spirit-world is outer give-and-take action. When considering the solar system in the galaxy, the relationship between the sun and the earth is inner give-and-take action, whereas the relationship between the sun and the galactic center is outer give-

Fig. 35 The Inner Quadruple Base and the Outer Quadruple Base of a Family

IQB = Inner Quadruple Base
OQB = Outer Quadruple Base
sm = spirit-mind
pm = physical mind

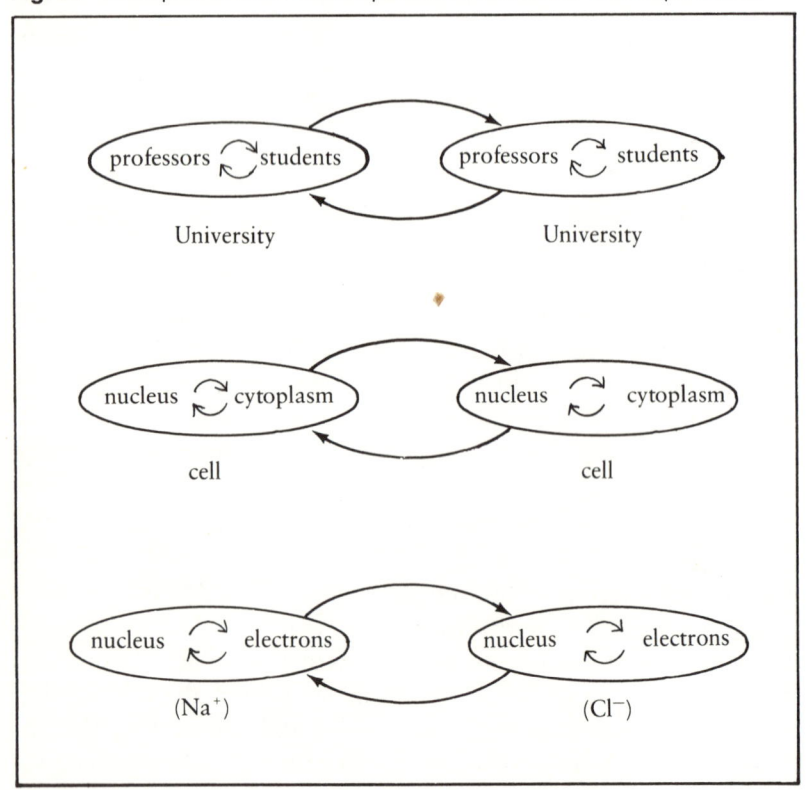

Fig. 36 Examples of Inner Quadruple Bases and Outer Quadruple Bases

and-take action. Furthermore, when considering the earth in the solar system, relationships within the earth are inner give-and-take actions, whereas the relationship between the earth and the sun is outer give-and-take action. This means that inner and outer give-and-take actions are always performed unitively in every stage; in other words, no being exists by itself.

In a nation, the inner give-and-take action between the government (subject) and the people (object) makes the inner quadruple base, whereas the outer give-and-take action between that nation and other nations makes the outer quadruple base. The inner quadruple bases are formed in a university by the inner give-and-take actions between the university president and the professors, between the professors and the students, between faculty members, etc.; at the same time, the university engages in outer, give-and-take action with other universities and organizations, which form outer quadruple bases. The inner give-and-take action between the nucleus and cytoplasm in a cell form an inner quadruple base, and the outer give-and-take actions between that cell and other cells form outer quadruple bases. The same applies for nucleus-electron and atom-atom relationships. (Fig 36)

From the smallest particles to the massive heavenly constellations, all things exist and develop according to inner give-and-take action and outer give-and-take action. If all these relationships are not conducted in a harmonious, principled way, the result will be confusion and ruin.

B. THE SPHERE OF THE GIVE-AND-TAKE ACTION

The give-and-take actions thus far discussed are mainly ontological in nature. We should, however, consider other aspects as well, such as the relationships between man and the rest of creation. There are basically two kinds of relationships: in one, man simply recognizes the things to which he relates; in the other, he dominates them as well. The give-and-take action for recognition is epistemological; that for domination is related to such enterprises as natural science, industry, economics, art, and so on.

We should, likewise, consider interpersonal give-and-take actions in the fields of ethics, education, politics, economics, etc. (In economics, which is a field of man's domination over creation, human relations are of paramount importance.) (Fig. 37)

Fig. 37 The Give-and-Take Action between Man and the Creation, and between Men

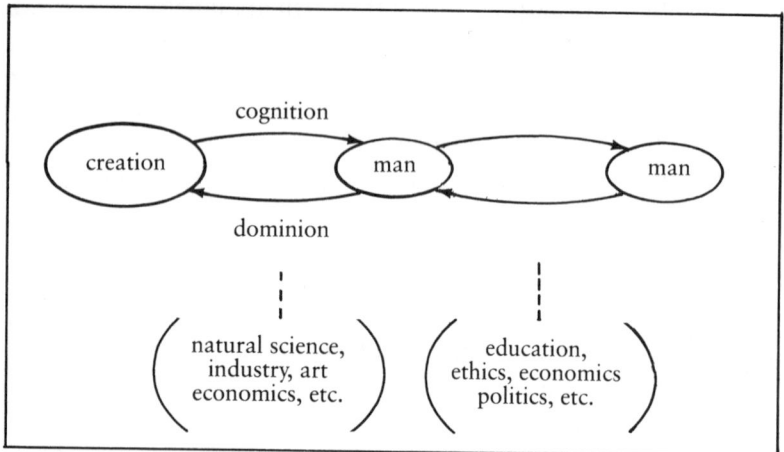

The world of thought, which is related to logic, obeys give-and-take laws. The subject (functional) part of the mind consists of intellect, emotion, and will, while the object part consists of ideas, concepts, original law, and mathematical principles. Thinking is achieved by the give-and-take action between the subject and object parts. (Fig. 38)

Fig. 38 The Give-and-Take Action in Man's Mind

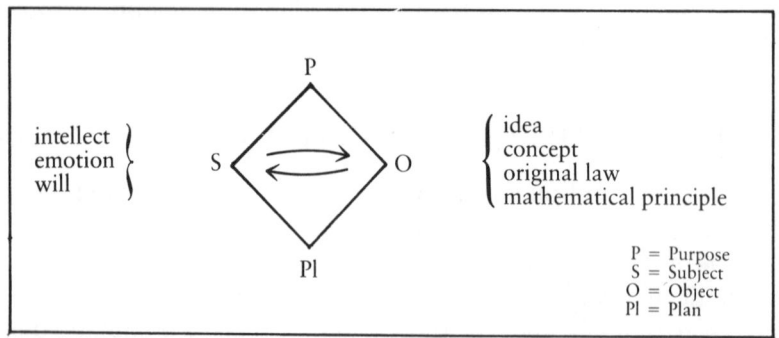

The concrete contents of the object part are the impressions of what has been experienced. When we want to go on a picnic, we base our thinking on past experiences and may conclude by stating for example, "That's a good mountain, let's go there!" Since God is the Creator, He did not need past experiences upon which to base His original thinking; but man does. Man creates new ideas by the combination and synthesis of ideas from past experiences. Ideas from past experiences are gathered and made to enter into give-and-take action with the intellect, emotion, and will, in order to create new plans and ideas.

Judgment, also is based on the give-and-take law. The judgment, "This flower is a rose," is based on the collative give-and-take action between 'this flower' and 'a rose', the former being an idea formed from sense-impressions from the outer world, the latter being an idea previously existing in man's mind. Conversation also, is based on the give-and-take law. If I mumble on randomly, you will not be able to understand what I say. If, however, you can understand what I say, it is because your laws of thinking and my laws of speaking coincide. Truly, all phenomena occur through the give-and-take laws, and we can say that we have a unique and universally true methodology.

C. TYPES OF GIVE-AND-TAKE ACTION

1. Bilateral Autonomic Type

You are listening to my lecture now. We are engaged in give-and-take action, with myself in the subject-position and you in the object-position. In this case, both you and I are engaged consciously. The type of give-and-take action in which both the subject and the object are engaged consciously is called *bilateral (mutual) autonomic give-and-take action*. Other examples are: man as subject and an animal as object, animals as subject and object, etc.

2. Unilateral Autonomic Type

The give-and-take action I am conducting with this piece of chalk in writing on the blackboard is *unilateral autonomic give-and-take action*, since I am doing so consciously, but the chalk is not. When only one party is engaged consciously, the relationship is called autonomic give-and-take action.

3. Unconscious Type

During the daytime, plants emit oxygen and take in carbon dioxide, while animals always exhale carbon dioxide and inhale oxygen. Plants do not intentionally emit oxygen for the sake of animals—it happens to be a by-product of photosynthesis; neither do animals exhale carbon dioxide to oblige plants—it is a by-product of respiration. By doing so, however, both help each other in what may be termed *unconscious give-and-take action*. In unconscious give-and-take action, neither the subject nor the object engage consciously, even if both or one of them have consciousness (autonomy).

4. Heteronomous Type

When both subject and object are inanimate beings and they are engaged in give-and-take action by the will of an outside agency, this type of give-and-take action is called *heteronomous give-and-take action*. The earth and the sun are engaged in give-and-take action in the solar system, since they are forced to do so by God. The parts of a clock are engaged in give-and-take actions in such a way as to tell time, since they are forced to do so by the will of man who made it. These are examples of heteronomous give-and-take actions.

5. Contrast Type (Collation Type)

When man contrasts or collates two or more beings (elements) and he finds harmony in them, he considers that they are engaged in give-and-take action, which may be called *contrast type (collation type) give-and-take action*. In many cases, the contrast is performed unconsciously. We feel harmony and beauty when we see mountains, the sea, clouds, and flying birds, or we see a house with a red roof in the middle of a green forest. These feelings of harmony come from the contrast type of give-and-take action. In this give-and-take action, what generally happens is that man unconsciously places one of the things in the subject position, and the others in the object position; their being engaged by an observer means that the give-and-take action is of the contrast type.

This type of give-and-take action is often applied intentionally, in order for man to obtain joy. Art is a good example. Artists apply it to arranging colors, light and shadow, lines, concave and convex parts, and so on, in order to produce a harmonious work of art.

Even in logic, thinking is formed through this type of give-and-take action. For instance, the proposition, "This flower is a rose," is formed by a process of give-and-take action. 'This flower' is subject; 'a rose' is object; and 'is', which is a logical term, is the contrasting, or judging element of the action. In cognition, we collate the sense-impressions of the object we see—that is, shape, color, aroma, etc.—with the corresponding prototypes we have inside us.

By the way, it must be noted that a contrast type give-and-take action is always accompanied by a unilateral autonomic type give-and-take action between man, who contrasts, and things, which are contrasted with each other.

D. CHARACTERISTICS OF GIVE-AND-TAKE ACTION

The characteristics of give-and-take action are as follows: (1) correlative elements (paired elements); (2) purpose and centrality; (3) order and locality; (4) harmony; (5) individuality and relationship; (6) identity-maintenance and development; (7) circular motion (in space and time). These have already been explained as the Seven Natures of Cosmic Law, in "Ontology."

III. A CRITIQUE OF TRADITIONAL METHODOLOGIES VIEWED FROM UNIFICATION METHODOLOGY

The purpose of this critique is to provide additional clarification of Unification Methodology.

A. HERACLITUS

Heraclitus, in saying that all things in the universe are changing and growing, considered only the equivalent of the developing give-and-take action in Unification Methodology. He neglected the identity-maintaining aspect.

B. ZENO

Zeno tried to prove that everything is unchangeable, immovable, immortal, and not-born. Contrary to Heraclitus, Zeno was concerned only with the identity-maintaining aspect, and he neglected the developing aspect.

C. SOCRATES

A and B initiate a dialogue in order to arrive at truth. This is outer give-and-take action between A and B centering on the purpose of finding truth, and their multiplying new truth is the outer developing quadruple base. Socrates' dialogic method, then, demonstrates the outer developing give-and-take action in Unification Methodology. (Fig. 39)

Fig. 39 Give-and-Take Action through Dialogue

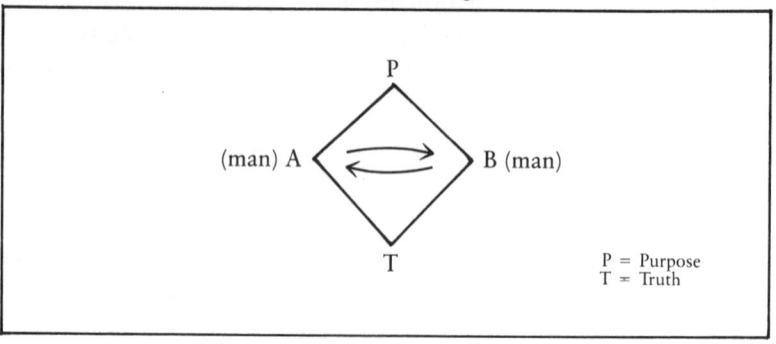

```
           P
(man) A ⟨⇌⟩ B (man)
           T
                        P = Purpose
                        T = Truth
```

D. PLATO

Plato studied the world of Idea. He can be said to have studied, unintentionally, the world of the Inner *Hyung Sang* of God. There are numerous ideas and concepts in the Inner *Hyung Sang*. Plato classified these, making a hierarchy of Ideas. Classifying them involves a collative give-and-take action. For example, collating the concept of 'animal' with the concept of 'horse', we conclude that the concept of 'animal' is generic, while the concept of 'horse' is specific. All this is collation type and inner give-and-take action.

E. ARISTOTLE

Aristotle's deductive method employs syllogisms, in which a universal truth is stated, then a more limited truth, and from these a conclusion is finally obtained. The conclusion (C) 'Socrates will die' is obtained by collating the two propositions: (A) 'All men die' (major premise) and (B) 'Socrates is a man' (minor premise). This inference is a collation type give-and-take action. Moreover, the proposition, 'Socrates is a man', is itself obtained by comparing 'Socrates' and 'a man'; i.e. by a collation type give-and-take action.

Aristotle's deductive method, therefore, is an expression of the collation type and inner give-and-take action. The collation type completing quadruple bases, which I have explained in Chap. 5 Logic, are formed through this give-and-take action, both in making a conclusion in the syllogism and in establishing each proposition.

F. BACON

Bacon maintained that we must free ourselves from our prejudices *(idola)* and make careful experiments and observations in order to arrive at the truth. Suppose the results of observations A, B, and C are all P. We can then make a general law, with P as the conclusion. For example, Mr. A dies, and so do Mr. B and Mr. C. We can then make the general law, 'All men die'. This is the inductive method. The inductive method, therefore, involves contrast-type give-and-take action.

The inductive method is based on experiments and observations which involve outer give-and-take actions. Also, it involves collation type give-and-take action, since a conclusion is drawn by comparing various observations. We see, therefore, that Bacon emphasized outer give-and-take action and collation type give-and-take action.

G. DESCARTES

Descartes doubted the existence of all things; he doubted the real existence of mountains, of rivers, even of his own body. Then he arrived at the famous proposition, "I think, therefore I am." For him, this proposition is the only believable truth. From the viewpoint of Unification Thought, the setting up of his proposition is the equivalent of his recognition of the inner quadruple base both in God and in man. But how was Descartes able to arrive at that proposition? Doubting all matter *(Hyung Sang)* means denying God's creation of the world. Then, what is left? It can be nothing other than God's thinking before beginning Creation. Descartes can be said to have unconsciously dealt with God's thinking, which, is actually His *Sung Sang* (Inner Quadruple Base).

H. HUME

The relationship of cause and effect is not purely subjective—as Hume maintained—but is both subjective and objective, as explained in Epistemology. (See ch. 4, I, B, 2.) Besides denying the existence of the material substance, Hume denied also the substantial reality of the *self,* saying that the *self* is nothing but a bundle of perceptions (impressions and ideas). He considered a bundle of perceptions the only believable existence. In Unification Thought terminology, Hume limited himself to the study of the *Inner Hyung Sang,* which contains perceptions.

I. KANT

According to Unification Principle, man is the integration, or encapsulation, of the universe; thus, he possesses all the elements of the outside world representationally as prototypes inside himself. As explained in the previous section, one of the characteristics for give-and-take action is correlativity. Cognition cannot be achieved with an outer element only. Both inner and outer elements must be related.

The inner element may seem to be transcendental, and Kant was convinced that it is, but actually it is not. A newborn baby, as he has only an incomplete prototype, does not understand anything clearly. His prototype is gradually completed with his growth. What he has experienced is included in his prototype, and the new prototype becomes the standard of cognition for the next experience. The prototype in Unification Thought, therefore, has both a transcendental and an empirical element. (We call this concept *priority of the prototype,* as explained in Epistemology.)

Both Kant and Unification Thought are in accord in considering that cognition is accomplished through the reciprocal relationship between outer and inner elements. For Kant, what comes in from the outside are sensible qualities, such as color, shape, aroma, etc., and what is in the inside are the forms of intuition and the forms of synthesis. The object of cognition is synthesized by these *a priori* forms inside.

According to Unification Thought, however, what is inside are content (image of content) as well as thinking forms—prototypes consist of both of them—and what is outside are sensible qualities (content) with existing forms. For Kant, the object of cognition is synthesized by the subject. In Unification Thought, however, subject and object are collated in cognition. Kant's transcendental method (theory of synthesis) can be said to be Kant's style of manifesting the theory of collation, which is established on the basis of the give-and-take action theory. (Fig. 40)

J. HEGEL

Instead of explaining the development of thinking and that of the universe as the process of *Chung-Boon-Hap,* Hegel explained it as the process of thesis-antithesis-synthesis. Also, he thought that God is Logos. Logos, however, is not God Himself, but the multiplied being of the give-and-take action between *Inner Sung Sang* and *Inner Hyung Sang* in God. Logos is the product of the Inner Developing Quadruple Base, which performs give-and-take action with

Critique of Traditional Methodologies

the *Hyung Sang,* centering on Purpose, to create existing beings.

Hegel had no concept of Quadruple Base, but thought that the universe had developed directly from the Logos. Accordingly he had to create an antithesis *(Nothing)* to explain this development. He regarded the relationship between thesis and antithesis as one of contradiction, and thought that new things were born as the synthesis of the interaction between these contradictory elements. This can be said to be his style of understanding the manifestation of give-and-take action between correlative elements, but they are quite different. He did not know that the development is brought about by the give-and-take action centering on purpose, that is, by the formation of a quadruple base. (Fig. 41)

Fig. 40 Kant's Transcendental Method (in Unification Notation)

(Internal World) TF ⇄ SQ (External World)

P = Purpose
C = Cognition
TF = Thinking Forms
SQ = Sensible Qualities

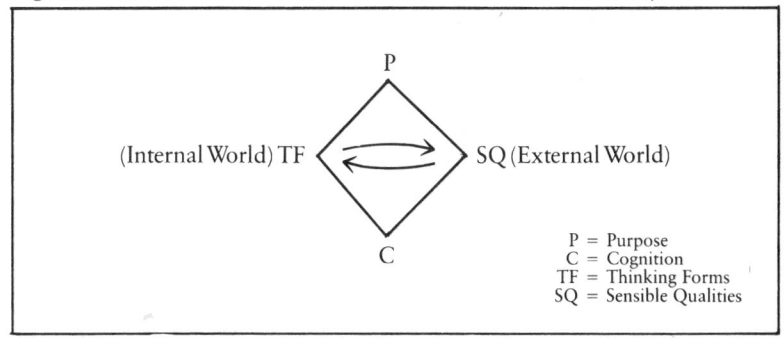

Fig. 41 The Dialectic of Thesis-Antithesis-Synthesis

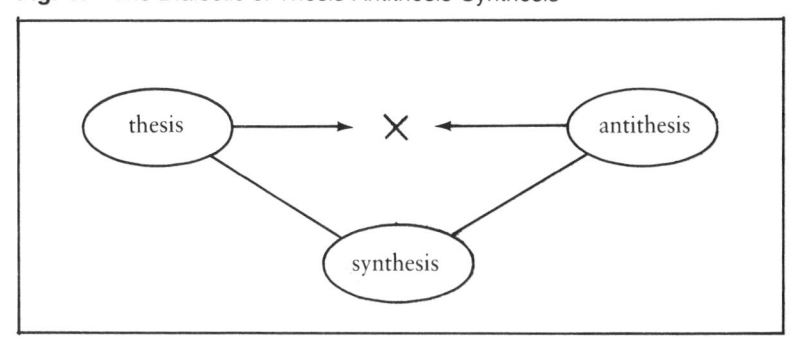

thesis → X ← antithesis
synthesis

K. MARXISM

The fault of the most fundamental law of the materialistic dialectic, the law of the struggle of opposites (the law of contradiction), has already been mentioned in Chapter 2 Ontology. In the Unification Thought view, development is made not through contradiction, that is, through the struggle of opposites, but through the harmonious give-and-take action of the correlative elements in nature, society and thinking.

With regard to the law of the transformation of quantity into quality, Unification Thought asserts that quality *(Sung Sang)* and quantity *(Hyung Sang)* are relative aspects of an existing being, so quality and quantity develop simultaneously. In the Unification Thought view, quality is expressed through quantity since quality and quantity are in the relationship of subject and object, contrary to the materialistic dialectical view that quantitative change is the cause with qualitative change as the effect. Also, Unification Thought asserts that a sudden change of quality is not a general phenomenon, but a gradual change of quality is a general one.

With regard to the law of negation of negation, which claims that a new state is attained by the negation of an old one, Unification Thought asserts that the new state is attained affirmatively from an old one through the give-and-take action of the correlative elements in it. Materialistic dialectic claims that the original state is restored in a more developed form through the negation of negation without any reason. Unification Thought, however, clarifies that such a restoring phenomenon appears through circular motion in time (spiral movement), one of the characteristics of the give-and-take law, by which every living being maintains its eternity. Clearly, such a phenomenon cannot be applied to the social revolution as Marx claimed.

L. HUSSERL

Husserl describes three stages of cognition: the cognition of reality (the fact, without the perceiver's subjectivity), the cognition of essence, and the cognition of pure phenomena.

The realm of the 'fact itself' *(Sachen selbst)* is the realm of scientific cognition. In Unification Thought, this is the cognition of the united body of *Sung Sang* and *Hyung Sang* of the existing being. (Most scientists, however, study only the *Hyung Sang* aspect.) Essence in the second stage corresponds to the *Sung Sang* of that being. Husserl asks us to suspend our judgments of the outside world (phenomenological *epoche*) in order to analyze pure consciousness. Having done this, we can understand that pure con-

Critique of Traditional Methodologies

sciousness consists of a thinking part and a thought part—that is, a functional part and an objective part. This is no more than the equivalent of the Inner *Sung Sang* and Inner *Hyung Sang* of man's mind in Unification Thought. (Fig. 42)

Fig. 42 Husserl's Phenomenological Method and its Correspondence in Unification Thought

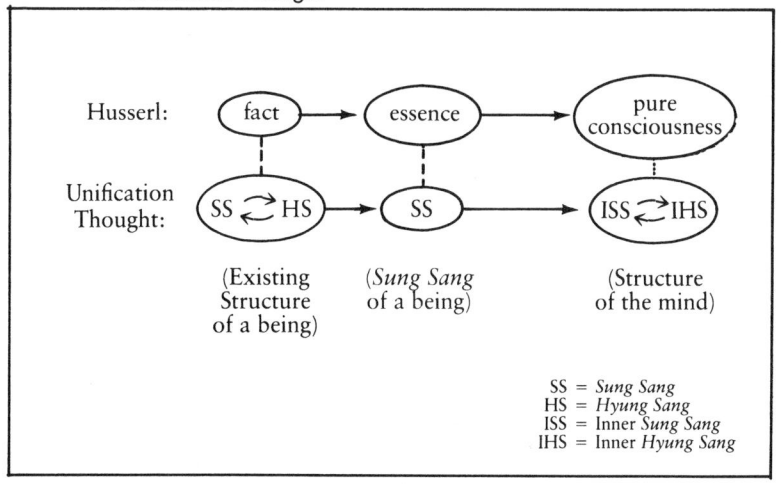

```
Husserl:           (fact) ──► (essence) ──► (pure consciousness)

Unification
Thought:           (SS ⇄ HS) ──► (SS) ──► (ISS ⇄ IHS)

                   (Existing      (Sung Sang     (Structure
                    Structure      of a being)    of the mind)
                    of a being)

                                              SS  = Sung Sang
                                              HS  = Hyung Sang
                                              ISS = Inner Sung Sang
                                              IHS = Inner Hyung Sang
```

M. THE ANALYTIC METHOD

Analytic philosophers are concerned only with the mathematical accuracy and logical consistency of a system of thought. Their analytic process is carried out through an intellectual inner give-and-take action. We have seen in the chapter on logic, (see Ch. 5, III, B) however, that inner give-and-take action includes both an intellectual aspect (logos) and an emotional aspect (pathos). We can say, therefore, that the analytic method deals only with one aspect of the inner give-and-take action.

* * * *

A Concluding Remark

I have explained Unification Thought, which is the systematization of Rev. Moon's thought. As already mentioned in the preface, the contents of this book come from my several lectures on Unification Thought, and having found some vague points in them in the process of editing, I have revised or supplemented them to express Rev. Moon's thought as accurately as possible. Here, in completing the explanation of Unification Thought, I would like to introduce a part of the Rev. Moon's keynote address at the ninth International Conference on the Unity of the Sciences, 1980.

> Peace is not desired on the world level alone, but also on the level of nations, societies and families as well. Even individuals yearn for peace between their minds and bodies.
>
> Of these various levels of peace, which level should be established first?
>
> It is easy to think that if world peace were established first, then on that basis the peace of nations, societies, families, and eventually individuals would also be established.
>
> But this is a wrong viewpoint. It is actually the reverse of the sequence necessary to establish peace. Individual peace must first be realized. Then family peace can soon follow, and only on that foundation can the peace of societies, nations and the world be expected. This is because individuals are the basic units of families, and families are the basic units of societies and nations.
>
> Frequently leaders believe that through outstanding organization and superior thought they can restore both the order of society and world peace. In reality, however, the peace of mankind can never be realized through these two means alone. International organizations such as the United Nations and thought systems such as communism, democracy, etc., have all tried to realize world peace in their own ways, but peace is still far from our grasp, and the world is experiencing more confusion as days go by.
>
> Unless the quest for peace starts from the peace of an individual, it is bound to fail again and again.
>
> Then how can the peace of an individual be achieved? It can be achieved by an individual having absolute love and practicing it. This is true because love is the precondition for all unity. Unity can be established on the basis of love, and peace on the basis of unity.
>
> Needless to say, the peace of the world comes into being only on the foundation of the peace of all nations. When each nation ceases to place all its emphasis on trade and other ways to secure its so-called national interests; when each nation begins to serve other nations and the world with absolute love; and when each nation

maintains such an international atmosphere consistently, the eternal peace of mankind will have been secured.

Thus it becomes apparent that world peace begins with individual peace and expands through families, societies, and nations to ultimately become world peace.

At this point I would like to mention absolute love and absolute values. It is on the foundation of love that the values of truth, goodness and beauty are formed. For example, the practice of love is evaluated as goodness. That is, when love is practiced, it appears as goodness. Therefore, it follows that when practicing absolute love, which is God's love, absolute goodness appears. The actions of an individual practicing absolute love for the sake of peace are goodness (absolute goodness). Likewise the actions of a family practicing love for the sake of peace are also goodness. The same is true for societies, nations and the world.

In other words, in order to realize true peace, the individual, family, society, nation and world must all realize the absolute values which are absolute truth, absolute goodness and absolute beauty. The practice of absolute goodness is most urgently required because then no element of evil can intervene and destroy order.

Since the spiritual values of truth, goodness and beauty are formed on the basis of love, without knowledge of absolute love, which is God's love, absolute truth, absolute goodness, and absolute beauty can not be realized. And where these absolute values are not realized, there can not be true peace.

Thus, for the true peace of mankind, absolute love must be practiced. But before it can be practiced, absolute love must first be understood.

I have already stated that absolute love is love which acts for the benefit of others, which serves others, and which is unchanging and eternal. Then, why does absolute love serve the whole and remain unchanging? And why can peace be realized only through love?

These questions require answers. But in order for these questions to be completely answered, the absolute being and his motive and purpose for creating the universe and mankind must first be fully clarified. The motive and purpose for creation particularly serve as indispensable standards for the practice of love and the establishment of peace. Before any plans can be put into actions, there must first be a definite purpose. Any action without purpose is meaningless.

If man was created by the absolute being and meant to practice the absolute being's love, then it is certain that there is a motive and purpose for the creation of man. In order for that motive and purpose to be clarified, an explanation of the absolute being, that is, a correct concept of God, must first be established. By establishing the correct concept of God, His motive and purpose of creation will be clarified, and accordingly, the reason why the absolute being's love must be practiced in order to realize peace will also be clarified.

Thus I submit that for the true peace of mankind, it is necessary to understand the absolute being correctly so that we can practice His love and finally realize His absolute values.

As seen from this address, Rev. Moon appeals to people first to have the correct understanding of God, then to understand the purpose and motive of God's creation of the universe and mankind, and finally to receive God's love and practice it in order to realize true world peace. His profound teachings about the true concept of God, the purpose and motive of God's creation, and absolute love are the core of Unification Thought. I pray with my sincere heart that, through this *Explaining Unification Thought*, though incomplete in its expression it may be, Rev. Moon's thought will be correctly understood by as many people as possible, as deeply as possible, and that they will respond to his sincere appeal.

Appendix: Various Types of Category

Category of Aristotle

1. Substance
2. Quantity
3. Quality
4. Relation
5. Place
6. Time
7. Position
8. State
9. Action
10. Passivity

Category of Marx

1. Content and Form
2. Essence and Phenomenon
3. Necessity and Contingency
4. Cause and Effect
5. Possibility and Actuality
6. Universal and Particular

Forms of Kant

JUDGMENT FORM

1. Quantity
   - Singular judgment
   - Particular judgment
   - Universal judgment

2. Quality
   - Affirmative judgment
   - Negative judgment
   - Infinite judgment

3. Relation
   - Categorical judgment
   - Hypothetical judgment
   - Disjunctive judgment

4. Modality
   - Problematic judgment
   - Assertoric judgment
   - Apodeictic judgment

THINKING FORM

1. Quantity
   - Unity
   - Plurality
   - Totality

2. Quality
   - Reality
   - Negation
   - Limitation

3. Relation
   - Substance
   - Causality
   - Reciprocity

4. Modality
   - Possibility
   - Actuality
   - Necessity

Forms of Unification Thought

EXISTING FORM

1. Self-Existence and Force
2. *Sung Sang* and *Hyung Sang*
3. Positivity and Negativity
4. Subjectivity and Objectivity
5. Position and Settlement
6. Relation and Affinity
7. Action and Multiplication
8. Time and Space
9. Original Law and Mathematical Principle
10. Infinity and Finiteness

THINKING FORM

1. Existence and Force
2. *Sung Sang* and *Hyung Sang*
3. Positivity and Negativity
4. Subject and Object
5. Position and Settlement
6. Relation and Affinity
7. Action and Multiplication
8. Time and Space
9. Original Law and Mathematical Principle
10. Infinite and Finite